COMPARATIVE THEORIES OF

COMPARATIVE THEORIES OF NONDUALITY
THE SEARCH FOR A MIDDLE WAY

Milton Scarborough

continuum

Continuum International Publishing Group

The Tower Building	80 Maiden Lane
11 York Road	Suite 704
London SE1 7NX	New York NY 10038

www.continuumbooks.com

British Library Cataloguing-in-Publication Data
A catalogue record for this book is available from the British Library

ISBN-13: PB: 978-1-4411-5902-1

Typeset by Newgen Imaging Systems Pvt Ltd, Chennai, India
Printed and bound in the UK by the MPG Books Group

I dedicate this book to ALL of my teachers, but especially,

R. L. Winstead, my math teacher at Gulfport High School, who taught me that learning was both fun and important;

Dwight Van der Vate, my philosophy professor at the University of Mississippi, who taught me how to think logically;

Bob Soileau, my theology professor at New Orleans Baptist Theological Seminary, who liberated me from naïve religion, a major turning point;

William H. Poteat, my religion professor at Duke University, who pointed the way to a new philosophical framework;

Victoria Scarborough, my dear wife, who teaches me everyday much about love and life.

CONTENTS

ACKNOWLEDGMENTS

Writing a book is by no means a solitary effort. If it does not quite take a village, it does take more than a few colleagues and friends. At the outset Tom Kasulis gave me encouragement to put my ideas into book form. Rob Colter helped me distinguish the received from the revisionist Plato. Ken McIntyre supplemented my views of Locke's social theory. Patrick Miller read Chapters 2 and 3 and made suggestions that helped mask my lack of expertise in biblical studies. Computer whiz Michael Bradshaw converted my hand-drawn illustrations to digital form. Candace Bonnett tweaked and prepared the images for transmission to the publisher. Brian Cooney corrected my sometimes skewed view of the Western philosophical tradition and forced me to think through ideas once more. Rabbi Marc Kline helped me locate an elusive midrash. Brad Nystrom, my office mate, tutored me in unknown capabilities of my computer. SUNY Press gave me permission to quote a passage from a former book, and Terry Muck, editor of *Buddhist-Christian Studies*, allowed me to reprint almost all of my "In the Beginning: Hebrew God and Zen Nothingness" as part of Chapter 7. My longtime friend and colleague Eric Mount was the only person other than my wife to toil dutifully through all eight chapters of the manuscript. He improved my writing, funneled countless helpful articles and books to me, and offered personal encouragement to pursue the project. My editor, Haaris Naqvi, guided me skillfully and patiently through the mysteries of the publication process, as did editorial assistant Dominic Mattos. P. Muralidharan of Newgen Imaging led the typesetting team and assisted me in making revisions to page proofs and in creating an index. Finally, my wife Victoria, my severest and best critic, read every word, made invaluable suggestions, and formatted the manuscript. I thank them one and all and absolve them of the errors that persist in the book, perhaps because I did not always take their advice.

In addition, I wish to thank President John Roush and Dean John Ward of Centre College for granting me a sabbatical leave near the end of my career and for providing me with a splendid office in retirement. Thanks are also due to Dean Stephanie Fabritius for helping me with incidental expenses.

Chapter 1
Western Dualism and Buddhist Nondualism

*If you are in opposition to anything, then this creates duality. Then you are stuck
with self and others and gain and loss, and you are unable to walk upon the open
ground of reality.*[1]

Yuanwu

The West is dualistic. Asia, by contrast, is nondualistic. These two statements are
a partial unpacking of what Kipling may have meant when he said, "East is East
and West is West and never the twain shall meet." He was mistaken, of course,
about the latter clause. As Huston Smith observes so dramatically:

> We hear that East and West are meeting, but it is an understatement. They are
> being flung at one another, hurled with the force of atoms, the speed of jets,
> the restlessness of minds impatient to learn the ways of others. When historians
> look back on our century, they may remember it most, not for space travel or the
> release of nuclear energy, but as the time when the peoples of the world first came
> to take one another seriously.[2]

I can hardly disagree, given that within 35 miles of my home there are four
Buddhist communities (Zen, Nicheren, and two Vajrayana groups) and a Hindu
temple. Within 100 miles there is a second Hindu temple, a Taoist group, and a
Buddhist retreat center affiliated with a Korean Zen lineage. The retreat center
nestles on a spot selected by Korean masters of *feng shui* (the white tiger mountain to one side, the blue dragon on the other, the red pheasant before it, and the
black turtle behind it), and the temple has a steeply sloping and curving blue-tiled
roof designed by Korean architects.

---

1. Thomas Cleary, trans., *Classic of Buddhism and Zen*, vol. 2 (Boston, Massachusetts
and London: Shambala, 1999), 226.
2. Huston Smith, *The World's Religions* (New York: HarperSanFrancisco, 1991), 6–7.

While residents of California or New York may view such a description as normal, I live in rural, central Kentucky! The presence of these Asian institutions here is clear evidence that the immigration of Asian thought and practice has reached America's heartland. It is one of the many faces of globalization, for globalization is not simply about economics. Years ago I would begin the first meeting of my college course surveying the world's religions by showing images of the Hindu temple (in Louisville) and the Zen temple (in Powell County, Kentucky) and asking students where in the world these buildings were located. At that time, "India" and "Japan" were the only answers given. Recently, however, it has become more difficult to fool the students. The presence of Asian institutions, thought, and practice in the Bluegrass has also begun to permeate cultural consciousness here. Now, most students know that "the United States" and "Kentucky" are the correct answers.

But what about Kipling's first clause? Perhaps there is no need to ask. It is a truism, and like many truisms, it is largely true. As for the clause interpreted in terms of Western dualism and Asian nondualism, who can deny the metaphysical dualism of Descartes's *res extensa* (spatially extended substance, body) and *res cogitans* (thinking substance, mind) or Kant's phenomenal realm (what appears) and noumenal realm (the reality hidden behind appearance), or Bultmann's outer world of time and space and his inner world of subjective decision making? Certainly not I! As for Asia, equally undeniable are the absolute cosmological monism of Shankara, the ethical middle way of the Buddha, the epistemological nondualism of Zen, and the metaphysical nondualism of Hua-Yen Buddhism.

In the natural course of things, however, truisms are generalizations, and generalizations, being merely general, do not reflect all the relevant particularities. Almost always, there are isolated, hidden, marginal instances that do not fit the broader pattern. There are minority opinions, movements against the grain, countercurrents, and undercurrents. Such is the case here. Asian nondualisms arose in reaction to Asian dualisms, and vice versa. Shankara's *Advaita*, for example, was a critique of the dualism of *Samkhya*, while Madhva's dualism, on the other hand, was a response to monistic *Advaita*. In other words, dualism and nondualism shared a cultural terrain.

But what about the West? Has it not been solidly dualistic from the start, utterly free of nondualistic undercurrents? The answer may seem to be an obvious "Yes." It is that spontaneous certainty that I wish to challenge. To be sure, Plato, at least the received Plato, is credited with (or, more often, blamed for) establishing dualism as paradigmatic for much of Western philosophy and theology, and I do not wish to challenge that claim. Instead, I want to point to a largely neglected and under-appreciated nondualistic root of Western civilization. It is possible that it offers a clue to a middle way for the West, one analogous (but not identical) to that found in Buddhism. I refer to the pre-Jewish culture of ancient Israel and to its contemporary resonances in the West. Its presence testifies against complete Western uniformity with regard to dualistic thought. For now, however, that exploration must wait because there are two prior questions: What is dualism and what's the problem with it? The answers to both questions can be found in the following true story.

Dualism Observed

In the second week of August of 1962, I left the University of Mississippi, having graduated in May and having stayed through the summer to work for the United States Department of Agriculture measuring cotton, including that of William Faulkner! During my junior and seniors years at Ole Miss, rumors persisted that the university—at the time an all-white institution—was going to be desegregated. Such rumors were the subject of much discussion across the campus. Students who helped out in the matriculation process were instructed in what to do if an African American were to appear in order to register. All students were forced to consider how they would feel and what they would do if the school were to become racially integrated for the first time in its history. The northern chapters of several fraternities on campus were trying to change their national charters to allow the inclusion of non-white members and were pressuring their southern counterparts to pledge blacks. Everyone was anxious. Yet nothing happened for two years following the onset of the rumors. Only a few weeks after my departure from Oxford, however, significant, riveting changes broke out, changes that would forever alter the university, the state, and the South. The changes were precipitated by the arrival on Ole Miss's doorstep of James Meredith, who was black. One attempt to enroll, however, would not be sufficient to get the job done.

The first effort to register James Meredith at the University of Mississippi took place in Oxford on September 20, 1962. Governor Ross Barnett flew up from Jackson, the state's capital, to order a halt to the attempt. He had appointed himself the official registrar of the university, and in that capacity he turned Meredith away. The second try took place on September 25th in the state office building in Jackson, where the Board of Institutions of Higher Learning and also university officials, under orders from the Fifth Circuit Court of Appeals, were prepared to register Meredith. At the last minute, however, Governor Barnett, who came from a meeting with legislators at the capitol, entered the room. Standing before television cameras, he told Meredith, who was accompanied by U.S. Chief Marshall James P. McShane and John Doar of the Justice Department, that entrance into Ole Miss was not possible. The third attempt occurred the next day on the Oxford campus, where McShane, along with unarmed federal marshals, faced Lieutenant Governor Paul Johnson and a large contingent of state police. Eighty-two Mississippi sheriffs were also present. When McShane attempted to push through a line of state troopers and initiate the registration, a brief shoving match between the two sides ensued. Then McShane, the marshals, and Meredith left, having demonstrated publicly and on television that Mississippi stood in violation of federal law. It was the fourth attempt, however, that was memorable, violent, and ultimately successful.

On Sunday, September 30th, when students were returning from Jackson, where, on the previous day, Ole Miss had played a football game against Kentucky, McShane led 200 federal marshals onto the campus. This time they wore helmets and were armed with pistols and tear gas guns. They took up positions in a ring around the Lyceum, a pre–civil war building that housed Ole Miss's administration, including the registrar. It was and remains today the symbol of the Ole Miss campus; its image adorns the school's logo. Once the marshals were in place,

Meredith was flown to Oxford from Millington Naval Air Station in Memphis, then driven into the campus via a side entrance and hidden in a closet in Baxter Hall, a student dormitory. Allegedly, a mattress was shoved into the closet to hide and protect him, and a marshal was stationed inside the room. The marshal was prepared to shoot anyone who came into the room and to ask questions later.

Students, unaware that Meredith was on campus, formed a crowd in front of the marshals at the Lyceum, some merely curious as to why the officers were there. State troopers were also present, forming a wider ring around the entire campus. Earlier, Governor Barnett had promised President John Kennedy and Attorney General Robert Kennedy that the state police would assist the marshals in the operation. In fact, however, the troopers kept out journalists and let in "outsiders" looking for trouble. They came from everywhere, some as far away as Georgia and Texas. The arriving "outsiders" joined the students at the Lyceum, changing the makeup of the crowd.

At dusk, the crowd turned hostile, taunting the marshals. Then someone began to throw stones. Later, people in the crowd began to throw whole bricks, which, mysteriously, seemed in plentiful supply. Others broke into the chemistry building and brought out acid and threw it on the marshals. Reportedly, the state police, rather than helping the marshals, looked on and laughed. The bricks and acid began to take a toll on the marshals. Finally, they fired tear gas canisters, and the crowd dispersed. Some in the crowd, however, left but returned with their guns.

At 8:00 p.m., just as President Kennedy went on television to address the nation about the crisis, rifle bullets began exploding out of the darkness at the marshals. The marshals requested permission to return fire, even though they carried only handguns. McShane phoned the Kennedys, seeking approval of the request. The Kennedys, probably hoping to prevent the situation from deteriorating further, refused to give it. This refusal left the marshals in an extremely precarious position. The building's columns provided little cover. The consequence was that all through the night the marshals remained at the Lyceum and took the deadly violence being hurled at them. Amazingly and inexplicably, they just stayed and took it! Their sole weapon was tear gas, which was effective only in keeping the shooters, protected by darkness and the surrounding trees, at a greater distance. As the night dragged on, the supply of tear gas ran low.

When a federalized National Guard force of 5,000 men, sent by the Kennedys, arrived at dawn and opened the door of the Lyceum, which a century earlier had served as a hospital during the Civil War, the long hallway was lined with the bodies of wounded marshals. Between 150 and 160 of the 200 were injured; 28 to 35 had been struck by bullets. By some miracle, only Paul Guihard, a French journalist, and Ray Gunter, a local worker, were killed. The National Guard took control not only of the entire campus but also of the town of Oxford. It was the first time an American city had been occupied by a military force since the Civil War. They also arrested retired General Edwin A. Walker, a Texan who was suspected of having encouraged and directed the rioters and who was seen on the campus during the hostilities. Previously, he had made a speech urging people from across the nation to come help defend Mississippi against the federal government. Later that same morning, October 1st, the regular registrar officially enrolled James Meredith as the first African-American student at Ole Miss.[3]

Why did such a terrible and irrational event happen? What were its causes? What writer of fiction could have imagined such a drama? The answers lie in a web of events stretching backward in time for more than a century at least, a web too complex even for historians to explain fully. I wish merely to call attention to a single element of that complicated event, namely, dualism. The face of Ole Miss that day in September of 1962 was the face of dualism, one of its ugliest.

Dualism Defined

What is dualism? Some attempt at definition is necessary because there seems to be some confusion about it. Let us see if some clarity is possible, at least with respect to the way the term will be used in this chapter. If monism has to do with one, then, quantitatively speaking, dualism has to do with two of something, anything at all. Linguistically speaking, dualism is expressed by binary terms; however, binaries are employed in a broader range of circumstances than simply to express dualism. Let's begin by examining those other possibilities.

First of all, binary terms may express simple difference. "Yellow" and "heavy," used to describe a table, for example, illustrate both two-ness and difference. The same would be true of "cold" and "hard" applied to ice. The two terms merely point to different features or aspects of something. This is mere distinction or difference.

Yet binaries are more often understood as standing in a relation of opposition to each other. If, for example, someone argues that the eruption of Mount St. Helen is a natural event and another person asserts that it is an historical event, then the juxtaposition of "natural" to "historical" amounts to a relation of opposition. In this instance, however, both could be true; their meanings are not necessarily mutually exclusive. There is some overlap, some possible mediation or middle ground.

Some oppositions are said to be "polar opposites." Such opposites lie at the extremes of a spectrum or sliding scale of positions or options. If the American political landscape, for example, consists of the radical right, conservatives, moderates, liberals, and radical leftists, then although all the groupings may be distinguished from each other and all oppose each other in some respects, only the radical right and the radical left are polar opposites. They represent the two orientations most distant from each other. Republicans and Democrats are opposites, but not polar opposites. Anarchists and Fascists would be polar opposites. The term "polar" is derived from the north and south poles of our planet. Although the poles are as far away from each other as is possible on the planet, they are continuous with, not separated from, the rest of the globe. Again, there is middle ground.

---

3. For Meredith's own account of many of these events, see his *Three Years in Mississippi* (Bloomington: Indiana University Press, 1966).

The final kind of relation expressed in binary terms is contradiction. Any conjunction of a term or concept and its negation amounts to a contradiction. The simultaneous assertion of "It is raining now" and "It is not the case that it is raining now" is a contradiction. While "black" and "white" are opposites, even polar opposites, a middle ground of gray lies between them. "Black" and "non-black," however, are contradictories. This is the sharpest kind of opposition; there exists no middle or common ground between them, only an either/or. The absence of middle ground is also known as a "dichotomy," when used, as I shall use it, in its strong sense. Thus, difference, opposition, and polar opposition constitute a progression away from an undifferentiated unity or monism in the direction of a dichotomy or contradiction.

Distinguishing, opposing, or contradictory terms juxtaposed together constitute a pair in a merely quantitative sense. If the juxtaposition of two terms becomes habitual, however, the binaries turn into a stable couple, if you will. "Left" and "right," "sacred" and "profane," and "black" and "white" are such pairs. If one is practicing free association, the mention of one term of such an established pair will almost certainly call to mind the other.

It is important to state that mere difference, opposition, polar opposition, or even contradiction, however, still do not in the strictest sense constitute dualism. For both the West and Asia, dualism consists of a dichotomy in which the paired terms, concepts, or things have a static substance or fixed essence. Descartes's metaphysical dualism of mind and body consists of "thinking substance" and "extended substance." Substance is an unchanging, underlying, metaphysical reality in which the qualities or attributes of a thing inhere. A fixed essence consists of changeless attributes, qualities, or meanings that are essential to the nature or identity of a concept or thing. Contradictions or dichotomies with substances or fixed essences are dualisms. Sometimes distinctions or oppositions "harden" into dualisms by losing sight of common ground and acquiring substances or fixed essences. In this chapter, then, whenever I assert the nonduality of two terms, concepts, or things, I intend, at a minimum, to reject dualism as just defined.

But what about distinctions? Often, of course, mere distinctions and the binary terms that usually express them are helpful. They demarcate semantic domains, enabling us to be discriminating. In fact, in logic classes philosophers or mathematicians often represent such distinguished meanings with Boolean circles that depict inclusion and exclusion, enclosing and closing off, separating this from that. Without distinctions we could not differentiate reflectively red from green, color from shape, triangles from rectangles, right from wrong, temperature from humidity, plumbers from carpenters, the judicial branch of government from the legislative branch, debits from credits, bronchitis from asthma, July from August, sociologists from economists, fantasy from reality, or truth from falsity.

Such distinctions make us intelligent and civilized, give us increased clarity and control, defuse arguments, ease our journey in myriad ways, and even delight us. For both philosophy and other modes of thinking, they are the coin of the realm, the air thought breathes, the energy that propels it forward. They are the indispensable tools for acknowledging boundaries and the ticket price for entry into intelligible reflection or discourse. They are not to be abandoned or disparaged.

Indeed, they cannot be abandoned because they are unavoidable. If we think about the matter realistically, utter silence is not an option.

Recently, with the appearance in the West of postmodernism, binary oppositions and even binary distinctions have become the objects of criticism; such binaries are not, it turns out, utterly innocent. For one thing, they are a first step, a necessary one, toward dualism. This fact alone is not sufficient cause to reject them, but perhaps it should send up a red flag of warning. Moreover, despite being essential to reflection, distinctions are dangerous because of the variety of ways in which they can mislead us into distorting our experience of reality.

One rather common and simple way they can mislead us is by prompting us to draw boundaries too narrowly and precisely. Years ago I took students several times to New Mexico to study Native Americans. We drove south, then west across Arkansas into Oklahoma. A guidebook depicted Arkansas as a woodland state dotted with lakes; Oklahoma was said to be a plains state. Yet as we drove across the state line from Arkansas into Oklahoma, the woods did not vanish, the land did not flatten out. Grass, trees, and lakes persisted. Where were the promised plains that should have appeared at the "Entering Oklahoma" sign? Only after continuing for 75 miles or so into Oklahoma did the landscape, which had changed imperceptibly slowly, suddenly appear different. "Woodland" and "plains," to be sure, are not altogether wrong. In a rough-and-ready way they are helpfully descriptive, yet compared to the actual terrain, they are clearly simplifications. They aroused, or at least permitted, expectations that were not fulfilled or not exactly fulfilled. Such experiences, we may hope, are instructive, leading us eventually to a more sophisticated reading of guide books and also to conceiving more realistic expectations.

A second way binary distinctions distort is by numerical simplification. Are all situations best understood in terms of two causes, classes, or features? Why not one, three, or ten? Consider sex, for example. It is usually described by a binary opposition that has become a full-blown dualism. Whether in theology ("male and female created He them") or biology, we have believed that there are but two sexes, male and female. But why merely two? Is it because there are two kinds of chromosomes (XX and XY) involved in the genetic determination of sex? Yet the dualism of the sexes preceded our knowledge of chromosomes. And why choose the two-ness of the chromosomes as the definition of sex? Isn't that a form of reductionism? Must one be a reductionist in order to understand sex? More recently, other possibilities have been suggested.

Anne Fausto-Sterling has argued that to the two "standard" sexes one could add "herms" (true hermaphrodites), "ferms" (persons with female sex parts but vestigial male ones), and "merms" (persons with male sex parts but vestigial female ones).[4] That would bring the number of sexes to five. My colleague William Weston, a sociologist, notes, perhaps a bit playfully, that if each of these five has homosexual or heterosexual brain structures or hormone washes, the number climbs to ten. If each of the ten is transgendered, then the number of sexes becomes twenty.

---

4.   Anne Fausto-Sterling, "The Five Sexes: Why Male and Female are Not Enough," *The Sciences* (March/April, 1993), 20–25.

Statistically speaking, of course, the number of such non-standard sexes is small; however, the additional categories are biological, plausible, and sensitive to differences. What might be the social consequences of acknowledging a larger number of sexes? Might it not be to reduce the variety of tensions that sometimes swirl around the standard dualism of male and female? Analogously, the number of races could be multiplied (or is "recognized" a more accurate term?), perhaps to the point of virtual elimination of distinctions among racial groups. Could it be that we prefer to speak in terms of two of anything largely because it is numerically simple and because it accords seamlessly and effortlessly with our already well-established habit of thinking in terms of binary oppositions?

There is a third distortion, one that characterizes dualism in particular. To speak of an essence or substance that is fixed, permanent, or eternal is to deny time and change. Perhaps during the era of Parmenides and Heraclitus it was possible to point to the flowing water of a river as an example of change and to a mountain as an example of the unchanging. At least as late as Newton one could still speak of the "fixed stars." Edmund Halley, a contemporary of Newton, was the first to understand that even the so-called fixed stars move. Until Charles Lyell, geologists did not understand that rocks were still being laid down by water and also that due to ice, wind, sand, and water were being altered by erosion. Until Charles Darwin, biology continued to speak of fixed species. Until the arrival of the Big Bang theory, astronomers and other physicists could speak of fixed physical laws. Nowadays, we talk of "natural history." We understand all of these former fixities as flowing; stasis is merely what moves relatively more slowly than other things. If there is something absolutely eternal or fixed, it is beyond perception. At best, such concepts survive largely as "limiting concepts."

Fourth, perhaps the apparently irresolvable dualisms or oppositions help account for the seemingly endless pendulum swings of Western culture, what I term the "zigzag effect." Descartes, Leibniz, and Spinoza, for example, established a rationalist epistemology that affirmed the power of unaided reason to arrive at clear and certain knowledge by means of innate ideas, deduction, intellectual intuition, or *a priori* categories. This was the zig. Locke, Berkeley, and Hume launched a contrary movement that emphasized the role of sense data generated, in most cases, by causal relations with an external, physical world. Here was the zag. Both movements were overstatements, lacking descriptive sensitivity and nuance.

Kant's attempt at a synthesis of the two positions, based as it was on the oppositions of *a priori* vs. *a posteriori*, phenomenal vs. noumenal, form vs. content, and theoretical reason vs. practical reason was no more satisfactory than the long disintegrated and overly simple "medieval synthesis" of revealed theology with natural theology and faith with reason. There was merely the substitution of one set of oppositions for another, a sleight of thought that brought but a temporary and illusory relief. The real culprit, the intellectual habit of reliance on simple binary oppositions, was left unidentified and, thus, "allowed" to perpetuate its deleterious effects.

Then Voltaire, Condorcet, Condillac, La Mettrie, Laplace, D'Holbach, Paine, Butler, and Deism zigged in the Enlightenment's reliance on a combination of reason and experience. The Romanticism of Wordsworth, Coleridge, Goethe, Burke,

Pietism, and Methodism, emphasizing creativity, feeling, intuition, imagination, and the concrete immediacy of living experience, zagged in rebellion.

To his credit, Hegel spotted this pattern of zig and zag and sought to domesticate it by incorporating it into a larger pattern, namely, the dialectic of thesis, antithesis, and synthesis, through which reason unfolded itself in history. Reason reached its culmination (so Hegel believed) in his own philosophy, a philosophy characterized by a final clarity and certainty in which all oppositions were eliminated. Yet this larger pattern, for all of its genius, does not fit all situations. Nowadays, virtually nobody believes absolutely in reason any longer.

Even after twentieth-century philosophy began to understand itself as an enterprise that studies the logic of language, the zigging and zagging continued. Logical Positivism, a school or method that aspired to a rigorous empiricism, believed language was or could be made rational and objective by tying it tightly to observations, especially in science. Deconstruction, on the other hand, viewed language as arbitrary, subjective, and irrational or nonrational. Neither approach was capable of inaugurating a middle way.

If, despite the fact that we are sometimes able to recognize an extreme as an extreme, we cannot readily make the nuanced change to arrive at a balanced mode or manner of reflection, this failure is not unrelated to the largely tacit and still habitual reliance upon binary oppositions that are everywhere at work in our thought, rhetoric, and action. We are still better at criticism than creativity, at self-assertion than self-transformation, at destruction than understanding, at iconoclasm than expressing the wonder of the world.

Fifth, when we elevate one of the oppositions or dualities over the other, we create a hierarchy that privileges the one at the expense of the other: men over women, straights over gays, youth over age, the rich over the poor, Christians over Muslims, Jews over Palestinians, Anglos over Hispanics, human artifacts and activities over the natural environment, religious right over secular left, etc. While in theory there is no necessary reason why this favoritism must occur, it almost always does. Indeed, one might begin to suspect that it is precisely the desire to establish such hierarchies that prompts the creation of dualities.

In a general way, we have reviewed the meaning and implications of dualism in the West. Perhaps now we are in a position to understand better the role it played in what happened at Ole Miss.

Dualism Applied

It was not the case that the South in which I grew up merely *distinguished* whites from blacks (the term "African American" did not exist then). The distinction had hardened into a dualism. Blacks were not simply human beings who differed in visible but superficial ways from whites. Like classes (*varnas*) and castes (*jatis*) in India, blacks and whites were virtually different species, one vastly inferior to the other. Indeed, blacks were not even blacks; they were "Niggers." Whites and "Niggers" did not belong together except in precisely defined circumstances that manifested their hierarchical relation, one in which whites were securely ensconced on top. Perhaps for some whites, blacks were even viewed as

Native Americans in the New World were viewed by some Spanish conquistadors, namely, as nonhumans. They were humanoid in form but lacking in rational souls, the defining feature of humans according to Aristotle.

"Separate but equal," a judicial doctrine concerning the racial segregation of schools, had a *de facto* application to many other dimensions of life as well. In neither case, of course, was there any actual equality. From birth to my mid-20s, I never drank from a water fountain from which any black person had drunk, ate at a restaurant in which any black person had eaten, stayed in a motel or hotel room in which any black person had slept, sat in a classroom in which any black student had sat, attended a church where blacks worshipped, attended a sporting event at which blacks were present as spectators or participants, or attended a movie theater in which any black person sat anywhere but in the balcony. The same could be said by virtually every Southern white prior to the sixties, and, for the most part, blacks could say the same with respect to whites.

The consequences for all were negative; for those on the bottom, they were devastating. The hardening of distinctions, their reification and essentialization, is social and cultural arteriosclerosis. By analogy to its clinical counterpart, this sclerosis leads to sociocultural *rigor mortis*. It effects entrenched positions and a cessation of dialogue. It makes the other dispensable. It resulted in 4,743 lynchings,[5] and those who eluded the noose were relegated to a humiliating and spirit-crushing existence. For Emmit Till, a 14-year-old black boy who whistled at a white woman, it resulted in the fact that his dead body was thrown from a Mississippi bridge into the Tallahatchie River.

Binary oppositions and dualisms, however, are not simply *products* of thought; they are also *ways of thinking*. As soon as discourse gets underway, it seems to bifurcate itself into opposing concepts and viewpoints. Why is this so? Are they the effect of innate structures of the human mind, as Structuralism claimed? Do they follow inevitably from opposable thumbs or bicameral brains, as some biologists or neurologists might be inclined to say? Are they caused by the subject-predicate form of Indo-European languages, as philologists or philosophers might aver? Is not this question itself dualistic, making the assumption that language is separate from thought and that one takes precedence over the other? Is such an assumption another piece of evidence that dualistic thinking is ineluctable? Or are binary oppositions simply habits that can be altered by vigilance and practice? Is it a combination of the above working together in some interactive fashion? For the time being, at least, there is no clear consensus about the answers.

In any event, dualism as a way of thinking is motivated. It serves a human purpose, but it does not necessarily facilitate the quest for dispassionate, objective

---

5. The number 4,743 refers only to documented cases that took place between 1882 and 1968. Three of every four victims were black. Although most took place in the South, they took place in nearly every state in the nation. Moreover, they were not always held in the secrecy of the woods by marginal figures in a community but also in public squares by community leaders. As AP writer Rebecca Carroll reports, nearly 200 anti-lynching bills were introduced into the U. S. Senate during the first half of the twentieth century; all were defeated. Rebecca Carroll, "Senate apologizes for anti-lynching failures," *The Advocate-Messenger* (Danville, Kentucky), June 14, 2005.

truth or harmony or even cooperation. John Welwood speaks in dramatic and negative terms about such motivations:

> The dualistic mind is essentially a survival mechanism on a par with fangs, claws, stingers, scales, shells, and quills that other animals use to protect themselves. By maintaining a separate self-defense, it attempts to provide a haven of security in an impermanent world marked by continual change, unpredictability, and loss. Yet the very boundaries that create a sense of safety leave us feeling cut off and disconnected.[6]

One need not endorse Welwood's claim without reservation in order to acknowledge some truth in it. For example, Plato—at least the received Plato—faced with the skepticism of the Sophists and the frightening flux of Heraclitus, gave himself over to dualistic thinking, dividing reality into two worlds, walling off the flux in one and asserting its ultimate unreality while locating his true identity and home inside the safety of the unchanging eternity of the other world.[7] Descartes, floundering in the wake of the shattered medieval synthesis, found unanimity neither within academia nor in the wider world. In his search for absolute certainty, he, too, turned to dualism, pushing all that could be doubted into an outside in order to disclose the indubitable "I think" within.

The impulse to self-defense, of course, is to be found in all of us; it is virtually omnipresent. Perhaps not coincidentally, at least if Welwood is correct, the number of binary oppositions and dualisms is virtually endless. Here are but a few of the oppositions and/or dualisms that we have inherited or created. They represent the result of a mere 5 minutes of recollection on my part: nature vs. history, works vs. grace, supernatural vs. natural, intelligible world vs. material world, empiricism vs. rationalism, phenomenal vs. noumenal, catastrophism vs. gradualism, creation vs. evolution, mind vs. body, psychology vs. logic, steady state vs. big bang, essentialism vs. existentialism, particle vs. wave, superstructure vs. deep structure, transcendent vs. immanent, inside vs. outside, idealism vs. realism, covering law vs. continuous series explanations, nucleus vs. cytoplasm, sperm vs. egg, Romanticism vs. the Enlightenment, nature vs. culture, revealed theology

---

6. John Welwood, "Double Vision: Duality and Nonduality in Human Experience" in John Prendergast, Peter Fenner, and Sheila Krystal (eds), *The Sacred Mirror: Nondual Wisdom and Psychotherapy* (St. Paul, Minnesota: Paragon House, 2003), 139.

7. Plato's writings are sometimes divided into three periods, each containing certain of his writings. My colleague in philosophy, Rob Colter, classifies them as follows: Early (Euthyphro, Apology, Crito, and Meno); Middle (Phaedrus, Phaedo, Cratyllus, Gorgias, and Republic); and Late (Timaeus, Laws, Theaetetus, Parmenides, and Sophist). He also points out that the Meno could really go anywhere, Phaedrus could easily be late, some books of the Republic are early, and Theaetetus and Parmenides are, perhaps, transitional between middle and late. Some current scholars argue that the claim that Plato is a dualist is based on the early dialogues and represents a reading of Plato influenced by Plotinus. The later dialogues, they say, do much to undermine the traditional view. Others, however, defend the traditional view. The debate is ongoing. In this chapter, I follow the traditional or received view, primarily because my concern is not with what Plato may have intended but how he was actually understood by and affected subsequent thinkers.

vs. natural theology, faith vs. reason, monism vs. dualism, reason vs. emotion, nominalism vs. realism, subject vs. object, potential vs. actual, good vs. evil, right vs. wrong, beautiful vs. ugly, simple vs. complex, necessary vs. contingent, meaning vs. referent, real vs. imaginary, raw vs. cooked, background vs. foreground, conscious vs. unconscious, action vs. contemplation, theory vs. practice, freedom vs. determinism, diachronic vs. synchronic, Apollonian vs. Dionysian, appearance vs. reality, one vs. many, change vs. stasis, conscious vs. unconscious, literal vs. metaphorical, cognitive vs. emotive, immanent vs. transcendent, inside vs. outside, vice vs. virtue, red states vs. blue states, and life vs. death. These are a few of the better known ones, but almost any reader could add indefinitely to this list. All are instances in which oversimplification or some other form of distortion occurs.

By now we ought to know well enough that "map is not territory." Taken literally, the expression refers merely to simple, territorial cases for which fairly simple perceptions can settle most differences. By contrast, most of the oppositions in the foregoing list are vastly more abstract, complex, and frustrating; their epistemological status and ontological status are not easily settled. Indeed, they may never be.

In the West the intellectual practice of drawing distinctions to the point of creating dichotomies is not, however, regarded as a rogue practice to be eliminated, used infrequently and with great discretion, or merely tolerated. It is a common practice endorsed and justified by one of the laws of logic formulated by Aristotle, namely, the law of excluded middle. The law can be stated for things, classes, or propositions. With respect to propositions, it says that any proposition is either true or false. For things, it says that anything is either A or not-A. It is held in the West to be essential to rationality, the paradigm of correct thinking. Like its companions, the laws of identity and non-contradiction, it is judged to be a tautology—always true, regardless of the empirical data or phenomenal circumstances.

Even if one regards the law as unimpeachable in and of itself, there is, however, the matter of its applicability to reality. If the law is true under any and all empirical or phenomenal circumstances, then it cannot be a generalization derived from the experience of concrete particulars. Its authority must rest, then, solely on an intellectualist intuition. Unless one is prepared to grant that such an intuition stems from a passionless, transcendent, universal, or infallible mind, then it is an intuition that is motivated. Its apparent motivation is similar to Descartes's, namely, a desire for clarity and certainty even at the price of divisiveness, a desire that at its extreme does not hesitate to ride roughshod over lived, experienced reality.

Western thought has not been altogether unaware of the aforementioned difficulties. Kant's antinomies are a moment of insight in this regard. With respect to being-in-general, he articulated four traditional metaphysical theses and their antitheses: (1) the world has a temporal beginning and is spatially limited vs. the world is infinite spatially and has no beginning, (2) existence is comprised of simple substances or composites made of them vs. there are neither composites nor simples, (3) freedom exists vs. all things are determined by the laws of nature, and (4) absolutely necessary being exists vs. no absolute being exists. Since both the theses and the antitheses can be proven to be true (so Kant held), we cannot know being-in-general but must limit our investigations to the phenomenal realm.[8] These antinomies are binary oppositions expressed in propositional form.

Whether dimly or acutely sensing the problems with thinking dualistically or in terms of binary oppositions, the West has devised strategies to deal with them. These strategies are reflected in the great number of phrases and concepts employed to characterize the relation between binary opposites. Among them are the following: holding them "in tension"; "oscillating" between them; seeing them as "complementary"; connecting them "dialectically"; noting their "intersection"; calling their relation "paradoxical"; keeping them "in balance"; "substituting" for the original oppositions a pair of terms whose meanings are similar but not so dichotomous; "mediating" between them; understanding them as connected by "betweenness" or the "in between"; "straddling" them; allowing them to "interact"; focusing on the "interval" between them; "deconstructing" them; "synthesizing" them; and seeing them as "overlapping," "interlacing," "interfacing," or "interlinking."

The tactics mentioned in this list are indicative of several things. First, the users of the aforementioned terms are unwilling to give up either of the binary opposites that preoccupy them. Both of the opposites are valued as necessary. Even the materialist, who rejects the mental or spiritual in an ontological or metaphysical sense, relies on the conceptual/linguistic opposition of material vs. spiritual to define his position. Second, there is an unwillingness to surrender the clarity or rationality that binaries allegedly provide, even while acknowledging to some degree that such goals are problematic. Third, virtually all the images portray the relationship connecting the terms as lying on a single logical and/or ontological level. This arrangement allows of no possibility of a complete resolution of the dualism and little opportunity even to lessen the tension, slowdown or halt the oscillation, or end the dialectic. The language describing the relation between binary opposites functions largely in the two-dimensional conceptual and imaginative environment of flatland. This idea will be elaborated in Chapter 8.

Process thought is an exception, having employed at least two strategies to deal with opposing pairs. One is to see binary opposites as parts of a whole. Pistons, rings, engine blocks, carburetors, spark plugs, rods, etc. are parts of engines. In this case, however, Process thought is unwilling to call an engine a genuine whole but sees it as an assemblage or "aggregate," a mere summation of the parts. Atoms and human beings, on the other hand, are regarded as examples of proper wholes or "actual entities." But what are their parts? Electrons and protons? Bodies and minds? Did these alleged parts, like the carburetor and engine block, exist as discrete entities prior to being assembled into a whole atom or whole person? If not, then the use of "parts" seems problematic. The resolution is to say that hearts, lungs, brains, and kidneys are not discovered or manufactured and then assembled but are gradually differentiated from the cells of a single fertilized egg. The parts of

8. Mulunkyaputta, one of the Buddha's disciples, complained and threatened to quit the *sangha* because the Buddha maintained that it was not useful to concern oneself with trying to answer 14 questions. The questions included whether or not the universe had a beginning, whether it will have an end, and whether the self survives death (*parinirvana*).

genuine wholes, by contrast to the parts of aggregates, are at least partially internally, rather than merely externally, related. They are organic wholes.

A second device used by Process thought[9] is abstract/concrete analysis. If parts or aspects are internally or organically related to wholes, then they are abstractions and the wholes are concrete. The former are derived from the latter by the operations of a thinking that limits its attention, simplifies what is more complex, and makes more determinate what is more inchoate.

For the most part, however, the West has simply learned to live among the contraries and contradictions, as anthropologist Elsie Clews Parsons lived among scores of snakes, both poisonous and nonpoisonous, on the floor of a Hopi Snake Clan kiva.[10] Indeed, Existentialism in particular often seems to heighten such tensions deliberately and to delight in them. But given that the oppositions are so frequently held absolutely, whether in thought or action, the life lived according to them has often been one of strife. From the perspective of absolutism, acts of yielding, compromising, negotiating, seeking middle ground, and adopting a more moderate or nuanced stance can only be seen as weakness, loss, or selling out.

Asia, by contrast to the West, has a long tradition of nondualism. Indeed, Asia is its birthplace. Of the Asian traditions, Buddhism, especially Mahayana Buddhism, has attracted the most attention in the West. Can Buddhism supply the requisite assistance to generate a more satisfying future for the West? Can it offer clues leading not to a *faux* middle way, a mere clinging to both extremes, but to a genuine one? Let us see.

Buddhist Nondualism and the Middle Way

According to legendary accounts, Siddhartha Gautama, the Buddha, grew up in the lap of luxury in Kapilavasthu, the capital city of the principality of Shakya, of which his father, Suddhodana, was the ruler. As Suddhodana's eldest son and designated successor, Siddhartha received the finest education locally available. Shortly after Siddhartha's birth, Asita, a seer, predicted that if the boy encountered suffering in his life, he would become a great religious teacher. If not, he would become a great political ruler. In order to ensure the latter outcome, the father arranged to provide his son with a sheltered life. To forestall boredom, the boy was moved about among three palaces, and 40,000 dancing girls were assigned to entertain him. Here, then, was an extreme form of living, a life of self-centered indulgence.

9.　Existentialists, phenomenologists, and individuals in other philosophical traditions also make use of abstract/concrete analyses.

10.　Dr. Elsie Clews Parsons studied the Hopi tribe. On one occasion, she was invited to enter and remain in the Hopi Snake Clan kiva during the 8 days and nights leading up to the snake dance in the village plaza. As she sat on the kiva floor making notes, rattlesnakes crawled across her lap. She is reported to have said, "God, how they make me creep!" See Frank Waters, *Masked Gods: Navaho and Pueblo Ceremonialism* (New York: Ballantine Books, 1970), 314.

Siddhartha's increasing insistence upon seeing the outside world led to a chariot ride (or rides) through the city streets, in which he encountered an old man, a sick man, a dead man, and a monk. Collectively, these are known as the "Four Holy Sights." Through the first three he learned that the destiny of all sentient beings was disease, old age, and death. From the monk, serene in the face of the knowledge of such suffering, Siddhartha received the insight that there might be a way to defeat such "enemies." Soon afterward, in what would be called "the Great Renunciation," Siddhartha slipped out of the palace and Kapilavasthu under cover of darkness, leaving behind his parents, wife, and newborn son, and headed for the forest, where he took up the life of an ascetic. He threw himself fully into the rigors of self-mortification, pushing himself to the limit. Karen Armstrong, relying on traditional accounts, describes these rigors as follows:

> Gotama went either naked or clad in the roughest hemp. He slept out in the open during the freezing winter nights, lay on a mattress of spikes and even fed on his own urine and feces. He held his breath for so long that his head seemed to split and there was fearful roaring in his ears. He stopped eating and his bones stuck out "like a row of spindles . . . or the beams of an old shed." When he touched his stomach, he could almost feel his spine. His hair fell out and his skin became black and withered.[11]

One day, weak from severe fasting, he fainted and might have died had others not gotten some food into him. At that moment, Siddhartha had arrived at the polar opposite of his former self-indulgent life in the palace.

Once revived, he happened to overhear a conversation in a boat passing on the nearby river. A musician was saying to his student: "If you tighten the string too much, it will snap, and if you leave it too slack, it won't play." These words triggered an insight into their applicability to his existential dilemma. He saw that a healthy body is a necessary condition for the pursuit of spiritual transformation. Food is neither to be rejected nor pursued gluttonously but ingested as medicine. Neither extreme asceticism nor lavish living eliminates ego; both strengthen it. He had arrived at the notion of an ethical middle way between self-indulgence and self-abnegation. The Noble Eightfold Path, which he created later, lays out the specifics of a praxical middle way.

More important for the purposes of this volume, however, is the notion of a metaphysical middle way, which is expressed in the Buddha's doctrines of no-self (*Anatman*), impermanence (*anicca*), and dependent co-origination (*pratityasamutpada*). In the sixth century BCE, only two possibilities were available for speaking philosophically about existence—permanent existence (*astitta*) and no existence (*nastitta*). These two options constitute a metaphysical dualism. For Hinduism, buried deeply within several peripheral and illusory layers (sheaths) of the self lay the *Atman*, the true and real self. It was an eternal, unchanging substance and was declared to be identical to *Brahman*, the generalized consciousness that pervades the world and the only genuine reality there is. The Buddha rejected such a self both because he had not experienced

11. Karen Armstrong, *Buddha* (New York: Penguin, 2001), 63.

Atman during his years of practicing *raja yoga* under the supervision of two of Hinduism's leading gurus, Alara Kalama and Udrakka Ramaputta, and also because it was incompatible with his doctrine of *anicca*, the experienced-based idea that everything is impermanent and changing. Nevertheless, he was reluctant to deny the existence of any self whatsoever, for experience testifies against that possibility also. Here was an opening for conceiving a self that constituted a metaphysical middle way. That self was the *namarupa* (name and form), a holistic self comprised of the *skandhas*, five interacting processes (body, feelings, perceptions, dispositions, and consciousness). Such a self was changing and, therefore, consistent with *anicca*.

Another of the Buddha's contributions to a metaphysical middle way was his doctrine of causality, *pratityasamutpada* (dependent co-origination), which developed initially in the context of philosophical anthropology. One rival school, the *Ajivakas*, advocated complete determinism. Another school, the *Lokayatas*, rejected the view that one event causes another in favor of the notion that each event causes itself. The Buddha's position was comprised of three elements. First, every effect has multiple causes rather than a single one, a claim with which both Aristotle and Freud would concur. Second, causality is circular rather than linear. Erik Erikson affirms such a circular causality in his theory of the human self as being created by the ongoing interaction of three processes—the biological, the sociocultural, and the psychological. Each process influences and is influenced by the other two.[12] In the Buddha's case, the circular causality is at work in the interaction of the five processes of the *namarupa* and in the interaction of the self with others. Both multiple causes and circular causes are illustrated by the twelve links in the chain of causality that was used to explain how ignorance (the first link) leads to suffering (the last link).

The third element of the Buddha's theory of causality is that one of the multiple causes is always *karma*, understood as the consequences arising from both past and present actions. The former (past) is a nod to determinism, while the latter (present) affirms some limited scope for freedom. Dependent co-origination, then, is a middle way between total determinism, on the one hand, and absolute freedom, on the other. It is also a middle way between no permanent self and no self at all. Taken together, these three forms of causality rule out the concept of an independent self in favor of an interdependent one; the self is constituted by and in a web of causal relationships.

Such a metaphysical middle way also implies an epistemological middle way. If the self is constituted in and by a web of causal relations, it is not independent of the world. Thus, while there can be a subject-object distinction, there can be no subject-object dualism. The absence of an inner-outer, subject-object gap to be inexplicably crossed means that the necessity of complete skepticism is ruled out. On the other hand, since knowledge is based on the self's experience as part of the web of interacting events, absolutely certain knowledge is rejected as well.

---

12. Erik Erikson, *Childhood and Society*, rev. ed. (New York: W. W. Norton & Company, Inc., 1963), 46, 137–138.

The self cannot step outside the web in order to view it as an object arrayed with utter clarity before either the eye or the mind's eye.

Of the many schools of early Buddhism, the Theravada school, established originally in Sri Lanka, is of special importance both because it was the last Hinayana school to survive but especially because it produced the first redaction of the Buddha's teachings. Much of Theravada praxis emphasizes restraint and non-attachment. The latter is helpful in understanding Buddhist logic and rhetoric concerning nonduality as the middle way.

Attachment is a form of that egoistic craving or addiction (*tanha*) that the Buddha identifies in his Four Noble Truths as the cause of suffering and dissatisfaction in life. It enslaves persons to habitual actions aimed at the satisfaction of ignorant desires that cannot be realized or that do not bring the expected fulfillment. Like the Buddha, Theravada recommends the practice of non-attachment. Unfamiliarity with Buddhist rhetoric might lead one to assume, mistakenly, that non-attachment is the opposite of attachment. In fact, the binary opposite of attachment is detachment; non-attachment, by contrast, is the middle way between them.

Gluttony, for example, is an addiction to food. Its opposite is self-starvation, as the Buddha well knew from his own experience of eating as little as one bean a day during his years of extreme asceticism but also from the Jain practice of *sallakhana* (self-starvation that aims at death). The middle way with respect to eating does not consist simply of ingesting a quantity of food intermediate between the amount eaten by the glutton and that eaten by the ascetic. Non-attachment recognizes that both positions are but different ways of satisfying egoistic desires related to food. Non-attachment rejects the preoccupation with food itself, the very attempt at ego-gratification through food. Non-attachment, then, lies on a different level than attachment and detachment. Indeed, one would be as justified to speak of non-detachment as to speak of non-attachment. Since there are probably more gluttons in the world than ascetics, however, "non-attachment" is usually the more pertinent expression. Another name for non-attachment is "equanimity," a middle way between the extremes of craving and aversion.

Centuries after the Buddha's *parinirvana* (death), Buddhist intellectuals undertook the further analysis of the *skandhas* into several underlying levels of constituents: first, *ayatanas*, then *dhatus*, then *dharmas*. Ultimately, the Sarvastivadins, a Hinayana sect, postulated *svabhava*, a permanent substance or essence, as the rock bottom reality underlying and sustaining all the others. Here was another of kind of *Atman*, a material rather than a spiritual one, and it called for another Buddha to exterminate it as Siddhartha had expunged the original. This exterminator or "second Buddha" was Nagarjuna, a second century CE south Indian monk. His method was philosophical dialectics based on the doctrine of *sunyata* or emptiness, which he declared to be identical to the Buddha's dependent-origination. He applied these tools to a variety of Buddhist concepts (time, causality, *nirvana*, and *samsara*, etc.), all of which he believed to be dependent on the very un-Buddhist idea of *svabhava*. A look at his treatment of time will be instructive.

Normally, when we think or speak of time, we do so by relying on such terms as "past," "present," and "future." These terms appear (both visually and audibly) to be quite distinct. If asked to what do the terms refer, we might reply, "To the concepts 'past,' 'present,' and 'future.'" These three apparently distinct concepts, in turn, might lead us to suppose that they refer to three separate and distinct realities, each with its own permanent, unchanging essence or *svabhava*. But such an outcome makes it impossible to understand how the present could ever "turn into" (changes) the past or how the future could ever be transformed (changed) into the present. After all, each is believed to be totally independent of the others. (See Figure 1.1.)

On the other hand, if asked to define "present," we would almost certainly do one of two things: (1) supply a synonym for "present" or (2) offer a definition that includes a reference, tacit or explicit, to "future" and/or "past." In the first case, one might say that the present is "now" or "this very moment," which may not be helpful because those terms themselves may need to be defined. In the more likely second case, one might say, "The present is what comes after the past and before the future." Nagarjuna's tactic is to focus on the second case, pointing out that the meaning of any one of the three terms is dependent on the meaning of the other two. Consequently, the terms are interdependent. Viewing the words as interdependent leads to viewing the three concepts of time and then the three realities of time as interdependent, and the interdependence of the three realities eliminates their fixed essences and allows for the change that makes time flow. (See Figure 1.2.)

Nagarjuna's dialectic, then, is an application of emptiness (identified as dependent co-origination) to language, and it shows that words, too, lack *svabhava*—that is, an independent definitional essence or fixed meaning. This insight destabilizes all linguistic distinctions, oppositions, and dichotomies.

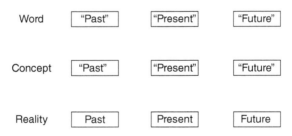

Figure 1.1 *Time as dualistic.*

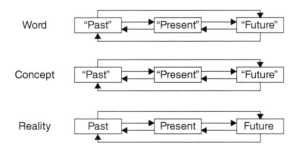

Figure 1.2 *Time as nondualistic.*

Eventually, Buddhism migrated eastward to China. There, it encountered the indigenous religion, Taoism. Among the claims of Taoism is that *yu*, the namable world of being—both the whole of it and its parts—arises ultimately from *wu*, unnamable and undivided non-being. In other words, *wu* is the formless and mysterious potential or source of all that becomes actualized, formed, and rational. According to Tom Kasulis, *Ch'an* Buddhism (and, later, *Zen*) integrates this Taoist idea of "nonbeing-as-source" with Nagarjuna's *sunyata* to create the concept of nothingness (Chinese *wu*, Japanese, *mu*).[13] An important difference here, however, is, as Kasulis notes, that while Taoism is interested in the source of everything (the universe), *Ch'an* and *Zen* are interested in "the source of our experience of the universe," although the focus is more frequently on the experience of the self than on its wider context. The importance of nothingness for this chapter is that it is the more comprehensive and ultimately unbounded context from which distinctions, binary oppositions, and dichotomies arise and into which they may, perhaps, be dissolved. Nothingness, then, is essential to the Buddhist middle way. From this perspective, emptiness and nothingness are not empty of reality but full. Reality is simply too rich for the simplifications of language.

Another vehicle for arriving at the Buddhist middle way is the doctrine of the Two Truths, enunciated by Nagarjuna. In chapter 24 of his *Mulamadhyamikakarika* he writes:

> The Buddha's teaching of the Dharma is based on two truths: a truth of worldly convention and an ultimate truth. Those who do not understand the distinction drawn between these two truths do not understand the Buddha's profound teaching. Without a foundation in the conventional truth, the significance of the ultimate cannot be taught. Without understanding the significance of the ultimate, liberation cannot be achieved. (Ch. 24:8–10)[14]

Some interpreters take Nagarjuna to be negating conventional truth in favor of *sunyata* (emptiness) understood as an unconditioned or absolute or ultimate truth. Indeed, earlier Buddhists had identified the doctrine of dependent co-arising with ultimate truth. For Nagarjuna, however, "emptiness" had a double meaning, a conventional one and an ultimate one. The conventional meaning is found in verse 18 of chapter 24 of his *Mulamadhyamikakarika*: "We state that whatever is dependent arising, that is emptiness. That is dependent upon convention. That itself is the middle path."[15] The equation of emptiness with dependent co-arising is Nagarjuna's conventional meaning of emptiness; it is necessary in order to lead people to the ultimate view.

What concerned Nagarjuna is that if people became bound to the doctrine of emptiness, then liberation would elude them. After all, clinging to views is itself a form

---

13.   T. P. Kasulis, *Zen Action/Zen Person* (Honolulu: University of Hawaii Press, 1981). See chapter 3.

14.   This translation is by Jay Garfield in his *The Fundamental Wisdom of the Middle Way* (New York: Oxford University Press, 1995), 297–298.

15.   Here I quote David J. Kalupahana's translation in his *Nagarjuna: The Philosophy of the Middle Way* (Albany, New York: State University of New York Press, 1986), 399.

of clinging (*tanha*), the principal cause of suffering, according to the Buddha's Four Noble Truths). Clinging to "right view" (Buddhist teaching that leads to awakening) itself binds one to suffering. The ultimate meaning of emptiness, then, is the cessation of clinging to any views at all, even Buddhist ones.[16] This second meaning of "emptiness" is ultimate truth. In other words, Nagarjuna aims at dissuading people from doing philosophy and encouraging them to return to the practice of meditation.

Paul Williams, who thinks that the two truths might be better understood as "two levels of reality," offers the following explanation:

> The everyday conventional world must be accepted not as an ultimate world but precisely as what it really is—the everyday conventional world. That is, it must be seen correctly as lacking inherent existence. The other point Nagarjuna is making is that when the everyday conventional world is thus seen correctly it is apparent that emptiness (the ultimate truth) and the world are not opposed to each other but rather mutually imply each other.[17]

In other words, Nagarjuna does not eliminate the conventional world in favor of the ultimate world but dissolves the *sclerosis* of the conventional world in the solvent of *sunyata* so that the conventional world can be properly affirmed. This interpretation is confirmed by his statement that between the two truths "there is not the slightest difference whatsoever"[18] (*Mulamadhyamikakarika* (*MMK*) 25:20). Later, the Chinese T'ien-t'ai Buddhist thinker Chih-I developed a doctrine of three truths: the "provisional" (conventional) truth of the Abhidharma scholastics; the "ultimate" truth of Madhyamika; and the "complete" truth of the Lotus, Avatamsaka, and Nirvana Sutras. In so doing, he makes even clearer than did Nagarjuna that convention emptied by *sunyata*, not mere *sunyata* by itself, is the middle way.[19]

One format employed by Nagarjuna to dissolve the sclerosis of discrete, fixed essence and identity is the *catuskoti* or tetralemma, which lays out the four logical options for understanding assertions. They are as follows:

1. X is Y.
2. X is not-Y.

16.   Buddhists speak of Buddhism (both its teaching and practice) as a raft that takes one from one side of the river (*samsara*, a life of suffering) to the other side (*nirvana*, the cessation of suffering). Having reached the far side, one leaves the raft behind.

17.   Paul Williams, *Mahayana Buddhism: The Doctrinal Foundations* (New York: Routledge, 1989), 70.

18.   Nagarjuna, *Mulamadhyamikakarika* (*MMK*) 25:20. In Kenneth K. Inada, *Nagarjuna: A Translation of his Mulamadhyamikakarika with an Introductory Essay* (Tokyo: Hokuseido, 1970).

19.   Gordon Kaufman interprets the "two truths" doctrine as a distinction between "first-order" knowledge or truth and "second-order" knowledge or truth. The former is ordinary knowledge about everyday experience. The latter is a "metaknowledge," in which elitists admit that first-order knowledge is but an approximation of reality and has mere "pragmatic utility." Yet this metaknowledge shares the same limitations as first-order knowledge. See his *God, Mystery, Diversity* (Minneapolis, Minnesota: Fortress Press, 1996), 177–178.

3. X is both Y and not-Y.
4. X is neither Y nor not-Y.

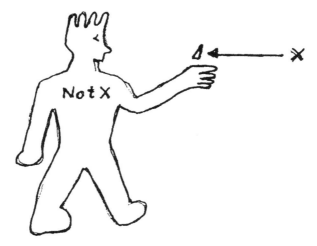

Figure 1.3 *Thumb as dualistic (thumb separated).*

Nagarjuna's dialectic is intended to discredit all four on the grounds that all four assume *svabhava* or inherent existence.

Here is a simple illustration. If Figure 1.3 represents true reality, then the tetralemma allows for four possible statements.

1. The thumb is X.
2. The thumb is not-X.
3. The thumb is both X and not-X.
4. The thumb is neither X nor not-X.

The first lemma, then, is clearly true, and the remaining three lemmas are clearly false. Conventional language works well here because X and not-X are taken to have discrete essences (*svabhavas*); language and reality are suitably matched.

In Figure 1.4, however, none of the alternative lemmas is utterly true or utterly false because neither X nor not-X is a discrete essence or *svabhava*. Thumbs, hands, arms, legs, torsos, heads, feet are not, first of all, separate parts that are then assembled and related externally. Fingers, hands, arms, etc. are differentiated from within the embryo. They are from the start interdependent and internally related. Conventional language cannot readily reflect that interrelatedness. To point to an interrelated thumb is, to some degree, to point to the entire body, because there are no fault lines dividing the body into discrete parts that can be named distinctly by nouns.

A. L. Herman illustrates the tetralemma in a particularly helpful way by applying it to the concept of causality as it relates to the production of cheese from milk. This example of one thing turning into another reflects the Indian context

Figure 1.4 *Thumb as nondualistic (thumb joined).*

for causality rather than the Western notion, based on purely external relations such as billiard balls striking each other. Each lemma is associated with a particular school of Indian philosophy.

1. *Self-Causation.* In this case, milk is the cause and cheese is the effect. But the Buddhist Sarvastivadins and Hindu Samkhya philosophers held that cause and effect are identical. If so, then no change occurs and milk merely produces itself (milk). No cheese is produced. If the claim is made that milk and cheese, although different, share a common, underlying substance that accounts for identity, then Nagarjuna can claim that such a substance is analogous to the *Atman* (unchanging self), which the Buddha rejected.

2. *Other-Causation.* The Sautrantikas, another Buddhist school, held that cause and effect are different. Nagarjuna simply points out that if they are both independent and unchanging substances, then they have no relation, causal or otherwise. Neither can effect a change in the other; milk cannot be the cause of the cheese.

3. *Self-Causation and Other-Causation.* The solution proposed by the Jains is that both identity and difference are involved in causation. Herman observes that Nagarjuna points out, however, that if both X and Y are unitary entities, then the Jain position is contradictory because it amounts to asserting both X=Y and not X=Y. Alternatively, if X and Y are composites, then asserting that causation links the parts of X and Y that are identical amounts to a reversion to the self-causation position. On the other hand, if the causal connection links the parts that are different, then other-causation is asserted. Both these options, however, have already been eliminated.

4. *Neither Self-Causation nor Other-Causation.* This final option, put forward by the Materialists and Skeptics, has prompted a variety of interpretations.

Tom Kasulis suggests that applying the term "identical" to a relationship between cause and effect is a category mistake, like positing that the color of knowledge is red. Herman views the fourth lemma as claiming that cheese appears "uncaused and at random." Nagarjuna himself objects that it lacks reasons to support it and is, therefore, dogmatic. Robert Magliola views the fourth lemma as the least wrong and as "the rhetorically most effective," pointing out that in some instances Nagarjuna himself affirms provisionally assertions of that form.

A final tool in the Mahayana Buddhist tool kit is the logic of *soku-hi*, advanced in more recent times by Nishida, Kitaro and the Kyoto School of Zen Buddhism. It is expressed in the Japanese phrase "*zettai mujinteki jiko doitsu*," which is often translated as "the self identity of absolute contradictions." Tom Kasulis emphasizes that this is not to be understood as a biconditional between A and not-A, which would violate the logical principle of non-contradiction. It is saying that A exists only insofar as it is distinguished from not-A. Thus, he often expresses it as "A *vis-à-vis* not-A."[20] Steve Odin prefers to call it "the absolute contradiction of self-identity."[21] In any case, it is a logic of affirmation and negation, of is and is not. Its value is in mediating between oppositions. For example, a famous line from the *Heart Sutra* says, "Form is emptiness, and emptiness is form." If form and emptiness are read as self-identical and as absolute opposites, then in Western absolute logic the statement becomes A and not-A. This is a contradiction and makes no sense. Read as "Form *soku* emptiness," the statement says, in effect, "Form is like emptiness in some respects and unlike emptiness in other respects." In this non-absolute Buddhist logic, the contradiction or dichotomy (but not the simple distinction) vanishes.

We have been examining Mahayana Buddhist resources for eradicating dualism and finding the middle way. Let's review them now.

First, Mahayana denies the existence of fixed essences, inherent existence, or substances such as *Atman* or *svabhava*. All things are empty of such essences. Second, it affirms that all things are causally conditioned. Nothing is independent; rather, all things are interdependent. Third, it affirms that words are relationally defined. This is an application of the Buddha's *pratityasamutpada* and Nagarjuna's *sunyata* to conceptualization and language. Fourth, the source of the conceptualized, objectified world is nonbeing. *Sunyata* places all things into a wider, interdependent context, often characterized as a net or web. A web or net, however, is two-dimensional. Thing and context seem to lie at the same logical or ontological level. What nonbeing as source does is to add a third dimension, the dimension of depth. This lower logical and ontological level is an even more potent solvent for both dualisms and binary oppositions. While Hinduism's *Atman* transcends the higher mind of intellect and reason, Mahayana's nothingness

---

20. Kasulis' views here appear in my notes on his lecture of 7/18/97 in an NEH (National Endowment for the Humanities) Summer Seminar on Zen philosophy that took place at Ohio State University.

21. Odin's preference appears in my notes on a lecture he gave as part of the NEH Summer Institute on Nagarjuna at the University of Hawaii in the summer of 1989.

transdescends them. Here is the basis for the West's characterization of Asia as "inscrutable." Fifth, there is the doctrine of two truths. Sixth, there is the logic of *soku hi*. Given such tools in its toolbox, Asia is far better equipped than the West to deal with all varieties of dualisms and other binary oppositions.

To this point we have examined the meaning of dualism in the West and in Asia. We have also surveyed some of the ways the two cultures cope with dualism. It may now occur to the reader to inquire as to what meaning "dualism" and "non-dualism" will have in the remainder of this volume. The answer is that I will use them in one or more of the following senses. First, the assertion of nonduality will be intended to reject ontological dualisms based on unchanging substances, fixed essences, inherent existences, or fixed identities, whether in subjects or objects, concepts or things. Second, the assertion of nonduality will deny the absolute independence of all binaries, whether they refer to things, conceptions, or linguistic meanings. Third, the affirmation of nonduality intends to point to a wider, deeper, more comprehensive context as the source of dualities. Fourth, "nonduality" will also be used to call attention to the fact that while distinctions may be both necessary and legitimate, they do not picture concretely and exhaustively the realities they purport to describe; rather, they picture things abstractly and selectively. In other words, binaries both represent and misrepresent reality. Language is often adequate to achieve its purposes, but it is not a perfect mirror. Finally, in affirming nonduality, I also intend to issue a warning and a reminder that binary distinctions and oppositions can all too readily harden into full-blown dualisms. Such a warning is meant to forestall that outcome.

Now that dualism has been observed, defined, and applied, perhaps the next question is this: How can it be avoided? More particularly, how can the West avoid it? Surely the West can no more cease speaking, thinking, and acting than can Asia, and the West is unlikely to convert to Buddhism. The reasons for such conclusions will be elaborated upon in later chapters but can be indicated now in a preliminary way. Buddhism is a religion rooted in monasticism. Its rhetoric is significantly negative. Conceptually, it is often nihilistic (whether or not it intends ultimately to be). And the tactics of Zen practice (certainly Rinzai), for example, present the religion from the point of view of an unenlightened person. One is expected to arrive at a more complete and positive perspective on reality by meditative practice, especially in a monastery and under the direction of a master. Although some American Zen masters—Charlotte Joko Beck and Philip Kapleau, to mention but two—have been experimenting with an "everyday" form of Zen, this movement remains minuscule in size.

Is the West utterly, then, devoid of any trace of homegrown nondualism? Is it bereft of any wherewithal for dealing effectively with dualism? The West does, of course, contain its own tradition of monasticism, but it is frequently dualistic, too, based as it often is on Plato. It also contains a tiny tradition of negative theology associated with mysticism and Plotinus. In any event, Christian monasticism and negative theology have been and remain largely rejected by the vast majority of persons in Western society and culture, and there is no basis for expecting that to change.

But is that all that can be said? Is it just possible that a neglected or forgotten stream of thought at the root of the Western intellectual tradition possesses unexpected and unutilized resources for eliminating dualism? Mahayana, which developed centuries after Theravada, said that its new teaching had come from the Buddha himself, who at his death had left it in the care of the *nagas* (serpents living underground) or, alternatively, with a hermit in the Himalyas, until the time was ripe for revealing it to the people. Are there "*nagas*" or "hermits" in the West? And do they hold the key to an alternative middle way, one that the West can wholeheartedly embrace as its own?

The following two chapters will explore the possibility that there are clues to a Western middle way in ancient Hebraic culture. Hebraic culture, however, is pre-philosophical. Hence the clues we may find there will necessarily lie beneath or prior to philosophical reflection as we now know it. Let us see what they are.

Chapter 2
Hebrew Pre-philosophical Nondualism

Derrida's critique of the metaphysics of presence . . . is actually just good old Jewish theology.[1]

John Caputo

Frustrated by the dualism of the West, we are searching for another way. Inspired by the nonduality of Asia, we are searching for a middle way, a middle way between the extremes of Western dualism. But if East is East and West is West, how can Asia's middle way take root in the West? Would it not be too inscrutable, too alien, and too unworkable? Aren't East and West themselves binary oppositions, even dualities? Perhaps, first of all, before we can find a Western middle way, we need to find a middle way between East and West? Is such a task possible? In fact, there is, I believe, a neglected possibility for doing so, and it will now become our focus.

Lying between Asia and the West, at once separating and connecting them, is a land bridge, namely, the Middle East (or Western Asia). As such, of course, it is merely a geographic middle and, therefore, holds out no promise for what we seek. But the Middle East is also a cultural reality, one with an intimate connection to the West. Indeed, it forms one of the three principal roots (Greece and Rome being the others) of Western Civilization. To be more specific, I am alluding to Hebraic culture, whose presence among us continues in the Bible, Judaism, Islam, and Christianity. By "Hebraic," however, I do not necessarily mean "Jewish." Judaism, as I understand it, began to emerge in the postexilic period with the emphasis by Ezra and Nehemiah on purity and exclusiveness and was further shaped by the rabbis in the period of the Roman destruction of the temple in 70 CE. In this volume, "Hebraic" will refer largely to the pre-Jewish culture and religion of ancient Israel (preexilic, exilic, and postexilic) insofar as it manifests itself in the Hebrew Bible (Old Testament).

---

1. John Caputo, "Beyond Sovereignty: Many Nations Under the Weakness of God," *Soundings: An Interdisciplinary Journal* 89 (Spring/Summer 2006): 31.

The promise of Hebraic culture for the present project is associated with the observation, made repeatedly by some biblical scholars, that in important respects Hebrew thought is nondualistic. If a Western middle way indebted to Hebraic culture could be discovered, then perhaps the West could more easily and fully embrace that middle way as its own. On the other hand, if Hebraic culture has significant resonances with Asian culture, then a middle way indebted to Hebraic culture might lead to a middle way not for the West only but to a middle way between East and West. Finally, in the process of articulating such a middle way, the West may be able to move beyond not only Modernity but also Postmodernity (which I call "pseudo-postmodernity"), its rebellious child. Such a middle way would require retaining crucial elements of Greek culture and integrating them creatively in relation to a recovered Hebraic culture having important connections to Asia.

To be sure, Hebraic culture was not monolithic, and it must not be essentialized. It contained elements drawn from such sources as Mesopotamia, Egypt, Canaan, Persia, and eventually Greece and Rome, and its makeup was ever changing. Consequently, my interpretation of it will of necessity be a selective activity, drawing from such disparate genres as myth, saga, history, drama, and law and from events widely separated in time. Sometimes the selection is deliberate, at other times unconscious. The same must be said for Greek culture, although I will pay much less attention to it and that attention will be narrowly focused on Parmenides, Heraclitus, and the Socratic thinkers (Socrates, Plato, Aristotle).

So how is Hebraic culture nondualistic? There is one obvious way, namely, that, unlike Socratic Greece, it is a pre-philosophical culture. Anyone who wishes to speak philosophically about such a culture will need to effect a creative, interpretive development of its possible philosophical implications, and I intend to do that. In so doing, however, I will be walking in the footsteps of many others who have done so before me.

In this and the following chapter I will examine metaphysical, epistemological, and social issues in Hebraic culture, taking note of the extent to which they can be illuminated by the Asian, especially Mahayana Buddhist, concept of nonduality. Where there is some overlap between the Asian and Hebraic concepts, we may find the basis for Western *nonduality*. Perhaps where the two sets of concepts diverge, we will find clues to *Western* nonduality.

Metaphysical Nondualism and the Bible

Classical Christianity was the culmination of a long interaction between Hebraic and Greco-Roman culture. At least as early as the Alexandrian conquest, Jerusalem was introduced to Athens. Intense and sustained contact, however, began when Seleucus, one of Alexander's generals, founded the Seleucid dynasty and began promoting Hellenistic culture among his subjects, which included the Jews. Eventually, resistance by Jews led to the Maccabean Revolt and to a brief period of independence from outside rule, but the advance of Hellenism was not to be halted.

As early as the second century BCE. the Hebrew Bible was translated for the first time into Greek. In the process, the resultant Septuagint incorporated some of Plato's technical, philosophical vocabulary. This was especially true of Plato's cosmological concepts, which were useful in translating the creation accounts in Genesis. Next, the apocryphal *Book of Wisdom*, written anonymously by an Alexandrian Jew, made frequent use of terms that can also be traced to Plato's *Timaeus*. Then Philo, another Jew of Alexandria, produced a theology that even more deliberately and systematically sought connections between Plato and the Jewish scriptures. These incorporations of Greek philosophy into biblical transla-tion, interpretation, and theology paved the way for the appropriation of Neo-Platonism by the early church fathers of Christianity.

From the perspective of translator Benjamin Jowett, the fathers' incorporation of Plato was based on a "misunderstanding," one in which "they seemed to find in his writings the Christian Trinity, the Word, the Church, the creation of the world in a Jewish sense."[2] More important for the focus of this chapter is the fact that Christianity incorporated Platonic dualism and used it to shape Christian theology.[3] From the perspective of Postmodern thinkers unhappy with what Heidegger termed "onto-theology," taking in Greek dualistic philosophy might be viewed as accepting a Trojan horse. Let us examine a few of these dualisms and juxtapose them to corresponding Hebraic conceptions as a way of understanding Hebrew nonduality.

Heaven and Earth

First, classical Christianity posits a metaphysical dualism of heaven and earth. In the main, the origins of such a conception are located in Greece. When Parmenides concluded "What is, is; what is not, is not," he identified the real with the permanent, with what is eternally unchanging. Here also lies the philo-sophical origin of the principle of identity that philosopher Jacques Derrida has so passionately attacked. By contrast, Heraclitus argued that there is only change or flux. His most remembered saying is that one cannot step into the same river twice. Subsequently, Plato found himself gifted, or saddled, with this double and apparently incompatible inheritance.

Unable or unwilling to choose decisively one or the other, or, alternatively, see-ing a way to gain an advantage against the skepticism of the Sophists, he kept both, albeit not without ultimately privileging Parmenides' position. This double legacy prompted him to conceive the novel possibility of not one world but two. The lower and less real world was characterized by temporality, change, and imperfection; this was the world of Heraclitus. The more original and troubling

<hr>

2.   Benjamin Jowett, ed. and trans., *The Dialogues of Plato*. 4th ed. 4 vols. (Oxford, 1953) cited in Jaroslav Pelikan, *What Has Athens to do with Jerusalem: Timaeus and Genesis in Counterpoint*, the Thomas Spencer Jerome Lectures (Ann Arbor: The University of Michigan Press, 1997), 24.

3.   As indicated in Chapter 1, some recent philosophers have challenged the received view that Plato was a consistent dualist. In this volume I will rely on the received view since it is, whether correct or not, the one that has influenced Western intellectual history.

speculation concerned an upper, unchanging, real, and perfect world of intelligible Forms, according to whose patterns the lower world was made by a divine craftsman. This upper world was the true home of human souls, which inhabited earthly bodies for a limited time. This world owed much to Parmenides.

Early Jewish and Christian thinkers, believing that Plato had been given divine wisdom by Moses or the Holy Spirit, noticed the similarities between the upper and lower worlds described in the *Timaeus*, on the one hand, and the heaven and earth of the Bible, on the other. In the interplay of interpretations that followed, heaven and earth, but perhaps heaven especially, were conceived or reconceived as having a largely Platonic structure. Heaven, like the Intelligible World, was eternal, unchanging, perfect, and truly real by comparison to the earth, whose features were the binary opposites of those of heaven. Here is the origin of the metaphysical divide between eternity and time as well as matter and spirit. For classical Christianity, heaven became a divine realm, the proper home of a divine being, both of which utterly transcended the earth. Here, too, is the origin of a host of insoluble epistemological problems for theology and the philosophy of religion.

Do we not have here another instance of what Jowett called a "misunderstanding"? Rather than looking at Timaeus, let's look at Genesis. The first verse says, "In the beginning of creation, when God made heaven and earth."[4] What seems clear here, although often overlooked, is that heaven, not simply the earth, is created. It is part of creation. It, too, is a "creature." Since it had a beginning, it cannot be eternal. As a consequence, all the associated, sharp oppositions— matter vs. spirit, eternity vs. time, changing vs. unchanging, reality vs. illusion— are blurred or undermined. Almost certainly, they do not square with the biblical picture.

For Hebrew thought, God's abode lies not in another world and not in "this world" as the opposite of "another world" but in *the* world, the only world there is. The world is a comprehensive entity that includes both heaven and earth. Indeed, Patrick Miller, Professor of Old Testament at Princeton Seminary, agreed with my suggestion that, so far as the Bible is concerned, God's dwelling place is more like another room of the same house than like another world.[5] Recall from the discussion of Buddhist nonduality in Chapter 1 that by placing "non" in front of a term, one disavows a dualism named by that term and its opposite. Applied here, it means that "non-heaven"—or, for that matter, "non-earth"—is a rejection of any dualism of heaven and earth. The Hebrew or biblical middle way, then, would be a reality that encompasses both and is designated as "non-heaven." This encompassing reality is the abode of both God and God's creatures.

Such an interpretation makes sense also of the following apocalyptic passage from the opposite end of the Bible: "I saw the holy city, new Jerusalem, coming down out of heaven from God . . . I heard a loud voice proclaiming from the throne: 'Now at last God has his dwelling among men.' "[6] What is envisioned here

---

4. Unless otherwise stated, all biblical quotations are from *The New English Bible*.

5. Patrick D. Miller (Professor of Old Testament, Princeton Theological Seminary) in conversation at Centre College, March 12, 2002.

6. Rev. 21.2–3.

is not the coming together of two metaphysically distinct kingdoms whose natures are defined by logically opposite attributes. Instead, the passage announces the healing of the long standing alienation between God and the creatures that is spoken of in the story of the fall. What Revelations is depicting is the realization of the goal of a return to the intimacy of heaven and earth we have already seen early in Genesis. This reuniting is possible because heaven and earth were from the outset part of the same larger reality.

And are there not implications here for God, also? If the biblical God's abode is neither heaven nor earth *understood as a pair of dualities*, then God must be the sort of "being" that can inhabit or act in such a middle world, a "being" that can move between heaven and earth understood as merely distinguished parts of a comprehensive realm.[7] That is precisely the kind of God depicted in Genesis. Although the heavenly part or room of this nondual and created world is God's normal abode (Psalms 115:3), the Bible does depict God as walking in the Garden of Eden with Adam and Eve, even carrying on a conversation with them. God has ready access to the primordial pair, although they do not have a symmetrical access to God. Later in Genesis, Abraham shares a meal with God, who appears in the form of a traveler.

Taken literally, of course, such stories make no sense. Classical Christian theology, however, read the Genesis material as a narrative symbolization of an onto-theological dualism. But must it be read that way? Can it not, with equal or better justification, be read as articulating a middle way between the extremes posited by Plato and the Fathers (especially the Latin ones) of Classical Christianity? Karen Armstrong makes the following observation:

> The ancient religions had believed that the deities, human beings, and all natural phenomena had been composed of the same divine substance: there was no ontological gap between humanity and the gods. But part of the distress that precipitated the Axial Age was that this sacred or divine dimension had somehow retreated from the world and become in some sense alien to men and women.[8]

Armstrong's use of "substance" is not appropriate for the biblical narrative in Genesis, but, apart from that, it seems to support my earlier, nondual interpretation.

I do not mean to suggest that the authors and/or editors of Genesis were consciously aware of and deliberately reacting to Plato. Merely in terms of chronology, that approach is problematic. Yet given the later encounter between Athens and Jerusalem, the juxtaposition of the difference between them, however artificial, seems both warranted and illuminating in view of the subsequent course of Western intellectual history.

---

7. In I Kgs 8.27, however, Solomon prays: "But can God indeed dwell on earth? Heaven itself, the highest heaven, cannot contain thee." This verse suggests to me that at least some Hebrews not only reject a dualism of heaven and earth, but also realize the hazards of drawing mere distinctions, especially with respect to metaphysics.

8. Karen Armstrong, *Buddha* (New York: Penguin, 2001), 53–54.

Finite and Infinite

Also bearing on the classic theistic conception of God is the finite-infinite duality. As the negation of "finite," "infinite" means "not finite." Its simplest definitions are "without end" or "without limits." More philosophically and subjectively, it can mean that the human intellect is not capable of conceiving the endless or the limitless. Buddhists use the term to mean that no limit or end has been experienced. Perhaps the first thinker to use the term, at least in the West, was Zeno of Elea (sixth century BCE). He seemed, however, to view infinity as an attribute, and it is his view that played a role in shaping the classical theistic conception of God. Human nature was said to be finite, while the divine essence or nature was infinite. In particular, such attributes of God as goodness, power, knowledge, and presence, for example, were said to be infinite. Put positively, God is all-good or infinitely good (omnibenevolent), all-powerful (omnipotent), all-knowing (omniscient), and everywhere-present (omnipresent). Humans, by contrast, are characterized by partial or limited goodness, knowledge, and power, and were present only here or there at the point of the location of their material bodies.

Again, the biblical picture is a very different one. The Hebrew Bible contains at least 20 verses in which God is said to "repent," "relent," "think better of," or say "I am sorry" concerning actions undertaken. I Chronicles 21.15, for example, reads: "And God sent an angel to Jerusalem to destroy it; but, as he was destroying it, the Lord saw and repented of the evil and said to the destroying angel . . . 'Enough! Stay your hand.' " The God who committed an "evil" act is clearly not omnibenevolent, although He[9] may be credited with acknowledging His own evil. Neither is this God omniscient, for surely He would not have initiated an act that He foresaw would end with His repentance. Moreover, if God could not control His own impulse to an evil, destructive act, then God is not omnipotent; this God lacks the power of self-control. Leading Israel's armies into battle during the conquest of Canaan; ordering the holy massacre (*herem*) of the spoils of war, including all living humans and animals; and sending bears to kill children who had teased the prophet Elijah clash sharply with later claims of God's utter goodness. Not knowing that the created order would be good prior to creating and observing it, not foreseeing that the human race would go so terribly awry as to warrant destruction by a flood, and allowing Himself to be dissuaded by certain patriarchs and prophets from carrying out His initial intentions are difficult to square with omniscience.

Moses talked God out of destroying those who made the golden calf at the foot of Mount Sinai, and Abraham persuaded God not to destroy Sodom and

---

9.   Hebrew society was patriarchal, and Yahweh was male. As a consequence, I will, like the Bible itself, use masculine pronouns when describing that God. The view of Yahweh as masculine is one of the serious limitations of Hebrew religion. A few biblical passages do describe Yahweh as possessing qualities or exhibiting behaviors that we typically associate with the feminine. Beyond that, the household religion of the ancient Hebrews included worship of *asherah*, the cult of the Queen of Heaven was popular, and Yahweh was sometimes held to have a consort. These beliefs and practices were the target of prophetic critique.

Gomorrah, provided that a sufficient number of righteous persons could be found in them. All in all, the Hebraic portrait of God, only part of which I am emphasizing here, is strikingly at odds with the portrait painted by Christendom with its related dualism of finite and infinite.

According to Abraham Heschel, the central characterization of God given by the Hebrew prophets is *pathos*, yet in so doing, he insists, they are not investing God with a metaphysical attribute.

> To the prophets, the divine *pathos* is not an absolute force which exists regardless of man, something ultimate or eternal. It is rather a reaction to human history, an attitude called forth by man's conduct; an effect, not cause . . . it has not a reflexive, but rather a transitive character . . . The basic . . . features emerging from the above analysis indicate that the divine *pathos* . . . is not conceived as an essential attribute of God. The *pathos* is not felt as . . . something objective, as a finality with which man is confronted, but an . . . expression of God's will; it is a functional rather than a substantial reality. The prophets never identify God's *pathos* with His essence, because it is . . . for them not something absolute, but a form of relation . . . If the structure . . . of *pathos* were immutable and remained unchanged even after the people . . . had "turned," prophecy would lose its function.[10]

There is here the implication that, for the prophets, what is said of *pathos* is also true for all of what Classical Christianity might understand as the attributes of God's personality.

Essence and Existence

For Heschel, God's personal attributes are part of God's existence and are immanent in history, but God's essence or nature is transcendent. This dualism of essence and existence, however, is nowhere to be found among the ancient Hebrews, including the prophets. An obvious reason for this omission is that the Hebrews, unlike the Socratic Greeks, knew no distinction between essence and existence. You may recall that the elimination of essences, or fixed natures, is precisely what Buddhism's emptiness (*sunyata*) or nothingness (*wu* in Chinese, *mu* in Japanese) sought to achieve; it is central to Asia's middle way. By the second century BCE, however, the essentialist concept 'being' was applied to the biblical God, most significantly, in the story of Moses at the Burning Bush (Exodus 3). In that passage, the Septuagint, which dates from the second century BCE, translated the Tetragrammaton (the four Hebrew consonants indicating God's name) as ὁ ὤν ("he who is"), while the *Book of Wisdom*, written by an Alexandrian Jew in the first century BCE, read it as τον οντα ("him who is"). Both interpretative translations define God in Parmenidean terms as a permanent, unchanging being. In the first century CE, Philo of Alexandria not only adopted the Septuagint's ὁ ὤν, but

---

10. Abraham Joshua Heschel, *Between God and Man: An Interpretation of Judaism*, selected, edited, and interpreted by Fritz A. Rothschild (New York: The Free Press, 1959), 117–118.

also placed God's self identification in verse fourteen (the Tetragrammaton passage) ahead (both in order and significance) of the very different one in verse six, where God says, "I am the God of your forefathers, the God of Abraham, the God of Isaac, the God of Jacob." The switch emphasized God's "true nature" as unchanging being. For Philo, God is saying, in effect, "No name at all can properly be used of Me, to whom alone existence belongs."[11] Jaroslav Pelikan goes on to observe that by the fourth century of this era God's identification with being became an unquestioned assumption, requiring no justification.

It is well known, however, that in the Masoretic text the vowels of the Tetragrammaton are absent. Scholars assume that once there were specific vowels, known to the ancient Hebrews, that should be tacitly supplied when reading or hearing this passage, but by now they have long been forgotten. The result is a situation in which the meaning of the Tetragrammaton depends in part upon someone's choice of possible vowels. Obviously, each such choice would yield a different translation and interpretation of this significant word. Among the suggestions that have been made are "I will be what I will be" or "I will cause to be what I will cause to be." Neither of these alternate readings defines God in terms of unchanging being. In fact, the former can be read simply as a tautology, adding nothing new but merely reaffirming what has already been said. It can even be read as a refusal on God's part to disclose the mystery of His self-identity, as if to say, "That's not any of your business." On the other hand, it can be read as saying, "If you want to know who I am, watch what I do." In fact, this last interpretation has been used by Existentialist thinkers to suggest that, like humans, God has no fixed essence but is creating one by the choices that God makes. Such an interpretation introduces temporality into God's existence, an existence that takes shape in the history of God's interaction with creation, especially people. For the ancient Hebrew, then, there is no dualism between God and the creatures based on a distinction between fixed essence and changing existence. In Buddhist terms, God has no *Atman* or *svabhava*. The absence of such a fixed essence is, you will recall, a central feature of Asian nonduality.

Body and Soul

For the received Plato, the human being is a compound of two metaphysically distinct elements, a body and a soul. This dualism is made necessary because anthropology must be understood in relation to the double world adopted by Plato to reconcile the disparate positions of Parmenides and Heraclitus and to challenge the epistemological skepticism of the Sophists. The soul, which is an eternal substance, belongs fundamentally to the upper or intelligible world of permanent forms, from which it came and to which, at death, it will return. The body, on the other hand, shot through with conflicting passions, is part of the lower or material world. In certain of Plato's dialogues, the body is pictured as an "oyster shell" (*Phaedrus* 250c and *Phaedo* 66b) or a "prison" (*Cratullus* 400bc) or even a "tomb" (*Gorgias* 493a). The body is the source of bad actions, and,

---

11. Philo, *De vita Mosis* 1.75, cited in Pelikan, *Athens* 69.

therefore, it must be controlled by the rational soul. From such negative circumstances, death, which is a separation of soul and body, is a liberation. Indeed, the purpose of philosophy, as stated by the Plato's character Socrates, is to get the separation process underway, even in this life.

The Hebrews, by contrast, have a more unitary and positive view of earthly existence. "*Gewiyya*," the rarely employed Hebrew term for body, is used only in such special instances as referring to the body of an angel, to a corpse, and to the "manpower" or labor of slaves.[12] The more commonly used terms for the human self are "*basar*" and "*nephesh*." Although the former term is sometimes translated as "flesh" and the latter as "soul," there is broad agreement among biblical scholars that these terms do not point to a metaphysical dualism but either to two aspects of a unitary self or simply to two ways of speaking about the unitary self.

The Anchor Bible Dictionary says: "What man is can only be understood in a wholistic way. Man does not possess a soul and a body, rather he is both soul and flesh." The soul is merely the life of the body. By and large this view continues in the New Testament. Biblical scholar Oscar Cullmann states that "the Jewish and Christian interpretation of creation excludes the whole Greek dualism of body and soul."[13] This assessment is echoed by Lynn de Silva, who says: "Biblical scholarship has established quite conclusively that there is no dichotomous concept of man in the Bible, such as is found in Greek and Hindu thought. The biblical view is holistic, not dualistic."[14] This is true even in the case of Paul, who often plays off flesh against spirit. For him, however, the terms refer to contrasting orientations to life by the person as a whole. Hence, "flesh" designates the whole person's being fundamentally given over to a life of sin, slavery, and death while "spirit" refers to the whole person's fundamental orientation to a life in Christ.

For philosopher Michael Foster, the absence of dualism among the Hebrews, both in cosmology and anthropology, is the result of the nature of creation in the P-account of Genesis, where matter, on the one hand, and form or spirit, on the other, are not conceived as primordially separate but are constituted simultaneously and from the outset as integrated.[15] In other words, matter and spirit are always already inseparable. In such an understanding, there is no place dualism can establish a foothold.

An important text for demonstrating the unitary nature of the human person is Genesis 2.7, which says: "Then the Lord God formed a man from the dust of the ground and breathed into his nostrils the breath of life. Thus the man became a living creature." This second version of the creation of man in Genesis is from the earlier Yahwistic or J-account. In it, God is depicted as creating in the manner of

---

12. "Body" in *The Anchor Bible Dictionary*, vol. 1, 768.

13. Oscar Cullman, *Immortality of the Soul or Resurrection of the Dead?* (New York: Macmillan, 1958), 30 cited in Ian G. Barbour, *Religion and Science: Historical and Contemporary Issues* (San Francisco, California: HarperSanFrancisco, 1997), 271.

14. Ibid.

15. Michael Foster, "The Christian Doctrine of Creation and the Rise of Modern Natural Science," in Daniel O'Connor and Francis Oakley, eds., *Creation: The Impact of an Idea* (New York: Charles Scribner's Sons, 1969).

a potter shaping clay. Greco-Roman Christianity, committed as it is to a mind-body dualism, interpreted God's act here as that of inserting a soul into Adam's or man's body. Even today, official Catholic doctrine maintains such a view. In its encounter with modern science the Roman church has gradually accommodated itself to Darwinism by acknowledging that the human body evolved in accordance with evolutionary theory. Souls, however, are completely different. They are purely spiritual substances altogether outside of the evolutionary or biological process; consequently, God is said to create each individual and unique soul and insert it into the body when the body is developed to the appropriate point, either in an evolutionary or an embryological sense.

This is not, however, the only way to read the text, and it is certainly one at odds with both what is otherwise understood by scholars to be the Hebraic view of the person and with the text's own language. The word for soul (*nephesh*) is translated in this passage as "living creature." It can also be translated as "person." Even today we say, "There were 101 souls present at the event" or "We had seven bodies present." These modern instances, in which both terms mean "persons" or "human beings," reflect the holistic understanding of the Hebrews. The word "*ruach*," which in noun form means "spirit" or "breath," is used in this passage in a verb form, making it clear enough that God is being depicted as simply breathing so as to start or trigger the breathing process in man, much as we do today when administering CPR to someone whose breathing has stopped. In this passage man is not a soul-substance added to a body-substance but enlivened dust.[16] This interpretation is reinforced by Psalm 104. 29–30, which says: "When thou takest away their breath, they fail and they return to the dust from which they came; but when thou breathest into them, they recover."

At the other end of life, death is not a separation of body and soul. In fact, early on, there is no indication in the Hebrew Bible that human beings survive death at all. Later, the Bible speaks of *sheol*, a gloomy, underground place where the dead, both the righteous and the wicked, apparently still embodied, lead a diminished form of existence. Even later, under the influence of Persian dualism, the righteous and wicked dead are segregated into separate realms, heaven and hell. Yet the Hebrew cannot conceive of life, before or after death, as devoid of bodies. Even Paul invents the motion of a spiritual body with which the dead are clothed in an early Christian version of the afterlife.

Time and Eternity

Like so much else in Plato's thought, time, also, is understood in the light of the contrast between the possibilities presented by Parmenides and those presented by Heraclitus. Time is a topic that acknowledges and takes account of change. For Plato and ancient Greeks more generally, the real or the divine is what does not change; it is the permanent. This changelessness is, consequently, beyond time

---

16. One of Gary Trudeau's "Far Side" cartoons shows a field covered with very tall rye through which two intersecting paths have been cut. Down each path, headed toward the intersection, is a hospital orderly pushing a gurney containing a corpse. The caption reads: "When a body meets a body coming through the rye."

and is known as "eternity." For Plato, eternity characterizes the intelligible world of changeless, divine forms. It transcends this world, the material world, which is characterized by change and is, therefore, subject to time. Both human and nonhuman life in the material world consist of shifting events that, nevertheless, follow in cyclical fashion the eternal patterns of the forms. There is no notion of history as irreversible movement toward an open future. Time and eternity, then, constitute a metaphysical dualism, one that is related to and meshes with the other forms of dualism in Platonic thought.

For the Hebrews, however, time was conceived differently. It is understood as history, but a history that is rather unique. First of all, it is dynamic and moves toward an open future. This is the prophetic understanding. Later, of course, apocalypticism will view history as leading inevitably toward a climactic event that is determined in advance by God and that terminates time. Here, history is not open.

Hebrew history, unlike most modern views, is not limited to the sphere of human action; it also includes the acts of God. As we have already noted, for the Hebrews, God and humans share a single, though differentiated, world, so history in this broader sense embraces all significant events that occur within that one reality. The distinction between myth and history is not one they draw. History is eschatological in the sense that it aims at a future in which Yahweh will be acknowledged as the god of all creation. Clearly, however, humans have something to say about that, and achieving a universal covenant community is not a foregone conclusion. Hence, history is both an experiment and an adventure. God is, nevertheless, faithful in his purposes and actions, whether humans are or not.

Although the Greek and Hebraic views discussed so far, were developed largely independently of each other, at least prior to Alexander's conquest, it is legitimate to observe that once they are juxtaposed, the Hebrew view can be said to be nondual with respect to the Greek view.

Epistemological Nondualism and the Bible

The metaphysical dualism of Plato is not unrelated to his epistemological dualism. The Sophists had claimed that the only possible human source of knowledge was the senses. Yet, the senses give access only to the changing events of the phenomenal world, yielding a mere shifting, unstable "knowledge" not worthy of the name and leaving man to be "the measure" of all things. From Plato's perspective, the Sophists were handicapped by having only a single, material world and only a material knower. Adding a second world, on the one hand, and conceiving human beings dualistically as compounds of body and mind, on the other, Plato opens up the prospect of a more promising epistemological outcome. It permits Plato to agree with the Sophists that the human body with its senses tracks the dynamic material world, but to affirm also that the human *mind*, by contrast, is able to contemplate the permanent, unchanging, divine Forms that constitute the intelligible world. The resultant unchanging, stable knowledge (*episteme*) is knowledge, indeed.

The problem of how to link the two worlds is solved, first of all, by an origin myth according to which the divine craftsman manufactures the material world using the intelligible Forms as patterns. Second, Plato postulates that prior to its embodiment in the material world, the human soul or mind existed in the intelligible world, where it "saw" the forms, which are the only true objects of knowledge. Subsequently, embodiment had the effect of inducing forgetfulness in the rational soul; hence, of necessity, earthly knowing became a matter of recollecting (*anamnesis*) of the mythical, preexistent knowing. The copy forms molded into matter serve to remind thinkers of the eternal forms of the intelligible world, which are the true objects of knowledge.

As a pre-philosophical culture, the Hebrews had no formalized epistemology. We can assume, however, that, like peoples everywhere, they used their eyes to determine if the wine jars were empty, their ears to determine if visitors were at the door knocking, their noses to detect the smoke that indicates fire, their tongues to tell whether food is thoroughly cooked and tasty, and their hands to determine the roughness or smoothness of a piece of wood being shaped into a usable object. In such relatively unproblematic cases, no theoretical reflection is likely to arise.

More important and more problematic was the focus of the Hebrews on history. Here lies their principal epistemic concern. Whereas in the West, historiography is devoted to generating, with the help of critical methods, a description of and explanation for what happened in the past, the Hebrews, although deeply interested in the formative events of the past, were also oriented toward the history yet to come. Their concern for the future was grounded in the stories of deliverance from slavery in Egypt and what they took to be the promises of God contained in the covenants with Noah, Abraham, Moses, and David. The future was, they believed, where those promises would be finally and completely fulfilled.

There was, however, no single Hebrew way of reading the future. Among the techniques or methods employed to do so were dream interpretation (Joseph, Daniel), trance (the ecstatic prophets), precognition (the seers), numerology, and divination (the casting of lots, or the *urim* and *thummim*,[17] by the priests, especially prior to undertaking military action). Most of these ways of knowing were shared among the various sociocultural groups of the wider region. The first book of Samuel 9.9 indicates that these knowers-of-the-future were once called "seers" but later called "prophets."

There was little uniformity among the prophets in either method or location. Some prophets did not restrict themselves to a single method but employed several. Samuel, perhaps the earliest Hebrew prophet, is a case in point. Some prophets were attached to the royal court, others to the temple and shrines. Still others were itinerant, moving about among the festivals. Some moved about in bands; others were solitary. Some were professionals; others, like Amos, were amateurs.

Biblical scholarship often distinguishes the practice of "foretelling," sometimes attributed to a seer (*roeh*), from the "forthtelling" of a prophet (*nabi*), although

---

17. *Urim* and *thummim* are sometimes said to be analogous to dice, but scholars admit they have no clear idea as to what they are.

some prophets practiced both. The former seeks by precognition to part the curtain dividing the present from the future and see what will inevitably occur, regardless of what humans choose to do. The forthteller, by contrast, announces what will happen if the people do not repent and change their behavior. Both make predictions, and both understand the ultimate source of such knowledge to be God. In the former case, however, the predictions are unconditional, while in the latter, they are conditional. My focus will be on forthtelling, the kind of prophecy most often associated with Hebraic thought and characteristic of the "writing prophets" of the eighth century and afterward.

Foretelling or precognition is a method homologous with a view of reality as fundamentally static. The future is not open but already determined by God. Forthtelling is appropriate for a worldview in which the future is yet indeterminate in the present. The foreteller believes that God's will and the future are best discerned by an inner communication with God. The forthteller believes that God's will and a conditional future are best discerned in present historical events. Hence forthtellers often describe in great detail current human behavior and the ways in which it stands in violation of covenantal requirements. A more secularized account might say that conditional future consequences were extrapolated from a knowledge of current trends.

Anchoring the prophecies or extrapolations in an awareness of present historical circumstances is indicative of an empirical dimension to prophecy, one not present in the other methods. Because there is no necessity that the present trends continue, the prophesied consequences of those trends can be avoided. All that is required is that the people amend their ways, returning to the path spelled out in the instruction (*Torah*). In fact, (with the exception of Jonah) to effect such a change of behavior is precisely the prophet's intent. Indeed, he cannot discover with certainty what the future holds because the people's actions are unpredictable and also because, although Yahweh is regarded as faithful to His promises, He is also a surprising God whose ways are beyond calculation.

For the purposes of this chapter, it is important to note that prophecy takes place within the Hebrew ontological context previously described—that is, there is no metaphysical dualism between heaven and earth or between mind and body. Consequently, there is not and cannot be any epistemological dualism analogous to that of Plato. It is the whole person, relying on the integration of all of his or her finite powers, that prophesies; and the prophecy occurs within the context of a single, if rich and variegated, world. This single, nondual mix of empirical, passional, and reflective aspects that was relied on while advancing toward a future whose actualities cannot be known with certainty because they are not yet actualities is faith.

Speaking of the second account of creation (Gen. 2.4b–25), biblical scholars Christian Hauer and William Young say, "There is a spontaneity in this account, as though the creator is pursuing an experimental process."[18] For the Hebrews,

18.   Christian F. Hauer and William A. Young, *An Introduction to the Bible: A Journey into Three Worlds*, 4th edition (Upper Saddle River, New Jersey: Prentice Hall, 1998), 61.

the entirety of history is an ongoing experiment and, therefore, an adventure; and it is so not only for the Hebrew people, but also for their God. Epistemologically, then, such a context has no room for absolute knowledge, not even absolute divine knowledge. Indeed, with respect to the future, there is simply no viable alternative to some kind of faith.

But if there is an empirical element in Hebraic knowing, what about the references to God, to God's action, to God's giving messages to prophets? Modernity would attribute such ideas to myth; there certainly seems to be nothing empirical about them. Indeed, how did the Hebrews know even that God exists? It is often said by scholars that they merely assumed it. Although such an answer seems partially correct, it also foreshortens the search for another possibility that fills out the picture a bit more. Philosopher of science Stephen Toulmin says:

> The existence of God . . . is not something to demand *evidence for*; nor is the sentence, "God exists," one to be believed if, and only if, the evidence for its truth is good enough. The very last question to ask about God is *whether* He exists. Rather, we must first accept the notion of "God": and then we shall be in a position to point to *evidences of* His existence.[19]

While Toulmin's claim is, in fact, an instance of the invalid logical form known as "affirming the consequent,"[20] it reflects precisely how science often goes about attempting to verify the existence of theoretical entities that are not themselves observable. And "pointing to the evidences," of course, is not always convincing and never yields absolute proof. Both in scientific and Hebraic epistemology it is always possible that there is more than one theory or story that can account for the evidence, and new evidence is always arriving from the future.

What Toulmin is suggesting can be illuminated, I believe, by the example of buying a new pair of shoes, a notion first put forward by Ian Ramsey to illustrate what he called "empirical fit."[21] Suppose you are walking down a street and pass a shoe store. You notice in the display window an attractive pair of new shoes. You stop for a moment, look down at the shoes you are presently wearing, and observe that their condition has imperceptibly deteriorated since you bought them 3 years ago. You notice, for example, that the tread is gone and that there is a small hole in the sole, and you decide that a new pair of shoes would be in order.

You enter the store and tell the clerk that you wish to look at a pair of shoes like those displayed in the window. The clerk brings them out in the size you indicate and hands them to you. You examine them, taking note of the supple leather uppers, the Vibram sole, the arch support inside, the double stitching, and the

---

19. Huston Smith, *The World's Religions* (New York: HarperSanFrancisco, 1991), 224–225.

20. Such an argument goes like this: If X (a theory or doctrine) is true, then Y (an empirical effect) will be observed. Since Y has been observed, X must be true. The problem is that other theories or doctrines also may account for Y, and these alternative possibilities have not been or cannot be ruled out.

21. Ian T. Ramsey, *Models and Mystery* (London: Oxford University Press, 1964), 17. Here, I have elaborated on his analogy of buying shoes.

padding in the heel. The evidence of their quality revealed by this examination leads you to the next step—you put them on. The clerk pinches the tip of the shoe to ascertain if there is sufficient room for your toes. You stand up and see how they feel when bearing your full weight. If all is still well, you walk about the store, or perhaps outside, checking for comfort. If they are, in fact, comfortable and if their price is within your budget, you are ready to take the next step. You reach for your wallet.

Purchasing the shoes amounts to a commitment to the shoes. Yet you are not, at this point, in a position to say that these are the best shoes you have ever owned. The only way to know how good they are is to wear them, and the only way to wear them is to make the *prior* commitment to buy them. Having bought them, however, the preliminary testing is over and the real testing can begin. Do they loosen up a bit and become more comfortable? Do they resist scuffing when you inadvertently kick a table leg? Do they leak when you step into a puddle? Do they have good traction when you walk on snow or ice? Are they durable over a long period of time? They may turn out to be the best pair of shoes you have ever owned, or they may suddenly fall apart this afternoon.

In an analogous fashion, the only way the Hebrews can come to know the truth concerning God's existence and promises is to accept them, live according to God's instruction, and watch history to see what happens. This is faith in the Hebrew sense. As Wright and Fuller put it:

> It is clear that the knowledge of God . . . is not a static faith floating through a man's consciousness; it was something to be done. Knowledge and truth in the Bible involve things to do, not simply a belief in a God of nature or an experience of God within . . . He is to be known by what he has done and said, by what he is now doing and saying; and he is known when we do what he commands us to do.[22]

History, of course, has to be interpreted, and not all interpretations will agree. Minor setbacks will not likely undermine commitment to the Yahweh theory; they can be set aside as anomalies. Conquest by Assyria, exile in Babylon, or the destruction of the temple in Jerusalem, on the other hand, count as major pieces of negative evidence, prompting apostasy, a patient waiting for the tide of history to turn, or a fundamental rethinking of theology. Also, as in science, it is nearly always possible to make auxiliary assumptions that save the theory. The notion that misfortune was God's punishment for Hebrew disobedience was such an assumption. It said, in effect, that God will take care of Israel, provided that Israel lives up to its covenant promises and not otherwise.

The persistence of Canaanite religion among the Hebrews can be accounted for, in part, by the fact that the agricultural technology associated with *Baal* proved effective: it functioned informally as an experiment that produced evidence in support of the associated Canaanite theology. Again, I do not claim that the Hebrews had a formalized epistemology consisting of a logic of verification that they explicitly applied to history. Yet such a logic and epistemology seem to be adumbrated

---

22.   G. Ernest Wright and Reginald H. Fuller, *The Book of the Acts of God*, Anchor Books (Garden City, New York: Doubleday & Company, 1960), 22–23.

in the biblical account of their struggle to discern history's meaning, and it was nondual with respect to the Greek and Modern dichotomies between myth and history and between subject and object.

As the content of biblical tradition, however, was increasingly forced into the dualistic conceptual categories of Plato, Plotinus, and Aristotle, nondual Hebraic conceptions were cracked open. This is true of faith, also. Greek anthropological dualism divided unitary Hebrew faith into an inside (the activity of mind or soul) and an outside (bodily action or works).[23] But because, for Greeks, bodies were not valued as real, because simply possessing bodies did not distinguish humans from lesser creatures, and because bodies became in later centuries increasingly depicted as machines, the outside aspect of faith gradually eroded. Faith became associated primarily with the inside. And since the inside consisted fundamentally of the rational soul, faith became, at least for Greco-Roman Christianity, a matter of belief in doctrines regarded as orthodox by the church. A Christian soul thinks about approved Christian ideas. Thus, the recitation of the Nicene or Apostles' Creed during a worship service is said to be a "confession of faith," a confession of what one believes. This understanding of faith is why of all the world's religions, Christianity is the most orthodoxic in its fundamental orientation; correct belief trumps approved practice. The other religions are far more orthopraxic: what you do matters more than what you think. Later, in the light of Martin Luther's critique of reason as a "whore," faith, for many Protestants, became understood as trust, which was an attempt to recapture its biblical meaning. In the light of the Greek-inspired inside-outside dichotomy, however, trust was largely confined to the inside. Its biblical connection to action (trusting action) was not fully retrieved.

Such departures from the nondualism of the Hebraic notion of faith underlie differences between Catholics, Muslims, and Jews, on the one hand, and Protestants, on the other. Generally speaking, the former hold that faith must be *accompanied* by deeds or works; the latter assert that faith alone is sufficient for salvation. Roman Catholics, who have a preference for the Gospel of John and the Catholic epistles, can cite as evidence for their position James 2.24, 26, which says: "You see then that a man is justified by deeds and not by faith in itself . . . As the body is dead when there is no breath in it, so faith divorced from deeds is lifeless as a corpse." Protestants, who owe much of their theology to Paul, cite Ephesians 2.8: "For it is by his grace you are saved, through trusting him; it is not your own doing. It is God's gift, not a reward for work done."[24] That scripture can be marshaled in support of such opposing stances indicates that the aforementioned splitting was already well underway in the first century.

23.   My colleague at Centre, glass artist and ceramicist Stephen Powell, visited artists and art schools in Moscow and Leningrad in the 1990s. He found that in both places—and the practice continues today—a distinction was made between designers and makers of glass art. According to this distinction, makers rely on their bodies and are considered mere craftsmen. Designers, by contrast, use their minds and are the real artists. Makers and designers may confer about the making process, but nobody is both a maker and a designer. This is a contemporary instance of the ancient Greek ideal.

24.   The bulk of modern biblical scholarship rejects the traditional view that Paul is the author of Ephesians.

From the Hebraic perspective, both Catholics and Protestants have mistakenly read scripture dualistically and misunderstood both Ephesians and James. How, then, are faith and action to be related? Suppose you and I are hiking through the woods. We come to a chasm a couple of yards wide. We pause to contemplate our options. I ask, "Do you believe you can jump across?" You reply, "Yes, I believe I can." Is that faith? For both Christendom and modern Christianity, it is. For most of the Bible, it is not. Catholics, of course, would say that to such genuine faith must be added works. For their part, Protestants would say that genuine faith, although complete in itself, will or ought to manifest itself in the external world in the form of deeds. Deeds are not faith but the evidence of faith, which is internal. In effect, both views reduce faith to belief. Suppose, on the other hand, that I jump from the hither side of the chasm with the intention of committing suicide. Or suppose that I stumble at the edge and frantically try to turn that stumble into a leap to the other side. Is either of these faith? Not for a Hebrew. While both of these latter options involve action, they lack proper belief.

The two options just posed are dualistic; they represent the binary oppositions of actionless belief, on the one hand, and beliefless action, on the other. It is precisely this dualism that James is trying to deconstruct. When he says that faith without deeds is lifeless, is a corpse, is dead, is he not saying that just as the dead do not exist, so an independent faith to which deeds can be added or not added, does not exist? There is no such thing. The Hebraic position is that faith is the interdependence of belief or trust and action. Even that formulation is somewhat misleading in that it suggests that there are two things and that each expresses itself in or influences the other. It would be more accurate to say that faith is always already unitary belief-in-action, believing action, or trusting action.

Moreover, it is ongoing belief-in-action, as indicated by the word "faithfulness," which is used as a description of God's behavior and as a goal for human behavior. When Jesus said to the woman with a 12-year-long uterine hemorrhage, "Take heart, my daughter; your faith has cured you" (Matt. 9.22), he was pointing to the fact that she had believingly *walked* from her village to find him and believingly *stretched out her hand* to touch his garment. So far as we know, sitting at home with belief in her heart did nothing; it produced no curative effects.

In the account I have given of a particular, and perhaps distinctive, Hebraic view of faith, I have spoken of "action" or "deeds" rather than "works." The last term conjures a picture of God as a heavenly accountant and of salvation as doing, from any motive, a specified number of things on God's checklist of the 613 commandments. In my estimation, such a view has no biblical basis. Action, on the other hand, is necessary because having faith means living one's faith, and, for embodied existence, to live necessarily entails action and involves the body. In Greek, unlike English, "faith" has a verb form (*pistein*, "to faith"); hence, one can faith. The life of faith is faithing. Given the foregoing, we can now say that Jews, Muslims, and Catholics are right to insist on the necessity of deeds. For their part, Protestants are correct to speak of faith alone because faith, Hebraically and nondualistically understood, necessarily already includes action.

Below is a summary in chart form of what has just been said discursively concerning Greek dualism and Hebrew nondualism.

Greek/Apollonian	Greek/Dionysian	Hebraic
Reason	Passion	Action
Knowledge	Opinion/Ignorance	Faith
Universal	Particular	The Concrete
Eternity	Time	Story, History
Soul	Body	Person
Being	Becoming	Existence
Spiritual or Ideal	Material	Embodiment
Parmenides/Plato	Heraclitus/Sophists	Abraham/the Prophets

Obviously, I have borrowed Nietzsche's terms "Apollonian" and "Dionysian" but am using them here simply as a convenient way to designate the two dualities of Socratic Greek thinking.

In conclusion, I want to suggest, but not argue, that for each line of the chart, the term representing the Hebrew perspective embraces a significant aspect of the meaning of both the Greek terms with which it is paired. Put another way, it is possible, I believe, to see the Greek terms as abstractions on the part of a relatively more philosophical form of thinking, abstractions from a more unified meaning represented by the Hebraic terms, whether or not precisely such an abstraction occurred in history.

Clearly, metaphysics and epistemology are rather abstruse philosophical enterprises remote from everyday social reality. If one wants to make the case that the ancient Hebrews, or any identifiable group of them, were genuinely nondualistic, it is not sufficient to limit the argument to metaphysics and epistemology alone. The case must be made for Hebrew social reality as well. It is to such social reality that we now turn.

Chapter 3
Hebrew Nondualism and Social Reality

Israel is no wallet.[1]

Covenant as Sunyata

The idea of covenant is found in the Hebrew Bible, the New Testament, and the Qur'an, and it continues to comprise the framework for much of the doctrine and practice of Judaism, Christianity, and Islam. "Testament" means "covenant"; hence, the New Testament and what Christians know as the Old Testament are elaborations of the implications of the covenant idea. If so fundamental an idea as covenant can be shown to possess a nondual structure, then, to a considerable extent, the case for Hebrew nonduality will have been successfully made. The central feature of Nagarjuna's nonduality is *sunyata* or emptiness, the notion that all things are linked in a network of mutual causation and are, therefore, interdependent, even mutually constitutive of each other. Can this be said of covenant? There are several obstacles to an affirmative answer to this question. One is the propensity to substitute for covenant the concept of contract, an idea significant for modern social theory in the West and familiar to us in both business and law. Although covenant and contract share in common the feature of being an agreement made among several parties, the two cannot be equated, and distinguishing between them is a common element in virtually all introductory textbooks in biblical studies. A typical statement of the difference is provided by Eric Mount, whose view is informed by William May and H. Richard Niebuhr:

> A contract constitutes an alliance of individuals for the satisfaction or guarantee of mutual interests; a covenant unites people with common allegiances to shared values or norms in a commitment to the long-term well-being of the community members.

---

1. My own twist on an illustration used later in the chapter by Thomas Kasulis.

> Contracts tend to be minimal, short term, and presumptive of little or no community bonding. Covenants presuppose community, lasting commitment to the other's total well-being, and the assumption of obligations to each other and to shared values that change one's life.[2]

Another misleading linkage is to see, as some have done in the past, an identity between a covenant and the suzerainty treaties of the ancient Near East, a connection made apparently plausible by the frequency with which the Bible refers to God as a king. There are, indeed, some similarities between these international treaties and the most complex forms of the covenant bond; however, there are also significant differences. A suzerainty treaty is made by an absolute monarch, bound by no restraints, with his vassals, who lack any power and are conscripted involuntarily for the treaty's obligations. A biblical covenant, by contrast, is freely chosen by all parties and involves obligations that bind God also and do so for the benefit of the Children of Israel. Also, the covenantal structure of Israel borrowed heavily from the structure of the Israelite family and tribe. Carol Meyers makes the following observation concerning that point.

> The affairs of a household thus took on a public character, with the integration of private and public domains mediated by the socio-religious life of the village community . . . The social sphere served to weave the family household units into the fabric of the larger village community on which they depended . . . Many features of family dynamics, of marriage patterns and kinship values, were no doubt altered during the momentous changes brought about by state formation and national institutional systems. Yet it is also true that many patterns and values associated with early Israelite family structures were incorporated into the legal systems and community values of subsequent Israelite life.[3]

A more serious challenge to understanding covenant as *sunyata* is posed by Tom Kasulis, whose recent work has focused on contrasting Asia and the West in terms of their emphases on differing clusters of values dubbed "Intimacy" and "Integrity," respectively.[4] As I read it, his Intimacy is an elaboration of *sunyata* as applied specifically to human beings and their social relations; hence, if covenant fulfills the definition of "Intimacy," it does so for *sunyata* as well. I will take up the features of Intimacy and Integrity one at a time and comment on them.

1. First, Kasulis states that whereas Integrity regards knowledge as public verifiability, Intimacy regards knowledge as objective, but personal rather than public. If we accept these without quibble as generally accurate descriptions, then under which category are we to classify the Hebrews? As already indicated in the previous

2. Eric Mount Jr., *Covenant, Community, and the Common Good: An Interpretation of Christian Ethics* (Cleveland, Ohio: The Pilgrim Press, 1999), 21.

3. Carol Meyers, "The Family in Early Israel" in Leo G. Perdue, Joseph Blinkinsopp, John J. Collins, and Carol Meyers, eds., *Families in Ancient Israel* (Louisville, Kentucky: Westminster John Knox Press, 1997), 40–41.

4. Thomas P. Kasulis, *Intimacy or Integrity: Philosophy and Cultural Difference.* The 1998 Gilbert Ryle Lectures (Honolulu: University of Hawaii Press, 2002).

chapter, Hebrew knowing concerns itself largely with understanding God's faithful and caring acts in history. The story of the deliverance of the Hebrews from bondage in Egypt is an important example. Clearly there is a public and objective aspect to this knowledge claim. That the Hebrews were slaves in Egypt at some point in time and later were neither slaves nor in Egypt is something objective, as in both Intimacy and Integrity, and verifiable in principle (at least by themselves, their contemporaries, and modern historical scholarship) as in Integrity. This is the case despite the fact that Egyptian records make no mention of the Hebrews as their slaves or of their escape. But that God is the sole or principal agent of this liberation from slavery is not publicly verifiable in the modern sense; here, according to modern thinking, the Hebrews go beyond verifiability to faith.

Yet they do not distinguish reason or verifiability from faith, and their faith is not blind. In the previous chapter we saw the ways in which Hebrew prophecy was, broadly speaking, empirical. Doubtless, the Hebrews considered alternative explanations but were unable to imagine that a lowly, enslaved people without any military capability were capable of freeing themselves from the superpower of their day. In other words, their conclusion was reached, in part, by means of what we might recognize as a yet unthematized disjunctive syllogism, namely, eliminating all possible explanations save one. Thus, they incorporated a rational element in their epistemology.

On the other hand, this piece of knowledge is public in the limited sense that it is held not simply by isolated individuals but jointly by the Hebrew people. In other words, it is publicly given in the tradition. In other contexts, God's existence, presence, and will are known through both public worship and in the "still small voice" of solitude. In short, Hebrew knowing includes some features from Intimacy, some from Integrity, and some from both, as well as others found in neither. With respect to Kasulis' two categories, then, let us say that the Hebrews' stance is one of "Hebrew nonduality." It cannot be described neatly as fitting into either one or the other of the two categories constructed by rational thought. One might also describe the situation, using Kyoto school Zen logic, as "Integrity *soku* Intimacy."

2. A second distinction Kasulis draws between Intimacy and Integrity is that the former consists of internal relations whereas external relations comprise the latter. Kasulis illustrates the two possibilities by the use of Boolean circles. An external relation is depicted by two circles whose boundaries lie completely outside each other. Internal relations are represented by the overlapping area of overlapping circles. Verbally, the two kinds of relations are distinguished in four ways. (1) In external relations the terms or related things exist independently, whereas an internal relation is a constituent of the essence of the related things. (2) An external relation is an add-on to the individuality of things, whereas an internal relation indicates that the related things are interdependent. (3) Dissolving an external relation is merely a disconnection, leaving the relatents essentially as they were, whereas a dissolved internal relation involves their transformation. Finally, (4) in an external relation something "belongs-to" another. For example, Kasulis says that a wallet "belongs to" John. In an internal relation something "belongs with" another. A family photo album belongs *with* the family whose life is displayed therein. Such things

as wallets are interchangeable; family photo albums are not. Clearly, a focus on internal relations reflects Mahayana Buddhism's emptiness and nothingness, essential elements of the middle way. Now let us see if internal relations reflect the character of covenant in the Hebrew Bible, also.

First, do God and the Hebrews exist independently? Very likely, one's immediate response is to say, "Yes." Moreover, Greco-Roman Christianity's doctrine of aseity (God's self-existence or independent existence) would agree, at least with respect to God. Yet in the biblical view, by contrast, God and the people are constitutive of each other. Abraham Heschel observes that "the Bible tells us nothing about God in Himself; all its sayings refer to His relations to man.'[5] The biblical story, he holds, is the story of these relations. Later in this chapter we will see that the story includes God's relation to the rest of creation, also, but that correction does not negate Heschel's main point. At Sinai, God acted not like an oriental potentate, laying down the law about how things henceforth must be. As John H. Hayes notes:

> The law is not only to be obeyed, it asks for an inner assent, a commitment . . .
> This inner assent to the law is synonymous with the Israelite's love of Yahweh.
> One should love Yahweh with "heart, soul, and might" and the words that
> Yahweh commands should be upon "the heart."[6]

In fact, God appears to act more like a suitor on bended knee, making a proposal of marriage. The deliverance from Egypt, the pillar of fire by night, the cloud by day, the manna from heaven had been elements in a courtship, one in which God tried to impress the coy and complaining Hebrews not by His looks, wealth, or athletic prowess but by the efficacy and fidelity of His care. The Hebrews had played hard to get. Even at the foot of Sinai they showed themselves hesitant to make a commitment and still ready to "play the field" with other gods. But when God proposed, "You will be my people and I will be your God," and the people gave their assent and commitment, God became, that is to say, turned into, the God of Israel, and the people became or turned into the "Children of Israel."

A teacher without students cannot really be said to be a teacher, and vice versa. Teacher and students need each other. Only in a functional relation can the one be a teacher and the others be students. It is the same with Yahweh. Yahweh without a people cannot be a God, and certainly not the God depicted in the Bible. "God," after all, is not fundamentally a proper name but a function, although, for some, it has become a proper name. A being cannot be a God (cannot fulfill the God function) unless there is a people or reality in relation to which that function is exercised. God-ing, like teaching, is a functional role.

---

5.   Abraham J. Heschel, *Between God and Man: An Interpretation of Judaism*, from the writings of Abraham J. Heschel, Fritz A. Rothschild. ed. (New York: The Free Press, 1959), 111.

6.   John H. Hayes, *Introduction to the Bible* (Philadelphia, Pennsylvania: The Westminster Press, 1971), 198.

Yahweh and the people need each other, constitute each other in their roles and identities.[7] Together they constitute the greater whole, the covenant community of Israel, the single reality that is, broadly speaking, the subject of the biblical narrative. Patrick Miller asserts that this reality is characterized by an *"intimate* connection between the community as a whole and its individual members,"[8] one in which each member is not focused on his or her own rights but upon responsibility to the other. (Emphasis added.) Thus, as Paul Lehman says, this single reality (the covenant community of Israel) is characterized by an ethos of "reciprocal responsibility."[9]

The whole, then, has an intrinsic connection to the parts, another of Kasulis' requirements for internal relations. Just as, according to J. L. Austin, the performative utterance "I now pronounce you husband and wife," provided that all the appropriate "felicities" obtain, brings a new reality into being,[10] so in the performance of the covenant ritual Israel, an interdependent covenant community, including both God and the people, came into being.

If the covenant brings a new reality into being; if God becomes the God of Israel or the God of Abraham, Isaac, and Jacob; and if the Hebrews become the Children of Israel or the People of Israel, then both God and the people have begun a process of transformation. Eric Mount's definition of "covenant" cited earlier notes that it involves an "assumption of obligations to each other and to shared values that *change one's life."*(Emphasis added.) John H. Hayes says that both the prophets and the Deuteronomic historian understood that what was required in order to prevent a repetition of Israel's rebellious past was "a spiritual transformation, an inner change in the Hebrew Man."[11] It follows that a dissolution of the covenant relationship would also necessarily involve a corresponding transformation.

The transformation that constitutes the covenant community of Israel begins at Sinai but is an ongoing process. It does not happen willy-nilly but through the implementation (by both God and the Hebrews) of the instruction (*Torah*) provided by God. Although S. Dean McBride, Jr. acknowledges the frequency with which *"Torah"* is translated by modern commentators as "instruction" or "teaching," he finds this to be "too facile" because it ignores the "sanctioned

---

7. Using more pious language, Buber writes: "You know always in your heart that you need God more than anything, but do you not know too that God needs you—in the fullness of His eternity needs you? How would man be, how would you be, if God did not need him, did not need you? You need God in order to be—and God needs you, for the very meaning of your life." Martin Buber, *I and Thou*, 2nd ed. (New York: Charles Scriber's Sons, 1958), 82.

8. Patrick D. Miller, " 'That It May Go Well with You': The Commandment and the Common Good" in Dennis P. McCann and Patrick D. Miller, eds., *In Search of the Common Good* (New York: T&T Clark, 2005), 18.

9. Paul Lehmann, *The Decalogue and a Human Future: The Meaning of the Commandments for Making and Keeping Life Human* (Grand Rapids, Michigan: Eerdmans, 1995), cited in Miller, "May Go Well," 20.

10. J. L. Austin, *How to Do Things with Words* (Cambridge, Massachusetts: Harvard University Press, 1962).

11. Hayes, 236.

political policies," "treaty-stipulations," "statutory rulings," and "the statutes and ordinances," and judicial dimensions in favor of "simply admonitions and sage advice" serving to "guide the faithful along a divinely charted path of life."[12] While his critique provides a helpful reminder of the diversity of materials to be found in Deuteronomy, he has isolated the judicial and political material from the narrative that frames it. That narrative consists of Moses' instructing the people. Also, he has understood "instruction" too narrowly as moral wisdom aimed at individuals rather than also as instruction of the kind that might be contained in courses in political science or constitutional law given in universities or law schools. In order to reflect the comprehensive character of Moses' instruction we might imagine a course such as Community Building 101 or Nation Building 102. McBride also believes that "instruction" overlooks the "normative, prescriptive force" of *Torah*. That force, which is surely there, is conditioned and tempered, however, by the overall goal of *Torah*, namely, "that it may be well with you."

This instruction by Yahweh through Moses is contained in summary form in the Decalogue or Ten Commandments. According to Patrick Miller, however, recent scholarship has shown that the Deuteronomic Code (Deut., chapters 12–26) "is ordered or structured along the lines of the Decalogue and so is to be understood as a development, specification, and illustration of the meaning and force of the Commandments."[13] What is found there has striking parallels to Confucianism, another form of Asian nondualism.[14] Confucius's task was to reorder an entire society that had sunk into political-social-moral chaos and urge it toward a new, ethical harmony. In the manner of a choreographer or dramatist, he sketches out roles, patterns, or precedents (*li*) for people to play or follow as they gave a form to their lives in a way that meshed with the lives of others to produce happiness in this-worldly life. As Hall and Ames put it, Confucianism is about "making persons."[15] The ideal form of these roles is spelled out in the Five Relationships (husband-wife, father-son, elder brother-younger brother, elder friend-younger friend, and ruler-subject).

Similarly, the Decalogue and Deuteronomic Code choreograph what Patrick Miller describes as

> a variety of complex relationships and systems: power relationships (e.g., king and subject, master and bonded servant, husband and wife, employer and employee, priest and lay person, lender and borrower, judge and plaintiff, landowner/property owner and landless, and so on) family relationships, communal relationships, property definition, systems of loans, systems of welfare, accessibility to economic goods, management of agricultural systems, and animal needs, judicial structures, and the like.[16]

12.   S. Dean McBride, Jr., "Polity of the Covenant People: The Book of Deuteronomy" in *Interpretation*, 41 (July 1987) 232–234.

13.   Footnote 1, Miller, "May Go Well," 14–15.

14.   See David L. Hall and Roger T. Ames, *Thinking Through Confucius* (Albany: State University of New York Press, 1987).

15.   Ibid., 71–83.

16.   Miller, "May Go Well," 19.

Such ideal patterns were intended, as Paul Lehman puts it, not for "being and staying human but *making* and *keeping* human."[17] (Emphasis added.) The goal of such a program of transformation and constitution is simply "that it may go well with you" (Deut. 5.16). Miller puts it this way: "*Life* is the goal, reward, and outcome of proper conformity to the responsibilities defined by the covenantal relationship and suggests an implicit correlation of the good and life."[18] As Miller notes, God is depicted as putting it this way: "Today I offer you the choice of life and good, or death and evil . . . Choose life" (Deut. 30.15, 19).

The final point concerning internal relations is that Yahweh and the people "belong with" each other. When the Babylonians conquered Judah, destroyed the temple in Jerusalem, and deported a significant part of the population to Babylon, including all of the leadership, the exiled Jews lamented, saying, "We have hung our harps on the willows, for how can we sing the Lord's song in a strange land?" (Psalms 137.2) Babylon was no substitute for the Promised Land. The emphasis here appears to be on the land, but is this not a synecdoche for the whole of the covenant reality they experience as lost—God, temple, family, state, community, and land? Wendell Berry would think so. He speaks of "an ancient system of analogies that clarifies a series of mutually defining and sustaining unities: of farmer and field, of husband and wife, of the world and God."[19] The covenant life in Israel is not interchangeable with any other life.

As for God, that the Children of Israel belong with Him is evident not only in the way He guides and provides for them, but also in the way He punishes them for their transgressions. Both are aspects of what Ed Farley calls "divine empathy,"[20] what Heschel calls God's "pathos," and what in the following passage is called "care."

> If the prophets have a single message, it may be summed up thus: God can be counted on to care. When his people have succumbed to corruption or to overweening pride, his care shows itself in punishment; when they are in despair or have been overrun by an arrogant enemy, his care shows itself in encouraging and restoring them. (Introduction to Micah, NEB, 997)

Clearly for God, Israel is no wallet!

3. A third feature of Intimacy, according to Kasulis, is its affective quality. Both the Hebrew Bible and the New Testament attest to God's love for his people, not just his chosen people, but all his creatures. If the "care" of the preceding passage is understood not only in the sense of "taking care of" but also in the sense of "caring for," then God's love is evident enough. The love and intimacy between Yahweh and Israel is reflected by the use of such analogies as parent-child, shepherd-flock, and husband-wife. Perhaps it is the prophet Hosea who in the Hebrew

---

17.   Lehman, cited in Miller, "May Go Well," 20–21.

18.   Miller, "May Go Well," 22.

19.   Wendell Berry, *A Continuous Harmony: Essays Cultural and Agricultural* (New York: Harcourt Brace Jovanovich, 1970), 159–160.

20.   Ed Farley, *Divine Empathy: A Theology of God* (Minneapolis, Minnesota: Fortress Press, 1996).

Bible depicts the relation of God to Israel as most intimate. He uses as an analogy for the God-people relation his own relationship with Gomer, his wife, who caused him enormous suffering by reverting to a life of temple prostitution. Like Gomer, Israel has repeatedly committed adultery (apostasy) by consorting with other gods. Like Hosea, God never gave up the effort to win back his wayward spouse. In the following passage Hosea depicts God as agonizing over his people: "How can I give you up, Ephraim, how surrender you, Israel? . . . My heart is changed within me, my remorse kindles already. I will not let loose my fury" (Hosea 11.8–9). Such persistence and such a willingness to forgive and take Israel back were not the result of mere duty but of an affective connection. Hosea does not hesitate to call it "love" (*hesed*), indeed a special love that remains faithful and loyal no matter what. Hence God says, "I will heal their apostasy; of my own bounty will I love them" (Hosea 14. 4).

Likewise, the people agonize over their disrupted relation with Yahweh. At the conclusion of Lamentations, which sometimes sounds like an account of a lover's quarrel, the author speaks for the people: "Why wilt thou quite forget us and forsake us these many days? O Lord, turn us back to thyself, and we will come back; renew our days as in times long past" (Lamentations 5.20–21).

4. A fourth feature of Intimacy is its somatic dimension. Already in Chapter 2 we have seen that for the ancient Hebrews, there is no mind-body dualism. An implication of this understanding is that all human activity, of whatever sort, is bodily. According to Jeremiah, for instance, when God longs for and calls for a covenant community in which the commandments are genuinely honored, not merely in the breach or in name only or without genuine conviction, he envisions a new covenant: "But this is the covenant which I will make with Israel after those days, says the Lord; I will set my law within them and write it on their hearts." (Jeremiah 31. 33). If Jeremiah's language doesn't quite make clear the bodily nature of the new covenant, Ezekiel does. In similar circumstances, he has Yahweh say to His people, "I will give you a new spirit within you; I will take out the heart of stone *from your body* and give you a heart of flesh" (Ezekiel. 36.26, emphasis added). Both the old and the new heart are bodily. Given the Hebrew view of the self as an embodied person, it cannot be otherwise.

5. Fifth and finally, according to Kasulis, Intimacy is characterized by knowledge that is not generally reflective or self-conscious of its own grounds. Already we have noted that Hebrew culture was pre-philosophical and that the Hebraic mode of knowing is faith. Doubtless, these facts in themselves are sufficient to locate the covenant community of Israel near to Intimacy. But there may be here an ambiguity with respect to the term "grounds." If, on the one hand, the term is understood as a theoretical presupposition of a foundationalist sort, then nothing of the kind is operative among the Hebrews. On the other hand, clearly Israel was aware that its polity, priestly system, and ethical teaching were derived from a covenant life rooted in a story linking them to a particular God who made promises and offered up instruction for their well-being.

Almost certainly, Kasulis' paradigm for "Intimacy" is contemporary Japanese society insofar as it is Shinto and/or Mahayana Buddhist, while his paradigm for "Integrity" is contemporary Euro-American society with its legacy stemming from the Enlightenment. With respect to these two options, Hebraic culture, we may say, is nondual in the sense that it cannot be forced readily into either alone.

One aim of *sunyata* is to reject the fixity of essence that denies the Buddhist doctrine of *anicca* (the experienced impermanence of all things) and the independence that such fixity reflects and supports. Are not the commandments of Yahweh fixed? And if so, does that not undermine the genuine interdependence of the covenant community? Eric Mount asserts, "Covenants should be dialogues in progress rather than simply regulations in stone."[21] Speaking of a moral framework or moral space as the presupposition of common ground, Patrick Miller addresses the issue of fixity in a way that applies equally to covenant.

> The danger of such concepts also becoming static and fixed is offset if both *structure* and *space* are set in a temporal and spatial *arc of understanding*. This is a trajectory of meanings, acts, and effects that receive their grounding in the moral framework and their orientation in the moral space but attend to the ever changing contexts of varying sorts (personal, communal, historical, geographical, economic, and so on).[22]

There is, in other words, an ongoing practice of interpretation of the covenant, even within the biblical narrative itself. Miller notes that Moses gives the Decalogue at Mount Sinai. Later, however, having led the Hebrew people to the brink of entry into Canaan, Moses "teaches them the Commandments *afresh* on the plains of Moab"[23] (emphasis added). Although he hearkens back to Sinai, he teaches the people "what is the meaning of covenantal existence in the new territory, now far from the wilderness of Sinai."

Many centuries later, the Talmud, the so-called "oral law," represents the persistence of that changing "arc of understanding" that the *midrashim* of Rabbinic Judaism carry forward today. In fact, by its very spatial and commentarial organization, a typical page of the Talmud insists on and attempts to guarantee continuing dialogue. An area along the left side and across the bottom of the page contains the commentary of Rashi, the great Talmudic scholar from the eleventh century. Another area across the top and down the right side of the page contains the commentaries of Rashi's students from the twelfth and thirteenth centuries. The opposing interpretations of Shammai and Hillel from the second century are located at the bottom of the middle. At the top of the middle is commentary of three centuries later from the Amoraim and Tannaim. According to Darrell Fasching, the significance of such a page arrangement is this:

> These parts express the voices of the rabbis throughout the ages all juxtaposed on the same page. The Talmud is not a finished book, but an ongoing dialogue among Jews not only of the same time period but from age to age . . . Rather than

---

21.   Mount, 34.
22.   Miller, "May Go Well," 32.
23.   Ibid., 33, footnote 42.

being led to a single conclusion, . . . it is more likely that the total impact will be experienced as an . . . invitation to enter a debate that spans the centuries. Nor is the Talmud . . . really meant to be studied alone. Talmudic study is a community . . . project that requires at the very least a partner with whom one can . . . interact, dialogue, discuss, and debate the meaning of a given page, . . . drawing on the wisdom of the dialogue partners through the ages.[24]

Ongoing dialogical study of the Talmud is, of course, a form of the covenant as a "dialogue in progress" called for by Mount.

The foregoing interpretation makes, I believe, a strong, point-by-point case that within the Hebrew Bible can be found grounds for claiming that a strain of ancient Hebrew life can be described as homologous with the definition of *sunyata* and Kasulis' related concept of Intimacy.

The Prophets *and* Sunyata

The foregoing interpretation of the covenant community opens up the possibility of a reinterpretation of the intent of the prophets. Nearly always, the fulminations of the prophets against the iniquities of the people point to violations of the covenant. In light of the covenant as *sunyata*, the violations can be understood as a "fall" into a variety of dualisms, the very dualisms that the covenant seeks to eliminate. Among them are king vs. subject, priest vs. laity, rich vs. poor, and Israel vs. the nations. Violating the covenant means seeing each member of these pairs as having a distinct and fixed essence and in elevating one member of the pair over the other in a way that diminishes life for both members of the pair, the pattern we saw in chapter one to be present in the racially segregated South.

King and Subjects

It would be difficult to overestimate the transformation of Israel's life and culture effected by the rise of monarchy. It was from the beginning and remained a matter of controversy. Israel already had a king, namely, Yahweh, and the assertion that Yahweh was king was understood to include the unspoken addition "and not any human being." The fact that surrounding nations had kings, giving them an advantage in marshalling military forces, made Israel seem vulnerable, especially in relation to the nearby and aggressive Syrians and Philistines. Yet when calls arose for a king "like the nations," the prophet Samuel warned that monarchy would result in a return to slavery for a people whom Yahweh had liberated from slavery in Egypt (I Sam. 8.11–13).

While Saul, the first king, was hardly more than the leader of the loosely coordinated Twelve Tribe League, the kingship of David and Solomon proved how accurate Samuel's warning had been. The covenantal theology of the tribal

24. John L. Esposito, Darrell J. Fasching, and Todd Lewis, *World Religions Today* (New York: Oxford University Press, 2002), 133–134.

league, with its democratic, egalitarian, and participatory values, was transformed into a royal theology that absolutized kingship. The heart of the royal theology was that henceforth kingship, which previously had been conditional, would become hereditary, dynastic, and unconditional. This royal theology was given a mythic foundation by the prophet Nathan's pronouncement from Yahweh: "Your family shall be established and your kingdom shall stand for all time in my sight, and your throne shall be established forever" (2 Samuel 7.16). Moreover, the king was regarded as Yahweh's adopted son. Speaking of this Davidic covenant, Miller says:

> There the earlier covenantal forms were transformed into the royal ideology of divine sonship by adoption and unconditioned rule by eternal decree. Such an ideology, which had as its central foundation the choice of David and Zion, the king and the temple place, served to give powerful support to the structures and prerogatives of monarchy by linking them to the cult.[25]

Here is the opening of a serious breach between the people and their leader, between the covenant theology and the royal theology. It is the essentializing of king and subjects as opposing dualities and the privileging of the former.

The changes wrought by David and Solomon were extensive. For his part, David united the northern and southern tribal confederacies into a single nation, chose Jerusalem as a neutral capital, and set up bureaucracies to run his administration. The military bureaucracy included two generals, one for the regular Israelite army and another for mercenaries from a variety of foreign countries. In the political domain he created such positions as secretary of state, recorder or herald, and minister of public works. Finally, with respect to religion, he appointed a personal priest and two chief priests to handle cult responsibilities. Each of these "cabinet" officials had a sizable staff. In addition, there would have been interpreters of foreign languages, especially Akkadian, which was probably the international language of the time. He established a school at the court to ensure that members of the administration were properly trained for their work; the classical writings in the various languages studied were used as textbooks.[26]

Solomon operated on an even grander scale. To defend the country he built a force of 1,400 chariots and 4,000 horses distributed across the country in designated chariot cities, each of which required barracks, supply depots, and stables. Numerous towns were rebuilt using casemate construction to serve as defensive outposts. He established 12 administrative districts throughout the country, each with an administrative head; built a fleet of ships and a port for use in trade; took full advantage of the overland trade routes linking Egypt with Syria and Mesopotamia; and launched mining operations for copper and iron. He ornamented the capital city with a palace and such royal buildings as the House of the Forest of Lebanon, the Hall of Pillars, and the Hall of the Throne. He acquired a harem consisting of hundreds of women from many countries, each bringing with

---

25. Patrick D. Miller, *The Religion of Ancient Israel* (Louisville, Kentucky: Westminster John Knox Press, 2000), 190.
   26. Hayes, 111–112.

her foreign cultural and religious values. Finally, he built a temple to house the sacrificial cult dedicated to Yahweh.[27]

The effects of these changes were many. Military operations, formerly defensive in nature, were undertaken to acquire land and economic advancement. Political decisions were no longer made according to covenantal ethics but expediency. Political and economic power shifted from the rural areas to the cities, especially those with governmental installations. A money economy replaced one based on land, slaves, or agricultural products. Culturally, an interest in international literature focusing on practical and theoretical wisdom arose. In short, a new and elite class appeared in Israelite society, one that was educated, affluent, and international in outlook, one that was out of touch with more traditional and ordinary people. Herein are the beginnings of other social dualisms in Hebrew society.[28]

The prophets of both the northern and southern kingdoms sought to rein in any royal acts that exceeded the boundaries laid down by the covenant. In the south, when David became infatuated with Bathsheba and arranged for her husband Uriah to be killed in battle, the prophet Nathan came and told David a story of a rich man who took a poor man's only lamb and served it to a visitor to his home. Filled with moral outrage at the rich man's meanness, David burst out, "As the Lord lives, the man who did this deserves to die." Then Nathan replied, "You are that man" and spelled out the consequences the king would have to endure for his actions, including the death of his son by Bathsheba (2 Sam. 12).

In the southern kingdom, when king Ahab took up the worship of Baal, the god of his wife Jezebel, building an altar to him in Samaria, Elijah exclaimed to him, "I swear by the life of the Lord the god of Israel, whose servant I am, that there shall be neither dew nor rain these coming years unless I give the word" (I Kgs 17.1). Later, Ahab desired the vineyard of Naboth of Jezreel and offered to buy it. When Naboth refused, Ahab's wife Jezebel, arranged to have Naboth falsely accused of cursing God and the king. For these crimes he was stoned to death. Then Ahab took possession of the vineyard. The prophet Elijah confronted Ahab with these words: "Where the dogs licked the blood of Naboth, there dogs shall lick your blood" and "Because you have sold yourself to do what is wrong in the eyes of the Lord, I will bring disaster upon you" (I Kgs 22.19).

The prophets also concerned themselves with foreign policy. When Rehoboam, Soloman's successor to the unified throne, refused to lighten the burden of forced labor and taxation laid by his father on the people, the prophet Ahijah of Shiloh, which is in the north, approached the king's brother, Jeroboam, and tore his own cloak into 12 pieces, saying, "Take ten pieces, for this is the word of the Lord the God of Israel: 'I am going to tear the kingdom from the hand of Solomon and give you ten tribes'" (I Kgs 11.31). This action encouraged Jeroboam to lead Israel to secede from the kingdom, dividing it into two separate nations.

When Rezin of Damascus and Pekah of Israel (the northern kingdom) revolted against Assyria, the aggressive superpower of the region, they urged Ahaz of Judah to join them. When Ahaz, a pro-Assyrian ruler, refused, the forces of Rezin and

27. Ibid., 116–124.
28. Ibid.

Pekah attacked Judah. Ahaz rejected the prophet Isaiah's advice to remain neutral and appealed to Assyria for military assistance. He even went so far as to strip the temple and the treasury of the royal palace of their gold and silver and send them to Tiglath-pileser, the Assyrian ruler, as a bribe. The Assyrians responded to Ahaz' plea and Judah was spared. The cost, however, as Isaiah had predicted, was high. Judah became a vassal state to Assyria and was forced to pay tribute. Beyond that, Ahaz made changes in the temple in Jerusalem to conform to the demands of Tiglath-pileser. For example, he installed a second altar in the temple, thus providing one for the worship of Yahweh and the other for rites honoring Assyrian deities. This act violated both Yahweh's prescriptions for the design of the temple and the covenantal commandment to worship Yahweh exclusively. These are but two of many instances in which the prophets sought to bring kings back into conformity with covenantal instruction and to restore wholeness to the covenant community.

Rich and Poor

A gulf opened up also between rich and poor. The vast public works projects undertaken by Solomon required a large supply of manpower, a need met by forced labor. An enormous amount of money was also needed. Tribute from vassal states and revenues from taxes on the use of the trade routes were insufficient; consequently, a tax was levied against the people, one particularly burdensome for the poor. These oppressive conditions were largely the cause of the former northern kingdom's secession from the unified kingdom, leaving Jerusalem to make up for the lost taxes and labor by squeezing Judah even harder. The northern kingdom of Israel, however, began its own public works projects in Samaria, Dan, and Bethel. Moreover, covenantal stipulations aimed at protecting the poor—for example, the one abolishing debts after 7 years—were ignored, especially in Judah. Among merchants, moral restraints related to cheating and lying were discarded in favor of acquisitiveness. Indeed, among groups positioned to take advantage of the boom, sumptuous lifestyles and lavish displays of wealth were pursued without any regard for those members of society who could barely scrape by.

The prophets, committed to the instruction of the covenant, took the side of the poor and politically oppressed. Hosea, for example, prophesying in Israel, complains that "false scales are in merchants' hands and they love to cheat" (Hos. 12.7). Amos uses even stronger language:

> For crime after crime of Israel I will grant them no reprieve, because they sell the innocent for silver and the destitute for a pair of shoes. They grind the heads of the poor into the earth. And thrust the humble out of their way. Father and son resort to the same girl to the profanation of my holy name. (Amos 2.6–7)

What the prophets' appeal to the covenant makes clear is that taking the side of the poor was not what Liberation Theology calls "a preferential option for the poor," if that is taken to mean an absolute commitment to the poor alone. It is not a matter of taking sides in class warfare. That in itself would be a form of social dualism. The covenant includes all the people, and the efforts of the prophets were aimed at correcting an economic imbalance that had negative consequences for all members of society, even those who had an economic advantage. Living well is not to be defined in exclusively economic terms. Its dimensions are qualitative as well as quantitative. Only insofar as the rich were sensitive to the plight of their neighbors, as the terms of the covenant required, could they truly enjoy their wealth and live well.

Priests and Laity

Previously, there had been priests who were in charge of the Ark of the Covenant and the Tent of Meeting. With the building of a permanent temple and the establishment of a school to produce trained functionaries, however, there arose a professional, priestly class. One way the budding dualism between priests and laity manifested itself was in different interpretations of the interrelated categories the holy and the profane (or common) and the pure and the impure. Certain places, things, persons, and times were regarded as holy, according to Patrick Miller, "not because of anything inherent within them, any *mana* or potency with which they were laden" but because they were "set apart" or dedicated to Yahweh, who was holy. To be sure, things do have potency and are dangerous—the Ark is an example—but only because God has so decreed. Purity has to do with the conditions that protect one from danger or death when the Holy is encountered.[29] Conceptually, holiness and purity and their opposites are nondual in the sense that the meaning of one set of these categories is required for the definition of the other, and vice versa, but ancient Israel knew no dualism of conceptuality vs. reality.

The problem is that the priests, whose job description included divination (using the *ephod* and the *urim* and *thummim*), teaching the Torah, and running the sacrificial ritual, came to understand holiness in a very narrow sense as including only the sanctuary, the priests, and the sacrificial ritual. Other people and things ordinarily existed in a profane state but could be made holy only temporarily and by special steps.

The countervailing view is expressed in the Holiness Code (Lev. 17–26) and by the prophets. Here, the entire land and people of Israel "existed in a state of holiness and were always under obligation to demonstrate that holiness, to achieve or maintain it by the whole realm of human conduct, moral and social as well as ritual."[30] Miller cites Milgrom as using "ascription" and "achievement" and Eilberg-Schwartz as using "static" and "dynamic" to describe the two views of holiness, respectively.[31] The view of the Holiness Code, Deuteronomy, and the prophets is the dominant view, and it is grounded in the covenant relation, which includes all Israelites, not just the priests. Thus a prophecy of Amos has Yahweh roar hatred for sacrifices, offerings, and pilgrim feasts and proclaim his preference

29. Miller, *The Religion of Ancient Israel*, 132.
30. Ibid. 156.
31. Ibid., see also footnotes 67 and 68.

for righteousness and justice (Amos 5.21–24). Isaiah's language in addressing the same problem is even more biting:

> Your countless sacrifices, what are they to me? I am sated with whole-offerings of rams and the fat of buffaloes; I have no desire for the blood of bulls, of sheep and of he-goats. Whenever you come to enter my presence—who asked you for this? No more shall you trample my courts. The offer of your gifts is useless, the reek of sacrifice is abhorrent to me. New moons and Sabbaths and assemblies, sacred seasons and ceremonies, I cannot endure. I cannot tolerate your new moons and your festivals; they have become a burden to me, and I can put up with them no longer. When you lift your hands outspread in prayer, I will hide my eyes from you. Though you offer countless prayers, I will not listen. There is blood on your hands; wash yourselves and be clean. Put away the evil of your deeds, away out of my sight. Cease to do evil and learn to do right, pursue justice and champion the oppressed; give the orphan his rights, plead the widow's cause. (Isaiah 1.11–17)

Such prophecies target both the priests who officiate at the ritual sacrifices and the laypeople who participate in the temple cult. For Amos and other prophets, holiness is manifested more significantly in the moral decisions of daily living, especially as they bear on caring for the widow, the orphan, and the poor. While it may or may not be the case that Amos and Isaiah opposed the sacrificial cult under all circumstances, it is clear enough that any attempt to separate cultic activity from moral living and to privilege the former at the expense of the latter is a dualism they vehemently reject.

Recall, too, that the priests were responsible for instructing the people in the ways that were pleasing to Yahweh. That instruction included the moral teaching of the covenant and was intended to promote living that "goes well." When Hosea complains that there is "no knowledge of God in the land" (Hos. 4.1) and that the people "have forgotten the teaching of God" (Hos. 4.6), he is pointing to the broken oaths, theft, murder, adultery that he everywhere observed and that are prohibited by the terms of the covenant. In fact, he explicitly connects lack of knowledge of God with breaking the covenant (Hos. 6.6–7). At the same time, he is indicting the priests for failing to fulfill their obligation to teach how a covenant people ought to live. He may also be indicting the king, who, as we have seen, is also a priest of the city-state of Jerusalem. Jeremiah also links knowledge of God to concern for the poor. Speaking of Josiah, God says: "He dispensed justice to the lowly and poor: did not this show he knew me?" (Jer. 22.16) The prophetic view seeks to deconstruct the emerging dualism of priesthood and laity, holiness and morality, and to recover the nonduality of covenant life.

Israel and the Nations

References to Moab, Edom, Ammon, Gaza, Syria, Egypt, Assyria, Tyre, Sidon, and Babylon, etc. are virtually omnipresent in the Hebrew Bible. Collectively, they are known as "the nations." The prophets seem constantly to compare and contrast Israel and/or Judah with one or more of them. If the people of the covenant community are Yahweh's "special possession" and raised "high above all the nations" (Deut. 26.18–19), they are so by contrast to the people of the nations. What makes Israel distinctive is that Israel is holy.

In what way were the Israelites set apart or distinctive? In what does their holiness consist? It consists in the different way of life they are committed to live, a way that sets them apart from the people of the nations: they live according to the terms of the covenant. Walter Brueggeman says that the Egypt that enslaved the Hebrews was the paradigm of a nation for that era. It was a nation whose religion was a "static triumphalism" and whose politics was one of "oppression and exploitation."[32] For Daniel Elazar, Egypt is the classic example of a state originated by conquest—hierarchical and authoritarian. Its modern forms are Fascism and Nazism.[33] Brueggeman sees Moses as the genius who set out to create a different kind of nation, one embodying a "counter-culture," a nation of freedom and criticism in a dynamic history; it is what Elazar terms a "federal model."

Israel, it seems, was defined, first of all, by contrast to Egypt, then later by contrast to a larger group of nations. Israel was to be a new paradigm. The assertion of a strong contrast between Israel and the nations certainly appears to be dualistic. And at times, Israel certainly seems to have behaved in a dualistic, exclusivistic manner. Some foreigners (Ammonites and Moabites) were excluded from the "assembly of the Lord" (Deut. 23.3–7). Foreigners were excluded from temple worship (Ezek. 44.5–9) and from partaking of the Passover meal (Exod. 12.43). Under Nehemiah and Ezra, even harsher forms of separation were enforced, as we shall see.

Yet such an assessment requires qualification. If Brueggeman is claiming that Moses/Israel defined itself in terms of a relation of contrast with the nations, particularly Egypt, then such definitional interdependence is an aspect of the interdependence that is *sunyata*. We have already noted that holiness, for the Hebrews, is not an innate quality or fixed essence. Holiness is not a *svabhava*. Again, Israel is holy or distinctive by virtue of behavior, and the covenant is conditional upon behavioral faithfulness. God "chose" them. In addition, they chose Yahweh. He would be their god and they would be his people. Here is the double choice and double commitment that is at the root of the covenant.[34] Yet, Yahweh's steadfast love (*hesed*) prompts enormous patience with Israel, despite its waywardness.

If the Ammonites and Moabites were prohibited from inclusion in the "assembly of God," it was not because they were essentially unholy but because of specific

---

32. Walter Brueggemann, *The Prophetic Imagination* (Minneapolis, Minnesota: Fortress Press, 1978), 16.

33. Daniel Elazar, "Federal Models of (Civil) Authority" in *Journal of Church and State*, Vol. 33, No. 2 (Spring 1991), 232.

34. God's original choosing of Israel and leading them out of exile in Egypt, however, were apparently not based on Israel's holiness. Deuteronomy 7.7–8 says:

> It was not because you were more numerous than any other nation that the Lord cared for you and chose you, for you were the smallest of all nations; it was because the Lord loved you and stood by his oath to your forefathers, that he brought you out with his strong hand and redeemed you from the land of slavery, from the power of Pharaoh king of Egypt.

hostile actions: they did not provide food and water to the Hebrews exiting Egypt and they hired Balaam to revile the Israelites. Other nations, Edom and Egypt, for example, were not excluded from the assembly (Deut. 23.3–7).

At least by the time of Deutero-Isaiah, Yahweh was understood by Israel to be the God of all the nations, not just Israel. He used other nations to carry out his purposes. In at least one instance Yahweh chose the Assyrian king to be the "deliverer" who rescued Israel from Syrian oppression (2 Kgs 13.5). Deutero-Isaiah saw Cyrus, king of Persia, as a redeemer-savior for those under the thumb of Babylon and has Yahweh say: "I roused one from the north, and he obeyed; I called one from the east, summoned him *in my name*" (Isa. 41.25, emphasis added). An even more stunning passage is found in Amos 9.7: "Are not you Israelites like the Cushites to me? says the Lord. Did I not bring Israel up from Egypt, the Philistines from Caphtor, the Arameans from Kir?" This suggests that God has redemptive relations with other nations, perhaps embodied in other exodus stories.

By the time of Trito-Isaiah, foreigners were permitted to enter the temple and pray.

> So too the foreigners who give their allegiance to me, the Lord, to minister to me and love my name and to become my servants, all who keep the sabbath undefiled and hold fast to my covenant: them will I bring to my holy hill and give them joy in my house of prayer. Their offerings and sacrifices shall be acceptable on my altar; for my house shall be called a house of prayer for all nations. This is the very word of the Lord God, who brings home the outcasts of Israel: I will yet bring home all that remain to be brought in. (Isa. 56.6–8)

By the third century BCE there was a formal process by which foreigners could convert to Israel's religion. In contrast to foreigners, resident aliens, according to Milgrom, were required to keep the religious law's "prohibitive commands" but were neither required to keep nor prohibited from keeping the "performative" ones.[35] Presumably, resident aliens, having lived among the Hebrews for an extended time, had already adopted much of the Hebrew way of living. Miller observes that although the Deuteronomic Code does distinguish treatment of neighbors and resident aliens from the treatment of foreigners, it is also the case that "the Commandments open the issue for the community as a whole vis-à-vis others outside the community and do not let the question of the neighbor remain a purely intra-community definition."[36] In other words, the issue of "the nations" is not to be solved simply by patiently waiting for their conversion but by including voices from the nations in an expanding reflection and discussion of the question of the meaning of "neighbor" and thus, the covenant. Miller goes so far as to say that implicitly Deuteronomy goes even further in the direction of some kind of pluralism.

> The gods whom Israel is not to worship have been "allotted to all the peoples everywhere under heaven (Deut. 4.19; cf. 29.26; 32.8–9). There is an implicit assumption

---

35. Miller, *The Religion of Ancient Israel*, 201.
36. Miller, "May Go Well" 18, n 11.

that the worship of other nations, identified in relation to other deities and other religious systems, is, in fact, a provision and work of the Lord of Israel.[37]

Finally, in the Babylonian Talmud there is a midrash that says that as Pharoah's army was drowning in the Red Sea (or Sea of Reeds), ministering angels in heaven proposed to sing a song rejoicing at the victory of and escape by the Hebrew slaves. God, however, rebukes them saying, "My handiwork (the Egyptians) is drowning in the sea, would ye utter song before me!"[38]

In sum, whereas all the nations might not share the same understanding concerning their relation to Yahweh, some Hebrew prophets held that, in time, such an acknowledgement would be made. Here, there is an eschatological dimension to Yahweh's relation to the nations. Clearly, views about the nations were not uniform, and they changed over time. My claims about Hebrew nonduality, however, as I indicated at the outset, are based on a selective reading of the Hebrew scriptures. Clearly too, there are some Hebrews who do not hold, in thought or behavior, that there is a Hebrew vs. the nations dualism.

Good and Evil

Beyond the threats of dualism already considered, any claim that Hebraic thought is nondualistic is faced with the daunting task of making that case with respect to the distinction between good and evil that is everywhere present in the Bible. No less a figure than Nietzsche saddles the Jews with the responsibility for subverting an aristocratic ethic of good vs. bad and replacing it with an altruistic ethic of good vs. evil. The latter he calls a "slave ethic" or an "ethic of the common man." He says:

> It was the Jew who, with frightening consistency, dared to invert the aristocratic value equations good/noble/powerful/beautiful/happy/favored-of-the gods and maintain, with the furious hatred of the underprivileged, that "only the poor and powerless, are good; only the suffering, sick, and ugly, truly blessed. But you noble and mighty ones of the earth will be, to all eternity, the evil, the cruel, the avaricious, the godless, and thus the cursed and damned!"[39]

Nietzsche is saying more than that the ethical prescriptions of aristocrats are different from those of the poor and that his preference is for the former. The shift from an ethics of good vs. bad to one of good vs. evil that he describes is a shift from a relativistic ethic to an absolutistic one, a hardening into dualism.

Where to begin? First, except for mentioning Jesus, Nietzsche is not very specific about who is to blame for what he sees as a tragedy. This lack of specificity itself seems to be a stereotyping and essentializing of Jews and the Bible, as if all

37.   Ibid., 34.
38.   Sanhedrin 39B.
39.   Friedrich Nietzsche, *The Birth of Tragedy and the Genealogy of Morals*, trans. Francis Golffing, Anchor Doubleday Book (Garden City, New York: Doubleday & Company, Inc., 1956), 167–168.

Jews held the same views and at all times. It is the case, of course, that the pre-exilic prophets criticized the rich and sought justice for the poor. Yet, as we have already noted, this is no sclerosis of social distinctions, no creation of a reverse social hierarchy, no absolute privileging of a single social group. The rich were criticized not for being rich *per se* but for the unethical manner in which their wealth was acquired, for the foolish ways in which that wealth was spent, and for their insensitivity to the poor. And the prophets championed the poor not because poverty in itself is viewed as morally or spiritually superior but out of a concern for the stability, intimacy, and well-being of the entire covenant community, including both the rich and the poor.

Second, the hardening of such distinctions as good and evil, holy and unholy, pure and impure, and Jews and non-Jews, a hardening that did occur, took place not at the instigation of pre-exilic, exilic, or early post-exilic prophets but largely by the priestly class of the second temple period. It was during that period that the priests were not merely in charge of cultic matters but were also in control of the government. Nehemiah, for example, although not himself a priest, shared their exclusivism. He had the Ammonite ruler Tobiah, who had married a Jewish woman, thrown out of Jerusalem; he forbade commerce on the Sabbath, locking the city gates and posting guards to enforce the prohibition; and he insisted on a pledge from male Jews who had married non-Jews not to arrange marriages for their children with non-Jews. In some cases he used cursing, beating, and pulling out hair to extract such a promise. Ezra, a priest, went a step further, demanding that Jewish men divorce their non-Jewish wives and drive out the children of those marriages.

While such actions do reflect a form of social dualism, it is not one that privileges the poor, slaves, or the common people. However ill-advised such actions may be, their aim was simply to ensure the survival of the handful of Jews who had suffered the destruction of their city, their temple, and their nation. It is situational, reactive, and qualified.

By contrast, the hardening of the categories of good and evil in the direction of a metaphysical dualism is almost certainly attributable to the rise of apocalyptic movements. According to them, God will very soon intervene in the world to overturn present reality and vindicate the righteous. Such views are generally regarded as arising during the postexilic period. Their sharp dualism between good and evil may have been borrowed from Persian sources or developed within Israel itself.

The figure of Satan or "the adversary" or "the accuser" appears not only in the well-known story of Job, but also in I Kings 22.21–22, I Chronicles 21.1, and Zechariah 3.1–2. Patrick Miller sees such passages as "not in the biblical literature reflective of a forthright dualism" but as the "seeds of dualistic thinking" or a "subdued dualism" or "incipient dualism." Such a Satan is different from the Satan of the intertestamental period. For Miller, both Persian dualism and the incipient Israelite dualism amounted to a critique of the view that "the reality of human sin and divine judgment" could "alone carry the moral burden of accounting for all the evil that happened."[40] Nietzsche may well be right with respect to

---

40. Miller, *The Religion of Ancient Israel*, 28.

later postexilic Judaism but not with respect to the preexilic, exilic, and early postexilic Hebrew thought that are my principal concern. An essentialist dualism of good and evil is not consistent with a God who changes, humans who change, and a covenant that changes.

The foregoing interpretation of the connection of prophecy with covenant can be summed up in the following passage by Christian Hauer and William Young:

> All of the prophets assume the special relationship between the Lord and Israel expressed in the Sinai Covenant. They frequently base their indictment of the people and leaders of the nation on violations of the covenant. The prophets are *covenant advocates* or *covenant mediators*, who remind the nation of its responsibilities because of its special relationship with the Lord.[41]

If, as I have argued, covenant is *sunyata*, then the prophets are also *sunyata* advocates and mediators, the promoters of a Middle-Eastern middle way.

Recall from Chapter 1 the Mahayana story that the Buddha left the wisdom of the middle way with the *nagas* (mythical serpents) until a future age when it would be needed. Perhaps the Hebrew prophets are "*nagas*," guarding the wisdom of a middle way for the West.

Alleged and Real Differences between Asian Nondualism and Hebrew Nondualism

To this point, I have emphasized only the similarities between Buddhist *sunyata* and Hebrew covenant. As one might reasonably expect, there are also differences between the concepts, and these differences deserve some attention. The Hebrews, after all, are Middle Eastern, not Eastern.

1. First of all, the Mosaic covenant was made with Israel, a mere subset of the human race. Buddhist *sunyata*, by contrast, embraces the entire human species. In other words, the covenant is particular while *sunyata* is universal. This observation, however, requires to be set in context. First, the God of the Bible is depicted as having created all human beings and as loving and acting in the best interests of all of them universally. We have already noted how even non-Israelites have been recognized as saviors by some Hebrew prophets and that other religions were understood as a provision of Yahweh, who led exodus events for some nations other than Israel.

Second, the Mosaic covenant is not the only one mentioned in the Tanak, but the third of five, although, arguably, it is the most important. The first covenant, the one made with Noah, is universal in character, and there is no reason to assume that it is to be regarded as in any way abrogated by the subsequent making

---

41. Christian E. Hauer and William A. Young, *An Introduction to the Bible: A Journey into Three Worlds*, 4th edition (Upper Saddle River, New Jersey: Prentice Hall, 1986), 139.

of the covenant at Sinai. According to Daniel Elazar, the Talmud supports such an interpretation.

> Yet the Bible teaches us that God's covenant with Israel must be viewed in the larger context of God's covenant with all men. The Talmud teaches that the beginning of this covenant relationship is implicit in God's relationship with Adam, particularly after man acquires knowledge of good and evil, but the first formal covenant was made with Noah after the flood (Genesis 9). Through Noah, the Talmud teaches that covenant is binding on all people as the basis for universal law.[42]

Third, the Abrahamic covenant, which Patrick Miller suggests is "the turning point in the biblical narrative" and is "in some ways, the link between the Noahic covenant and that of the Mosaic covenant,"[43] supports the inclusiveness of the covenant. In Genesis 12.3 and 18.18 God promises that through Abraham "shall all the families of the earth be blessed." In these verses the Hebrew God's universal intent is manifest.

Fourth, both entrance into and exit from the Mosaic covenant was an ongoing possibility. Periodic covenant renewal festivals allowed not only for pledging anew to live according to God's instruction but for making an initial commitment to the covenant life, and one could choose not to participate in them.

Finally, we have seen that there is an eschatological dimension to the covenant in the form of a hope, expressed in many places in the Hebrew Bible, especially in Deutero-Isaiah, that some day all peoples will belong to the covenant community. Indeed, this eschatological feature is essential to the voluntary and conditional character of covenant membership. Covenantal relations are not a matter of nature but are an achievement in history.

2. The future-oriented perspective of the covenant could be seen, however, as indicating a second difference between it and Buddhist *sunyata*. Mahayana Buddhism asserts that the Buddha nature is present both now and always in all sentient beings. This is misleading, however, when one recognizes that although some Buddhists seem to have so regarded it, the Buddha nature is not an essence or substance but a mere potential for enlightenment. Analogously, one can say that from a biblical perspective all peoples have an ever-present potential for covenant membership. One can infer such a potential from the priestly account in Genesis of the creation of humankind: "Then God said, 'Let us make man in our image and likeness' . . . So God created man in his own image; in the image of God he created him; male and female he created them" (Gen. 1.26–27). The so-called *Imago Dei* has had a long history of varying interpretations. It has been identified with reason, immortality, conscience, creativity, rule, and response-ability, to name a few. More recently, process and feminist theologians, taking notice of the shift from "him" to "them" in the final clause of the previously quoted biblical passage, have understood the *Imago* as "being in relation." Paula Cooey, for example, sees the story

---

42.   Daniel J. Elazar, "Covenant as the Basis of Jewish Political Tradition" in *The Jewish Journal of Sociology*, 20 (June 1978), 7.

43.   Patrick Miller, email to Milton Scarborough, February 2, 2007.

of the creation of Adam and Eve as the creation of difference within relationship. She says:

> Because the divine life requires differentiation within relationship, to be created in the image of God means that God intends humans for relation with God, with other humans, and with the rest of God's creation . . . It clarifies theologically that the image of God borne by all humans is borne, as in the case of God, in relationship with others rather than in isolation from them.[44]

Cooey's reference to differentiation and relationship within the divine life, however, reflects a trinitarian perspective, according to which the three divine persons are related but different. This theological reading puts back into Genesis, with virtually no textual basis for doing so, the Christian doctrines of God the Son and God the Holy Spirit. Alternatively, with ample justification, much of which has been provided earlier in this chapter, one can conceive divine relatedness and difference in relation to the creatures.

Relatedness to others, then, is a central feature of both God and humans. In any case, there is a parallel between the inherent human potential for being in covenant relationship and the inherent human potential for enlightenment: the Elohim-nature is analogous to the Buddha-nature.

Also, just as there is an eschatological dimension to the Hebraic hope for a universal actualizing of that potential, so there is one in Mahayana Buddhism. When a *bodhisattva* vows not to enter *nirvana* until even the grass is enlightened, at least implicitly and in principle, he or she posits a future goal toward which to aim.

3. A third difference is that whereas covenant, at least in popular understanding, includes members of the human race only, Buddhist *sunyata* embraces all "sentient beings"—dogs, giraffes, elephants, mice, fleas, etc. This is an implication of the doctrines of *karma* and *samsara*, according to which creatures are repeatedly reborn into various species, depending upon the morality of their past actions. In fact, for some Buddhist sects, *Hua-Yen* for example, even the inorganic realm is included. All things equally possess the Buddha-nature and as such, "preach *dharma*," i.e., manifest Buddhahood. The Buddha-nature extends, as Tom Kasulis once pointed out, to "piss" and "shit."

The popular conception of covenant on this point is, however, a misconception. Among the many relationships concerning which the covenant provides instruction and lays down obligations is the relation of humans to animals and land. The clear implication here is that these latter creatures are included in the covenant. Exodus 23.11–12, for example says:

> For six years you may sow your land and gather its produce; but in the seventh year you shall let it lie fallow and leave it alone. It shall provide food for the poor of your people, and what they leave the wild animals may eat. You shall do likewise with your vineyard and your olive grove. For six days you may do your work,

---

44. Paula Cooey, *Family, Freedom, and Faith: Building Community Today* (Louisville, Kentucky: Westminster John Knox Press, 1966), 45.

but on the seventh day you shall abstain from work, so that your ox and your ass may rest, and your home-born slave and the alien may refresh themselves.

Some interpreters have seen the commandment about letting fields lie fallow as reflecting an early insight into the importance of crop rotation and, consequently, as reflecting concern merely for humans needs. Such needs would include not only that of the poor, who are mentioned explicitly, but also landowners, for whom crop rotation would promote continued productivity over the longer term. A rested and refreshed ox and ass could work harder and last longer in the service of mankind. Even the reference to wild animals, which at first glance might seem to escape this interpretation, can be seen as a way of ensuring a plentiful supply of game animals for human consumption.

There are instances, however, in which helping animals cannot be so readily reduced to helping humans. Deuteronomy 22.4 says, "When you see your fellow-countryman's ass or ox lying on the road, do not ignore it; you must help him lift it to its feet again." Exodus 23.5 extends the injunction to helping the ass of "one who hates you." Deuteronomy 25.4 prescribes that an ox that is threshing corn should not be muzzled. A Jewish commentary on the verse asserts that the reason for the rule is so that the animal will "not be tortured by its inability to satisfy its hunger."[45]

What is important to understand, however, is that the idea of covenant involves the notion that members of the covenant community are to contribute to the good of the other members. Given that animals are part of that community, it is appropriate to think of their service as their contribution to the life of the whole. In any case, regardless of the motive, the inclusion of animals and land in the covenant reflects a level of concern and care for them that works to their benefit, even if it also benefits humankind.

Moreover, the fact that God is said to love and care for the things God has created provides a basis for valuing animals and land apart from their utility to humans. Much later, the New Testament says that "the created universe waits with eager expectation for God's sons to be revealed." Although it now "groans in all its parts" (perhaps because of covenant violations on humanity's part), the "universe itself is to be freed from the shackles of mortality and enter upon the liberty and splendour of the children of God" (Rom. 8.19–22). Obviously, the universe includes animals and land.

The Psalms, of course, are filled with passages that sing the praises of nature for its beauty and, more significantly, as a vehicle for manifesting God's glory. On the whole, however, it must be acknowledged, that both divine and human concern for nature in the Bible are not so prominent as is the concern for humans. And there are certainly no stories there to compare with that of the bodhisattva who, from compassion, slit his own throat with a piece of sharpened bamboo and lay down in front of a mother tiger that, due to lack of nourishment, could not feed her hungry cubs. Doubtless, such stories reflect the Buddhist view that all

---

45. *The Torah: A Modern Commentary*, rev. ed., W. Gunther Plaut and David E. S. Stein, eds (New York: Union for Reform Judaism Press, 2005), 1337.

creatures in the cycle of rebirth (*samsara*) are future Buddhas and that Siddartha Gautama himself had lived many previous lives in animal form.

4. Such considerations bring to the forefront another difference between the Hebrew covenant and Mahayana Buddhist *sunyata*, namely, the presence of an ontological hierarchy in the former and its absence in the latter. Although Elohim loves all the creatures and proclaims them to be "very good," humans alone are made in god's image. Indeed, the entire biblical story is, as we have noted, largely about the relation of God and humans. Clearly, these facts are evidence of an incipient ontological hierarchy. By contrast, we have seen that in some schools of Mahayana, all beings "preach" *dharma* equally with the highest of celestial Buddhas. For Hua-Yen, that assertion holds for even non-sentient beings. Purged of all obvious anthropocentrism, Mahayana Buddhism is, at least in this respect, the radical ecologist's dream ideology.

Imagine, for example, that a person strolling through a park hears anguished sounds coming from a nearby lake. Rushing to the lake, he or she discovers a dog and a human child drowning. Both are going down for what appears to be the last time. No other help is available. There is time to save but one; the other will surely die. Which one to save? Almost certainly, a Westerner would save the child, regardless of its health or moral status. The Asian, on the other hand, will find no clear resources in Mahayana Buddhism to make such a decision. Very probably, a Japanese or Chinese person will also save the child but will do so on Confucian grounds, not Buddhist ones. Here is a significant difference between covenant and *sunyata*.

5. *Sunyata* is a decentered reality. The various constituents of its web-like structure are of equal value to the whole. For classical Christianity, however, there is an undisputed center, namely, God. All humans, sometimes even all creatures, are viewed as directing their worship and adoration away from themselves toward a divine being that is in itself indifferent and self-sufficient. Adherents to such a view have "found" it in the Hebrew and Christian scriptures. It should be obvious to the reader that this chapter takes a different position. God and the creatures are mutually dependent or interdependent. Elohim or Yahweh cannot even be God without a relation to the creatures.

If "decentered" means the absence of an *absolute* center of value, then the Hebrew covenant of ancient Israel is decentered. For ancient Hebraic religion, the covenant community itself, including God, not God alone, is the center, a dynamic center that aims in hope to embrace all others. Here the scripture seems to be at odds with classical Christianity. This does not mean, however, that all elements of the covenant community contribute *equally* to covenant life, as Buddhism might hold. As the active instigator of history, both natural and social, God has a privileged position in the covenant community. Between the extremes of decentered and equal (Buddhism), on the one hand, and entirely God-centered (classical Christianity), on the other, ancient Hebrew religion represents a distinctive middle way.[46]

46. The Talmud contains a story in which Rabbi Eliezer ben Hyrcanos disagrees with other Rabbis concerning an interpretation of the law. To prove that his view is the correct one, Eliezer works a series of miracles, but the other rabbis remain unconvinced. Finally,

6. Finally, although both covenant and *sunyata* involve internal relations, the internal relations are not identical in nature. According to Stephen Pepper, cosmological theories are constructed from "root metaphors," metaphors about the whole of things. During the Newtonian era, for example, the world was understood as a "machine," the dominant root metaphor of the time. Coupling this image with the notion of divine creation yields the view that the world was *manufactured* by God. Other root metaphors are emanation (Plotinus), birth, growth of a tree (Vishnu's creation of world), word or poem (P-account of creation in Genesis), thought (Zuni), a ceramic vessel (J-account of creation in Genesis), vivisection (Indra's creation from the carcass of Vritra), and sacrifice (Prajapati's offering himself as the sacrificial substance). A myth of origin or creation selects and establishes a culture's root metaphor. The world thus created is structured according to the "logic" of the root metaphor.

Japanese Buddhism is influenced by its centuries-long association with Shinto, the indigenous Japanese religion. In one Shinto origin myth the world is born from the sexual union of Izanagi and Izanami. Its root metaphor, then, is birth. The logic of birth is that the progeny share the same nature as the parents. The offspring of a cow is itself a cow and all the "children" of cows are essentially the same in virtue of possessing equally the cow-nature. Hence, for Shinto, all the constituents of the world—humans, animals, plants, and minerals—despite their obvious differences, share the same nature because all are children of Izanagi and Izanami. Insofar as Japanese Buddhism has been affected by such considerations, internal relations have a mythico-biological or racial character.

In the case of the machine metaphor and the ceramic metaphor the logic is different. Neither the machine nor the clay pot shares the same nature as the manufacturer or potter, except that all are physical. When such root metaphors are employed in a theological context, however, as in Deism or classical Christianity, even this physical similarity is eliminated to emphasize the "wholly other" character of God in relation to the creation.

But what about the P-account of creation in Genesis? If the world spoken into being by Elohim possesses the character of words or speech, does its share the same nature as the speaker? Here the logic of speech is ambiguous. Insofar as a word arises from the mindbodily being of the speaker, it is internal to the speaker. Insofar as it is launched from the tip of a tongue into the public space of discourse where its meaning is finally determined by the interpretive response of the hearers, it is external. Also, a child grows up in a world already containing language. A word, then, is both internal and external to the speaker; hence the world structured by words is both internal and external to the creator, both somewhat determined by and somewhat free of the creator. This simultaneous affirmation and

---

Rabbi Eliezer calls on God to vindicate him. Indeed, a voice from heaven declares that Eliezer is right. Speaking for the others, however, Rabbi Joshua replies to God and Eliezer that the Torah states that the majority view is to be followed. Rather than being offended, God is said to have laughed joyfully and said, "My sons have defeated Me. My Sons have defeated Me." Cited in Esposito, Fasching, and Lewis, p. 135. This story illustrates the ambiguous standing of God in the covenant community.

denial displays the Zen logic of *soku hi* and the middle way. In other words, the words are internal in some respects and external in others. Yet these respects lack fixed essences and precise conceptual fracture lines.

The point is that although I have argued that both the Hebrew covenant and *sunyata* are characterized by internal relations, those internal relations are not identical in the two cases. The latter are more biological, racial, and natural, whereas the former are relatively more linguistic, habitual, and intentional. Such differences in the self-understanding of origins might be useful in explaining other socio-cultural differences between the West and Asia, but that enterprise lies beyond the scope of this chapter.

From our position in the present, we have taken a backward glance in search of resources in the West itself for creating and affirming a Western middle way, a way that might prevent excesses, if not errors, as we perpetually create the present from the past and the imagined future. Searching for and sketching the contours of a contemporary Western middle way, one inspired by the West's Middle Eastern or Hebraic root, will occupy us in the remainder of this volume.

Chapter 4
From Omniscience to Ignorance

I have known what the Greeks did not: uncertainty.[1]

Jorge Luis Borges

By even speaking a phrase to you, I have already doused you with dirty water.[2]

Yuanwu

So far, this volume has sought to make four broad points. The first is that in the West binary oppositions pervade speaking, writing, and thinking and that intellectual endeavors of all kinds are faithfully wedded to conceptual and ontological dualisms, sometimes even when dualism as an explicit doctrine is rejected. The second is that dualistic thinking, whether formal or informal, prompts and/or justifies dualistic behavior, which often has negative political and social consequences. One need only recall James Meredith's difficulties in gaining admission to the University of Mississippi in order to appreciate this point. The third is that Asian philosophy and practice, especially Mahayana Buddhism, employ a variety of tactics to counter dualism and point to a nondualistic middle way. These points were made in Chapter 1. The fourth point, made in Chapters 2 and 3, is that part of the West's intellectual, religious, and social heritage is a kind of pre-philosophical Hebraic nondualism; consequently, even though this part of our heritage has been marginalized or ignored, perhaps it can open our minds to the possibility of a form of nondualism more suited to and assimilable by the West than Asian versions. Beyond that, as part of the Middle East, Hebrew culture may contain clues to a middle way between East and West. Before attempting to lay out a Western

---

1. Jorge Luis Borges, "The Babylon Lottery" in *Ficciones* (New York: Alfred A. Knopf, 1993), 45.
2. Quoted in Thomas Cleary, trans., *Classics of Buddhism and Zen, vol. 2* (Boston, Massachusetts: Shambala, 1999), 183.

middle way, however, I wish to examine in a cursory way the history of Western dualism and where it has led us.

The Foundations of Western Epistemological Dualism

Dualism has had a long history in the West. Its precursors include the distinction made in Homeric times between mortals and immortals. In philosophy alone dualism goes back to the Pre-Socratic and Socratic thinkers of ancient Greece. The Pre-Socratics attempted to comprehend reality in terms of such binary oppositions as change vs. stasis, appearance vs. reality, and the one vs. the many, with philosophers lining up on one side or the other of these options.

The classic formulation of dualism, properly-so-called, was articulated by Plato and Aristotle. We have already seen that the former found himself confronted with both Heraclitus' view that change is real and Parmenides' assertion that the real ("what is") never comes into being, goes out of being, or changes. For Parmenides, the real is characterized by a fixed, permanent, unchanging identity; consequently, anything that changes is unreal.

These two differing opinions (along with others about whether reality was a single thing or many; whether the senses were reliable or not; and whether nature was comprised of earth, the boundless, fire, water, or atoms) gave rise to skepticism with respect to the possibility of genuine knowledge, a position argued strongly by the Sophists. Theirs was a view that favored Heraclitus's principle of change and appealed primarily to the testimony of the senses. If, however, what is regarded as reality is constantly changing and if every knower of that reality is changing, too, then what passes for knowledge must also be changing. But a putative knowledge that won't stay put, that proclaims one thing today and announces something else tomorrow, is of little or no value. Surely it is no genuine knowledge.

These conflicting perspectives of Heraclitus and Parmenides posed a dilemma for Plato, yet he conceived a clever way to embrace both viewpoints. The material world, the world given to the senses and characterized by change, was the world dominated by the views of Heraclitus and the Sophists. This world, of course, was accepted by everyone. Plato's genius, however, lay in conceiving a second world, one very different from the ordinary one. It was an intelligible world, an unchanging world, reflecting Parmenides' views. The intelligible world was, however, a supersensible world and not, therefore, apprehensible by the senses. Such a world required a novel kind of object of knowledge and alternative way of knowing, a way other than perception.

Plato's new objects of knowledge were ideas, not simply the ideas we conceive of inside our individual human minds, but ideas having a separate reality of their own. In fact, they are forms or patterns used by the divine craftsman, according to Plato's *Timaeus*, in the construction of the lower, material world, to which the senses have access. These forms, totally devoid of matter, are pure, eternal intelligibilities. The constantly changing particulars of the material world, however, maintained the general pattern (copy forms) of the original patterns in whose likeness they had been made, much as the shape of water in a swimming pool remains constant even when water is always entering and exiting the input and output valves. The new way of knowing, namely, thinking or reasoning or theorizing, was an operation of the intellect alone. It consisted in the contemplation of the eternal ideas, forms, or patterns. These two worlds, then, determined the first formalized epistemological dualism, which became paradigmatic for the future.

Spanish existentialist philosopher Ortega y Gasset describes this historic event in appropriately dramatic fashion.

> There was a moment, the chronology of which is perfectly well known, at which the objective pole of life, viz., reason was discovered. It may be said that on that day Europe, as such, came into being . . . Parmenides and Heraclitus had reasoned, but they did not know it. Socrates was the first to realize that reason is a new universe, more perfect than and superior to that which we find, spontaneously, in our environment. Visible and tangible phenomena vary incessantly, appear and vanish, pass into one another: white blackens, water evaporates, man dies; what is greater in comparison with one thing turns out to be smaller in comparison with another. It is the same in the internal world of man: desires and projects change and contradict them-selves; when pain lessens it becomes pleasure; when pleasure is repeated it grows wearisome or painful . . . On the other hand, pure ideas, or *logoi*, constitute a set of immutable beings, which are perfect and precise. The idea of whiteness contains nothing but "white"; movement never becomes static; "one" is always "one," just as two is always two. These ideas enter into mutual relation without ever discomposing one another or admitting vacillation: largeness is inexorably opposed to smallness . . . It must have been with unparalleled emotion and enthusiasm that men saw, for the first time, the austere outlines of ideas, or "rationalities" rise before their minds . . . There was no doubt about it: true reality had been discovered; and in contrast with it the other world, that presented to us by spontaneous life, underwent an automatic depreciation.[3]

The double world and the double faculties of perception and thinking made necessary a new understanding of the knower. Consequently, Plato conceived of the human self as comprised of two parts, the body and the soul, each of which was associated with one of the worlds and one of the faculties. Body, perception, material world, and change were paired, as were soul, thinking, intelligible world, and permanence. The body, which was merely a temporary home for the mind, disintegrated at death and could not, therefore, be real. Because mind or the rational soul, unlike the body, was immortal and merely returned at death to the intelligible world, which was its proper home, the real or true self was defined in terms of reason or mind alone. Moreover, because divinity (along with the real) was understood to be whatever was permanent, the self (reason), the forms, and the unchanging essence of nature were also divine. This conception of divinity would affect the conception of the Christian God when early church fathers articulated Christianity in Greek philosophical categories.

___

3.   Jose Ortega y Gasset, *The Modern Theme*, trans. James Cleugh (New York: Harper and Row Publishers, 1961), 54–55.

The essential harmony between the unchanging being of the knower (identified as reason or mind) and the unchanging, intelligible reality (ideas or forms) produces an unchanging and genuine knowledge. Indeed, this harmony implies the identity of the real and the rational. If something is rational, it is also real; if something is real, it is also rational. The real and the rational are convertible. When Aristotle, Plato's pupil, created from the thought patterns utilized in Socratic discourse a formalized logic, the rational became defined in terms of this logic, and Aristotelian logic gradually assumed control of all serious intellectual discourse. The outcome is an identity linking reality, rationality, permanence, logic, and divinity. This identity stood in binary opposition to another defined in terms of the unreal, the irrational, change, passion, and the human or mortal.

Moreover, it is not even necessary for the human mind to *acquire* knowledge because the rational soul had already acquired it in its pre-existent state in the intelligible world, where it had viewed the forms directly. Once relocated inside a material body at birth, all that remained was for reason to remember what it had apprehended earlier. A more solid foundation for knowledge can hardly be imagined.

The moves described above laid the foundation for Western philosophy from that time to the present. Notice, however, the multiple oppositions that are part of that foundation: the intelligible world vs. the phenomenal world, reason vs. the senses, being vs. becoming, time vs. eternity, change vs. stasis. In each of these dualisms, both the realities and the concepts that mirrored them were held to have fixed identities. The paired concepts were fixed by logical definitions and expressed in language by binary oppositions.

Given that terms, concepts, and realities shared fixed and completely distinct identities, no overlapping or blurring of boundaries was possible. The possibility of a middle way is always ruled out from the start. The alleged middle way of Plato, namely embracing central ideas of both Heraclitus and Parmenides, would, according to Nagarjuna's judgment, be no middle way at all. It is merely a statement of the third lemma of the Tetralemma or Catuskoti (X is both Y and not-Y), one that installs dualism as part of the foundation for the view that both reality and knowledge are intelligible, logical, and fixed. Nagarjuna would also observe that the skepticism of the Sophists and the rationalism of the Socratics developed in relation to each other; they exhibit the unrecognized dependent co-origination of the philosophical world of ancient Greece. Such dependent co-origination, the reader will recall from Chapter 1, is what Nagarjuna identified with *sunyata* or emptiness, which undermines any dualism.

The Slippery Slope into Ignorance

One of the traditional areas of philosophy in which dualism appears is epistemology, which is proposing theories concerning the nature of knowledge and also offering critiques of those theories. It asks and attempts to answer such questions as: Is knowledge possible? What is truth? What are the criteria for assessing knowledge claims? Are there limits to knowledge?

Dualism appears in epistemology in at least two basic forms. The first is that of knowledge vs. ignorance, a dualism found in the ancient world, as we have seen, and one that is reappearing in the postmodern world. The epistemology of the modern world, by contrast, wrestles primarily with the dualism of subject vs. object, asking whether knowledge is determined by the object, the subject, or a combination of the two. The two dualisms are, as we shall see, related.

Allusions to skepticism and ignorance may seem untimely in our era, which has witnessed a so-called "explosion" of knowledge. The alphabet, writing, printing, the scientific method, travel, public schools, exploration, electronic communication, computers, research universities, corporate and governmental research are some of the elements that have contributed to an ongoing acceleration in the generation of knowledge. In fact, knowledge production has become an industry. The Genome Project sought, for example, to unravel the mysteries of DNA; such knowledge can identify the basic causes of diseases and lead to gene therapies. Every year, new species of creatures by the thousands are discovered on our planet (most of them microscopic), and we have hardly begun to explore the oceans' depths or extraterrestrial space. Physicist Ian G. Barbour, speaking of the "unboundedness of nature," captures the prevailing mood.

> Today each scientific discovery raises a dozen new questions, and each problem solved becomes the starting point of a dozen others. It looks more like a divergent than a convergent series; far from tapering off, science seems to be following an accelerating curve. There is a sense of inexhaustible challenge, of surprises yet to come, and of permanent mystery remaining.[4]

And all of this says nothing of the oft-postponed exploration of so-called "inner space," which is now underway.

Finding space for storing our vast quantities of knowledge has become problematic. New libraries have had to be built and old ones expanded. The shelving of *Chemical Abstracts* alone imposes such a burden that many libraries exclude it, even if they can afford it. Books and periodicals have had to be transferred to microfilm or microfiche, and now computer databases are coming to the rescue.

In view of such considerations, any talk of skepticism seems misplaced. But philosophers, it must be understood, march to a different drummer and seek to satisfy more demanding standards. Let us trace briefly the gradual slide of some of them into a strange form of ignorance.

Skepticism is the energy that fuels the movement from belief in knowledge to its opposite, from epistemological zig to epistemological zag. We have already noted that Plato's philosophy was formulated in relation to the skepticism of the Sophists. His ingenious conception of reason, the forms, and two worlds, modified and buttressed by the massive corpus of Aristotle's writings, were the levees that stemmed the rising tide of that earlier skepticism. Everywhere they turned, whether to this world or another, whether in science or metaphysics, they found what they regarded

---

4. Ian G. Barbour, *Issues in Science and Religion* (Englewood Cliffs, New Jersey: Prentice-Hall, Inc., 1966), 286.

as genuine knowledge. But our Socratic philosophical engineers were unaware of the frequency and intensity of the storm surges to come.

When the early church fathers embraced reason as part of the articulation of first Jewish and then Christian religious ideas into Greek philosophical categories, the concept of rational knowledge was reinforced and disseminated more widely with the expansion of Christianity. The power of human reason within the Christian framework was, however, limited because man was regarded not as divine but as a creature characterized by finitude.

For Augustine, whose Platonism reached him via a Neo-Platonic filter, philosophy and theology were virtually identical, as were Christianity and Platonism themselves. He held that, indeed, we humans can know with certitude certain eternal and necessary truths but only because our finite minds receive divine assistance: the incorporeal divine light of God illuminates our judgments, enabling us to transcend finite limitations. In other words, but for God, such matters would be permanently beyond our knowing. For Plato and Aristotle, by contrast, the power to know such things was inherent in the rational soul; no divine revelation was required. Augustine's view, then, could be considered a tiny but significant early step on the slippery slope to ignorance, even if it was not so considered at the time.

Aquinas, whose theology was intimately entwined with Aristotle's philosophy, had a more robust estimate of reason. Not only was it able to know the essence of natural things, but even without supernatural assistance, it could demonstrate by various rational arguments the existence and nature of God. Yet for him—unlike Augustine—philosophy and Christianity were not identical. In fact, the specifically Christian features of divinity—the Trinity and Incarnation, for example—were accessible to faith alone. Faith, of course, was capable of prodigious feats. Aquinas' faith alone, for example, could produce nine books about angels. For him, philosophy and reason were merely the handmaidens of theology and faith. The scope of genuine knowledge reason and philosophy can provide us was diminished.

In fourteenth century Florence the Medicis founded a new Academy, which launched a Neo-Pythagorean[5] revival that began to change the intellectual landscape of Europe. It emphasized the works of Plato (especially *Timaeus*), whose influence in the late Middle Ages had been eclipsed by those of Aristotle. Whereas quantity or number was merely one of ten Aristotelian categories for analyzing reality and was subordinate to logic, Neo-Pythagoreanism promoted the primacy of mathematics. Indeed, it held to the proposition that the universe is somehow made of numbers.

This idea prompted Johannes Kepler, a Neo-Pythagorean, to draw a distinction between primary and secondary qualities in things. Among the former were length, width, breadth, shapes, positions, directions, velocities, and accelerations; all were measurable and expressible in mathematical terms. Secondary

---

5. Neo-Pythagoreanism was a revival in the first century BCE and beyond of the emphasis by Pythagoras in the sixth century BCE on numbers and their metaphysical significance. Neo-Pythagoreanism was revived in Florence in the fourteenth century CE.

qualities—color, smell, taste, touch, and sound—were not quantitative. Galileo, another Pythagorean, who believed that with respect to mathematics human knowledge and divine knowledge did not differ, adopted Kepler's distinction but added that only primary qualities were real. They actually existed in the things of the natural world, while secondary qualities existed in the mind only.

The two scientists justified the distinction on the Parmenidean grounds that primary qualities were unchanging, whereas secondary qualities changed under varying conditions. The length of an object was the same, whether measured in Bologna or Budapest. Color, however, varied according to the light, and taste varied with the taster. Yet, some interpreters say the distinction was based not so much on change vs. no change but on what is measurable and expressible in mathematics vs. what is not.[6] Whatever the basis for this distinction, it resulted in another loss of knowledge, one more severe and closer to home than that produced by medieval thinkers. This outcome is ironic, given that modern science is regarded as leading, in another sense, to a vast expansion of knowledge. E. A. Burtt sums up the loss in terms of ontology (what is real) rather than epistemology:

> Now, in the course of translating this distinction of primary and secondary into terms suited to the new mathematical interpretation of nature, we have the first stage in the reading of man quite out of the real and primary realm . . . His performances could not be treated by the mathematical method, except in the most meager fashion. His was a life of colours and sounds, of pleasures, of griefs, of passionate loves, of ambitions, and strivings. Hence the real world must lie in the world outside man.[7]

Here, skepticism and ignorance exist not just with respect to some transcendental world, but they also expand into an entire dimension of the natural world. Here, the slide into ignores gains momentum.

René Descartes, the so-called "father of modern philosophy," took the primary-secondary distinction of Kepler and Galileo and gave it a more systematic philosophical expression. Prior to Descartes, reason was understood to be objective, located in the world, because the God of Christendom had created a world order permeated by fixed, intelligible essences, which human reason was divinely designed to know. As a consequence, human thinkers faced outward toward the world, largely unaware of their own participation in creating the knowledge they obtained.

For Descartes, however, a problem arose. If reason is universally present in all humans and is everywhere essentially the same, how can one account for the enormous diversity of opinions among the inhabitants of the world? This diversity was all the greater in the wake of the Protestant Reformation and the disintegration of the so-called "medieval synthesis." Should there not be unanimity, a significant indicator of certainty in knowledge? He writes that as early as his college days he came to see "that there is no opinion, however strange, and however difficult

---

6. Barbour, 27–28.
7. Edwin A. Burtt, *The Metaphysical Foundations of Modern Physical Science*, rev. ed. (Garden City, NewYork: Doubleday and Company, Inc., 1932), 89.

of belief, which has not been upheld by one or other of the philosophers."[8] Even outside scholarly and scientific circles, in the "great book of the world," he says, "I met with nothing to reassure me."[9] The problem, Descartes surmised, is that the reason of Plato and Aristotle is merely theoretical. It lacks a deeper, more solid grounding in human experience, and it also lacks a sure method of operation.

In the search for that more solid foundation Descartes undertook a systematic or methodological doubt or *skepsis*, according to which his intention was simply to persist in doubting anything and everything until he stumbled upon something indubitable.[10] He cast out the testimony of the senses on the grounds that it can be confusing or contradictory, and that move led to a rejection of the view that he had or was a physical body. His doubt extended even to mathematical truths, which certainly seemed universally agreed to, on the grounds that he could imagine a God or demon who deliberately manipulated the circumstances so as to deceive him. Until this possibility, however farfetched, was ruled out, certitude was not possible.

Finally, the breakthrough he sought came with the realization that even when he is doubting, there must exist a self or I that performs the act of doubting. This cogito, the I or self that thinks, is the indubitable principle or cornerstone on which Descartes believed he could found a rational knowledge modeled after the distinctive characteristics of mathematics. In choosing the cogito as the starting point for his "universal mathematics," as he called it, he shifted the basis of certain knowledge from objective reason to subjective reason, that is, to the internal, solitary intuition of his individual mind, a shift with momentous consequences for the future. It is at this point that the knowledge-ignorance dichotomy coincides with the subject-object dualism. Knowledge is achievable and ignorance is eradicated only if the internal subject can cross the great divide to reach the reality (object) external to the self.

His immediate problem, then, was discovering a way to move from the *cogito*, which resides in an internal theater of solitude, to knowledge of the external world. The key was in discovering among the innate contents of his mind the idea of God. He reasoned that an imperfect being such as himself could never conceive of a perfect being; therefore, the idea of God can have come only from God. God, then, must be an existing being. From that conclusion, Descartes argued that a moral God (perfect morality was part of the idea of God he discovered) would never create humans such that they were always deceived about the nature of reality. Thus, whenever humans apprehend anything with both clarity and

8. René Déscartes, *Discourse on Method* in *Descartes Philosophical Writings*, trans. and ed. Norman Kemp Smith (New York: Modern Library, 1958), 104–105.

9. Ibid., 99.

10. Descartes's intentions to the contrary notwithstanding, he relied heavily and uncritically on a large number of scholastic ideas, including that of substance. See Etienne Gilson's *Index scholastico-cartesien* (Paris: F. Alcan, 1913) and his *Etudes sure le role de la pensee medievale dans la formation du systeme cartesien* (Paris: J. Vrin, 1930). Cited in Karl Jaspers, *Three Essays: Leonardo Descartes Max Weber* (New York: Harcourt, Brace & World, Inc., 1964), 171, n 1. If he had, in fact, extruded all dubitable thoughts from his mind, his mind would have been blank and all thought would have been paralyzed.

distinctness (the two qualities that characterize mathematical knowledge), God's goodness is the guarantee that such apprehensions are veridical or true.

It turns out that the only features of the external world that are both clear and distinct are the primary qualities identified by Kepler and Galileo: lengths, widths, positions, shapes, and motions. A world characterized by these qualities *alone*, however, is insensate. Animals and human bodies become nothing other than machines, whose parts are linked by merely external relations. The entire biological dimension of the world understood as living, not just human biology, disappears into ignorance. This obliteration of biological life that mediates between mind and matter, is an essential feature of his mind-body dualism.

As if that were not enough, there is another problematic feature of the Cartesian program. Descartes says, "The nature of matter or body in its universal aspect, does not consist of its being hard, heavy, or coloured . . . but solely in the fact that it is a substance extended in length, breadth, and depth."[11] Concerning this passage, William H. Poteat makes the following comment:

> It is here that the paralyzing incoherence appears. For the concept of homogeneous quanta of space by means of which an extended "substance" is defined does not of itself provide us with the grounds for imputing *substantiality* to it; and in the repertoire for the mensuration of mere quanta of spatiality, there are no resources by means of which to specify that the spatiality has within it vectors, is inherently vectorial—having length, breadth, and depth as radii from some point of orientation.[12]

In other words, a discarnate mind has no orientation or other means for understanding or carrying out a measurement. Whether tacitly or explicitly, a body is the location presupposed by all other locations. The latter are oriented in virtue of their relation to the former. One does not see, hear, smell, taste, touch, measure, or think from nowhere but from a specific place, at the center of which is one's body.

At the same time, Descartes's external world does not consist of spatial or extended *things* (including machines) but merely of unlocated and unlocatable spatial qualities. Moreover, since mind, which is utterly without extension, cannot be connected to any particular body, there exist no resources for identifying mind as belonging to any particular person. Indeed, within the Cartesian scheme of things, persons, as usually understood, cannot exist. Identifiable persons, life, and mechanical things, then, cannot be known. The reduction of knowledge and the augmentation of ignorance have moved beyond the transcendental world, human biology, and biological realm more generally and spilled over into the physical or material world itself. Ignorance is accelerating rapidly.

11. René Descartes, *The Principles of Philosophy*. Translated by Valentine Rodger Miller and Reese P. Miller. (Dordrecht, Holland, Boston, Massachusetts, and London England: D. Reidel Publishing Company in, 1983), 1.53.

12. William H. Poteat, "Persons and Places: Paradigms in Communication" in *The Primacy of Persons and the Language of Culture*, eds. James M. Nickell and James W. Stines (Columbia: University of Missouri Press, 1993), 31.

Across the channel a new philosophical movement was taking shape at the hands of John Locke, Bishop Berkeley, and David Hume. "Empiricism," as it was called, regards all genuine knowledge as originating in the sense data that arrive at the human knower via the bodily senses. All three men embraced Descartes's turn to the subjective, adopting as their epistemological starting point the mind within the body, the mind in its theater of solitude.

For Locke, the mind was a blank slate upon which experience writes. The senses deliver to the mind simple ideas of the qualities of external things. Such ideas are the raw material for knowledge. Other ideas are produced by reflection on these simple ideas or by combining them into complex ideas. One consequence of this view was the elimination of innate ideas, which had been essential to Descartes's position. On the other hand, Locke kept both God and substance (the metaphysical reality in which the perceived qualities or attributes of anything inhere).

It was a simple step for Bishop George Berkeley, who was more consistent than Locke, to eliminate matter and substance also by pointing out that we have no idea of them that originates, as empiricism requires, in the senses. What we call "the material world," then, is only a congeries of qualities (yellow, square, hard). Nevertheless, being a bishop, Berkeley retained God, the human mind, and other spiritual selves.

It was left to David Hume, a Scot, to carry the empiricist assumption to its logical and skeptical conclusions, paring away the metaphysical remnants from the views of his predecessors. By definition, God is imperceptible; consequently, we can have no knowledge of God. Moreover, introspection of the human mind yields no perception of a permanent, thinking cogito or I. In fact, we notice only a shifting procession of ideas. As for science, its central explanatory concept, causality, has no grounding in simple sensations. What we see, for example, is merely one billiard ball rolling up to another and the other one moving away. We have no sensation of a necessary connection between the behaviors of the two balls; the connection is merely a fiction made into a habit of thought. Finally, because causality is crucial not only to the possibility of scientific knowledge but also to knowledge generally, the inability to ground causality in experience, the only legitimate source of knowledge, implies that knowledge of all kinds is impossible. Here, it seems, skepticism has reached its limit. We are in possession of no rational knowledge, which is to say that we have been overtaken completely by ignorance.

Back on the continent, Immanuel Kant was shaken from his "dogmatic slumbers" by Hume's skeptical conclusions. Moreover, Isaac Newton, following up on the primary-secondary dichotomy and the experimental method of Galileo, had discovered the laws of motion. They led the scientist to the view that the universe was like a great machine, so mathematically precise were the movements of atoms (microscopic), baseballs (mesoscopic), and planets (macroscopic), for example. Kant was also concerned that Newton's mechanical picture of the universe would result in the elimination of God, morality, and human freedom. Thus, Kant was moved to undertake a critical assessment of the human powers of knowledge as a way of discovering what it was really possible for humans to know.

He agreed with Hume that what we call "knowledge" starts with the arrival beneath consciousness of sense data from the external world, but he held that these sensations do not constitute perceptions until met and organized by the human mind. So, as a first step (the "transcendental aesthetic"), the mind unconsciously imposes on the incoming data the "forms of intuition" (space and time) to create perceptions. A second step (the "transcendental analytic") organizes perceptions into conceptual knowledge with the aid of twelve "categories of understanding." Instead of our concepts having to conform to experience, experience, in Kant's scheme, must conform to our conceptual categories, which are like permanent pigeonholes into which experience must fit if it is to become organized and knowable.

By means of this two-level process theoretical reason yields rational knowledge of the world but only the world as it appears to us. The real or noumenal world, the world as it is in itself (as distinct from its mere appearance) cannot be known, and whereas the phenomenal world is governed by mechanical causality and necessity, this noumenal realm is not. It is in the noumenal realm, completely beyond the lawful restrictions of the phenomenal world, that Kant locates the ideas of God, freedom, and moral obligation. Although these ideas of pure reason (reason without the intuition of sense data) do not provide us with genuine theoretical knowledge, they do have a "regulative" value in the practical affairs of life, that is, they provide concepts (self, cosmos, God—none of which is given in experience) that unify our experience and tell us how to live in a practical sense. Despite his "Copernican Revolution" (making experience fit concepts, rather than the reverse) Kant, nevertheless, is unable to recover for knowledge anything that Hume had taken away, unless knowledge is understood as subjectively organized appearances. The forms and categories that organize appearances do not themselves arise from experience, hence it is possible to regard the results of their organizing operation as purely arbitrary.

The German Idealists (Fichte, Schelling, and Hegel) noticed quickly an important contradiction in Kant's thought. If, as Kant claims, we have no access to things in themselves, no sense impressions of them, how can we know they even exist? The Idealists concluded that we cannot and so simply dropped the idea of noumenal reality. Instead, they reclaimed Plato's notion that the real is the rational and vice versa. The implication of this move is that, freed from the inaccessible thing-in-itself, we can know everything (everything that is rational).

Yet again, this is not really to recapture what Hume's skepticism had excluded but to reduce reality to rational thought ungrounded in experience. In the hands of the Idealists, Kant's categories became not the transcendental conditions for the construction of thought but modes of being, that is, thought understood as reality itself. Matter and life became the idea of matter and life. The irrational, ambiguous, and unconscious were eliminated from reality and, consequently, from knowledge. Since for the Idealists knowing is being (and vice versa), God and the human self are, in effect, reduced to knowing, that is, thinking. They are, in Descartes's words, "thinking things," that is, tautologically and unhelpfully, "things that think." Indeed, human minds become momentary cells of thought in the Divine Mind, and reality is mental or spiritual.

Meanwhile, the nineteenth century saw the expansion of science as one after another new disciplines (geology, sociology, and biology, for example) differentiated themselves from the broader natural philosophy that preceded them.

Originally, these disciplines adopted a methodological positivism, that is, as a matter of method only they avoided metaphysical issues and restricted themselves to empirical phenomena. Soon, however, methodological positivism turned to a metaphysical positivism: nature is all that exists and the scientific method is the only avenue to knowledge.

Gradually, the sciences took over the subject matters formerly treated by philosophy, leaving the latter with nothing to do. In search of a distinctive task of its own, Analytic philosophy made the "linguistic turn." It took up the logical analysis of language, attempting to clarify the meaning and usage of propositions that were confusing, misleading, or meaningless. In so doing, it gave up such tasks as constructing comprehensive systems (like the Idealists) or discovering facts about the world (like science).

Analytic or Linguistic philosophy took three forms. The first was the short-lived Logical Atomism of Bertrand Russell. He sought to invent an artificial and ideal language based on logic and mathematics. Language, he believed, insofar as it was clear and logical, could be reduced to simple, atomic propositions ("That is red.") that would correspond to the true nature of reality. The problem, it was noticed, is that Logical Atomism had no place for general propositions ("All humans are mortal.") and could not account for the richer language in terms of which Russell explicated his philosophy and sought to persuade others of its merits.

Logical Positivism, the next development in linguistic philosophy, gave up metaphysics (except for what was implied by its method), combining Hume's empiricism with the newfound interest in logic. Its central principle, the verification principle, stated that only two kinds of statements are meaningful: (1) empirical statements and (2) formal definitions, tautologies (statements that are always true such as, "Today is either Tuesday or some other day."), and linguistic conventions (A triangle has three sides). All other statements are not simply false but are meaningless, that is, "vacuous pseudostatements."

Critics, however, pointed out that "meaningfulness" is not an observable quality, hence the verification principle is not an empirical statement. It becomes merely a recommended program of action based on emotive (subjective) considerations. Also, not only did Logical Positivism exclude the languages of metaphysics, ethics, and theology, but also much of the language of science itself. Temperature, for example, is not an observable property, and gravity is not an observable force. And what of the neutrinos, quarks, strings, and superstrings of today? Such concepts could be and were regarded as "useful fictions" (useful for keeping the work of science going), but fictions could hardly be equated with knowledge.

Faced with such serious difficulties, a new phase emerged. The emphasis shifted from the now-problematic *meaning* of a sentence to its *use*. The sentence "There's the door," for example, can be used either to point out to a house guest where the bathroom is located or to ask a rowdy party guest to leave. The phonemes (sound forms) and morphemes (visual forms) are the same in each case, but the words are used for different purposes. Language, it was now recognized, is used for an enormous variety of ends: to reject, affirm, encourage, praise, reprove, instruct, celebrate, warn, grieve, recommend, confirm, command, etc. Language was not limited to describing nature or reporting information about its causal mechanisms, as in science. Moreover, each discipline or culture has its own distinctive "universe of discourse" and "logic." Even ethics and theology, previously rejected by logical positivism, could now be reinstated by virtue of their having special proprietary logics and technical vocabularies.

Yet the shift from meaning to use did not imply or justify a recovery of or an increase in knowledge. Only scientific language was regarded as cognitive (about the real world external to the self); other universes of discourse were emotive (merely subjective expressions of the self). The early Ludwig Wittgenstein (a Logical Positivist) ended his *Tractatus Logico-Philsophicus* by saying, "The correct method in philosophy would really be the following: to say nothing except what can be said, *i.e.* propositions of natural science—*i.e.* something that has nothing to do with philosophy."

Later on, Wittgenstein rejected Logical Positivism and developed a new understanding of language by calling attention to the way using language is analogous to playing a game—chess or baseball, for example. Just as we play a variety of games, so we play a variety of language games. Such games do not mirror reality; rather, they conform to the rules of the particular game being played. These rules are created and transmitted by a culture to achieve the practical aims of living. Which game and which rules are appropriate are determined by the context in which they are employed. To say, "I want a black cow" at a cattle auction is to offer to buy a relatively large, four-footed, black animal. To say it at a soda fountain is to request a root beer float (root beer over vanilla ice cream). So long as we do not burden language with unrealistic expectations of speculative, theoretical, metaphysical knowledge, we will muddle along just fine. If confused language does mislead language-users in the direction of metaphysics, philosophy's appropriate task is a kind of therapeutic editing of the misleading statements, connecting them back to some ordinary, non-puzzling context. It seems, then, that we are ignorant (have no genuine knowledge) of everything, except in science.

Most recently, perhaps nobody has attacked the received tradition of reason and knowledge with such passion and ingenuity as the late Algerian-born philosopher Jacques Derrida. His program of deconstruction has generated both fervent support and severe criticism. One of his admirers, John Caputo, has written that, to his critics

> Derrida is the devil himself, a street-corner anarchist, a relativist, or subjectivist, or nihilist, out to destroy our traditions and institutions, our beliefs and values, to mock philosophy and truth itself, to undo everything the Enlightenment has done—and to replace all this with wild nonsense and irresponsible play.[13]

On the other hand, Caputo sees him, as he sees himself, as a conservative whose deconstructive method is

> turned toward opening, exposure, expansion, and complexification (*Points*, 429), toward releasing unheard-of, undreamt-of possibilities *to come* . . . to show that

---

13. *Deconstruction in a Nutshell: A Conversation with Jacques Derrida*, ed. with a commentary by John D. Caputo (New York: Fordham University Press, 1997), 36. Hereafter designated as *Nutshell*.

things—texts, institutions, traditions, societies, beliefs, and practices of whatever size and sort you need—do not have definable meanings and determinable missions, that they are always more than any mission would impose, that they exceed the boundaries they currently occupy.[14]

Put differently, Derrida intends by a serious and meticulous application of his method to dissolve the *rigor mortis* that reason, substance, essence, and identity effect so as to render the West open once again to the other, to fresh readings of texts, and to a novel future. In fact, his project takes aim at the whole of Western metaphysical thinking grounded in Socratic (and even Pre-Socratic) thought. This work has been more well-received and influential in linguistics, literary theory, and literary criticism than in mainstream philosophy. Whether he has been understood or misunderstood, however, his novel methodology, along with his minutely detailed and sometimes opaque writing style has made his work difficult to grasp, even for professional philosophers.

Perhaps readers familiar with Derrida's project will already have recognized its remarkable similarity to Nagarjuna's effort to undermine Buddhist scholasticism's concept *svabhava*. Both Derrida and Nagarjuna oppose fixity, defineability, and the sufficiency of logic and reason. Like most late twentieth-century Western philosophers, Derrida focused on the logic of language. Hence, Derrida and Nagarjuna share not only similar goals but employ similar methods of attack, namely, pointing out the contradictions in their opponents' arguments. In other words, both relied on a dialectics of language.

Derrida's point of departure was the structural linguistics of Ferdinand de Saussure. For Saussure, linguistic meaning consists of signs. A sign, in turn, is a binary combination comprised of a signified (an idea or concept) and a signifier (a linguistic term or phrase that mirrors the signified). Recall that the Platonic legacy is an understanding that genuine knowledge requires a rational knower, a fixed and rational object of knowledge, and a relation of perfect mirroring, correspondence, or representation between them. In the context of linguistic philosophy, this means that the signifier must have a fixed definitional essence or identity, that the signified must have a fixed or conceptual essence or identity, and that the former must mirror the latter. As a consequence, Derrida's attack on essence or identity will be directed at the signified-signifier equation.

Although Derrida employs a variety of weapons in launching his assault on identity, I wish to focus on one of them only, which will be sufficient for my purposes. Moreover, I intend to characterize that weapon in terms other than those he himself uses. The shift will, I believe, make more readily intelligible the nature and significance of his attack. Let us examine the case of giving a definition. In that case, the sign becomes analogous to the definition, the signified becomes a *definiendum* (that which is to be defined) and the signifier becomes a *definiens* (that which does the defining). Let us now suppose that we wish to define "justice," and let us use Plato's definition, albeit modified for political correctness. Here it is.

---

14. Ibid., 31.

Definiendum		Definiens
Justice	is	giving a person his or her due.

Now at first blush it appears that by identifying the *definiendum* with the *definiens* we have defined the term in question, and in some sense surely we have. One may not like the definition given, but a definition it is.

In my own terms, what Derrida does, in effect, is to point out that "justice" has been defined only if the terms of the *definiens* have also been defined. Clearly, they have not in this instance. One could argue, of course, that surely each of them has been defined at some other time and place. But Derrida would reply that if so, they were defined only in the same way we have, to this point, defined "justice," that is, in a merely partial or preliminary fashion.

What is required, in effect, if there is to be knowledge according to the exacting intellectual standards stemming from Plato, is that each of the terms in the *definiens* be made a *definiendum* and then defined. In other words, "giving," "a," "person," "his," "or" "her," and "due," must be defined before they can, strictly speaking, be used to define "justice." We could supply those definitions, of course, but that would be merely a delaying tactic, for the terms of each new *definiens* (the ones defining the seven new *definienda*) would themselves need definition. In short, the process of defining would never end, that is, would not terminate in a *definiens* comprised of terms that were already *completely* defined. In fact, the dualism of defined vs. defining is broken down because every allegedly defined term consists entirely of defining terms, which consist of other defining terms.

Ultimately, defining never succeeds. Indeed, it never can succeed. There is nothing to stop the process of defining—no anchor, no foundation, no closing of the circle of meaning; language seems to be free-floating. The grand consequence is this: if only what can be put into language (strictly defined, logical, and permanently fixed language) counts as genuine knowledge, then knowledge is impossible, even scientific knowledge. In other words, all of what we have previously judged to be knowledge has evaporated, and we are totally submerged in ignorance.

In the end, I have little quarrel with Derrida's critique of the received philosophical tradition. On the other hand, overall his results are disappointing. In my estimation, he did not take full advantage of an opportunity he helped to create. He seemed unable to take the final, crucial step that would have resulted in a complete revolution in our understanding of knowledge. The reasons for this assertion will soon be given.

Rummaging through the Ruins

Nobody, of course, uses the word "ignorance" when speaking of our present epistemological circumstances, but, given that nobody proposes a new conception of knowledge, that is clearly what it is. What we have been getting, instead, are various euphemisms under the broad umbrella of pragmatism.

For Friedrich Nietzsche, for example, knowledge, as an end in itself, as the discovery by reason of universal and absolute truths, does not exist. Reason is not a heavenly or divine faculty but an activity rooted in an earthly body—not the mechanical body of Descartes or the body of biologists, but one that is shot through with vitality, passions, and energy. It's similar in some ways to the Freudian subconscious but is not understood simply in terms of sexuality. What takes on articulate form in reflection has its beginnings in the life of the body. Moreover, knowing is not a matter of discovering a preexistent and ready-made world but of creating a world through the fictions of language in the service of our most fundamental drive, namely, the Will to Power, which aims at self-expression and the mastery of the challenges and opportunities of life. Life, in other words, does not serve knowledge; rather, knowledge, having become practical, serves life. With many of these points I agree. Whatever Nietzsche's intent, however, knowledge, for him, seems to be totally absorbed by and vanishes completely into life viewed as the will to power. But without his saying more, is this not another rebound from zig to zag, a move from a knowledge cut off from life (Plato, Descartes) to a life in which the concept "knowledge" no longer has a legitimate place?

Ludwig Wittgenstein's efforts to understand language, also, produced mixed results. In the end he reached the following conclusions: that language has no single, universal, fixed logical structure; that it is without rational grounding; that it is based on the actions, habits, beliefs, and socio-cultural traditions of peoples; that its uses are variable; and that it is ultimately mysterious in nature. Again, I share with him all of these conclusions. They led him, however, to propose that philosophers abandon any attempt at an explanation of language but, instead, restrict themselves to a description of its ordinary or everyday uses. The puzzles and problems that arise in philosophical reflection, particularly in metaphysics, are the consequence of taking ordinary language out of the familiar contexts in which it developed and in which it operates effectively and, instead, projecting it into strange and inappropriate contexts. In such instances, philosophy's task becomes a therapeutic one, that is, nudging language back to its familiar haunts and describing its proper uses there. This approach will, he believes, dissolve philosophical puzzlement and perhaps discourage future unfruitful dislocations of language. Here again, language and the thinking that it makes possible are understood purely pragmatically, and it seems to ignore the fact that the logical extension of language from one universe of discourse into another is one important way thought becomes aware of and gives expression to hitherto unnoticed realities and connections. Keeping language in its familiar haunts, if that were possible, would stifle such insight and creativity.

More recently, American pragmatist Richard Rorty is quite explicit in his assessment of the Western intellectual tradition's aspirations to knowledge. In his *Philosophy and the Mirror of Nature* he agrees with the hermeneutical tradition of Heidegger and Gadamer, which he describes as "an expression of the hope that the cultural space left by the demise of epistemology will not be filled."[15] Instead,

15. Richard Rorty, *Philosophy and the Mirror of Nature* (Princeton, New Jersey: Princeton University Press, 1979), 315.

he embraces a position that seems to draw on or accord with those of John Dewey, Ludwig Wittgenstein, Wilfred Sellars, and Willard van Orman Quine. Rorty terms his position "epistemological behaviorism" and characterizes it as follows:

> Epistemological behaviorism (which might be called simply "pragmatism," were this term not a bit overladen) has nothing to do with Watson or with Ryle. Rather, it is the claim that philosophy will have no more to offer than common sense (supplemented by biology, history, etc.) about knowledge and truth. The question is not whether necessary and sufficient behavioral conditions for "S knows that p" can be offered; no one any longer dreams they can. Nor is the question whether such conditions can be offered for "S sees that p," or "It looks to S as if p," or "S is having the thought that p." To be behaviorist in the large sense in which Sellars and Quine are behaviorists is not to offer reductionist analyses, but to refuse to attempt a certain sort of explanation: the sort of explanation which not only interposes a notion of "acquaintance with meanings" or "acquaintance with sensory appearances" between the impact of the environment on human beings and their reports about it, but uses such notions to explain the reliability of such reports.[16]

"Aquaintance with meanings" and "acquaintance with sensory appearances" are inner states; they allude to the Cartesian cogito or theater of solitude, the starting point for philosophizing for much of modernity. Rorty is not saying that such inner states are not ever to be mentioned but that we cannot "take knowledge of these 'inner' or 'abstract' entities as *premises* from which our knowledge of other entities is normally inferred, and without which the latter knowledge would be 'ungrounded'."[17] In fact, "S knows that p" is not "a remark about the relation of subject and object, between nature and its mirror"; rather, it is "a remark about the status of S's reports among his peers."[18] Rorty, then, embraces what might be called a "sociological theory of truth" and elaborates on it as follows:

> More broadly, if assertions are justified by society rather than by the character of the inner representations they express, then there is no point in attempting to isolate *privileged* representations. Explaining rationality and epistemic authority by reference to what society lets us say, rather than the latter by the former, is the essence of what I shall call "epistemological behaviorism," an attitude common to Dewey and Wittgenstein . . . It claims that if we understand the rules of a language-game, we understand all that there is to understand about why moves in that language-game are made.[19]

His argument seems to presuppose an inner-outer dichotomy that cannot be justified. Whatever kind of knowledge we have, it is a knowledge acquired and maintained by the total person incarnate in a social context. And where, specifically,

---

16. Richard Rorty, *Philosophy and the Mirror of Nature* (Princeton, New Jersey: Princeton University Press, 1979), 176.
17. Ibid., 177.
18. Ibid., 175.
19. Ibid., 174.

lies the authority by which society "lets us say" whatever we say? Neither the pope nor the *Academie Francaise* is able to prevent us from speaking ungrammatically, telling lies, making errors of judgment, and borrowing language from other linguistic traditions.

Moreover, he does not seem to be concerned by the affinity between "what society lets us say," on the one hand, and the informal logical fallacy of *argumentum ad populum* (the fallacy that truth is what popular opinion says it is), on the other. Finally, under Rorty's scheme is it possible for philosophy (or any other discipline) to exercise a critical function in society? If so, does that function consist of anything more than saying—on what basis?—to the wayward speaker, "Get back into your box" ("familiar haunts")? He seems naively positive about history and biology and excessively negative about other fields or ways of thinking.

But let us return once more to Derrida, both because perhaps nobody has recently attacked the received philosophical tradition with such intensity and genius as he has and because by exposing his basic assumptions we may be able to catch a glimpse of the fundamental problem of postmodern thought more broadly as it relates to the slide into ignorance.

Derrida has concentrated his deconstructive activity primarily on logocentric terms, that is, to the logically defined terms central to the tradition stemming from Plato. In the course of deconstructing such terms, he emphasizes their opposites. For example, he moves from identity to difference, from presence to absence, from center to margin, from logic to rhetoric, and from realism to a linguistic form of idealism. Language is not determined by reality but by its own internal and arbitrary rules and practices. But he sees that since "difference" and the other opposites to which he gravitates, are also logocentric, they, too, are problematic. Hence, if they are to be used and if logocentrism is to be avoided (otherwise, he merely replaces a zig with a zag), then the opposite terms must be placed "under erasure" or "crossed out," that is, used merely provisionally. Even so, they must be changed frequently so that they don't harden and become fixed.

Derrida calls this practice of relying on crossed out and provisional terms *"différance."* This policy of crossing out and changing terms often to escape sclerosis, he also calls "hymen," "spacing," and "proto-writing."

What gives crossed out terms such provisional legitimacy as they may have is some connection to experience, however tenuous. Beneath these terms, which function like a palimpsest, can be found experience, not in a fulsome sense, but merely a "glimmer" or "trace" of what appears or what happens. Yet these two concepts do little to ameliorate the heavily negative character of his philosophy. They are too much an afterthought, too half-heartedly or grudgingly mentioned and developed, too much at the margins to stave off dominance by the more powerful and more frequent rhetoric of absence and difference. Deconstruction's trace is less like the Natchez Trace and more like the chemical trace—a few parts per million. Like *sunyata* in some nihilistic Mahayana Buddhist schools, it is incapable of inaugurating a genuine middle way.

Robert Magliola pinpoints a major difficulty with Derrida's program.

> If all language is logocentric, and all experience is language, and experience is all that "goes on" for "us," then how does Derrida "appreciate" the difference?

To say he appreciates it *under erasure*, to say he appreciates the glimmer that shines beneath the crossing-out, is no answer. It is no answer because he has rejected both feelings and any "third" mode of appreciating, so we are left only with *reason*, with *Ratio*! And reason, as Derrida has indefatigably toiled to prove, is absolutely logocentric . . . Reason in no way accounts for the glimmer.[20]

So what does that outcome imply about the possibility of knowledge? Derrida's answer is found in a passage concerning *différance*.

As for what "begins" then—"beyond" absolute knowledge—*unheard-of* thoughts are required, sought for across the memory of old signs. As long as we ask if the concept of differing should be conceived on the basis of presence or antecedent to it, it remains one of these old signs, enjoining us to continue indefinitely to question presence within the closure of knowledge. It must indeed be so understood, but also understood differently: it is to be heard in the openness of an unheard-of question that opens neither upon knowledge nor upon some non-knowledge which is a knowledge to come. In the opening of this question we no longer know.[21]

I understand Derrida to be asking how we are to understand the meaning of "differing" (the practice of *différance*) in the light of his deconstructive program.[22] Is the word to be defined in a logocentric way as presence (specifiable and logical in its meaning)? "Yes," he answers, but also differently, namely, in terms of the mysterious "unheard of thoughts" that are not knowledge. But what are these "unheard of thoughts" and what are we to call this state in which "we no longer know" if not "ignorance?" And why must "knowledge" remain in bondage exclusively to the old definition of it in terms of presence? Here, Derrida offers no real help. In the end, his final counsel is simply that we persist in the never-ending work of deconstruction.

Canadian philosopher Mervyn Sprung is more upbeat than Derrida with respect to the state of ignorance in which we find ourselves. In his *The Magic of Unknowing: An East-West Soliloquy* he proclaims:

The idea-words "dream," "magic," and "source" claim preference to "knowledge," "reality," and "truth" in that, unlike these, they do not fail to fulfill themselves when put to the vivial test. Whereas "knowledge," "reality," and "truth" abandon the thinker at the very point where their promise should be kept, dissipating

20.   Robert Magliola, *Derrida on the Mend* (West Lafayette, Indiana: Purdue University Press, 1984), 43.

21.   Jacques Derrida, *Speech and Phenomena*, trans. D. B. Allison (Evanston, Illinois: Northwestern University Press, 1973), 103, cited in Magiola, *Derrida on the Mend*, 43–44.

22.   Derrida alters the normal French spelling of the word for "difference" to show that his differing is not simply the binary opposite of identity. In Buddhist terms, it's a nonidentity rather than a not-identity.

themselves in their failed fulfillment, "dream," "magic," and "truthing" evoke expectations which can be fulfilled.[23]

For Sprung, life "ceases to bewilder" and fulfillment is achieved as we abandon our desire for a "gnoseal" solution and embrace in its place a "vivial" one. Like Derrida, Sprung resorts to another pair of binary opposes ("gnoseal" and "vivial"), but by contrast to Derrida, Sprung seems joyfully to embrace the ignorance that follows in the wake of abandoning knowing for living. The influence of Buddhist teaching on Sprung becomes apparent from the fact that "magic" and "dream" are terms found in Nagarjuna and that Sprung's vivial solution turns out to be the practice of a "life-discipline."[24] "Gnoseal" and "vivial" are just another version of the dualism of knowledge and life. This volume, however, seeks a nondual solution.

Critique

The views just discussed are intended to be representative of the various portraits of the philosophical landscape in the wake of the deconstruction of rationalism. I find all of them to be disappointing. All seem too timid, still too committed, despite good intentions or protestations to the contrary, to the intellectual legacy of the ancient Greeks and to several forms of dualism, whether consciously aware of it or not. Where one might expect the excitement of a new beginning, one that has both learned from the mistakes of the past and also glimpsed a radical new vision, there appears to be merely a momentary irrational thrill among the literary theorists, on the one hand, and a solemn determination among postmodern philosophers to make the negation of a past that is not sufficiently past a permanent part of the future, on the other. In the end it is but another zag to rationalism's zig. Let me be more specific.

Given the traditional dualities of practice vs. theory, action vs. contemplation, coping vs. representing, living vs. thinking or knowing, so-called Postmodernism

---

23. Mervyn Sprung, *The Magic of Unknowing: An East-West Soliloquy* (Peterborough, Canada: Broadview Press, 1987), 154.

24. Some psychotherapists, under the influence of both Hindu and Buddhist nondual thinking, have begun to modify their approach to therapy in the light of this absence of knowledge. See *The Sacred Mirror: Nondual Wisdom and Psychotherapy*, eds. John J. Prendergast, Peter Fenner, and Sheila Krystal (St. Paul, Minnesota: Paragon House, 2003). John Prendergast writes, "As therapists learn to live in the unknown, increasingly free of conclusions, they are better able to assist their clients to do the same" (9). Sheila Krystal speaks of an "inner organizing principle . . . that evolves naturally toward wholeness and health and allows the emergence of the unknown" (124). Dorothy Hunt avers, "The mind must live in openness and unknowing, without an agenda, without an effort to 'get' something, for the Unknown and Unborn to present itself" (170). She acknowledges that therapist use methods and techniques but that "our effectiveness depends on how much we can *unlearn*, how much our minds can rest in unknowing" (181).

has embraced the former and abandoned the latter. Certainly Rorty and Derrida are aware of these binary oppositions and intend to transcend them. It is not at all clear, however, that they have succeeded. Indeed, it appears that they have not. The intention to overcome these dualities seems, paradoxically, to have reinforced them. One indication of this is the ascendancy of such terms as "life," "behavior," "practice," "praxis," and "discipline." Each of them, at least rhetorically, is the binary opposite of a term proprietary to rationalism; they are the hitherto lesser-used terms of the traditional pairs. Yet neither the denotations nor connotations of any of them are closely linked to knowledge or truth. Rorty does suggest the term "edification," which has the advantage of not being half of an established pair of binaries. If, however, "edification" means merely "moral or spiritual improvement," then intellectual improvement is left out. Yet even if "intellectual improvement" is included, that could easily be construed, according to a common dualism, as "knowing how" rather than "knowing that." In such an instance, "edification" would connote, for example, simply a refinement of skill in logic—mastering formal logic rather than merely informal logic. Edification, then, would seem to exclude a genuine gain in knowledge. There is no middle way between knowing and living here, at least not rhetorically.

But if rhetoric and concept cannot actually be decoupled, then there can be no *conceptual* middle way either. Knowledge disappears into its traditional opposite—life. If knowledge or thought is to be integrated with and not obliterated by (or, as in Buddhism, understood as always already integrated with) being or practice or life or edification, then none of these latter terms (understood as the binary opposites of knowledge or thought) can adequately describe the new integrated whole or an original whole, which must somehow include both conceptually and rhetorically both sides of the opposition or alleged opposition. In the strictest sense, of course, there are no wholes understood as absolutely independent, complete, and bounded entities. Relative, dependent wholes are situated in increasingly larger contexts often having ambiguous horizons rather than sharp boundaries.[25]

What seems to have happened, however, is that the new emphasis on life, practice, discipline, behavior, action, and edification coincides with the virtual disappearance of the terms "knowledge" and "truth" from the vocabularies of postmodern thinkers, except when such words are being denounced. This oddity hardly seems well calculated to integrate knowledge with life or theory with practice. Their *rhetorical* effect—whatever the intentions of the rhetoricians may be—is to dissolve knowledge, truth, and thinking in life, action, or practice—that is, to obliterate them in the solvent of their opposites. Gordon Kaufman, for example, in the course of interpreting Nagarjuna's two truths, distinguishes "metaphysical validity" ("how things really are") from "pragmatic utility" ("useful for guiding everyday life"). Since both of Nagarjuna's truths, however, lack "metaphysical validity," both can have only "pragmatic utility." Where is any reference here to

---

25. But references to wholes are not merely arbitrary. Atoms, molecules, cells, organs, individuals (human and otherwise), baseballs, planets, etc., are so constituted as to invite most people to experience them as wholes.

knowledge (of whatever kind)? Wouldn't one expect that language is successful in guiding life precisely because it does tell us *something* that is true about that life? Must "true" and "knowledge" be permanently identified with "absolute truth" or "absolute knowledge"?[26] For some postmodernists, the answer appears to be "Yes." But as Nagarjuna might point out, each term of a pair is defined by reference to the other. Such interdependence of meaning points to a wider context inclusive of both and from which both, cut off from that context, are but reified and distorted abstractions. In other words, the dualisms of metaphysical vs. everyday and philosophical vs. ordinary cannot be maintained.

Beyond such dialectical objections to these dichotomies, there is no clarity or consensus, so far as I am aware, as to what is included in each category. If when speaking by phone with someone at a nearby Pizza Hut, I say, "I want a medium, thin-crust, vegetarian pizza with mushrooms, banana peppers, and extra cheese," there would be few dissenters to the claim that such a statement belongs to ordinary language. But what if the statement becomes an example for interpretation in a philosophy class? Is it still ordinary? Or what if, having had a delicious mouthful of the pizza, I, whether I am a professional philosopher or not, exclaim enthusiastically, "Pizza is the salvation of the world?"[27] Wittgenstein, of course, would solve the problem by reference to its use, whether it was for philosophical or non-philosophical purposes. This ploy (yet another set of binary opposites) does not settle the matter. If a religiously pious Jew resorts to "God" language regularly, not only in a setting for worship, but also in the course of preparing and eating a kosher meal on days other than the Sabbath, is that an ordinary or metaphysical usage? The distinction, I suspect, is not nearly so neat as has been assumed.

And what about scientific language? Is that part of ordinary language or metaphysical language? Certainly, many philosophers would judge that science makes one of the most legitimate, least problematic uses of language, but is it part of ordinary language? Gordon Kaufman thinks it is, provided that scientific language is "about" everyday experiences.[28] But is the language of science used in ordinary situations either by nonscientists or by scientists? To be sure, many scientific terms have filtered down into the language of laypeople—"big bang," "natural selection," and "DNA" among them, although they are still not so well known as the majority of other terms in popular usage. Such terms as "quarks," "strings," and "superstrings," however, have become known to a relatively small group of intellectuals who are physicists or who read the popular writings of physicists such as Stephen Hawking, Paul Davies, and Brian Green. None of this language appears to be about ordinary experiences. Moreover, it remains the case

26. Gordon Kaufman, *God, Mystery, Diversity* (Minneapolis, Minnesota: Fortress Press, 1996), 177–178.

27. A recent television commercial for Yellow Book portrays a seeker of wisdom approaching a holy man sitting in meditation. To all of the seeker's questions, the wise man replies that the answers are to be found in Yellow Book. "Suppose pizza makes you happy," he suggests by way of illustration. Then he indicates that one can merely consult Yellow Book and order the pizza to be delivered.

28. Kaufman, 177.

that most of the vocabulary employed by scientists in refereed journals is not part of the language of ordinary laypeople and is not used in what most people would call "everyday situations" or about "ordinary experience."

When physicists discuss whether or not neutrinos or quarks are real, are not those who claim that they are (or, for that matter, that they are not) making metaphysical statements? For that matter, has anyone ever observed temperature (as distinct from feeling warm or seeing the mercury in a thermometer rise)? Most scientists understand their words and concepts to bear on realities, whether those alleged realities are directly observable, indirectly observable, or hardly observable at all. Such linguistic habits complicate any effort to distinguish the metaphysical from the ordinary on grounds of observability or of use by "the man on the street." Is there a common usage or definition for "ordinary" and "everyday?"

Perhaps such worrisome matters in physics lie behind the fact that Rorty mentions only biology as a science about whose language he is sanguine. I find myself wondering if Rorty's selection of biology while ignoring the other sciences does not indicate the lingering legacy of positivism. Yet biology is broader than its behavioral features. It, too, makes use of models and metaphors in its explanations, and biologists make ontological claims, not simply statements that are practically effective.

What is so appealing about Derrida is that he is more radical, that he goes beyond such half-hearted and halfway measures. To be sure, both Magliola and Caputo attempt to defend Derrida against his critics by assuring them that his deconstructive techniques are aimed at metaphysics alone, and I cannot say otherwise. But his alleged intention aside, his deconstruction of language in terms of the problematic linkage of signifier-signified, definiendum-definiens is indifferent to the metaphysical-ordinary, philosophical-everyday distinction or dualism. The fact is that when I use words to order a certain kind of pizza and within 30 minutes the very kind of pizza I ordered arrives at my door does not exempt my language from his critique. Such language, no more than language about God, for example, satisfies the traditional definition of "knowledge."

Here we come to the heart of the matter. What links all the thinkers discussed so far in this chapter, from Plato through Derrida, is their common subscription to one of the fundamental tenets of rationalism, and this common subscription is the obstacle to overcoming dualism, to leaving rationalism and modernism in the past, and to envisioning a hopeful way forward. Let me explain the situation by means of two sets of propositions.

The Rationalist, Modernist, Absolutist says:

> Presupposition: Knowledge, if we can have it, is absolute, certain.
> Supposition #1: We *can* have such knowledge.

The Anti-rationalist, Pseudo-Postmodernist, Relativist says:

> Presupposition: Knowledge, if we can have it, is absolute, certain.
> Supposition #2: We *cannot* have such knowledge.

What is almost always noticed and argued about is the second statement in each case, what I am calling the "supposition." What has gone largely unnoticed is the fundamental agreement between the two positions on the first statement, the presupposition. It is the common agreement about the presupposition that exposes the common commitment to rationalism. Rationalism and anti-rationalism, modernism and postmodernism, absolutism and relativism are, in fact, two species of the same genus, two sides of the same coin, two merely apparent dualities that are, in fact, parasitically dependent on one another.

Rorty, of course, would not be happy to be branded a relativist; yet we have seen that, rhetorically at least, he found no satisfactory escape hatch through his turn to pragmatism. Derrida, also, has no desire to endorse relativism and claims to reject it. In this claim he is correct in the sense that he does not subscribe unqualifiedly to Supposition #2. Instead, he puts it under erasure, accords it a merely provisional status. At this point he is on the verge of a more significant breakthrough. Yet he goes no further; disappointingly, it's as close as he gets. However distant from modernity and logocentrism he may be, he remains bound by their gravitational pull. He does not reach sufficient momentum to escape.

The more far-reaching step that he fails to make is the rejection of the presupposition. It is precisely this failure that prevents his offering anything in its place. For him, it seems, the category "knowledge" is already permanently filled by Plato, Aristotle, Descartes, and the Enlightenment and cannot be replaced. Speaking of Derrida, Magliola puts the matter this way: "But as a Cartesian 'rationalist to a fault' . . . he cannot concede a 'knowing' which is not consciousness-bound and logical."[29] We are left, then, with nothing but whatever works in a practical sense or the Sisyphusian injunction to keep negating, deconstructing, and erasing. In the end, neither Rorty, Wittgenstein, nor Derrida escapes the Modernist predicament. All give up on knowledge. All move toward the future, but do so looking in the rearview mirror.

Related Dualisms

The predicament just outlined—the knowledge-ignorance dualism—is embrangled with at least three other dualisms. This should not be surprising in light of the concept 'theory laden' put forward by Norwood Hanson. He pointed out that scientific theories are not independent but dependent upon a network of other theories. The same interdependence obtains outside of science, also. These other dualisms are difficult to see because, like the identity of knowledge with the rationalist interpretation of knowledge made by putative critics of rationalism, they are largely tacitly held.

The first of the three other dualisms, one which was mentioned earlier, is the subject-object dualism. It depends, as was pointed out, on another dualism, the Cartesian dualism of mind and body, *Res Cogitans* and *Res Extensa*. Let me be clear about what I am claiming and what I am not claiming here. I am not claiming that Derrida, for example, explicitly holds to a metaphysical dualism of mind and body. If asked about the matter, almost certainly he would deny it. Indeed, very few philosophers these days of any school or movement are dualists in that

29. Magliola, 124.

sense. What I am claiming is that other positions he takes, despite his intentions to the contrary, imply such a dualism.

This state of affairs is the result of the fact that Descartes, as the "Father of Modern Philosophy," not only postulated the doctrine of mind-body dualism but also inaugurated a broader critical rhetoric based on that dualism. The fate of his entire project to achieve certainty in knowledge hinges on separating utterly mind from body (body, given that he regards it as unintelligent, threatens to taint thinking) and on ensuring that intellectual understanding can function completely apart from all other operations of the mind (sense, memory, and imagination). While adherence to such a *doctrine* has largely disappeared, utilization of the *critical rhetoric* stemming from it, even after determined efforts to expunge it, persists. This rhetoric is pervasive and too often taken for granted. The dualism of scheme and reality, singled out by Donald Davidson and still frequently relied on, is an example.[30]

Behind the dualism of mind and body lies yet another one, the dualism of the divine and the earthly. The paradigm for its non-theistic, Greek form is Plato's intelligible world and material world. The dualism of God and creation represents its Jewish-Christian-Muslim theological form. Descartes's belief in the possibility of certain knowledge is inspired by divine omniscience, a condition for which is that God's mind utterly transcends the earthly creation. One clue to this connection between Descartes's certain knowledge and divine omniscience is the role God plays in Cartesian epistemology as the guarantor that whatever one perceives to be clear and distinct is veridical. Descartes's reliance upon the existence and nature of God for the validation of these two criteria of truth is reminiscent of St. Peter's receipt of the keys of the Kingdom of God. A Cartesian parody of the relevant scripture (Mt. 16.19) might read: "Whatever is apprehended as clear and distinct on earth, shall be (or shall have been) made true in Heaven."

Another clue to Descartes's reliance upon his conception of heavenly knowledge in the formation of a model for human certainty is discernible in his depiction of the nature of knowledge. Jacques Maritain shows that Cartesian knowledge is like angelic knowledge as described in Aquinas' *Treatise on the Angels*. Angelic knowledge has three features, and Maritain demonstrates that all three of them are found in Descartes's epistemology. First, angelic knowledge is "intuitive in mode." Angels do not reason; they have a single intellectual operation, at once perceiving and judging. There is no groping for what is merely glimpsed; instead, there is but an instantaneous flood of light that bursts upon its object and lays it bare and transparent *sub specie aeternitatis*. This intuitive power characterizes Descartes's "natural light of reason." Even his arguments consist of a chain of such intuitions.

Second, angelic ideas are innate. They are a "dowry of light," infused into the mind by God. Descartes, too, postulates the presence of innate ideas in human minds. As creator of humans and human minds, God placed them there. Third, angelic ideas are independent of things; they are not derived from experience of the world. Maritain quotes Augustine as saying that "God produced things

30.   Rorty 310.

intelligibly in the knowledge of spirits before producing them really in their being." Angelic ideas do not represent things but the ideas in God's mind that served as patterns for the creation of the world.[31] Given Descartes's starting point within the mind, the being of the world is obscured by the interposition of ideas, which alone the mind can apprehend directly. The world is not so much observed as it is argued into existence. To that extent, Descartes's knowledge is also independent of things.

Once, during a discussion with Burman, Descartes himself remarks that without a body, "*tunc essem sicut angeli, qui non imaginatur*" (I should then be like the angels, who have no power of imagery).[32] What I am suggesting here is that Derrida, and others who reject the possibility of knowledge, on the one hand, while clinging to a model of knowledge inspired by the certitude of heavenly knowledge (recall the absolutist presupposition mentioned earlier in this chapter), on the other, are tacitly and parasitically dependent on the subject-object, mind-body, and God-world dualisms.

Derrida once said, "So, you see, I am a very conservative person."[33] He is speaking of his attitude toward institutions, but we have seen that his conservatism is more extensive. It includes his unrecognized dialectical commitment to a view of knowledge, properly so-called, as rational, logical, absolute, and certain. Such a commitment is a barrier that blocks his entrance into a future he desires but too dimly sees.

Is there another way? Robert Magliola has argued that Nagarjuna achieves the same goals as Derrida—the deconstruction of identity, of permanent essence, of presence, of logocentrism—but without Derrida's inability (due to his rationalism) to embrace the limitations of language. Nagarjuna's advantage lies in his doctrine of two truths: the absolute or ultimate truth, on one hand, and the relative, conventional, empirical truth, on the other. In Magliola's words, this double truth "allows the reinstatement of the logocentric" so that "we can 'have it both ways.' "[34] The reinstatement is possible because Nagarjuna says that between the two "there is not the slightest difference whatsoever."[35] The ultimate reality is this very phenomenal world seen differently—that is, seen as *sunya* (interdependent and empty of fixed essences).

What conclusions are we to draw from this? That the West should embrace Buddhism? Already in the first chapter I have indicated that such a move is unlikely to be accepted by the vast majority of Westerners. Too often, Indian Buddhism expresses itself in excessively negative terms and, as a consequence,

31. Jacques Maritain, *Three Reformers: Luther—Descartes—Rousseau* (New York: Charles Scribner's Sons, n.d.), 66.

32. Cited in Norman Kemp Smith, *New Studies in the Philosophy of Descartes: Descartes the Pioneer* (London: Macmillan, 1966), 158–159.

33. Cited in Caputo, *Nutshell*, 8.

34. Magliola, 87.

35. Kenneth K. Inada, *Nagarjuna: A Translation of his Mulamadhyamikakarika with an Introductory Essay* (Tokyo: Hokuseido, 1970), 25:20. The verse, quoted from Kenneth Inada's translation, actually refers to *nirvana* and *samsara*; however, the former represents the ultimate or unconditional, and the latter the conventional or conditioned.

appears to be life-denying. "Emptiness," for example, appears in English as the binary opposite of "fullness," which the West finds more appealing. This negative reaction occurs despite the fact that if viewed from another standpoint (the so-called awakened standpoint), the empty self can also be understood as full (because it is interdependent with a reality much wider and richer than the narrow, disconnected self).

East Asian Buddhism is not much better than the Indian variety. Zen, for example, does not present itself from the awakened point of view but from that of the unawakened person. Such a presentation makes Buddhism initially baffling. Rinzai Zen especially—the first form of Buddhism to interest Americans (excluding Japanese immigrants)—deliberately intensifies this bafflement to precipitate an existential crisis that leads to the great doubt and then to the great death of the egoistic self. Even if Westerners in large numbers were disposed to and could embrace Buddhism, there are reasons, to be given in subsequent chapters, not to do so, at least not without making significant modifications.

What, then, do we do? Where are we to turn? How do we proceed? The epigram that opened this chapter was made by Richard Tarnas about Santayana's endorsement of skepticism, but in subsequent sentences Tarnas takes a surprising and hopeful turn.

> Skepticism is the chastity of the intellect, Santayana declared, and the metaphor is apt. The mind that seeks the deepest intellectual fulfillment does not give itself to every passing idea. Yet what is sometimes forgotten is the larger purpose of such a virtue. For in the end, chastity is something one preserves not for its own sake, which would be barren, but rather so that one may be fully ready for the moment of surrender to the beloved, the suitor whose aim is true. Whether in knowledge or in love, the capacity to recognize and embrace that moment, when it fully arrives, perhaps in quite unexpected circumstances, is essential to the virtue.[36]

Has the moment of surrender just alluded to arrived? Can ancient Hebrew nondualism offer any helpful clues? Can the hitherto inviolable link between knowledge and omniscience or certainty be broken without our being sentenced permanently to skepticism, relativism, and nihilism? Let us see.

---

36. Richard Tarnas, *Cosmos and Psyche: Intimations of a New World View* (New York: Viking, 2006), xiii.

Chapter 5
A Western, Nondual Epistemology

To think, analyse, invent are not anomalous acts, but the normal respiration of the intelligence.[1]

Jorge Luis Borges

If you want to understand the true essence of the way, do not get rid of sound and form, words and speech; words and speech are themselves the Great Way.[2]

Pao-chih

In the previous chapter we saw that the philosophical search for knowledge has ground to a halt, either in frustration and despair or with a gleeful sense of liberation, as what was once held to be knowledge has not merely dripped or dribbled away but fallen away in huge chunks like the collapse of the face of Mt. St. Helen. Moreover, we have been advised not to attempt to find a replacement for epistemology but to resort to accounts of life, behavior, ordinary language, practice, mysticism, or Asian nondual dialectics. Yet two telling facts raise questions about this putative plunge into what, eschewing euphemisms, I prefer to call "ignorance."

The first is that, despite the enormous differences in the philosophies of Descartes, Hume, Kant, Wittgenstein, Rorty, and Derrida, for example, these philosophers are united in their characterization of genuine knowledge as being absolute, infinite, eternal, rational, and perfect, even when they differ in their judgments as to whether such knowledge is achievable. In other words, despite their disagreement with respect to the suppositions concerning the prospects for attaining knowledge, what they have not sufficiently questioned or abandoned is

---

1. Jorge Luis Borges, "Pierre Menard, Author of Don Quixote" in *Ficciones* (New York: Alfred A. Knopf, 1993), 37.

2. Quoted in Thomas Cleary, trans., *Classics of Buddhism and Zen*, vol. 2 (Boston, Massachusetts: Shambala, 1999), 144.

the presupposition concerning the definition and nature of such allegedly genuine knowledge, a presupposition that, even when sometimes denounced, finds a way to survive as the *de facto* determinant of their philosophies. That is also why postmodernity is in reality merely a pseudo-postmodernity. It has by no means left modernity behind.

Even some who are sympathetic to the Buddhist middle way seem to embrace the equation of knowledge and absolutism and, consequently, give up on knowledge. Thus, Stephen Laycock, for example, urges with Hui-Neng that we "separate . . . [our]selves from views" and affirms that the Buddha's "right view" leads us naturally, progressively, and finally to embracing "no views."[3] Even if "no views" is taken to mean "no views regarded as absolute," it is a bit strange to write a book filled with declarative sentences that make assertions (including the assertion that one should embrace "no views") and at the same time to advocate adopting no views. This interpretation of the Buddhist middle way—shared by some Buddhists, but not all—is not the middle way we are seeking.

The second fact is that all of the skepticism (which I share) about the received view of knowledge notwithstanding, both ordinary speakers-thinkers-writers and also scientists (if scientific language is not regarded as ordinary) continue to believe that they possess knowledge in some very real sense. Even professional philosophers who, while sitting around seminar tables discussing academically the nature of knowledge, are able to convince themselves that they do not know what a pizza or justice is, find that their confidence with respect to knowing these things and more, effortlessly and inevitably revives so soon as they exit the seminar room. Belief that we know in some more significant sense than pragmatism or deconstructionism allows is, in my experience and that of others, virtually ineradicable.

Derrida himself, in the same passage cited earlier, follows up his statement that "we no longer know" by saying: "This does not mean that we know nothing but that we are beyond absolute knowledge."[4] This is a knowing, he continues, that "opens neither upon knowledge nor upon some nonknowledge which is a knowledge to come." These positive and potentially fruitful statements are as close as Derrida comes to a real breakthrough. Yet they are a missed or failed opportunity because he goes on to say that this knowledge beyond knowledge and nonknowledge is a knowledge for which "unheard-of thoughts are required." Moreover, these "unheard of" thoughts will "*legitimately* be understood as meaning nothing, as no longer belonging to the system of meaning." (Emphasis added.) Here, Derrida, who had just put his hand to the plow, turns and looks back, for the allegedly legitimate "system of meaning" to which he refers is the old, absolutist one. In other words, he is saying that in the absence of absolute knowledge there is nothing we can meaningfully regard as knowledge because meaningful knowledge remains, for him, identified with absolute knowledge. Unhappily,

    3. Steven W. Laycock, *Mind as Mirror and the Mirroring of Mind: Buddhist Reflections on Western Phenomenology* (Albany: State University of New York Press, 1994), 107.
    4. Cited in Magliola, *Derrida on the Mend* (West Lafayette, Indiana: Purdue University Press, 1984), 44.

the breakthrough Derrida seeks does not happen because Derrida himself seems either not to have heard or at least not to have articulated these "unheard-of thoughts."

Robert Magliola, who zeroes in on the expression "unheard-of thoughts," affirms against Derrida that such thoughts have already been both uttered and heard, and on that point I stand in agreement with him. Yet Magliola's proposal is to replace the definition of knowledge as rational with mysticism, a position that implies that he, too, has not fully rejected the equation of knowledge with certainty, presence, logocentrism, or absolutism. At least rhetorically—and recall that rhetoric and concept are difficult, if not impossible to de-couple—he has zagged from logic to mysticism, from the rational to the irrational. It is my intention in this chapter to attempt an adumbration of one version of the knowledge that is beyond knowledge and non-knowledge, beyond both rationalism and mysticism. In other words, I aspire to a more satisfactory epistemological middle way.

Markers of Unheard of Knowledge

Clues to this knowledge are found in ancient Hebraic thought. In order for such an outlook to be useful to us, however, its pre-philosophical nondualism must be made appropriately philosophical. That transformation, however, has already been largely accomplished in Chapters 2 and 3 because there Hebraic thought was described not simply in its own terms but in terms of its philosophical import. That import will be incorporated (although not in any stepwise or systematic way) into what follows in the hope of achieving a Western middle way with respect to knowledge. This incorporation is a philosophical project that seeks to meet the objections lodged by some postmodernists against epistemology. It may also amount to at least a partial characterization of Derrida's "unheard of knowledge."

In my judgment, ancient Hebrew thought is a clue to the aforementioned "unheard of knowledge." On that basis, creating an epistemological middle way for the West amounts to conceiving knowledge as homologous with certain conditions or markers derived from or consonant with ancient Hebrew thought. The first and most important such marker or criterion is that epistemology must vigorously reject once and for all the definition of knowledge as omniscient, absolute, perfect, eternal, wholly rational, logocentric, and infinite. That's easier said than done.

In the late 1960s, fellow graduate student Ed St. Clair recalls watching on television a controversial play during a World Series baseball game. A runner was called out at third base by the third base umpire. Managers and players from both teams poured onto the field to argue about the call. Meanwhile, telecasters did instant replays from each of the three cameras that were covering the game. From one camera position the runner appeared to be out. From another, he appeared to be safe. From the third, it was impossible to tell. Despite the fact that the rule book states that a player is out if the umpire pronounces him out, most people would persist in asking, "But was he *really* out?"

What would be required, technologically speaking, to answer such a question, St. Clair pointed out, is (1) an infinite number of cameras (2) viewed simultaneously, not to mention perfect eyesight, judgment, and memory. Notice the presence of the requirement "infinite." Only such an arrangement both leaves no possible perspective out of account and also integrates the multiple perspectives into a unity. In fact, to exclude no perspective would require further that the cameras themselves be infinitely small since the spatial gaps between and among camera lenses amount to ignored perspectives. All these requirements, however, are impossible to meet *in principle*, not just in fact. Cameras, as material objects, require in principle some quantity of space and, consequently, necessitate some impossible camera locations. Such an example illustrates the absurdity to which our desire—or *tanha*, to use a Buddhist term—for absolute certainty has led us. But the impossibility (in principle and in fact) of this view-from-everywhere means that it is, in fact, the view from nowhere. The new model of knowledge must embrace an experienced finitude, not an imagined divine or angelic infinitude. And its embrace of finitude must be thoroughly liberated from nostalgia for infinite knowledge. In Chapter 2 we saw that for Hebrew thought both humans and God were characterized by experienced epistemological finitude.

Second, this middle way with respect to knowledge must accord with Hebraic nonduality of mind and body, and it must do so not only in intention but conceptually and rhetorically. Because a body is almost universally acknowledged to be finite, mind or knowledge inherently incarnate in a body must also be finite. What is essential here is not a perfunctory disavowal of metaphysical dualism in anthropology but rather the creation of an epistemology in which the bodily character of all feats of actual knowing is not merely given lip service but plays a substantive role.

Third, a reconceived knowledge, one that truly leaves modernity behind, must also avoid such putative dualisms as absolute vs. relative, objective vs. subjective, theory vs. practice, action vs. contemplation, and thinking vs. doing. Indeed, it must forego all illegitimate dualisms while, nevertheless, allowing for the drawing of appropriate distinctions.

Fourth, such an epistemology must avoid foundationalism, the view that a knowledge is derived logically from some independent, indubitable principle (like Descartes's "I think, I am") that serves as its foundation. The attempt to identify an indubitable foundation is simply another way of seeking an escape route from finitude.[5] Moreover, it is a ploy that is parasitically dependent upon a dualism of foundation vs. superstructure. Whereas some epistemologies of the past have been foundationalist, it is not the case, as Rorty seems to assume, that this feature is essential to any philosophical discussion of the possibilities and

5.   One might object that this itself is parasitically dependent upon a dualism of finite vs. infinite. Recall, however, that in Chapter 2 ancient Hebraic pre-philosophical thought was articulated on a conceptual ground that was prior to such a distinction, much less such a dualism. Consonant with Hebraic thought, this chapter espouses what Buddhism might term "non-infinite." Although "non-infinite" also implies "non-finite," Western culture has erred in the direction of a quest for infinity. Consequently, "non-infinite" is more appropriate.

actualities of human knowing. In other words, the fact that past epistemologies
have been foundationalist is an insufficient justification for abandoning any and
every epistemology.

Fifth, the epistemology sought in this chapter does not assume that reflection
must begin with epistemology before it can proceed to ontology or other domains
of philosophical reflection. For any theory of knowledge, humans must be understood to be endowed with the relevant cognitive capabilities and logical resources
requisite for attaining the knowledge the epistemology prescribes, but the reverse
is also true. Thus, epistemology and anthropology (or other forms of ontology)
codetermine (dependent co-origination) each other in a benevolent circularity
that consistency demands. No reflective project makes an absolute beginning;
such beginnings are always, as we shall see, *in medias res.*

Sixth, a genuinely postmodern epistemology is not to be understood as the
privileged domain of philosophers. Philosophers are not necessarily the exclusive
masters of the mysteries of methodology, from whom persons in other disciplines
must seek permission and approval before proceeding with their own investigations. Critical reflection is interdisciplinary.

While these six criteria or conditions may not constitute an exhaustive specification of "unheard of thoughts," they are important ones. Can a new understanding of knowing, one that satisfies all these conditions and thus eludes the recent
objections to epistemology, be found? Let us see.

The Tacit Dimension

One of the persons who has, in my estimation, most clearly heard the "unheard-of
thoughts" Derrida dimly divines but does not articulate is Michael Polanyi, a
scientific colleague of Einstein's in Berlin. Along with Maurice Merleau-Ponty,
he appears to possess much of the marginalized wisdom of the ancient Hebrew
"nagas." His program, like Derrida's, seeks to undermine the excessive rationalism of the Western intellectual heritage. Both thinkers have Jewish roots.
Nevertheless, there are significant differences. Whereas Derrida is viewed as an
atheist and skeptical of metaphysics, Polanyi is willing to speak of God, even if
rarely and more than a bit unconventionally. While Derrida seems to draw most
heavily on rabbinic Judaism, with its focus on massaging fresh meaning from
ancient texts, Polanyi appears to be closer to ancient Hebrews of the sort I have
described in Chapter 2. Also, as a natural scientist, he is more concerned, at least
initially, with the natural order rather than the analysis of language, although he
goes on to write about language, economics, sociology, anthropology, history,
art, and religion.

While Derrida, as is common among French intellectuals (even those of Algerian
origin, it seems), often carries on a philosophical dialogue with literature, literary theory, and linguistics, the context of Polanyi's epistemological reflections is
physical chemistry and general science. His background in a so-called hard science is, in my estimation, a distinct advantage in the sense that he knows science
from the perspective of an insider and is, therefore, less given to setting science on
an epistemological or methodological pedestal, on the one hand, or deploring its

status within Western culture, on the other. He is able to appreciate its remarkable achievements and continuing possibilities while at the same time acknowledging its clay feet.

Unlike Derrida, Polanyi is not a professionally trained philosopher. This fact is significant in three respects, two positive and one negative. First, it means that the sixth of the criteria stated above is fulfilled: epistemology need not be done by professionally trained philosophers. Second, it means that he did not absorb to the same degree as many others who philosophize the critical rhetoric of Cartesianism, freeing him to think outside the inherited philosophical boxes. This fact alone goes a long way toward explaining the originality of his views. Often, as we shall see, what Derrida understands to be a negative is turned by Polanyi into a positive. By the same token—and this is the downside of his dearth of professional training in philosophy—because he often does not appeal to the vocabulary, concepts, and distinctions employed and taken for granted by most philosophers, the latter find it difficult to discern the way in which Polanyi's work operates at right angles to the entire modern tradition in the West. As a consequence, they are prevented from readily grasping its radical import. Despite the existence of The Polanyi Society and a journal (*Tradition and Discovery*), which are dedicated to exploring the implications of his thought, Polanyi never broke into the philosophical mainstream, except perhaps in the philosophy of science.[6]

It will not be my intention in what follows to give a thorough exposition of Polanyi's philosophy but rather to borrow freely some of his ideas and those of others, mixing and matching them with my own, in order to produce what I hope will be a persuasive collage that bears on an epistemological middle way between absolutism and relativism, certainty and ignorance, thought and life, and which does so in an idiom that the West can both understand and appreciate. To accomplish that goal I will deliberately interpret Polanyi in a novel way that highlights certain affinities of his thought with Mahayana Buddhist philosophy.

Perhaps the central concept of Polanyian epistemology is the "tacit dimension," an idea to which he was led by way of his acquaintance with experiments in subception. Psychologists presented experimental subjects with visual images of nonsense syllables, administering electrical shocks following particular syllables. The subjects soon learned to manifest behaviorally an anticipation of the shocks but could not tell how this anticipation was done. Similarly, in 1958 Eriksen and Kuethe administered shocks to a subject who happened to speak certain words designated as "shock syllables." The subject learned to forestall the shocks by avoiding the use of those terms, yet he did not know that he was doing so and could not explain how he did it once it was called to his attention.

Although Polanyi made no use of his work, French existential phenomenologist Maurice Merleau-Ponty called attention to similar phenomena. For him, capacities present but not readily detectable in healthy humans are sometimes more apparent in exaggerated forms in patients. One example is what Merleau-Ponty refers to as the "motor physiognomy of color." Various color stimuli were directed at subjects having diseases of the cerebellum or frontal cortex. The stimuli were

---

6. I myself am neither a member of the society nor a subscriber to the journal.

projected for such brief intervals and at such weak intensities that the subjects did not actually perceive the colors. Instead, for each color they experienced certain feelings and incipient movements. Once told which colors corresponded to which experiences, they could successfully identify the color stimuli without ever seeing the colors.[7]

Polanyi's conclusion from the experiments in subception is that we know more than we can tell, that we possess a knowledge that is not completely articulable.[8] Such conclusions were in accord with Gestalt psychology (another influence on Polanyi), which had demonstrated that one can recognize a whole of some kind by integrating the particulars that comprise the whole but without explicitly identifying those particulars. Polanyi, however, rejected the Gestaltists' mechanistic explanation for gestalt recognition, choosing to see it as "the outcome of an active shaping of experience performed in the pursuit of knowledge."[9]

These two influences, experiments in subception and Gestalt psychology, led Polanyi to formulate a theory of tacit knowing or a logic of tacit inference. Let us see how it works in the case of driving a nail with a hammer. One grasps the handle of the hammer with one hand and holds the nail at a designated spot with the other. One's attention, however, is not riveted on one's hand or the handle but on the nail, and if that attention wanders, one is likely to miss the nail and strike a thumb. Yet clearly one is also aware in some fashion of the hammer's handle because the pressure of the handle stimulates sensations in the hand that holds it.

Polanyi concludes that there are two kinds of awareness involved here, linking the two aspects of the act of hammering—the sensations in the hand and the perception of the nail. "Focal awareness" is directed toward the nail, whereas awareness of the handle is termed "subsidiary awareness." The inarticulate sensations in the hand wielding the hammer are the subsidiary clues to a successful act of striking the head of the nail. *Attending from* a subsidiary awareness of the impressions of the handle on the palm of the hand, one *attends to* the head of the nail. The sensations, then, are not known in themselves, as subception and Gestalt psychology affirm, but known in terms of their contribution to the driving of the nail. The subsidiary clues, he came to say later, being closer to the agent, are the "proximal" pole or term, and the nail is the "distal" pole or term of a feat of tacit knowing.

This vectorial or "from-to" structure in which meaning is partially displaced away from oneself Polanyi calls the "semantic function" of tacit knowing. At the same time, he says that such tacit knowing "has the structure of a skill, for a

---

7. Maurice Merleau-Ponty, *Phenomenology of Perception*, trans. Colin Smith (London: Routledge & Kegan Paul, Ltd., 1962), 209–211.

8. Bill Schweiker, Professor of Religion at the University of Chicago, notes that "we live deeper than we think." Spoken in the senior seminar in religious studies at Centre College, Danville, Kentucky in March 2007. Schweiker's formula, however, maintains, at least rhetorically, the distinction between thinking and living. Polanyi, by contrast, speaks of two kinds of knowing. There is, however, as we shall see, no dichotomy separating them.

9. Michael Polanyi, *The Tacit Dimension* (Garden City, New York: Anchor Books, 1967), 6.

skill combines elementary muscular acts which are not identifiable, according to relations that we cannot define." Indeed, the "from" pole always involves a skill, although the skills become increasingly sophisticated as the kinds of knowing become more complex. The dentist's use of a probe and the blind person's use of a stick, for example, are obviously similar to the use of a hammer, but in the former two cases there is simultaneously a concern for knowledge—knowledge of what lies in a hidden cavity or the challenges of an urban street.

Polanyi's writings are filled with such examples. A look at several more will exhibit the wide variety of contexts in which the basic structure of tacit knowing is manifest. The principle by which swimmers manage to keep themselves afloat is simple enough: when exhaling, they do not fully empty their lungs; when inhaling, they inflate their lungs beyond normal levels. In this way, buoyancy is maintained. Yet few swimmers know this, and almost none know it prior to learning to swim. Moreover, even if they were provided with explicit knowledge of this principle prior to the onset of swimming lessons, it would be of little or no value in developing the desired skill.[10]

The same is true of riding a bicycle. According to Polanyi, the principle at work in maintaining balance is that for any given angle of imbalance, one must turn the bicycle in the same direction as the imbalance so as to form a curve whose radius is proportionate to the square of the velocity over the imbalance. He adds, however, that "such knowledge, though true, is ineffectual unless it is possessed tacitly."[11]

Many times each day we recognize the physiognomies of the people around us. We do so, however, without having specified the particular features comprising the face. Again, our reliance on those features as clues to the facial whole is a subsidiary one. We attend from our tacit awareness of them in order to attend to the face as a whole. This fact explains why a husband can recognize his wife's face without being able to say what color eyes she has. Notice that in visual perception (by contrast with the tactile and kinesthetic uses of the probe, stick, and hammer) we have no explicit awareness of bodily sensations. We know, of course, that focusing of the eye is carried out by the operation of six muscles that function together to distort the shape of the eyeball, which, physiologically speaking, is what focusing is.

Polanyi also points to the work in biofeedback of Hefferline and his collaborators, who found that spontaneous muscle twitches occurring inside the body of a human subject and yet unfelt by that subject could be made observable externally by amplifying their electrical currents a million-fold. When an unpleasant noise was temporarily stopped during such twitches, the subject learned to increase the frequency of the twitches and to block out the noise much of the time once it resumed. The subject had no idea of the muscle twitches or the modification of their frequency. Polanyi concludes that in a similar fashion we rely on subliminal awareness of events deep inside the body to perceive objects outside of it.[12]

10.   Michael Polanyi, "The Structure of Tacit Knowing," a lecture delivered at Duke University on February 17, 1964, 10.

11.   Ibid., 11.

12.   Polanyi, *Tacit Dimension*, 14.

The from-to structure of subsidiary or tacit awareness is also essential in what Polanyi calls "connoisseurship." The arts of tasting wine, tea, balsamic vinegar, or olive oil are obvious examples. The ability of an expert to identify from a sip and whiff of wine its kind, vintner, and year is remarkable, yet no mere intellectual grasp of the many descriptive terms used in wine-tasting is sufficient for such an identification. In fact, acquiring such expertise requires a long apprenticeship under a master, for the expertise involved is not formalizable.

Falling into this same category are a variety of activities in the sciences and medicine. Classifying a plant or animal requires practice in the field with an experienced botanist or zoologist. Students of biology and chemistry require extensive time in laboratories under the supervision of experienced researchers. Polanyi notes that in some instances students pick up tacitly laboratory techniques or research skills of which even their seasoned instructors have no explicit awareness.

In medical diagnosis it is essential that a physician be able to recognize symptoms. In auscultation, for example, he or she must be able to recognize the accentuation of the second sound of the pulmonary artery. No verbal description of the sound will suffice. A medical student can acquire this knowledge, Polanyi says, "only by being repeatedly given cases for auscultation in which the symptom is authoritatively known to be present, side by side with other cases in which it is authoritatively known to be absent" and by demonstrating to an expert his or her ability to differentiate between them.[13]

Polanyi recounts the story of a distinguished psychiatrist who, along with his students, observed a patient undergoing an as yet undiagnosed fit. Later, the students discussed whether the man had undergone an epileptic or hystero-epileptic seizure. Finally, the psychiatrist settled the matter when he announced, "Gentlemen, you have seen a true epileptic seizure. I cannot tell you how to recognize it; you will learn this by more extensive experience." This diagnosis, Polanyi claims, resulted not from attending focally to the symptoms themselves but by relying upon them subsidiarily as clues to their integrated meaning.[14]

In describing the relation of the tacit to the explicit, Polanyi says the former may exceed, coincide with, or be left behind by the latter. The first is the "ineffable domain," where articulation is hardly possible. The last is the "domain of sophistication," where "symbolic operations" tend to "outrun our understanding and thus anticipate novel modes of thought." The examples of tacit knowing given so far belong to the domain of the ineffable, about which we can speak, he says, but not with absolute clarity or precision.

The middle domain, where the tacit and explicit are more balanced, is illustrated by listening to speech or reading an intelligible text.[15] In both cases, one is aware of the words (whether written or spoken) and their meaning but not in the

13. Michael Polanyi, *Personal Knowledge: Towards a Post-Critical Philosophy* (New York: Harper and Row, 1958), 54–55.

14. Michael Polanyi, "Faith and Reason" in *The Journal of Religion*. Vol. 41, No. 4 (October 1961), 239.

15. Polanyi, *Personal Knowledge*, 87.

same way. Clearly, one is somehow aware of the words; otherwise, their meaning could not be understood. But the awareness is a tacit one. The listener or reader attends from the tacit awareness of the words by relying on them to attend to their joint meaning. This fact, Polanyi avers, accounts for the so-called transparency of language, yet the necessary reliance on tacit awareness for knowledge of any kind implies that there are no "clear and distinct ideas" in the Cartesian sense of their being fully conscious and pellucid.

Polanyi illustrates the distinction between the tacit awareness of words and the explicit awareness of their meaning in the following account. He notes that he often receives mail in a variety of languages and reads these letters at the breakfast table. Occasionally, he may want to pass one of them along to his son to read, but must check the letter to see in what language it is written because his son knows English only. In other words, Polanyi knows perfectly well the message the letter conveys but is not explicitly aware of the language in which the message is written.[16]

Tacit awareness also plays a role in discovery, including scientific discovery. Here, there may be particulars aplenty, but the comprehensive entity or meaning they imply, if any, is not known. Rejecting the implication of Plato's argument in the Meno that searching or discovering is logically impossible and that our only alternatives are ignorance, on the one hand, or the remembrance of forgotten knowledge, on the other, Polanyi proposes that we have an "active foreknowledge" of a "hidden reality" by means of "intimations." The first step is finding or selecting a significant problem. This is itself, he says, an addition to knowledge and is the gift of original minds. Then, moved by "intellectual passion," scientists attend from the puzzling particulars that serve as clues in the "hope" and with the "faith" that their effort will be rewarded. Such passion, hope, and faith are absolutely essential because, according to Polanyi, "formal processes of inference cannot thrust forward toward the truth, for they have neither passion nor purpose.[17] The discovery, if there is one, usually follows a period of "incubation," and is the result of a tacit inference in which the meaning of the clues is found. It is the "grace" that follows hard work. For Polanyi, discovery is what Piaget terms an "irreversible process," meaning that a logical gap is crossed and that the steps of that crossing, because they were largely tacit, cannot be fully specified.

For Polanyi, the point of view from within the process of discovery, rather than the point of view acquired after a discovery is already made, becomes the proper paradigm of all knowing. This point can hardly be over emphasized. The latter approach is virtually certain to result in misleading textbook accounts of the scientific method in which all the wrong turns, dead ends, hunches, guesses, delays, confusion, etc. are retrospectively excised, ironed out, made straight, or otherwise rendered logical. By contrast, he asserts that "it is more illuminating to think of the way we struggle from a puzzled incomprehension of a state of affairs toward its real meaning."[18] He generalizes this position by saying that "our active

16. Polanyi, *Personal Knowledge*, 57.
17. Polanyi, "Faith and Reason," 243.
18. Ibid.

foreknowledge of an unknown reality is the right motive and guide in all of our knowing, from the dawn of discovery to the holding of established truth."[19]

If the search for knowledge is driven by intellectual desire and conducted largely by inarticulate powers, then the solution or discovery "carries conviction from the start."[20] There is an assurance of things hoped for because the discovery "emerges in response to our search for something we believe to be there." Thus, says Polanyi, "It arrives accredited in advance by the heuristic craving which evoked it."[21] Indeed, those same intellectual desires and inarticulate heuristic powers continue to accredit and sustain the discovery so long as it is sustainable. Knowledge discovered in this way is not infallible; mistakes can be made. Yet we accredit our feats of knowing as being competent, and the discovery or knowledge is sustainable so long as there continues to flow from it an indefinite range of "as yet undiscovered, perhaps as yet unthinkable, consequences."[22] Indeed, continuing to have consequences serves as Polanyi's abbreviated definition of "reality."

Once a discovery is made or once the integration of particulars into a whole that is their joint meaning has occurred, analysis of the whole becomes possible. Imagine, for example, that I am presented with the visual image of a circle, several ellipses, some lines, and a dot. They are juxtaposed to each other in a particular fashion. Initially, as I attend to them focally, these particulars have no special meaning. Following up intimations that there may be a greater significance here, I strain to grasp what it is. Suddenly, the gestalt changes as a tacit inference based on a subsidiary reliance on the particulars as clues discloses the image of a rabbit, a perceptual whole. Now, however, by shifting the newly minted whole into the tacit domain, I can rely on it subsidiarily to attend focally to the task of analyzing that whole into its parts, namely, the body, ears, feet, whiskers, tail, and eyes of a rabbit. The subsidiary awareness of the rabbit guides the analysis. Prior to becoming aware of the whole, the ears were mere ellipses, the body and head mere circles, the whiskers mere lines, and the eye a mere dot.

Most of the examples of Polanyi's epistemology given so far fall into what Rorty or Wittgenstein would regard as the "everyday" or "ordinary" realm. But Polanyi's use of "faith," "hope," and "grace" to characterize discovery generally and scientific discovery in particular are indications of his willingness to move, if tentatively, into metaphysics. This coincides with his aforementioned "domain of sophistication." He does not treat some of the more elusive "discoveries" of quantum physics, but, for some, these would qualify as metaphysical. George Gale, author of *Theory of Science: An Introduction to the History, Logic, and Philosophy of Science*, expressed surprise at the fact that in a graduate seminar in physics, his professor asked students to make a show of hands to indicate whether or not they believed in the existence of neutrinos.[23] Most did not. But the question

---

19. Ibid.

20. Polanyi, *Personal Knowledge*, 127.

21. Ibid., 130.

22. Polanyi, *Tacit Dimension*, 23.

23. George Gale, *Theory of Science: An Introduction to the History, Logic, and Philosophy of Science* (New York: McGraw-Hill Book Company, 1979), 175.

is analogous to questions as to whether or not one believes in God. Decades later now, a quick survey of the physicists at my own institution revealed that none of the five believes in strings and only two believe unequivocally in neutrinos.[24] Polanyi does, however, make rare, brief, and unorthodox remarks about God and religion.

Like the writings of Teilhard de Chardin, Polanyi's views of religion seem grounded in evolution, which generates ever ascending levels of reality as potentialities hidden in earlier levels emerge to be governed by more comprehensive laws that rely on lower, less comprehensive ones. Inanimate realities give rise to animate life, which in turn, gives rise to an emergent humankind. But what about the whole of reality? Polanyi says:

> I have mentioned divinity and the possibility of knowing God. These subjects lie outside my argument. But my conception of knowing opens the way to them. Knowing, as a dynamic force of comprehension, uncovers at each step a new hidden meaning.
>
> It reveals a universe of comprehensive entities which represent the meaning of their largely unspecifiable particulars . . . The vision of such a hierarchy inevitably sweeps on to envisage the meaning of the universe as a whole. Thus natural knowing expands continuously into knowledge of the supernatural.[25]

The possible presence of hidden meanings in religion, as in science, comes in intimations, which lead to a new understanding of religious ritual and practice. Worship, he says,

> sustains, as it were, an eternal, *never to be consummated hunch*: a heuristic vision which is accepted for the sake of its unresolvable tension. It is like an obsession with a problem known to be insoluble, which yet follows, against reason, unswervingly, the heuristic command: "Look at the unknown!"[26] (Emphasis added.)

The phrase "never to be consummated" makes clear that Polanyi is not proposing what Derrida calls "some nonknowledge that is a knowledge to come." Knowledge is eschatological, not teleological.

With the addition of religion into his theory of epistemology, Polanyi envisions, as Ian G. Barbour puts it, "a harmony of method over the whole range of knowledge."[27] Whether driving a nail, diagnosing an illness, classifying a new plant, discovering a new law of physics, or discerning the meaning of the universe as a whole, the person is undergirded from start to finish by the same from-to

---

24.   One said that if he believes in electrons, he has to believe in neutrinos. Another said that neutrinos are as real as electrons and protons. A third said that the evidence for neutrinos was strong.

25.   Polanyi, "Faith and Reason," 246.

26.   Polanyi, *Personal Knowledge*, 199.

27.   Ian G. Barbour, *Religion and Science: Historical and Contemporary Issues* (San Francisco, California: HarperSanFrancisco, 1997), 94.

structure, namely, the hazardous reliance upon tacitly generated intimations that are self-accredited as clues to knowledge.

Implications, Comparisons, Extensions

First, that knowledge arises from an ultimately unspecifiable tacit domain undercuts foundationalism and an understanding of knowledge as absolute. Thus, it satisfies two more of the criteria stated at the start of this chapter (criteria one and four). In imitation of Asian rhetoric one might say that the tact dimension is the epistemological foundation of no foundation, yet the tacit differentially grounds all knowing.

Second, beyond rhetoric, the concept of a tacit dimension has significant convergences with key Buddhist concepts. Like both Nagarjuna's *sunyata* (emptiness) and Zen's *mu* (nothingness) the tacit dimension functions to undercut dualistic thinking. Dualistic conceptions are the products of reflection and lie at the "to" pole of reflective acts. The absolute character of these dualities, however, is relativized or dissolved by the "from" pole, which is the inarticulate, shadowy, background that is the tacit dimension. In other words, the ultimately unspecifiable and inexhaustible tacit dimension is a kind of Western version of emptiness and nothingness, both in description and function. Because this Western emptiness, like its Asian counterpart, undermines in principle all dualisms, our criterion three is satisfied.

According to Tom Kasulis,[28] Zen nothingness adds to Nagarjuna's emptiness the Taoist idea of nonbeing as source. In Asian thought, nonbeing is not the absolute absence of being but the ambiguous or formless potential from which formed meaning and being can emerge. For Polanyi also, the formless and ultimately unspecifiable tacit dimension is the source of meaning, a meaning that can be made only partially explicit by reflection and can be only partially corrected by it. Reflection itself is always dependent upon its prereflective ground, namely, the tacit dimension. A reflection that cut out the tacit dimension would undercut itself.

Nonbeing as source, however, is not an exotic or inscrutable novelty but an appropriate phenomenological characterization of quite ordinary events. Consider that both writing and speaking depend upon an upsurge of meaning from one knows not where. For example, suppose you and I engage in a conversation. Whether the subject be politics or cycling, I have no experience of explicitly consulting my stock of words dealing with such topics, no experience of consulting a rule by which to make a selection from that stock, no experience of organizing those selected words into grammatical and coherent propositions to be communicated to you. Indeed, our powers of tacit inference make such explicit construction of meaning unnecessary. What I actually experience is the mysterious appearance of words at the tip of my tongue and of their launching

---

28. Tom Kasulis, *Zen Action/Zen Person* (Honolulu: University of Hawaii Press, 1981), chapters 2 and 3.

themselves into the public space we jointly occupy as we try to make sense to each other. I can, of course, silently and reflectively preview what I intend to say before I say it, and sometimes, especially in writing, I struggle to find the best word to use. Nevertheless, even the origin of the words to be previewed, weighed, and selected is obscured by the chiaroscuro of their tacit roots. We can deliberately summon word-candidates, but which candidates show up and when we do not reflectively control. They appear out of the peculiar and fulsome nothing of the tacit dimension.

Third, the foregoing remarks illustrate how the concept of the tacit dimension undercuts the cogency of the West's traditional and nearly exclusive reliance on a visualist imagination, which had its origins in the life-world of the ancient Greeks, especially their response to the peculiar light of the Peloponnesian peninsula. C. M. Bowra explains the connection between Greek light and Western visualism as follows:

> The beauty of the Greek landscape depends primarily on the light, and this has had a powerful influence on the Greek vision of the world. Just because by its very strength and sharpness the light forbids the shifting, melting, diaphanous effects which give so delicate a charm to the French or the Italian scene, it stimulates a vision which belongs to the sculptor more than to the painter, which depends . . . on a clearness of outline and a sense of mass, of bodies emphatically placed in space, of strength and solidity behind natural curves and protuberances. Such a landscape and such a light impose their secret discipline on the eye, and make it see things in contour and relief rather than in mysterious perspective or in flat spatial relations.[29]

Bowra goes on to link this "secret discipline" of light to the rise of Greek philosophy.

> Nor is it fanciful to think that the Greek light played a part in the formation of Greek thought. Just as the cloudy skies of northern Europe have nursed the huge, amorphous progeny of Norse mythology or German metaphysics, so the Greek light surely influenced the clear-cut perceptions of Greek philosophy. If the Greeks were the world's first true philosophers in that they formed a consistent and straightforward vocabulary for abstract ideas, it is largely because their minds, like their eyes, sought naturally what is lucid and well-defined. Their senses were kept lively by the force of the light, and when the senses are keenly at work, the mind follows no less keenly and seeks to put in order what they give it. Just as Plato, in his search for transcendental principles behind the mass of phenomena, tended to see them as individual objects and compared his central principle to the sun which illuminates all things in the visible world and reveals their shapes and colors, so no Greek philosophy is happy until it can pin down an idea with a limpid definition and make its outline firm and intelligible.[30]

29. C. M. Bowra, *The Greek Experience* (New York: New American Library, 1957), 23–24.

30. Ibid. Anaximander's *apeiron* (the boundless) is something of an exception to the rule.

According to Erich Auerbach, this predilection for the visual can be discerned in the literary style of the Greek poets, namely, the tendency to eliminate background in favor of foreground. Speaking of Homer's *Odyssey*, for example, he says that

> the basic impulse of Homeric style: to represent phenomena in a fully externalized form, visible and palpable in all their parts, and completely fixed in their spatial and temporal relations. Nor do psychological processes receive any other treatment: here too nothing must remain hidden and unexpressed . . . Homer's personages vent their inmost hearts in speech, what they do not say to others, they speak in their own minds, so that the reader is informed of it . . . and no speech is so filled with anger or scorn that the particles which express logical and grammatical connections are lacking or out of place . . . Never is there a form left fragmentary or half-illuminated, never a lacuna, never a gap, never a glimpse of unplumbed depths . . . The Homeric style knows only a foreground, only a uniformly illuminated, uniformly objective present.[31]

In this legacy of the visual imagination from ancient Greece we find the roots of visualism, which not only favors vision over the other senses but seeks to eliminate reliance on them altogether in matters intellectual. Contributing to the rise of visualism were Gutenberg's printing press, which transformed linguistic meaning into a fixed spatial phenomenon; the Neo-Pythagorean revival in Florence, which emphasized Euclidean geometry, whose figures were so obviously linked to vision; the invention of linear perspective by Renaissance painters, particularly Giotto and Masaccio, which converted the merely mathematical space of Euclid into an objective space in which people came to understand themselves to live. One might say that, in terms of the imagination, visualism defines modernity.

Visualism enters modern philosophy most powerfully and obviously through Descartes, who owed much to Galileo, a Neo-Pythagorean who declared sight to be "the most excellent of all the senses." Descartes's *Discourse on Method* was the first work of philosophy I ever read. It appeared in an Anchor-Doubleday edition that also included a treatise by Descartes on optics. Only years later did I appreciate the connection between the two works. Descartes's theory of knowledge was modeled after his understanding of the way he understood the eye to function. His key terms, such as "reason" and "intuition," were defined in terms of the imagery of light and sight. Ignorance was "blindness"; the problem to be eliminated was "darkness" or "obscurity" or "vagueness"; and the instrument for eliminating them was the "natural light of reason." The criteria for identifying genuine knowledge were "clarity" and "distinctness."

One passage explicitly connects intuition and visual perception interpreted in a visualist way.

> How the mind's intuiting powers may be best employed can be learned from the manner in which we use the eyes. For he who endeavors to view a multitude of

---

31. Erich Auerbach, "Odysseus' Scar," in *Mimesis: The Representation of Reality in Western Literature* (Princeton, New Jersey: Princeton University Press, 1953), 4–5.

objects all at once in a single glance sees none of them distinctly; and similarly anyone who is wont to attend to so many things at once in a single act of thought does so with a confused mind. But just as workmen who engage in tasks calling for delicate manipulation, and are thereby accustomed to direct their eyes attentively to distinguish things which are subtly minute, so likewise with those inquirers who refuse to have their thought distracted. Occupying themselves with the things that are simplest and easiest, these too become perspicuous.[32]

The epistemological theory Descartes here constructs is modeled upon an eye staring disinterestedly at a two-dimensional surface on which are inscribed the lengths, widths, shapes, and positions of Euclidian geometry. These are the "simples" that are paradigmatic for what is both "clear and distinct" in the external world, that is, what can be held to be certain. Philosopher Marjorie Grene has dubbed that surface the "blackboard of the mind." Indeed, it is on the blackboards of classrooms that geometry has traditionally been taught.

Unlike the bodily eye, however, Descartes's mind's eye has no location in a body or the natural world more generally; body and world belong to extended substance, an utterly separate and mechanical reality. Neither does this visualist, mental eye belong to a social world. Hence, the epistemological starting point and setting of Descartes's philosophy has been termed by William H. Poteat a "theatre of solitude." Without location, without a perspectival center, it has no orientation, either spatial or conceptual. It is a mental substance hovering over the universe like an angel or God.

The limitations of the model should be obvious. It leaves out of account whatever reality lies above, below, and behind the eye. Even for an embodied eye, which can turn in any direction, what appears to it must always appear in front of it. As for a disembodied eye, which is outside of all space, "in front of" and "turning around" can have no meaning. Moreover, Walter Ong has noted that so soon as knowing is pictured as an eye gazing at a surface, the surface is inevitably experienced as a wall that obstructs access to what lies behind it. Here, he claims, is the imaginative origin of Kant's phenomenal-noumenal dualism.[33]

Visualism, then, especially insofar as it is a model by which to understand both perceiving and thinking, promotes the very kind of specifiability and decidability that Polanyi and Derrida seek to eliminate. It also promotes dualism because the visualistic criteria of clarity and distinctness demand that reality be seen in black and white terms, including the social reality at Ole Miss in 1962. That Maurice Merleau-Ponty in his *Phenomenology of Perception* urges a return to the naïve and ambiguous perception that characterizes embodied existence in the lived world can be read as an attempt to blunt the fragmenting force of visualism. The same can be said of Zen's encouraging the practice of *mushin* (no mind or without thinking) as a way of recovering a world undivided by the naïve utilization of fixed, abstract categories.

---

32.   René Descartes, "Rules for the Direction of the Mind" in *Descartes's Philosophical Writings*, sel. and trans. Norman Kemp Smith (New York: The Modern Library, 1958), 39.

33.   Walter Ong, *The Presence of the Word: Some Prolegomena for Cultural and Religious History* (New Haven, Connecticut: Yale University Press, 1967), 74.

Fourth, so far, this sketch of some of the implications of Polanyi's thought reveals broad convergences between his concerns and those of what I have called "pseudo-postmodernism," but there are also significant similarities of a more specific sort. With respect to the meaning of words, for example, Derrida's concept of "undecidability" parallels Polanyi's "unspecifiability." The former reflects the fact, discussed in the previous chapter, that we cannot say explicitly what we mean when we speak or write because all alleged signifieds turn out to be merely signifiers. Signifiers attempt to spell out the meaning of terms but are never able to complete the task. Definitional meaning is always "disseminated," that is, is always deferred temporally and dispersed spatially as additional signifiers must be summoned in a futile effort to close precisely and permanently the circle of linguistic meaning. This incompleteness of definition is the opening in the circle through which meaning is always hemorrhaging.

Polanyi's "unspecifiability" refers to the pervasive presence of a tacit coefficient in all of our feats of knowing, including those involving our use of language. Although some of what is tacit in the utterance of one moment can be made explicit in another, the content of the tacit dimension as a whole cannot be specified and in that sense is inexhaustible. It is homologous with what Buddhism sometimes calls the "inexhaustible treasury." Moreover, he regards each use of a word as modifying, however slightly, its former meaning. There is no absolute meaning invariance. Linguistic meaning, one could say, is subject to Buddhism's *anicca* (impermanence). Even the broader frameworks of meaning we inhabit are always changing, at least incrementally. Such changes of meaning are part of a "lifelong" process.[34]

For Derrida, the implications of undecidability apply principally to the interpretation of texts. What is dispersed and deferred constitutes a "surplus" (a term Polanyi also uses) of meaning that thwarts all attempts at a final, definitive interpretation. At least part of this surplus is what phenomenology terms "sediment," that is, the residue of previous experiences. It amounts to an explanation of why complete agreement among interpretations remains elusive. Because the experience of individuals is at least somewhat different, the sediment of individuals is also somewhat different.

For Polanyi, unspecifiability characterizes both speech and texts generally, but as a philosopher of science primarily, he is more concerned to apply it specifically to presuppositions, theories, arguments, laws, and even mathematical formalisms. The implication is that these various forms of conceptualization cannot be justified either finally or impersonally. Language, he says, is "the product of man's groping for words in the process of making new conceptual decisions."[35] Obviously, groping is largely a tacit operation.

Although some may judge such views to have largely negative consequences, this is not the case for either pseudo-postmodernity or Polanyi. In the case of Derrida, for example, the deconstruction of absolutism, fixed identity, permanence essences, and universal truths is liberating. It opens up the possibility that

34. Polanyi, *Personal Knowledge*, 97.
35. Ibid., 112.

the differences contained in the widely varying surplus meanings we bring to texts and that result in a variety of interpretations of those texts can now be appreciated rather than deplored. The play of such differential meanings and interpretations is both enriching and delightful. One critic has characterized this new situation in glowing terms as "carnival." Another has called it "erring," a term used with approbation. Instrumentalism in the philosophy of science says that although scientific theories are not true, they are useful fictions that keep the work of science going. Analogously, deconstructionists seem to be saying that although the play of differential meanings cannot be regarded as genuine knowledge, it should continue because it sustains continued interpretation.

Polanyi, too, acknowledges the presence of a subjective element in human thought. The very title of his Gifford Lectures, *Personal Knowledge: Towards a Post-Critical Philosophy*, is a clue to that acknowledgement. The following characterization of the task of philosophy, however, makes the acknowledgement more explicitly.

> I believe that the function of philosophic reflection consists in bringing to light, and affirming as my own, the beliefs implied in such of my thoughts and practices as I believe to be valid; that I must aim at discovering what I believe in and at formulating the convictions which I find myself holding; that I must conquer my self-doubt, so as to retain a firm hold on this programme of self-identification.[36]

The Polanyian Difference

Although there are surely other consonances between Polanyi and postmodernity, I will turn now to the differences. It is the differences, I believe, that will reveal further why postmodernity is but a pseudo-postmodernity and how Polanyi's thought is nondualistic. For pseudo-postmodernity, the enriching play of textual interpretations carries with it the implication that knowledge is no longer possible, that it never really was. That's because, as we saw in Chapter 4, pseudo-postmodernity still clutches to its breast the definition of genuine knowledge as absolute, certain, rational, logical, and universal.

Polanyi, however, does not acquiesce to ignorance. By way of contrast, he asserts that he does not judge his views to be "merely subjective."[37] The "merely" leaves an opening for balancing that assertion with a claim to objectivity, a claim postmodernity is unwilling and unable to make. He announces his intention to take advantage of that opening when he states that what he seeks is a "personally grounded objectivity."[38] Sometimes, he calls his position a "paradox." My acquaintance with Mahayana Buddhism, however, leads me to interpret his position as a kind of Western nondualism with respect to knowledge and ignorance. At any rate, the surplus of the ultimately unspecifiable tacit dimension does not simply thwart

---

36.   Polanyi, *Personal Knowledge*, 267.
37.   Ibid., 65.
38.   Ibid., 115.

knowledge (as it does if omniscience is the paradigm for knowledge) but also makes knowledge possible (according to the paradigm of finitude). Indeed, it is the *sine qua non* of there being any knowledge whatsoever. What for pseudo-postmodernity is simply a negative is understood by Polanyi as a positive, also.

An epistemology not founded on the traditional dichotomies of knowledge vs. ignorance, of the subjective vs. the objective, requires a new conception of objectivity, one that does not depend on a perfect isomorphism of a conceptual scheme or verbal formula, on the one hand, and some object or reality, on the other. As both a scientist and a philosopher interested in science, Polanyi seeks that new definition largely in the context of the philosophy of science. It is not surprising, then, that "Objectivity" is the opening chapter of his major work. There, he begins with a discussion of the shift from the Ptolemaic to the Copernican view of Earth's relation to the planets and sun.

Prior to Tycho Brahe's observational data supporting Copernicus, the chief reason for adopting the heliocentric view, says Polanyi, was the "greater intellectual satisfaction" it provided.[39] That intellectual satisfaction involved a rejection of the testimony of the senses to the effect that in its rising and setting the sun obviously moves, whereas the earth clearly does not. Furthermore, it meant abandoning the terrestrial perspective in favor of one that, as Polanyi puts it, "equally commends itself to the inhabitants of Earth, Mars, Venus, or Neptune, provided they share our intellectual values."[40] He notes that while this does link greater objectivity more closely with theory, it does not constitute an abandonment of anthropocentrism; rather, it represents a shift from the anthropocentrism of the senses to the anthropocentrism of reason.[41] In other words, the views of both Ptolemy and Copernicus are anthropocentric, but they appeal to different anthropological faculties.

The preceding example is an indication that Polanyi regards the formulation and application of criteria for the appraisal of theories to be a legitimate methodological enterprise. The use of such criteria is common among philosophers of science. In this case, the criterion Polanyi appeals to can be stated in the following way: of two or more competing theories, the one that adopts the most comprehensive perspective is to be preferred. He goes on to formulate at least two more such criteria.

One of them has already been mentioned. It is sometimes designated by other philosophers of science as the "fruitfulness" criterion. If we not only can know more than we can say, but also can say more than we know, each saying of the latter kind is an act of hope that awaits future confirmations of our theories. Polanyi notes that 66 years after Copernicus' death, further confirmations of the heliocentric view appeared in Kepler's discovery that planets moved in elliptical orbits and that their angular surface velocity remained constant. After the passage of another 10 years he found that orbital distances are related to orbital

39. Ibid., 3.

40. Ibid., 4.

41. Implicit in an affirmation of an anthropocentrism of reason is to affirm that knowledge is finite, not infinite or divine.

periods. In another three-score and eight years, Newton realized that all these movements were expressions of the underlying force of gravity. Each of these confirmations, says Polanyi, "proved to be a token of a deeper significance unknown to its originator."[42] The intuition of an indefinite range of possible future confirmations of a theory is part of what constitutes fruitfulness and rationality; it endows the theory with "prophetic powers."[43]

Still another criterion is aesthetic in nature. Scientists, mathematical scientists most especially, speak of theories as exhibiting beauty. While some philosophers have attempted to define "beauty" more precisely as "simplicity" or "symmetry," Polanyi views such "pseudo-substitutions" as at best merely indicating the "marks" of rationality and objectivity but not fully expressing of the "exhilarating" beauty that connects scientists to profounder dimensions of reality. In other words, of two competing theories, the one that is more beautiful—all else being relatively equal—is to be preferred.

Other criteria of theory assessment have also been proposed by philosophers of science. The empirical or correspondence criterion, for example, states that the theory that best fits the data is more likely to bear on reality. "Best fits" is meant to include qualitative considerations. The comprehensiveness criterion regards as the best theory the one that fits the greatest quantity of data. The coherence criterion endorses theories that possess logical coherence, whether among the concepts internal to the theory or to the concepts belonging to other theories. Finally, some philosophers of science argue that in the end objectivity resides in the scientific community itself, especially as its views come to be stated in textbooks, an indication that a broad consensus has been achieved.

Polanyi holds that it is legitimate both to formulate and employ criteria of justification and other methodological rules. Unlike some others who embrace the use of such criteria, however, he does not suppose that their application can guarantee absolutely objective truth, either actually or potentially. For him, such formalisms are of the nature of "maxims," that is, rules ultimately grounded in the tacit dimension of the discipline or art they seek to govern. There are no formalisms to decide which criteria are to be brought to bear in the course of theory assessment, or how exactly they are to be applied, or what to do when multiple criteria yield conflicting assessments. Even if new rules were devised to deal with such issues, then by what rules would we choose among these new rules and what rules would govern their application? Formalization always remains parasitically dependent upon informal acts. In other words, criteria and rules make sense and possess authority only for those already engaged in the discipline or art in question. Formalized criteria are the culture on tiptoe, peering toward the farthest horizons in order to achieve such universality and objectivity as is possible at the moment. Such insight indicates that objectivity always remains in a nondual fashion connected to subjectivity. Again, criterion three is met.

Beyond that, we seek objectivity not only in the intellectual assessment of theories but also in perception. We appraise our perceptual performances,

---

42. Polanyi, *Personal Knowledge*, 5.
43. Ibid.

Polanyi says, and modify them so as to achieve clarity, distinctness, sharpness of contour, coherence among sensory data, and other perceptual values. We move closer to or back away from a source of sensory information, shield our eyes from glaring light, turn up or down the volume of television sets or stereos, don head phones or remove them in an effort to satisfy such standards. Many times, perhaps most times, such appraisals are conducted tacitly.

We also appraise verbal articulations, both our own and those of others, whether in speaking, writing, or silently reflecting. An obvious instance is searching for the right word. As each word-candidate comes to mind, we appraise its appropriateness for the intended use, whether that be to describe, explain, exhort, express, or demand. When we settle on a word as the right one, we are judging it to be the best one for our purposes. Writing second drafts of essays, poems, or documents clearly entails an appraisal of the initial draft. Both of the foregoing examples describe relatively more reflective appraisals. Yet more spontaneous linguistic performances indicate a prereflective appraisal of the best verbal response for the context of the moment. Polanyi himself makes the point in terms of tacit inferences.

> At each of the innumerable points at which our articulation is rooted in our sub-intellectual strivings, or in any inarticulate feats of our intelligence, we rely on tacit performances of our own, the rightness of which we implicitly confirm.[44]

Appraisals are not merely intellectual, nor do they focus on ourselves only. In a relatively more practical vein, participants, coaches, judges, audiences, and inspectors also appraise performances—those of others as well as their own—in sports, the arts, manufacturing, and the practice of the professions.

Appraisals, of whatever kind they may be, have in common that the standards or criteria (whether tacit or explicit) employed in conducting them, constitute an objective pole to the concrete acts of knowing we undertake. At the same time, we are the ones who create or endorse the standards or criteria we will follow. In that sense they are self-set. Having adopted them, we appraise our own effectiveness in following them. Polanyi calls this willingness to turn for guidance to our own creations, even while we are willing to appraise and modify them, the "Pygmalion" in us.

> We grant authority over ourselves to the conceptions which we have accepted, because we acknowledge them as intimations—derived from the contact we make through them with reality—of an indefinite sequence of novel future occasions, which we may hope to master by developing these conceptions further, relying on our own judgment in its continued contact with reality. The paradox of self-set standards is re-cast here into that of our subjective self-confidence in claiming to recognize an objective reality.[45]

It is important to be clear that, for Polanyi, our acknowledgement of the authority of our own conceptions is "not purely egocentric," not aimed at the satisfaction of

---

44. Ibid., 100.
45. Ibid., 104.

merely a private subjectivity; rather, we hold them to be "universally satisfying."[46] In other words, we affirm them with "universal intent." What Polanyi means by "personal knowledge" is not, as William H. Poteat correctly observes, "a soliloquy" that expresses his "idiosyncratic uniqueness" but the recovery of an ancient, pre-Cartesian, Augustinian model according to which what is confessed is

> both *given* and *shared*. This recovery of the pre-personal and personal historical roots of one's own knowledge leads, not, as for the Cartesian, to subjectivism and relativism, but to the recognition of the inescapable, because necessary, universal intent of all our affirmation.[47]

It is the "act of commitment," made with hope and a passionate sense of obligation to universal intent, that "saves personal knowledge from being merely subjective."[48] A skeptical reader might reply to the previous sentence as follows: "It may save the intention, but does it thereby rise to objectivity?" My reply is that Polanyi is not speaking of some bare intention—intention and nothing more. His is an intention at work in all of our appraisals, both reflective and prereflective, of the relevant clues, evidence, and criteria available to us at any point in time. The skeptic's comment reflects, I suspect, that same nostalgic hankering for certitude that expressed itself in the umpire's call of "out" at third base described in the previous chapter. Such hankering keeps us asking insistently, "But was he *really* out?"

The "intent" of "universal intent" is a reiteration of Polanyi's rejection of absolute knowledge. The tacit dimension, which makes knowledge possible, simultaneously renders it finite and differential. The tacit dimensions of no two people are identical. Difference is a genuine aspect of reality, and the change that occurs in every moment at every level of reality, from cells to ideas, is constantly generating novelty. Not only can difference not be ignored, but also it should not be ignored. It is more than simply real; it also adds richness and zest to life at every turn. Polanyi understands this. To reject modernity is to repudiate its attempts to ignore difference.

The "universal" of "universal intent," however, is a refusal to correct a zig by committing a zag. Polanyi's writing can be regarded as a paradigm for such a balance. It should be clear from the prior exposition of his thought that he would agree with Ed Farley's assessment—aimed at correcting deconstruction's near exclusive emphasis on difference—that although they fall short of being universal, there is a "perduring" of "types, patterns, and continuities" to be found in "everything from granite to complex, self-transcending individuals of higher mammalian species," that in terms of temporality there are "epochal features, influences, trends . . . and macro-movements." He affirms that people experience

---

46.   Polanyi, *Personal Knowledge*, 106.

47.   William H. Poteat, "Upon First Sitting Down To Read *Personal Knowledge* . . . . An Introduction," *Intellect and Hope: Essays in the Thought of Michael Polanyi*, eds. Thomas A. Langford and William H. Poteat (Durham, North Carolina: Duke University Press, 1968), 18.

48.   Polanyi, *Personal Knowledge*, 65.

these patterns and that they are "to some degree sharable and communicable (and intersubjectively verifiable)."[49] With respect to language he adds the following:

> The function of language cannot be reduced to the voicing of difference. To speak of malice or play is not to speak of mere difference but of something in which differentiation is ever at work.[50]

Doubtless with Derrida in mind. Farley is acknowledging difference in language while also affirming identity and commonality.

Put in terms of my Buddhist interpretation of him, Polanyi's universal intent, along with his "personally grounded objectivity" is his attempt to articulate for the West the nonduality of objectivity vs. subjectivity, universal vs. particular, identity vs. difference. There is a greater reality from which all these binary oppositions are abstracted aspects.

At a time when globalization (economic, cultural, and religious) is accelerating, "universal intent" urges us not to abandon but rather to continue the search for common ground and common grounding so that we are able peaceably to enjoy the innumerable delights of pluralistic diversity. Here, then, is the middle way between identity and difference, which Western common sense can both understand and appreciate.

The Body

So far there has been no mention of Polanyi's view of the body. But if the tacit dimension is central to his thought, the body is hardly less so. That is because of the essential connection between them. Like the tacit dimension, the body is bashful, preferring the shadows to the limelight's glare. Polanyi says of it: "Our own body is the only thing in the world which we normally never experience as an object, but experience always in terms of the world to which we are attending from our body."[51] We can, of course, see our hands and feet and our reflection in a mirror, but such sights are relatively infrequent by comparison to the body's other uses, and the body is never seen as a mere object but as part of oneself. Although the body hides itself, Polanyi regards it as "the ultimate instrument of all our external knowledge, whether intellectual or practical."[52] Indeed, he affirms "the bodily roots of all thought, including man's highest creative powers."

We have already mentioned the six muscles that, by changing the shape of the eyeball, make possible focused visual perception. Other bodily activities, including neural ones, make possible the other forms of perception as well as thinking. All the traces of past experience—memories, habits, skills (linguistic and

49. Edward Farley, *Good & Evil: Interpreting a Human Condition* (Minneapolis, Minnesota: Fortress Press, 1990), 3.

50. Ibid., 7.

51. Polanyi, *Tacit Dimension*, 16.

52. Ibid., 15.

pre-linguistic), perceptual generalizations, intellectual generalizations, beliefs, myths—have their bodily roots and form part of the tacit dimension that is the "from" pole of the "from-to" structure of knowing. Indeed, they are a Wordsworthian *a priori* (not prior to experience, but prior to reflection) that is essential to thought.[53] In fact, Polanyi can speak of muscle movements as "premises" of thought. If this conception startles us, it is because we bear within ourselves the deeply entrenched legacy of Cartesian mind-body dualism, and Polanyi's expression alerts us to the degree to which he has overcome it and its secondary ciphers, such as the logic-psychology dualism.

The body of which he speaks is not the objectified body of the natural sciences but similar to the "lived body" of existential phenomenology. Thus it cannot be defined merely in physiological or biological terms. The body as a living, fleshly power underlying and making possible knowing of all kinds is not static. Not only does it grow and change physically, but also its epistemic boundaries expand and contract like an accordion. The body is the tacit dimension made flesh.

Consider the example of the blind person's stick. Initially, what its user experiences is the sensations of pressure made by the near end of the stick in the palm, not awareness of the street that lies at the stick's far end. But with practice the sensations are "transposed" inward, becoming part of the body, enabling the user to rely on them for attending to the world explored at the stick's distal pole. Polanyi terms this inward transposition both "incorporation," in which clues, whether sensations or language, are taken into the body, and also "indwelling," in which the body pours itself into sensory or linguistic particulars, converting them to clues. The body and the tacit dimension are, then, functionally indistinguishable. Both are coextensive with whatever we rely on, that is, attend from in order to attend to something else. Moreover, any expansion of knowledge is accompanied and made possible by an expansion of tacit reliances and, thus, an expansion of functional bodying. Here, criterion two, the rejection of a mind-body dualism, is fulfilled. Minding is an emergent activity whose source and ongoing ground is such bodying. Here, too, is the satisfaction of criterion five, namely, the rejection of the modern view that epistemology must precede ontology. Like all philosophy, epistemology arises *in medias res*. It merely seeks to clarify a world that preceded it and from which it is an upsurge.

Recall that Descartes's aspirations for certainty hinged upon the elimination of the body as a factor in knowing because he recognized, correctly, that its concreteness and particularity were obstacles to his goal. Perhaps Derrida's inability to make a definitive break with absolute knowledge is related to the abstract and bodiless character of his deconstructive analysis. Terry Eagleton, for example, says of Derrida's undecidability of language:

> Meaning may well be ultimately undecidable if we view language contemplatively as a chain of signifiers on a page; it becomes "decidable", and words like

---

53. In his "Ode: Intimations of Immortality from Recollections of Early Childhood" Wordsworth wrote that "the child is father of the man." As the child precedes and gives rise to manhood, so prereflective experience precedes and shapes reflective experience.

"truth", "reality", "knowledge", and "certainty" have some of their force restored to them, when we think of language rather as something we *do*, as indissociably interwoven with our practical forms of life. It is not of course that language becomes fixed and luminous; on the contrary, it becomes even more fraught and conflictual than the most "deconstructed" text. It is just that we are then able to see, in a practical rather than academicist way, what would *count* as deciding, determining, persuading, certainty, being truthful, falsifying and the rest—and see, moreover, what beyond language itself is *involved* in such definitions.[54]

Polanyi makes a complaint similar to Eagleton's, but it is directed to Wittgenstein.

Disagreement on the nature of things cannot be expressed as disagreements about the existing use of words. Whether an alleged machine of perpetual motion is such a machine or not cannot be decided by studying the use of the terms in question. Whether the law is but "the will of the stronger" or the "command of the sovereign" or . . . etc., cannot be decided by linguistic investigations, which are irrelevant to the issue. These controversial questions can be attended to only if we use language as it exists to direct our attention to its subject matter and not the other way around . . . "Grammar is precisely the total of linguistic rules which can be observed by using a language *without* attending to the things referred to. The purpose of the philosophic pretence of being merely concerned with grammar is to contemplate and analyse reality, while denying the act of doing so.[55]

Both Eagleton and Polanyi are saying that there is no serious problem with the undecidability of language provided that language is not abstracted from the bodily and sociocultural context in which it is used. Indeterminacies are finally resolved, if they are at all, by our inarticulate powers, which we have equated with Polanyi's expanded understanding of the body. To acknowledge the existence of the body and to embrace wholeheartedly its essential role in knowing is tantamount to embracing the sort of knowledge of which embodied beings are capable, namely, finite knowledge. For finite knowledge, the body is the *sine qua non*.

David Loy makes a similar point. He argues that Hui-Neng, Dogen, and Eckhart are in agreement that there is nothing inherently defective about language. That view distinguishes them from Nagarjuna, Tung-Shan, Suzuki, Derrida, and Caputo.[56] Hee-jin Kim, commenting on a line from Dogen, says, "In spite of inherent frailties in their make-up words are the bearers of ultimate truth."[57]

---

54. Terry Eagleton, *Literary Theory: An Introduction* (Minneapolis: University of Minnesota Press, 1983), 146–147.

55. Polanyi, *Personal Knowledge*, 114.

56. David Loy, "Dead Words, Living Words, and Healing Words" in *Healing Deconstruction: Postmodern Thought in Buddhism and Christianity*, ed. David Loy (Atlanta, Georgia: Scholars Press, 1996), 33–51.

57. Hee-Jin Kim, "The Reason of Words and Letters: Dogen and Koan Language" in William R. LaFleur, ed., *Dogen Studies* (Honolulu: University of Hawaii, 1955), 57–58. Cited in Loy, 43.

Elsewhere Kim affirms that words are not "mere means or symbols that point to realities other than themselves but are themselves the realities of original enlightenment and the Buddha-nature."[58] Although neither Loy nor Kim mentions body in this context, Kim does say that words accomplish their task in our "existential metabolism,"[59] which resonates with Polanyi's body and tacit dimension.

The necessary presence of the functional body in all actual feats of knowing is already a rejection of a string of related dualisms that trouble those seeking to escape modernity: practical vs. theoretical, doing vs. thinking, action vs. contemplation, pragmatic vs. intellectual. Polanyi says, for example, that "if perception prefigures all our knowing of things, drive satisfaction prefigures all practical skills, and the two are always interwoven."[60] In another context he states that

> the arts of doing and knowing, the valuation and the understanding of meanings are thus seen to be only different aspects of the act of extending our person into the subsidiary awareness of particulars which compose a whole.[61]

Still elsewhere, when speaking of scientific and artistic genius, he elaborates the point as follows:

> The art of the expert diagnostician may be listed next, as a somewhat impoverished form of discovery, and we may put in the same class the performance of skills, whether artistic, athletic, or technical. We have here examples of knowing, both of a more intellectual and more practical kind; both the "*wissen*" and "*können*" of the Germans, or the "knowing what" and the "knowing how" of Gilbert Ryle. These two aspects of knowing have a similar structure and neither is ever present without the other . . . I shall always speak of "knowing," therefore, to cover both practical and theoretical knowledge.[62]

The similarity of structure to which Polanyi refers here is none other than the from-to structure of tacit knowing, which we have previously discussed. The "from" pole always involves both a desire or drive, on the one hand, and a skillful performance of some kind, on the other. The "to" pole is the knowledge sought, discovered, or sustained. Such a position also implies a rejection of any dichotomy between the everyday or ordinary, on the one hand, to the metaphysical, on the other. Here, too, such distinctions or dualisms, convenient and useful as they may be in particular contexts, are made within a more comprehensive context of nonduality.

Perhaps by now the reader has begun to suspect there is an Achilles heel to this argument for Polanyian nonduality. Does it not rest, in the end, on Polanyi's own use of such binary expressions as "from-to," "subsidiary-focal," or "tacit-explicit?"

58.   Hee-Jin Kim, *Dogen Kigen—Mystical Realist* (Tucson: University of Arizona Press, 1975), 110. Cited in Loy, 43.
59.   Ibid.
60.   Ibid., 99.
61.   Ibid., 65.
62.   Polanyi, *Tacit Dimension*, 6–7.

Here, as elsewhere, the distinctions are not dualities. Recall that at least some of what is tacit in one moment may become explicit in the next, and vice versa. The content of the tacit and the explicit is not permanently fixed but constantly shifting. Moreover, at any moment there is no sharp boundary between the tacit and explicit, just a shading from one into the other. Even the "from" and "to" as categories are, in my interpretation, but two poles, abstracted from a unified and temporal feat of knowing, that is, what Polanyi characterized above as "only different aspects of the act of extending our person." They point to the directedness or vectorial character of what phenomenologists call "intentionality," especially the operative intention of the late Husserl and Merleau-Ponty.[63] The "from" is analogous to what phenomenologists term the "noetic" (subject) pole of an intention, while the "to" is analogous to the "noematic" (object) pole. Finally, that the terms in each of these binary combinations define each other (as *sunyata* makes clear) reinforces, I believe, Polanyi's nondualistic aims.

Although overcoming the dualisms of the subjective vs. the objective and knowledge vs. ignorance are among the most significant of Polanyi's achievements, he opposes several other dichotomous pairs, also. First, he joins Quine in rejecting the dichotomy between analytic and synthetic statements, which was employed by Kant and later by Logical Positivism. Analytic statements, according to the Positivists, are universally and necessarily true because the meaning of the terms require it, whereas the truth of synthetic statements depends upon whether or not they correspond to empirical observations. Appealing to his distinction between the subsidiary and focal, the tacit and the explicit, Polanyi argues as follows:

> To take cognizance focally of a subsidiary element of a comprehension is a new experience, and an act which is usually hazardous. The conclusion thus reached is in the nature of an explanation. We see combined here the characteristics of an empirical observation with those of an analytic proposition. This is due ultimately to the fact that the dichotomy between analytic propositions that are necessary, and synthetic statements that are contingent, no longer holds when we can know the same thing in two different ways which cannot be transposed into each other by logical operations, but can be identified only by an inquiry of the Socratic type . . . We must *use* the word "justice", and use it as correctly and thoughtfully as we can, while watching ourselves do it, if we want to analyse the conditions under which the word properly applies. We must look, intently and discriminatingly, *through* the term "justice" at justice itself, this being the proper use of the term "justice", the use which we want to define . . . Only the the meaningful use of the term can indicate to us what situations we are to look at.[64]

Put more simply, the observation of our use of terms and the situations in which we use them (the empirical or synthetic aspect) and the analysis of the conditions under which we use them (the analytic aspect) are interdependent; they influence each other in a circular determination of meaning that disrupts or forestalls the dichotomy. They are nondual.

---

63. The distinction between operative and active intentionality will be discussed in subsequent chapters.

64. Polanyi, *Personal Knowledge*, 115–116.

Parenthetically, Polanyi's suggestion that we watch how and under what conditions we use words accords with Terry Eagleton's suggestion, cited above, that we do not think of language "contemplatively as a chain of signifiers on a page" but "rather as something we *do*, as indissolubly interwoven with our practical forms of life." Saussure's structural linguistics, on the other hand, is similar to what Polanyi views as "destructive analysis,"[65] that is, "dismemberment" of a meaningful whole into the particulars (the ones that can be made relatively explicit) that comprise it. For Polanyi, such an analysis has its appropriate uses but is not the only or the best way to understand language.

Another pair of opposites Polanyi subverts, one made popular by C. P. Snow's *The Two Cultures*, is that of the sciences vs. the humanities. The particular context Polanyi addresses is the distinction drawn by T. Lipps and Wilhelm Dilthey early in the twentieth century. Lipps held that to appreciate a work of art requires inhabiting the mind of the artist. Dilthey asserted that to know a mind necessitates reliving its operations. Both approaches are forms of interiorization, which, allegedly, stands in opposition to the externalization or objectification essential to the sciences. Existentialists claim something similar to Lipps and Dilthey when they distinguish distanciation from participation. Polanyi objects that his "analysis of tacit knowing shows that they were mistaken in asserting that this sharply distinguished the humanities from the natural sciences." For Polanyi, indwelling of tacit clues is essential to all forms whatsoever of knowing-perceiving-doing, without regard for disciplinary or other boundaries.

Finally, Polanyi's conception of the tacit dimension resolves the centuries-old dispute between faith and reason by enabling him to offer a new interpretation of the epistemology of St. Augustine. The latter said, "*Fides quaerens intellectum*" and "*nisi credideritus non intelligitis*." The former means "faith seeking understanding"; the latter can be translated as "Unless you believe, you will not understand." Both are similar to St. Anselm's "*credo ut intelligam*" (I believe in order to know). What Polanyi does is to link faith to the "from" and reason to the "to" of his "from-to" structure of tacit knowing.

> We must now recognize belief once more as the source of all knowledge. Tacit assent and intellectual passions, the sharing of an idiom and of a cultural heritage, affiliation in a like-minded community: such are the impulses which shape our vision of the nature of things on which we rely for our mastery of things. No intelligence, however critical or original, can operate outside such a fiduciary framework . . . This is our liberation from objectivism: to realize that we can voice our ultimate convictions only from within our convictions—from within the whole system of tacit acceptances that are logically prior to any particular assertion of our own, prior to the holding of any particular piece of knowledge.[66]

The "system of tacit acceptances," this surplus, this sediment, this nothingness is the "from" that we bring to any inquiry, whether practical or theoretical, whether

---

65. Polanyi, *Personal Knowledge*, 63.
66. Ibid., 266–267.

deconstructive or empirical. We bring it because it is the *sine qua non* of launching and sustaining such an inquiry or project. We do and must bring it because in virtue of our necessarily embodied reliance on it, we *are* that always expanding system of tacit acceptances. When we acknowledge this understanding, says Polanyi, "the contrast between faith and reason dissolves."[67] Like "from-to," "faith-reason" is nondual.

It should be clear enough that belief, as understood here, is not the assent of a separate and utterly disinterested intellect to the truth of approved doctrinal formulations lacking sufficient evidence. It is a confident reliance on tacit acceptances, a courageous indwelling of clues, and the passionate pursuit of intimations in the hope of a discovery or of fresh confirmations. It is the structure of all knowing-as-learning.

The tacit dimension also has implications for meditation. All of us occasionally have moments of great lucidity and clarity, but the presence of a tacit dimension would seem to rule out such extravagant claims for meditation and enlightenment as "absolute clarity" and seeing "without blinds spots."[68] Such claims would seem to require that the tacit dimension be utterly dispelled or completely penetrated and that such insights would be incorrigible by any future evidence or experience.

Such claims also seem to deny that meditation has its own cultural context. Yet a non-meditator is induced to take up the practice by someone's characterization of what meditation is all about. Meditation manuals and meditation masters instruct novice practitioners in the techniques of posture, breathing, ritual, and mindfulness. Centuries of meditational lore explains its significance, touts its benefits, and provides guidance around obstacles and through fallow periods. When strange experiences occur in meditation (*makyo*, for example), there is always an interpretation of them ready-to-hand, and if not, one is suggested and/or endorsed by a spiritual teacher. We never come to meditation absolutely empty but filled with particular tradition-laden expectations that shape to some degree the experiences we have.

At the end of Chapter 2 I raised the question as to how nondual Hebrew epistemology supported God's existence. My answer was to note Stephen Toulmin's view that one must not first seek evidence of God's existence before accepting it; rather, one must passionately accept the hypothesis of God's existence as a way of acquiring evidence for it. Toulmin's position was explicated in terms of Ian Ramsey's story of buying and wearing a pair of shoes as a necessary condition for acquiring knowledge about the shoes. The same question I asked of the Hebrews can also be put to Polanyi when he speaks of God.

For Polanyi, whose ontology we will encounter briefly in Chapter 7, evolution manifests itself as an ascending ontological hierarchy that results from the emergence of a series of increasingly more comprehensive and complex entities out of more limited and less complex ones. For him, when one retraces the steps of that ascent, the imagination "inevitably sweeps on to envision the meaning of the

67. Polanyi, "Faith and Reason," 244.
68. See Laycock, *Mind as Mirror*, 107, 109.

universe as a whole. Thus natural knowing expands continuously into knowledge of the supernatural."[69] Indeed, he understands the Christian faith to be "a passionate heuristic impulse which has no prospect of consummation."[70] Worship is the primary context in which talk about God occurs, and God-talk is the attempt to articulate the implications of worship. For Polanyi the scientist, worship itself, however, is understood as a response to the persistent heuristic command "Look at the unknown!"[71] Any putative knowledge of God that results from following that heuristic command exhibits the same epistemological grounding as scientific or any other knowledge, namely, the adventurous and hazardous willingness to indwell or embody relevant particulars as clues to a comprehensive entity that is their joint meaning, although the degree of risk is greater.

Polanyi himself says little about the clues to God except that they are found, first of all, in worship and include prayer, confession, ritual, readings from the Bible, the sermon, and the church itself. Other scholars, however, have identified elements or types of religious experience. These include the sense of vast space, timelessness, serenity, joy, harmony, peace, and the unity of all things that are often experienced in meditation. There is also the sense of dependence, finitude, wonder, awe, and fascination that comes in an encounter with something regarded as sacred or holy. Conscience that does not allow us to ignore responsibility, righteous indignation at injustices done to others, moral courage in the face of danger, and self-sacrifice are other clues, as is the experience of reconciliation following guilt and alienation. Further clues can come from personal relationships (marriage, for example) and the experience of significant events (the exodus of the Hebrews from Egypt, the Babylonian exile, and the holocaust). Finally, the experience of order, complexity, beauty, or adaptability in nature is such a clue.[72] Polanyi himself does say that clues may be found anywhere in human experience, even what is conventionally deemed to be nonreligious experience. Perhaps because he is a scientist, an especially seminal clue is the study of evolution.[73] Such so-called religious experiences are not, for Polanyi, facts from which God

---

69. See Laycock, *Mind as Mirror*, 246. Rhetorically, at least, Polanyi seems to slip into a dualism of the natural vs. the supernatural. Such a dualism, however, does not appear to be required, however, if he means to equate God with the whole of reality or even if God is the ultimate level to emerge in the hierarchy of reality. Unfortunately, Polanyi never defines the terms. As Chapter 2 points out, no such dualism exists for the ancient Hebrews.

70. Polanyi, *Personal Knowledge*, 280. It is impossible to know whether or not Polanyi's statements about the structure of belief in Christianity are meant to apply to religions other than Christianity. I am inclined to say that they do apply, although the language of the Judeo-Christian tradition as contained in the Bible points more directly to that structure than does the language of some other religions. This statement may also be taken to reflect the Judeo-Christian upbringing that forms part of my own tacit dimension.

71. Ibid., 199.

72. A more fulsome summary of the elements or types of religious experience is found in Ian G. Barbour, *Myths, Models, and Paradigms: A Comparative Study of Science and Religion* (New York: Harper & Row, 1974), 53–56.

73. Polanyi, *Personal Knowledge*, 283–285.

may be either induced or deduced; rather, they are intimations that become clues when incorporated into the body and relied upon in an effort to discover their joint meaning.

I can imagine that a philosopher of the Analytic school might scan the list of experiences or clues above and conclude that they are largely emotive rather than cognitive, that is, that they merely describe or point to subjective states of persons rather than to any reality transcending human beings. To make such a claim, however, is to revert to the dualisms of body vs. mind, subject vs. object, and emotional vs. intellectual, that is, to try to pry or tear apart what experience discloses as always already ambiguously together. Moreover, as critics of the cognitive-emotive dualism have pointed out, so-called emotive aspects of experience presuppose and are linked to cognitive ones. Dale Cannon, while in no way denying the presence of emotive aspects, makes the cognitive element clear in his description of the six ways of being religious (or spiritual, if you prefer).[74]

His "way of ritual," for example, is defined as "participation in the sacred archetypal patterns through which *ultimate reality* is manifest." The way of devotion consists of the "cultivation of a personal relationship with *ultimate reality*." The way of the mystical quest make use of ascetic and meditative disciplines in an effort to free oneself from "the obscuring limitations and distracting compulsions of ordinary life in order to attain a direct awareness of *ultimate reality*, come to be wholly one with it, and have life . . . grounded in it." A cognitive claim is explicit in each case, demonstrating the nonduality of the cognitive and the emotive. (Emphasis added in each case.)

Most persons, of course, do not place so high a value on intellectual concerns. Among the six ways, the one in which philosophers and theologians are most likely to have a proprietary interest is Cannon's "way of reasoned inquiry," which is "the rational, dialectical struggle to transcend conventional patterns of thinking in an effort to attain understanding of, and consciousness-transforming insight into, the ultimate what, how, and why of things." Here, the cognitive aspect is front and center.

Not everyone, of course, is drawn to the risky business of regarding life experiences as clues, of attempting to integrate them into a comprehensive entity (God or ultimate reality), and of testing the truth and viability of that integration by living according to it. For some, life without such an adventure appears to be quite satisfactory. Others may make the attempt at integration but fail. Some may achieve the integration but find that the result does not pass the test of living and ongoing reflection on that living. Moreover, because of different sedimented cultural experiences, Asians are more likely to conceive of ultimate reality as impersonal rather than personal. As for the West, the outcome of such an integration depends, in part, upon the degree and manner of reliance upon the elements of the Wesleyan Quadrilateral: revelation (scripture), tradition

74. Dale Cannon, *The Six Ways of Being Religious*. (Belmont, California: Wadsworth Publishing Company, 1996), p. 69.

(papal encyclicals, church councils, and writings of early theologians), reason, and experience.

At this point, with some help from Polanyi, we have sketched an epistemological theory whose from-to structure is constant across the spectrum that runs from so-called ordinary or everyday knowledge, to scientific knowledge, to religious or metaphysical knowledge, despite differences in their significance and degree of risk. Now it is time to link this view to the middle way and the Middle East.

The Middle Way

In Plato's dialogue named for him, Menon puts to Socrates a question. How can we go looking for something? For either we already know it, in which case there is no need to look for it, or, if we don't know it, then we will not recognize it, even if we stumble upon it by accident. Menon's question poses an epistemological dilemma whose two horns are, in effect, ignorance, on the one hand, and knowledge, on the other. Faced with such a stark choice, Socrates-Plato chose knowledge. The choice was made on both theoretical and pragmatic grounds. The latter are that by choosing knowledge, we are at least encouraged to keep on searching for it, whether or not we actually obtain it. The theoretical grounds are embodied in the myth that in a preexistent and disembodied state, all human souls contemplated the pure and luminous forms, intelligibilities, or patterns according to which all things in the lower or material world were made. These divine patterns are the only true objects of knowledge, a knowledge that the myth states we already possess and that we have only to recollect. Between such ideal knowledge and ignorance there is no middle way, at least not one that is endorsed as genuine knowledge. It is that fateful choice by Socrates-Plato that laid the groundwork, whether it was intended or not, for the absolutism of modernity.

Pseudo-postmodernity, whether in its pragmatic or deconstructive form, has added its voice to a growing number of persons who have come to the realization that Plato's choice is not tenable. For some postmodernists, that assertion leaves either the option of acquiescing to ignorance or the option of living in an unresolved dilemma, which amounts to the same thing. For me, such an outcome is simply a strong indication that our dualistic Greek intellectual legacy has been found wanting.

But what about our Middle Eastern, Western Asian, Hebraic roots?

Chapter 2 described an ancient Hebraic version of epistemological nonduality. Perhaps it is not surprising that in characterizing his own view of knowledge Polanyi, himself a Jew, should make a reference to Paul, the Jewish-Christian. Polanyi says that scientific discovery is

> a passionate pursuit of a hidden meaning, guided by intensely personal intimations of this yet unexposed reality. The intrinsic hazards of such efforts are of its essence; discovery is defined as an advancement of knowledge that cannot be achieved by any, however diligent, application of explicit modes of inference.

Yet the discoverer must labor night and day. For though no labor can make a discovery, no discovery can be made without intense, absorbing, devoted labor. Here we have a paradigm of the Pauline scheme of faith, works, and grace. The discoverer works in the belief that his labors will prepare his mind for receiving a truth from sources over which he has no control.

I regard the Pauline scheme therefore as the only adequate conception of scientific discovery.[75]

My own choice of a paradigmatic figure for reflecting on epistemology in a genuinely postmodern age is Abraham, who, according to Hebrews, left Ur of the Chaldees for the Promised Land "not knowing where he was going." Elsewhere, I have spoken (with some hesitation) of this passage as an "epistemological allegory" and elaborated on it as follows:

Abraham left Ur of the Chaldees without knowing his destination but not without a reason. He had been given the promise of a "land flowing with milk and honey" and of descendents as numberless as the grains of sand. Upon closer examination, however, the promise is incredibly vague . . . Is it a physical place or a spiritual condition? If physical, then no actual place bearing that name or description existed. It was not, like an Easter egg, hidden in advance for Abraham to find. Furthermore, Yahweh gave him no map, no checklist, no definition, no explicit criteria, no photograph, no surveyor's coordinates by means of which to identify the place if he should happen upon it. In fact, Abraham never did reach the land which subsequent patriarchs and judges came to call the Promised Land.

Reflecting upon this extraordinary state of affairs, one is led to the conclusion that Abraham will find it, if at all, only as he is transformed by the journey itself and only as he is able to create from some merely suitable place something more . . . To picture Abraham's movements as purely spontaneous suggests that he lives in a momentary present cut off from past and future. Abraham, by contrast, has dreams, intentions, ambitions that go beyond grazing.

He is searching for something, the Promised Land, but does not quite know what or where it is. The direction he travels is shaped not only by present circumstances but also by past experience and by the approach of a future whose possible scenarios he continually sketches, modifies, and resketches. His trajectory is not a circle, a straight line, or a spiral; it is nothing that can be plotted in advance or which even in retrospect can be adequately expressed by any geometrical figure, regular or irregular . . . He is confident some of the time that he is making progress, but is less than certain. Although he has no definitive proof that he is closer to the Promised Land today than he was a month ago, he is not without pertinent evidence. He can point to sunrises, sunsets, waterholes, mountain peaks and passes, and other features of the terrain as they are familiar, unfamiliar, or of doubtful familiarity. And he can point to the positions of stars. More importantly, however, he is grasped by a vision of a land of promise, and that vision is a framework in which features of the terrain or sky are able to become clues or evidence. However incomplete

75. Polanyi, "Faith and Reason," 246–247.

from an omniscient perspective his evidence may be, he is confident enough to press on.[76]

Here, in narrative form (the form on which the ancient Hebrews relied most heavily), is disclosed an entirely different epistemological possibility than is offered us by Plato, modernity, or pseudo-postmodernity. Abraham is neither stuck in the Land of Ignorance (Ur), nor has he arrived in the Land of Knowledge (the Promised Land). Instead, he traverses the Land of Learning. In Polanyian terms, Abraham's passionate intentional arc (both active and operative intentionality) exhibits the from-to, subsidiary-focal, tacit-explicit structure of personal knowing, prompted by largely inarticulate intimations of the possible discovery of a land "flowing with milk and honey."

Moreover, the Promised Land is not to be understood as an already completed reality, hidden in advance like an Easter egg for Abraham to find. It is not identical with the terrain where Abraham's physical migration came to a halt, nor was that halting the end of his journey. The terrain, with its inhabitants and natural resources were but the raw materials with which Abraham, relying on his ever-modified visions and fresh intimations, created/discovered such a Land of Promise as was possible. And that creating/discovering was itself the continuation of the journey. Indeed, at no place and time does creation ever cease; it is continuous. And we may choose to become cocreators with others and God in the next phase of that creation.

Recall that in Chapters 2 and 3 I argued that ancient Hebraic culture was a non-dualistic alternative to the dualism of our Greek inheritance, an alternative that perhaps the West can embrace. The epistemological nondualism of the Abraham passage becomes apparent if his "not knowing where he was going" is interpreted as "non-knowing" (a rhetorical formula indebted to Buddhism) for expressing the middle way between the extremes of knowing absolutely and not knowing at all (ignorance). Such nondualism is more likely to be appreciated in the West, however, if it is put into positive rather than negative terms. Hence, I propose that in a genuinely postmodern era knowing be understood as learning, a concept that is descriptive of Abraham's journeying, I believe, and of what Polanyi calls "personal knowledge" or "post-critical knowledge."

Like the rhetorical suggestions of the pragmatists, "learning" has connections to the practicalities of life. To learn is to adapt to one's circumstances, and adaptation occurs not only at the level of human existence but across the entire range of biotic organisms, organs, and functions. Living is adaptation and, therefore, is learning. But unlike the Pragmatists' linguistic choices, "learning" has clear and longstanding connotations that link it to intellectual life—to thinking, to arguing, to justifying, and to creating and contemplating theories.

It would be a mistake, however, to construe "learning" as a mere combination of bits of (absolute) knowledge and bits of (absolute) ignorance. Such a both-and

---

76. Milton Scarborough, *Myth and Modernity: Postcritical Reflections* (Albany: State University of New York Press, 1994), 127–128. Used with permission from SUNY Press.

interpretation, the reader will recognize from Chapter 1, is identical to the 3rd lemma of Nagarjuna's tetralemma. Nor, strictly speaking, can it be understood as neither knowledge nor ignorance, the 4th lemma. Even if the 4th lemma is sometimes taken to be the least objectionable, all of the lemmas of the tetralemma are, finally, dualistic.

Nor should it be understood along the lines of Teilhard de Chardin's vision of the "unanimisation" (being spread everywhere) of the "noosphere" ("thinking earth," "inter-thinking humanity," or "envelope of thinking substance").

> The curve of consciousness, pursuing its course of growing complexity, will break the material framework of Time and Space to escape somewhere toward an ultra-centre of unification and wholeness, where there will finally be assembled, and in detail, everything that is irreplaceable and incommunicable in the world.[77]

Here is the Cartesian dream temporarily postponed but finally fulfilled: mind freed utterly of body and the material world and possessing omniscient knowledge. Here is an instance of the "nonknowledge which is a knowledge to come" that Derrida rejects and that continues to reflect, however tenuously, belief in universal and absolute certainty.

Learning, however, is nondualistic. It is empty of both absolute knowledge and absolute ignorance. It is the always already ambiguous, finite condition from which both absolute knowledge and absolute ignorance are overly simplified, idealized, reified, and often problematic abstractions. Learning is the often hopeful, often passionate project that generates (according to a model of finite knowledge) answers in the form of new perceptions, new facts, new theories, new insights, new perspectives, clarifications, disagreements, and wider agreements and that, at the same time, arouses fresh curiosity, raises new questions, and catches glimpses of exciting intimations that perpetually propel us, with Abraham, along the way toward Canaan. Canaan, however, has its own from-to structure in the sense that its *from* is the always modified promise and vision Abraham brings with him from Ur. Canaan's *to* is what Abraham creates from the resources acquired along the way. Such a stance I find to be compelling, fruitful, and true.

Such a stance also overcomes the opposing emphases of East and West. While the West focuses on the goals or products of reflection and on such aspects of human experience as are amenable to rationalized history, Asia, generally speaking, is interested in the origins of experience beneath history in the emptiness or nothingness of the timeless present (*Nikon*, Japanese for "right now"). These differing emphases have sometimes been characterized as "root" (Asia) and "fruit" (West). In the Hebraic, Middle Eastern, or Western Asian, Polanyian scheme just elaborated, the root (the subsidiary, the tacit, the from, the beneath history, nothingness) and the fruit (the focal, the explicit, the to, and history) are always *already* inescapably linked in the finite, from-to structure of personal knowing that recognizes and acknowledges as fundamental the plant entire. This from-to

---

77. Teilhard de Chardin, *The Phenomenon of Man* (New York: Harper & Row, 1964), 180–181.

structure is intentional, but not a bare intentionality that links an already existing and independent from and to. It is the more ambiguous and comprehensive reality from which root and fruit are abstracted aspects. It is the active and operative intentionality that permeates interdependent mind/bodily-being-in-the-world. It is the Hebraic or Middle Eastern way that comprehends the emphases of Asia and the West.

Here, I believe, is an appealing middle way that motivates an ongoing quest for knowledge, acknowledges that there are limits to such knowledge, and promotes humility. It is a knowledge that eliminates or substantially reduces the traction of crusades, inquisitions, terrorisms, fundamentalisms, and other forms of divisiveness and cruelty as well as nihilism, skepticism, and relativism, all of which rest on the presumption of an absolute knowledge.

One feature of Polanyi's thought, however, appears to clash sharply with Buddhism, namely, his frequent and approving references to passion. Isn't passion precisely what the Buddha's second noble truth warns us against? Will it not inevitably lead to suffering (*dukka*)? First of all, the Buddha does not command that everyone must seek an end to suffering. The four noble truths are aimed at those who wish to avoid suffering. It is conceivable that someone might make the calculation that there is some goal worth the suffering involved in reaching it. Vietnamese Buddhist monks may well have done so when they practiced self-immolation during the Vietnam war.

Yet there is another way to think about this matter. The *tanha* that the Buddha sees to be the cause of suffering is not mere interest, enthusiasm, or even passion but the deep-seated craving and addiction that sustains a fundamentally egoistic stance toward life and threatens to destroy life. Given that interpretation, *Nirvana* is neither the elimination of passion nor the achievement of a permanent state of pleasure; rather, it is equanimity, mental balance, and unshakability in the face of life's tumults. From this perspective Buddhist practice can be understood as lowering one's spiritual center of gravity by rooting oneself more deeply in nothingness. The more deeply the roots go, the more passionately one is able to pursue a cure for cancer, the eradication of poverty, the elimination of war, the cleanup of the environment, and the discovery of unified field theory without being personally destroyed by failure, either temporary or long term.

Moreover, passion may arise within the larger, encompassing context of compassion, as when a scientist passionately seeks a cure for cancer not in order to win the Nobel Prize and fame for himself but in order to alleviate the suffering of the entire human population, including himself. Very likely, such compassion grounded the passion of the Vietnamese monks.

What might such a nonduality of passionate commitment to the discovery of universal truth, on the one hand, and the acknowledgement of limitation, finitude, ignorance, on the other, look like? Here is one example, taken from Gandhi's autobiography.

> What I want to achieve—what I have been striving and pining to achieve these thirty years—is self-realization, to see God face to face, to attain *Moksha* . . . All that I do by way of speaking and writing and all my ventures in the political field, are directed to the same end . . . Far be it from me to claim any degree

of perfection for these experiments. I claim for them nothing more than does a scientist who, though he conducts his experiments with the utmost accuracy, forethought and minuteness, never claims any finality about his conclusions, but keeps an open mind regarding them . . . One claim I do indeed make and it is this: *for me they appear to be* absolutely correct, and seem for the time being to be final. For if they were not, I should base no action on them. But at every step I have carried out the process of acceptance or rejection and acted accordingly. And so long as my acts satisfy my reason and my heart, I must firmly adhere to my original conclusions.[78] (Emphasis added.)

It is an example I believe Abraham and Polanyi would endorse and the Buddha could endorse in principle.

---

78.   Mohandas K. Gandhi, *Gandhi: An Autobiography: The Story of My Experiments with Truth*, trans. (from the Gujarati) Mahadev Desai (London: Phoenix Press, 1949), xi–xiii.

Chapter 6
Nondual Self and Other

When you make the two one,
and when you make the inside like the outside and the outside like the inside,
and the above like the below,
and when you make the male and the female one and the same . . .
then you will enter the Kingdom.[1]

Jesus, Gospel of Thomas

The Problem of Self and Other

In Chapter 1 we saw that Buddhism promotes not only an ethical middle way (between self-indulgence and extreme asceticism) and an epistemological middle way (between subjective and objective, knower and known), but also an ontological or metaphysical middle way (between the eternally existent and the not existent). The principal focus of its ontological concern is the self. In fact, Buddhism is often classified by scholars as a religion of the self (by contrast to religions of nature or of history). Nearly all of its doctrines bear on the proper understanding of the self, primarily because knowledge of self has soteriological implications. In other words, knowledge of self determines whether or not one attains nirvana.

Buddhism affirms that ignorance about the true nature of the self is the root cause of human suffering in the world and that knowledge of the true nature of the self brings relief. We are deluded, it claims, in thinking that there exists a permanent, unchanging, and independent self (*Atman*) and deluded in thinking that happiness is a consequence of serving the ends established by that ultimately illusory self's ignorant, selfish, and unrealistic desires.

By way of remedy, the Buddha taught three doctrines that bear on the self. First, the doctrine of *anatman* (no-self) asserted that there was no *Atman*, no permanent

---

1. Saying 22.

self. One reason for that understanding is that all things, including the self, are subject to *anicca* (the law of continual change). Moreover, *Pratityasamutpada* (dependent co-origination) entailed that the self was not independent but interdependent.

Centuries later, Nagarjuna rejected *svabhava*, an alleged permanent basis for the self, and declared that the self was *sunya* (empty). To say that the self is empty is to adopt a middle course between the claims of Hindus, on the one hand, who said the self is real (permanent, unchanging), and the several rival groups, on the other, that denied that any self exists at all. Against both extreme positions (a permanent, independent self vs. no self whatsoever), the Buddha and Nagarjuna held that there is a self but that it is an interdependent, changing one.

The idea of a permanent, independent self is essential to the most fundamental social dualism, namely, the self vs. the other. Independence and permanence apply to both self and other. The same logical pattern present in the opposition of self vs. other is at work in other social oppositions: male vs. female, black vs. white, Republican vs. Democrat, gay vs. straight, Muslims vs. Christians, rich vs. poor, liberals vs. conservatives, evangelical vs. mainline churches, Protestants vs. Catholics, and us vs. them.

In the West, the problem of the self vs. the other is manifest most obviously in the ideology of individualism, whose distinctive American form is especially antithetical to a sense of togetherness, solidarity, and common ground. Sociologist Robert Bellah has distinguished four varieties of it: John Winthrop's biblical individualism, Thomas Jefferson's civic individualism, Benjamin Franklin's utilitarian individualism, and Walt Whitman's expressive individualism.[2] While the first two conceived of individuality as part of some wider social context, the latter two did not. The individualism of Franklin and Whitman are particularly destructive of a sense of community and of the common good.

A key figure in the creation of American individualism is English philosopher John Locke. Locke was impressed that English physicist Isaac Newton, by his discovery of the laws of motion, had been able to achieve what was believed to be a complete understanding (at least in principle) of the entire physical universe. Both the explanation of present and past events in terms of their causes and the precise prediction of future effects depended ultimately on atom-like corpuscles—discrete, invisible particles, whose behavior consisted of motion in various directions with varying degrees of momentum and of their collisions with other such particles.

What Newton had done for the physical world, Locke aspired to do for both the inner, mental world and the outer, social world. He believed that in order to achieve these goals he needed something in each realm analogous to Newton's corpuscle. In the mental realm, the appropriate analogue was the sensation. A sensation is an isolated, fundamental, atom-like unit of perception. More specifically, it is a simple idea, passively received when an object impacts the body's

---

2. Robert Bellah, Richard Madsen, William M. Sullivan, Alan Swidler, and Steven M. Tipton, *Habits of the Heart: Individualism and Commitment in American Life* (Berkeley and Los Angeles: University of California Press, Ltd., 1996), 27–35.

sensory equipment. Subsequently, the mind operates to combine simple ideas into complex ideas.

In the social realm Newton's atom inspired a view of reality consisting of a multitude of discrete, autonomous selves—social atoms or islands. Each self is a separate being, a separate center of value and meaning; and relations among selves are, as in the physical and mental realms, purely external. They do, however, share in common a rational nature. Group structural relations are established by a contract, which is adhered to only so long as the contract serves the private interests of the individuals involved. Inevitably, the interests of individuals will conflict, but the ideology of individualism takes for granted that each individual is prone to give priority to his or her own desires over those of all others. Thus, the antagonistic stance of self vs. the other arises, whether the other be another individual or a collectivity (family, community, nation, etc). What we have here is social conflict defined, prompted, and justified in large measure by an ontological dualism (self vs. other). Genuine community, solidarity with the poor, and social justice for all are among its casualties. Enron's Ken Lay, motivated by greed, defrauded tens of thousands of people of their life savings and retirement income. This is but one recent and egregious example.

While many Westerners embrace, at least in practice, the privileging of self over the other, some persons, appealing to particular religious or spiritual considerations, urge altruism, namely, acting self-sacrificially in the interest of others rather than for one's self. For Buddhists and ancient Hebrews, both positions are extremes; neither includes both self and all others. In the Hebrew Bible, as we saw in Chapter 3, persons are intimately related by and through a covenant community. In the New Testament Jesus urges, as part of the Great Commandment, that persons love their neighbors *as themselves.* Jesus' approach, like the approach of the ancient Hebrews, rejects the privileging of either self or the other. As for Buddhism, the self is empty of a fixed nature and discrete boundaries; it is interdependent with not only all humans but also all other sentient beings.

Recently, Emanuel Levinas has reflected deeply about the relation of self and other, as did Martin Buber, a fellow Jew, before him. Levinas' self, like that of Nagarjuna, is constituted in interdependence with the other. Moreover, both theories come into view as a result of a complex philosophical dialectic. Westerners without philosophical training and perhaps even some philosophers trained in the Analytic tradition are not likely to be persuaded by such an approach. In addition, the Buddha's view of the self, like that of Nagarjuna, is described largely in negative terms, that is, in terms of what the true self does not possess (*an-Atman,* without an *Atman,* or *sunya,* without *svabhava*).

To a Westerner, "emptiness," because it appears in English as the binary opposite of "fullness," has connotations that are life-denying. This negative reaction occurs despite the fact that, if viewed from another standpoint (the so-called awakened standpoint), the empty self can also be understood as full (because it is interdependent with a reality much wider and richer than the narrow, disconnected self). Indian Buddhism in particular (Theravada) is often expressed in excessively negative terms, and Zen Buddhism (including Ch'an) does not present itself from the awakened point of view but from the point of view of the unawakened person. Such a presentation makes Buddhism initially baffling. Rinzai Zen especially—the first form of Buddhism to interest nonimmigrant Americans—deliberately intensifies this bafflement to precipitate an existential crisis that leads to the Great Doubt and then to the Great Death of the egoistic self. In short, the nihilistic Buddhist way of making the case for the interdependence of self and other is not likely to be intelligible and/or persuasive to a large Western audience.

What I propose to do, by contrast, is to offer a resolution to the self vs. other dualism in terms that are more accessible, familiar, and appealing to the West. Consonant with the more obviously life-affirming nondualism of the ancient Hebrews, it will rely heavily on biography, narrative, case history, particularity, and prereflective or operative intentionality rather than dialectics (Levinas, Nagarjuna) or description of types of relations (Buber's "I-thou" and "I-it" relations).

First of all, I will use Erik Erikson's psycho-historical theory to show how the *presence* of a series of significant others cogwheels with an always changing self to continually cocreate that self. Second, I will tell the story of Victor, the "Wild Boy of Aveyron," to demonstrate the consequences of the *absence* of crucial others for the development of a self. Finally, I will tell the story of a sight-challenged boy, Joey, to show how others shape even the self's capacity for perception, which is usually regarded as actualizing itself automatically and without social nurturing.

The Presence of Others and the Development of Self: Erikson's Stages

Erik Erikson is a psychoanalyst known for his theories of identity and the eight stages of the life cycle. Although indebted to Freud, he does not take up the psychoanalytic inheritance without making some significant modifications. By contrast to Freud, for whom the id is of primary importance and for whom the weak ego, caught between the id and the superego, is passive, Erikson makes the ego both strong and active. Erikson also rejects Freud's thermodynamic model of the self, thus eliminating the determinism inherent in Freud's conception of mechanical causality. Finally, Erikson expands Nicolai Hartmann's notion of environment to include the social world and understands that environment as being not only around us but in us.

For Erikson, the self is the result of three ongoing processes—a biological process, a sociocultural process, and a psychological process. These processes function according to the principle of relativity—that is, each one affects and is affected by the other two. Erikson's relativity, then, is similar to the Buddha's dependent co-origination (*pratityasamutpada*). Moreover, the three processes are three in number only in the sense that the entire self "lends" parts of itself to three distinct disciplinary methodologies (biology, psychology, and sociology), which Erikson views as at least second order abstractions (an abstraction from an abstraction). In Buddhist terms, the processes are empty (*sunya*) of separate, fixed essences; their distinctness is dissolved in the reality of the self as an always changing concrete whole.

The biological process includes (1) the long span of evolutionary history, (2) the nine-month-long embryological development within the uterus, and (3) the Freudian psychosexual stages of extrauterine or epigenetic life. These stages are: (1) oral-sensory-respiratory, (2) anal-urethral-muscular, (3) genital-locomotor, (4) latency, and (5) adult genital.

Subsequent to birth, libido, a general, pleasure-seeking energy, successively endows the orifices of a child's body with increased sensitivity, converting them into organs for exploring the world. The anatomical structure and function of each such "zone" teaches the child a generalized "mode" of relating to the world that at the social level becomes a "modality" of interacting with people. For example, during the first psychosexual stage (the oral-sensory-respiratory stage) the oral cavity is an anatomical *zone* that becomes the paradigm for the general mode of incorporation, which becomes the social modality of "getting." In other words, the mouth's taking in of food becomes generalized to include the taking in of perceptions, oxygen, affection, skills, others, and wisdom. As another orifice is sensitized by libido, other modes and modalities arise.

Erikson describes the sociocultural process in terms of three coordinates: (1) collective ego-space-time, which consists of a group's geographical and historical perspectives; (2) collective life plan (a group's economic goals and means); and (3) ideology (which is largely unconscious). Put differently, the members of a social grouping have a feeling for their place, they know what direction their action in time should take, and their lives make sense to them in terms of certain models.

One illustration of these social coordinates is provided by the Dakota Sioux. In terms of collective ego-space-time, they migrated from the upper Missouri and Mississippi to the high plains of the Dakotas and organized their lives around the hunt for buffalo. Hence, Sioux or Lakota social structure consisted of a "flexible system of 'bands,'"[3] which roamed the interminable plains, dragging upon travois the entirety of their earthly possessions, which could be unpacked and placed into hastily erected teepees. Secondarily, they hunted small game and raided other tribal groups to obtain horses. Geographically, they knew no borders except those set by nature. This unboundedness of space permitted voluntary gatherings but also centrifugal dispersions toward an ever-expanding horizon in pursuit of the buffalo.

The extent to which the Sioux depended upon the buffalo for their collective life plan can be indicated by the uses made of the animal's body.

> The buffalo's body had provided not only food and material for clothing, covering and shelter, but such utilities as bags and boats, strings for bows and for sewing, cups and spoons. Medicine and ornaments were made of buffalo parts; his droppings, sundried, served as fuel in winter. Societies and seasons, ceremonies and dances, mythology, and children's play extolled his name and image.[4]

3. Erik H. Erikson, *Childhood and Society*, 2nd ed., revised and enlarged (New York: W. W. Norton & Company, Inc., 1963), 115. Hereafter designated as "*Childhood*."
4. C. Wissler, "Depression and Revolt," *Natural History*, 1938, Vol. 41, No. 2, cited in Erik H. Erikson, *Childhood*, p. 115.

Nothing was wasted. Waste was a luxury they could not afford. From this buffalo-based economy stable social roles emerged.

Young males aspired to be hunter-warriors. They were to hunt game, women, and spiritual power. Childhood training was designed to teach them aggressiveness, generosity, and fortitude as well as the skills of using the bow, riding horses, and conducting warfare, which were required to maintain the nomadic life. Girls were taught sewing, cooking, conserving food, setting up tents, along with the virtues of bashfulness and fear, in preparation for the roles of wife and mother. They were also taught skills for protection against sexual assault.

Related to such a collective life plan was an ethic of generosity, an ethic reflecting an ahistoric outlook that gave little thought to the future. The central act of this ethic was the "give-away," a safety net for the poor. For example, a widow had no hunter to bring her food. So, the first act of males returning from a hunt would be to give away some buffalo meat, perhaps a hindquarter, to village widows. Likewise, warriors returning from a raid on a neighboring tribe to steal horses would give away some horses to those in their village who had none. The poor person was one with nothing to share, and the immoral one was the person who had something but would not share it.

For Erikson, "ideology," the third element in the sociocultural process, has neither pejorative nor merely political connotations. It is

> a coherent body of shared images, ideas, and ideals which, whether based on a formalized dogma, an implicit *Weltanschauung*, a highly structured world image, a political creed, or, indeed, a scientific creed (especially if applied to man), or a "way of life," provides for the participants a coherent, if systematically simplified, over-all orientation in space and time, in means and ends.[5]

It is the not necessarily conscious congeries of images and values embedded in the collective life plan and the collective ego-space-time.

Central to Erikson's theory is the psychological process, which knits together a person's experiences in the psychosexual stages with the various elements of the sociocultural process. This knitting is primarily the work of the ego, which cannot be identified with either the popular notion of inordinate self-esteem or the permanency of conscious experience (the I of philosophers). Largely unconscious, the ego is "a selective, integrating, coherent and persistent agency central to personality formation."[6]

The psychological process is the negotiation of a series of tasks that arise as the organism, which is undergoing psychosexual development, encounters "a widening radius of significant individuals and institutions."[7] Each task is to develop a favorable ratio between polar elements of identity so as to be ready for facing

5. Erik H. Erikson, *Identity, Youth and Crisis* (New York: W. W. Norton & Company, Inc., 1963), 189–190. Hereafter designated as "*Crisis.*"

6. Erik H. Erikson, *Insight and Responsibility: Lectures on the Ethical Implications of Psychoanalytic Insight* (New York: W. W. Norton & Company, Inc., 1964), 147. Hereafter designated as "*Insight.*"

7. Erikson, *Crisis,* 93.

later tasks. These encounters also offer the person the opportunity to develop a basic strength or virtue.

The eight stages of this process, identified by age, task, psycho-sexual stage, and virtue, respectively, are as follows:

1. infancy, trust vs. mistrust, oral-sensory-respiratory, hope
2. early childhood, autonomy vs. shame and doubt, anal-urethral-muscular, willpower
3. play age, initiative vs. guilt, infantile genital, purpose
4. school age, industry vs. inferiority, latency, competence
5. adolescence, identity vs. identity diffusion, puberty, fidelity
6. young adulthood, intimacy vs. solidarity, adult genitality, love
7. adulthood, generativity vs. self-absorption, adult genitality, care
8. maturity, integrity vs. despair, adult genitality, wisdom

These psychosocial stages, however, are not discrete compartments. All the psychosocial tasks and strengths are found in every stage, although one set becomes dominant in each stage.[8] Here, then, is a brief overview of Erikson's theory of the self.

The significance of the foregoing for overcoming the dualism of self vs. other comes into view only with the realization that the values, roles, skills, images, ideals, ideas, models, worldviews, ways of life, etc., are contributed and mediated by the "widening radius of significant individuals and institutions" previously mentioned. Moreover, institutions themselves are experienced largely in terms of the persons who belong to, run, or represent them.

Erikson identifies these persons and institutions and links them to the stages at which they typically make their most crucial contributions to the creation of a self. They are as follows: stage one—the maternal person; stage two—the parental persons; stage three—the basic family; stage four—the neighbors and the teachers and playmates at school; stage five—persons in one's peer groups, outgroups; stage six—partners in sex, friendship, competition, and cooperation; stage seven—divided labor and shared household; and stage eight—all humankind and "my kind."

The good mother (or maternal figure), for example, delivers to the child food, warmth, and love in the right quantity, at the right time, and with the right intensity to sustain its further development. She also teaches the child the cultural connotations of its bodily experiences and, thus, the most rudimentary elements of its cultural identity. Beyond that, she helps the infant resolve its first psychosocial task (trust vs. mistrust) and passes on to it what she herself has achieved of the vital virtue of hope. What the mother has to give is dependent, in part, upon the relation she had during her own childhood to her own mother. Insofar as the mother is the neonate's world, she assures the child through her care that the

---

8. The ongoing interaction of all psycho-social tasks and virtues in all psychosocial stages is analogous to the so-called feedback loops involved in the 12 links in the Buddha's chain of causality. Both illustrate how causality is circular.

world is a trustworthy place, and the child will develop a favorable ratio of trust over mistrust. Mistrust, however, is not altogether discouraged; otherwise, the child will become dangerously naïve and credulous. In similar fashion, the other significant persons and institutions, by both word and example, proffer ideals, images, values, skills, and roles to the budding child and, thus, play their part in the slow and ongoing process of creating a human self.

Like a Taoist tweaking the nose of a Confucian and true to his principle of relativity, Erikson notes that there is a sense in which "babies control and bring up their families as much as they are controlled by them."[9] This is because all adult caretakers, teachers, and employers are themselves in some stage of the life-cycle and are resolving their own psychosocial "crises" even as they assist the younger generation with theirs. Thus there is a dovetailing or cogwheeling of the generations such that one person "is activated in whatever strength is *appropriate to his age, stage, and condition*, even as he activates in the other the strength appropriate to *his* age, stage, and condition."[10] In this process of interactive development the boundary between self and other is blurred. The "doer" and "other," says Erikson, become "partners in one deed." Here he catches a glimpse of the nonduality of self and other. This partnership is his reformulated golden rule.[11]

Moreover, as this cogwheeling proceeds, the balance of power shifts from the older to the younger. Erikson explains:

> In youth the tables begin slowly to turn: no longer is it merely for the old to teach the young the meaning of life. It is the young who, by their responses and actions, tell the old whether life as represented to them has some vital promise, and it is the young who carry in them the power to confirm those who confirm them, to renew and regenerate, to disavow what is rotten, to reform and rebel.[12]

By conserving what seems true and purging what does not, youth fulfills its function of revitalizing social evolution.

All of us, of course, recognize a debt to our parents, teachers, and friends in the shaping of our lives, and sometimes we even own up to that debt and thank those responsible for it. Yet we may continue to believe that there is, nevertheless, a permanent core or ego (a kind of *Atman*) that receives and makes use of the elements of identity with which others gift us. There is no more support for such a view in Erikson's theory than in that of the Buddha. In fact, the two positions are remarkably similar.

For the Buddha, the self is a *namarupa* (name-form), a relative whole that is the integration of five *skandas* (body, feelings, perceptions, dispositions, and consciousness). There is no additional constituent such as a permanent self or ego. As for the *skandas*, they are subject to *anicca* (impermanence, change) and are construed as processes. For Erikson, too, the person or self is a whole, one that is the integration of three processes, but no unchanging ingredient or

9. Erikson, *Childhood*, 69.
10. Erikson, *Insight*, 233.
11. Ibid.
12. Erikson, *Crisis*, 258.

constituent exists.[13] For both there is a temporal shift that is ambiguous or nondual with respect to continuity and discontinuity. In addition, the mutual development of the cogwheeling generations could serve as an illustration of the Buddha's concept of dependent co-origination, which Nagarjuna identifies with emptiness. For both the Buddha and Erikson, then, persons, interdependently co-originate each other. The self vs. other dichotomy is obliterated.

The Absence of Others and the Self: Victor, the Wild Boy

Existential phenomenologist Maurice Merleau-Ponty holds that a person, in virtue of being an embodied subject, is a "being-in-the-world," that is to say, that prior to reflection, a self is constituted by a pre-reflective dialectic with the world as lived (rather than merely thought). In cases of illness or injury, this dialectic, which is normally hidden from view, is interrupted or distorted and, consequently, we are enabled to catch a glimpse of how human selves are normally constituted. The case history to which I now turn, however, is that of a young boy who is neither sick nor injured, at least in the ordinary sense of those terms, but is feral. I believe that the consequences of his being feral will, nevertheless, enable us, to place in sharp relief the normal contribution made by the other to the self.

In late eighteenth-century France, stories circulated in the Department of Aveyron about the sighting of a completely naked boy in the Caune Woods, where he was observed collecting acorns and roots. A few years later, near the end of September of 1799, three "sportsmen" spotted him again in the same area. Attempting to elude their pursuit, he climbed a tree but was captured and taken to a nearby village, where he was placed in the care of a widow. By week's end, however, he escaped and remained on the loose through a "rigorous" winter. Eventually, he was caught again in the Canton of Sernin, moved to the hospital of Saint-Afrique for several days and then on to Rodez for several months. Eventually, a minister in the government ordered him brought to Paris, where he arrived in September of 1800 and was placed in the National Institute for the Deaf and Dumb. There, he came under the care of a young physician, Jean-Marc-Gaspard Itard, who named him "Victor" and worked with him for a period of 5 years.

Victor's initial appearance and behavior differed sharply from Rousseau's picture of the noble savage. He was described as follows:

> A degraded being, human only in shape; a dirty, scarred, inarticulate creature
> who trotted and grunted like the beasts of the fields, ate with apparent pleasure

---

13. For both the Buddha and Erikson there is neither absolute continuity nor absolute discontinuity of the self as a whole or of its elements. For both there is gradual change through time that permits a recognizable identity in most cases. When I returned to my hometown for the 30th anniversary of my high school class's graduation, I was able to recognize many members of my class but unable to recognize others. Such recognition depended largely upon physical appearance. Even fewer classmates would have been recognizable on the basis of a continuity of ideas they held. The persistence of one's own self-identity is a matter of an ongoing creation.

the most filthy refuse, was apparently incapable of attention or even elementary perceptions such as heat or cold, and spent his time apathetically rocking himself backwards and forwards like the animals in the zoo. A "man-animal," whose only concern was to eat, sleep, and escape the unwelcome attentions of sightseers.[14]

Itard himself noted that the boy was "affected with spasmodic movements and often convulsions" and that he "bit and scratched those who opposed him." He "showed no affection for those who attended him" and "was in short, indifferent to everything and attentive to nothing."[15] Some years later he described Victor as follows: "His eyes saw nothing, his ears heard and did not listen . . . and in some measure he differed from a plant only in that he had, in addition, the ability to move and utter cries."[16]

This so-called Savage of Aveyron was, in fact, only the latest in a string of such wild children found in India and elsewhere in Europe. Linnaeus, the famed biological taxonomist, mentions ten cases between 1544 and 1731 of what he classified as a distinct species, *Homo ferus* (wild man). In Itard's day, medical opinion was agreed that such children were imbeciles or incurable idiots and that no form of therapy could substantially alter their condition.

Itard himself, however, was influenced by the widespread optimism of his era in the power of science to accomplish nearly anything, as well as by the philosophical writings of John Locke and Condillac, both of whom Itard understood to credit the human condition almost entirely to environmental factors. This led him to a diagnosis that saw Victor as "less an adolescent imbecile than a child of ten or twelve months, and a child who would have the disadvantage of antisocial habits, a stubborn inattention, organs lacking in flexibility, and a sensibility accidentally dulled."[17] He estimated that the boy was probably abandoned by his parents at age five and had lived a solitary life in the wild for seven years before his capture at age twelve, during which time he had forgotten his years in civilization and formed alternative habits. In short, Itard believed that a relatively brief exposure to a well-conceived regimen of socialization would restore the boy to full humanity.

To that end, he set five goals. They were: (1) to "interest him in social life," (2) to "awaken his nervous sensibility," (3) to "extend the range of his ideas," (4) to "lead him to the use of speech," and (5) to "make him exercise the simplest mental operations" upon both "objects of his physical needs" and "objects of instruction."[18]

---

14. George Humphrey, "Introduction," Jean-Marc-Gaspard Itard, *The Wild Boy of Aveyron*, trans. George and Muriel Humphrey (New York: The Century Co., 1932), vi–vii.

15. Jean-Marc-Gaspard Itard, "First Development of the Young Savage of Aveyron," in *The Wild Boy of Aveyron* (New York: The Century Co., 1932), 4. Hereafter designated as "Development."

16. Jean-Marc-Gaspard Itard, "A Report Made to His Excellency the Minister of Aveyron," in *The Wild Boy of Aveyron* (New York: The Century Co., 1932), 54. Hereafter designated as "Report."

17. Itard, "Development," 10.

18. Ibid., 10–11.

Work toward these goals was not done sequentially but simultaneously and with the assistance of Madame Guérin, who was Victor's governess, and clear progress was made on most of them. In what follows, however, I intend to concentrate on the 2nd and the 4th goals, the ones toward which Victor made the least progress.

Both Itard and others who examined Victor noted that his senses were dulled. With no apparent discomfort, he could pick up a hot coal from the hearth and replace it in the fire or completely immerse his hand in boiling water to procure a potato. He seemed hardly to notice pistol shots discharged near him, and human voices seemed insignificant for him. Snuff placed in his nose did not result in sneezing, and he had no taste for chocolate or other European sweets.

On the other hand, the sight of the sun and the various sounds and sights of a storm triggered "loud bursts of laughter," "almost convulsive joy," or "a kind of frantic rage."[19] The rays of the moon would sometimes induce "a sort of contemplative ecstasy . . . interrupted at long intervals by deep inspirations nearly always accompanied by a plaintive little sound."[20] Once, following a heavy snowfall, he escaped into the yard, eating and rolling in the snow while expressing his delight by "the most piercing cries."[21] It became clear that his perceptive faculties were attuned to the sensations that he was accustomed to encounter in the fields or forests and that related to survival rather than to those of civilized society.

Itard reports making good progress with the senses of taste, touch, and smell. With respect to touch, Victor was initially insensitive to both heat and cold. Besides picking up hot coals and plunging his hand into boiling water without noticeable pain, he would also sit half naked for hours on wet ground, indifferent to frigid temperatures and a wet wind. Itard began by giving him hot baths lasting 2 to 3 hours. Eventually, the boy became sensitive to cold and even refused to bathe if the water were merely lukewarm. This development led to his appreciation of clothes as providing warmth.[22]

Itard also placed both hot chestnuts and cold, hollow chestnuts into an opaque vase with an opening narrow enough only for a hand to enter. When given a cold chestnut, Victor learned to reach into the vase and retrieve a similar one, thus learning to distinguish it from the hot ones by mere touch. Distinguishing shape by means of touch was facilitated by placing acorns and chestnuts into the jar and having Victor fetch one resembling a nut Itard would show him. In a similar fashion Victor learned to differentiate size by means of touch. Finally, Victor learned to distinguish by tactile means metal letters of the alphabet.[23]

With respect to taste, Victor made much progress. Formerly, his diet had consisted largely of acorns, potatoes, and raw chestnuts. Itard managed to get Victor to eat with enjoyment many dishes that he had previously found to be unpalatable.

19.   Itard, "Development," 12.
20.   Ibid., 13.
21.   Ibid., 12–13.
22.   Ibid., 14–16.
23.   Itard, "Report," 62–63.

In fact, Victor came to enjoy eating out at restaurants with Itard and at the homes of Itard's friends. The boy never learned to like hard liquor, however, and always preferred water to wine, for which he did develop some appreciation.[24]

Smell was the one sense that was already well-developed. Early on, Victor explored all the new things he encountered by sniffing them, much the way a baby explores the things of the world by stuffing them in its mouth. Itard soon concluded that regarding the olfactory sense, the boy had nothing to learn from civilization.

With respect to vision, one of Itard's methods was to write a series of words on two blackboards, one for Victor and one for himself. The order of the words on the two boards was different. When Itard pointed to a word on his board, Victor was to point to the same word on his own board. If Victor made a mistake, Itard had him examine the letters comprising the two words until Victor understood that they were not the same. The words were not pronounced, and they carried no intellectual or emotional meaning for Victor. In this way, the focus of the exercise was on visual discrimination alone; yet improvement in visual perception was tardy in coming by comparison to the previously mentioned senses. Itard's explanation for this difference is that taste, touch, and smell are "only a modification of the organ of the skin." Hearing and sight, on the other hand, are "more subjective, enclosed in a most complicated physical apparatus, are subject to other laws and ought in some measure to form a separate class."[25]

The sense most recalcitrant to the changes Itard's schedule of treatments sought to effect was that of hearing, the sense that, according to Itard, "contributes most particularly to the development of our intellectual faculties."[26] In order to prevent visual distractions, Itard blindfolded Victor. Then, by graduated steps, he sought to have him recognize increasingly subtle sounds. The initial task was to distinguish the sound of a bell from that of a drum. Then, Itard would create other sounds by striking various objects with a rod. Next, Itard played on a wind instrument, which more closely approximated the human voice. Finally, Itard used his own voice to make a wide a variety of sounds, deliberately demonstrating the full range of intonations of which the human voice is capable. Once Victor had learned to recognize all such sounds, Itard taught him to recognize the sounds of the five vowels, the sign of such recognition being the raising of the one of his five fingers associated with the particular vowel.

It was at this point that an obstruction appeared that prevented any further progress. Victor took great delight in these exercises, but his expressions of "gaiety" became so disruptive that the lessons could not continue, even after Itard reluctantly punished Victor by striking his fingers with a drum stick. This event permanently damaged the relationship between the two and brought progress to a halt. Itard repeatedly tried to resume the lessons after the passage of long intervals of time, but eventually he gave up in despair. He said, "How many times did

24.   Ibid., 64–65.
25.   Itard, "Development," 20.
26.   Itard, "Report," 55.

I regret ever having known this child, and freely condemn the sterile and inhuman curiosity of the men who first tore him from his innocent and happy life."[27]

Itard's fourth goal was to teach Victor to speak. Those persons who held that Victor was an imbecile kept asking, in effect, "If he's human, then why doesn't he speak?" Even today, speech is often identified as that which distinguishes humans from other animals. Victor's voicebox appeared to be undamaged, yet not only did he not utter a word, but also he paid little or no attention to the speech of others around him. One day Itard noticed that whenever "Oh" was said, Victor would turn his head toward the speaker. The doctor tried to capitalize on this preference for "Oh" by coaxing Victor to say "eau" (water), withholding from him a glass of water until he said it, but efforts were to no avail. Later, however, Victor said "*lait*," his very first word, but it was said as a mere expression of pleasure at receiving milk, not beforehand as a request for milk. Next, he learned to say, "*lli*," probably a designation for Julie, Madam Guérin's daughter, who came to visit on Sundays. Even later, imitating his governess' exclamation "*Oh, Dieu*," (Oh, God) Victor would say, "*Oh, Diie*."

But despite the fact that in terms of intellectual development, Victor was clever and inventive in communicating his wants and needs by means of gestures, in learning to recognize the written form of many words and concepts (including nouns, adjectives, verbs, wholes and parts, and abstract qualities), and in acting in accordance with their meanings, he did not learn to speak. After 4 years Itard wrote the following negative assessment: "With respect to hearing, Victor could be considered a deaf mute although he was certainly much inferior to this class of unfortunates since they are essentially observers and imitators."[28]

Having failed to lead Victor to speech through the sense of hearing, Itard did not halt his efforts but adopted an alternative approach. He devoted more than a year to teaching speech by means of vision, believing that positive results were "both near and inevitable," but finally he was forced to admit that he had been "entirely mistaken." The results were "nothing but the emission of unformed monosyllables sometimes shrill, sometimes deep and still far less clear than those which I had obtained in my first experiments." In the end, he says, "I resigned myself to the necessity of giving up any attempt to produce speech, and abandoned my pupil to incurable dumbness."[29]

Early on in his stay at the institute, Victor spent his days squatting alone in a corner. He did learn to tolerate people, although when he tired of them, he would hand them their coats and direct them by gestures to the door. He did develop some affection for Itard and even more for Madame Guérin, who was so attentive to his needs. Also, he moved from complete self-absorption to some consideration of others, especially those few persons of whom he became fond. He displayed his affection for them by delightedly performing small services for them. He developed a sense of shame and sorrow for his misdeeds. But nature, especially in its more dynamic forms, remained more significant to him than humans. It was

27. Itard, "Report," 59.
28. Ibid., 85.
29. Ibid., 86.

nature alone that sparked in him moments of ecstasy. Itard concludes that such social advances as Victor made were, nevertheless, "subordinated to an utter selfishness" and that "pity is yet to be born in him."[30]

As indicated earlier, Victor's case is not unique. There were feral children before him and also several since him. In 1828 Casper Hauser was found in Germany. In 1930 two girls from India were found living with a pack of wolves, but they died of fever before coming to the United States. In the 1990's, Oksana, a Ukrainian girl deserted by her parents, was found at 8 years of age living with a mongrel dog. As a result of her 5 years with the dog, she moved on all-fours, lapped up water with her tongue, and panted like a dog. In 1999, social workers in Mirny, Ukraine, discovered Edik, a 4-year-old boy. He was living on the third floor of an abandoned apartment building. He, too, sought warmth and protection among stray dogs.[31]

Perhaps the most interesting case is that of Genie. She was found at the age of 13 and a half living in Arcadia, California, a suburb of Los Angeles. She was the size of a normal 7-year-old, was wearing diapers, and could neither walk nor talk. Her father, Clark Wiley, was mentally ill, and her mother, Irene, was physically ill. At the father's insistence, Genie was completely confined to a single room in their home. The blinds were shut and the room was kept dark. Later, neighbors would say they never knew she existed. By day she was strapped to a potty chair. At night she was locked in a cage made from chicken wire. Her mother brought meals to her, but the father forbade Irene or Genie's brother to speak to her.

None of these children could speak when found. Oksana is now able to talk in simple sentences but is not expected to develop any further, and she still reverts on occasion to dog-like behavior. Genie learned many words but could not speak in sentences. Doctors who examined her found that the left side of her brain— the part used for speech—was both smaller than normal and malformed. They attributed this condition to lack of verbal stimulation.[32] Edik, perhaps because he was found at such an early age, shows more promise than the others. He possesses many words, speaks grammatically, and continues to make progress.[33]

Speaking is not instinctual behavior built into our genetic code and/or brain structure, merely awaiting an external trigger in order to begin its preprogrammed operation. Neither is it the mere transference to an external domain by arbitrary, meaningless, independent means the meaning possessed or generated internally by pure mind. Speaking is a mode of being-in-the-world, essential to being a normal human. It requires, of course, the requisite biological and physiological capacities, and these must become engaged in and with a social world that speaks, that bears through time an inheritance of acquired meanings embodied in a particular vocabulary and grammar, and that employs particular intonations and auxiliary gestures as part of its principal way of communication.

30. Ibid., 100, 96.
31. "Wild Child: The Story of Feral Children," a video documentary, produced by Optomen Television for the Discovery Channel.
32. Ibid.
33. Ibid.

Humans are not humans independent of communication with others. Humans are not externally related to communication. Communication, especially by speaking, is itself human society's distinctive way of existing. Indeed, it is constitutive of what is often regarded as the fully human self.

As a mode of being-in-the-world, speaking is an intentional act, but its intentionality is primarily and fundamentally an operative intentionality that is always already incarnate in a world that is natural, cultural, and social—nondually so. It functions pre-reflectively in that world in the course of living that world. As a form of intentionality, speaking is motivated. Speaking begins when the adult participants in a particular speaking community speak in the presence of a babbling infant, who experiences the words directed toward it as a beckoning, as an invitation to join that community and as a covenant to help constitute the child as a speaking self that appropriately and fully belongs to that community. To respond to that beckoning and to enter the speaking world is to participate in an evolution of one's merely potential human self into an actual human self. It is also to amplify and transform the already existing connections between self and other.

Furthermore, the world in which selves as mind/bodily-beings-in-the-world exist is not given as completely determinate, objective, and permanent but as an incomplete, somewhat determinate, and changing world shaped in part by language. Thus, to join a community of speech simultaneously endows one with the possibility, even necessity, of contributing in the constitution of one's own self and that of others but also in the constitution of the story-shaped world or worlds in which such speaking selves live and move and have their being.

Victor was not a fully human self, and apparently, subsequent to his capture, could never have been. His was no fully human self because there was, at least during the crucial early years (when there is a neural developmental window for speech), no human other with whom his human selfhood could have been jointly created. Here, the nonduality of self and other becomes undeniable. The other that was available to him was a nonhuman other—the fields, forests, sky, plants, and animals. It is by engagement with this nonhuman other that his not-fully-human self was constituted. It was the self of a man-animal. Perhaps too harshly, Itard once described him as a "man-plant." The intervention of human selves was too little and too late. The window of opportunity for learning to speak—when babbling occurs, the impulse to imitation is strong, and the organs of speech are flexible—had passed. Virtually unbreakable habits had been formed. Moreover, Victor's daily interaction with Itard and Madame Guérin took place within an institution for the deaf and dumb that otherwise provided neither incentive for nor assistance in speaking.

Nowadays, in view of advancements in medical knowledge, one might say that Victor's condition was not the result of the absence of a human other but the presence of autism. Autism is actually five neurobiological disorders jointly named "Autism Spectrum Disorders" (ASD). Common to all of them, although in different degrees, are repetitive behaviors, problems with communications, and problems with socials skills. Medical investigators are not in complete agreement about the causes of ASD, but many believe that the problem has a genetic base. Clearly, Victor suffers from two of these three impairments.

There is, however, no necessary conflict here. The neurobiological condition impairs speaking precisely because it impairs social relations with other humans. And surely nobody holds that a genetically normal child isolated from human contact would develop normally. In fact, the recommended therapy for ASD is regular and intense contact with normal children and adult therapists, and the latter is precisely how Victor made such progress as he did.

Not only does the absence of human language-users prevent the development of a normal human self, but so does the significant presence of non-humans, at least in one notable instance. In 1931 comparative psychologists Luella and Winthrop Kellogg brought Gua, a chimpanzee of seven and a half months of age, to live in their home with Donald, their five-month-old son. For the next nine months Gua and Donald were reared in the same way and given identical tests to document their development. The experiment was abruptly halted, however, when an unintended consequence appeared. To the Kellogs' surprise, Donald began imitating the barks and yelps of the chimp. The Kellogs had conceived of the enterprise as an experiment on the chimpanzee, but it turned out to be equally an experiment on their own child. Clearly, the two infants provided an illustration of both the Buddha's dependent co-origination (*pratityasamutpada*) and Nagarjuna's emptiness (*sunyata*) as applied to human selfhood.

The Differential Other and the Self: Joey, the Sightless Boy

Both Joe Perez, a Puerto Rican emigrant, and his wife Lucille Perez, ethnically Italian, were blind. Lucille was totally blind from birth. Joe was legally blind (20/200); he could cross streets and was employed at making wallets. Both were students at the New York Institute for the Blind. Having been assured by a physician that their blindness would not be inherited by their offspring, they proceeded to have three children: Joey, Gary, and Monselue.[34]

Although Joey was premature (4 pounds, 7 ounces), his pediatrician pronounced him normal. Indeed, Joey did learn to eat and sleep normally; however, he seemed abnormally inactive and did not breathe well. Sometimes Joe would arise in the night and place a finger beneath Joey's nose to be sure he was breathing. Later, Gary's pediatrician, upon hearing a description of Joey's behavior, asked Joe and Lucille to bring him in. When the pediatrician examined Joey, he referred the child to a specialist, who determined that Joey had cerebral palsy. His parents were stunned.

Joey was given a walker and was soon "zipping around the house"; however, he frequently bumped into furniture. These accidents prompted Joe to bring in a sighted neighbor, who showed Joey photographs in a magazine, but Joey could not recognize the objects in the pictures. It seems he identified things primarily by touch. Worried by these revelations, Joe took Joey (without Lucille's knowledge) to a doctor for an eye exam, but the doctor, after having examined Joey's eyes and

34. Jhan and June Robbins, "The Boy Who Found the Sun," *Redbook*, December 1966.

conducted some tests, concluded that nothing was wrong with them and that Joey was not blind. When Joe asked if he should consult an eye specialist, the doctor gently teased him: "You'll be taking him next to a toenail expert!"

At age five, Joey entered a school for special-needs children. It was run by the New York Philanthropic League, which was a branch of the United Order of True Sisters. As part of the matriculation process, he was evaluated by a hospital, whose report was as follows:

> The patient, Joseph Michael Perez. Jr., is a 5-year-3-month male presenting a spastic quadriplegia (mild in uppers, moderate in lowers), the product of a premature delivery. Has two younger siblings—both normal and in good health. Mother totally blind. Father legally blind. Patient has some visual perceptual disturbance. Does not avoid simple hazards. Psychological testing yielded an IQ 44. It does not appear that the patient will make significant educational progress. No accomplishment exceeds those of average 2-year-old child.[35]

Based on these test results, Susan Samuels, the school's director, placed Joey in a class of mentally retarded students.

During the first eight lessons, she observed that he fell over things, did not know colors, never looked out the window, and identified things by touch. In short, she observed that he behaved like a blind person, but she was not entirely convinced. Acting on a hunch, she transferred him to a class for normal students. When Joey would send a toy fire truck whizzing across the room, the other students would yell at him, "Look at whatcha doin', for Pete's sake." One day the teacher overheard a bright boy named "Billy" say, "Joey, you nut, look at it! Why don't you look at it?" When the teacher attempted to explain to Billy that Joey was blind, Billy retorted, "Joey can see okay—he just doesn't know how to use his damn eyes!"

Over the course of the next few months, an astonishing change took place in Joey. He stopped groping and began reaching for things. He remarked to the teacher that certain blocks were missing from the pile. He would step back and appraise what he had painted with a brush to see if the colors were right. He called the teacher's attention to mud on her shoes. From the window, he yelled to his classmates that a yellow Mustang was passing by. To the surprise of all (except, perhaps, Billy), Joey learned to see. His teachers expected that his IQ would rise, and an orthopedist predicted that in the future he might no longer need his walker.

A private psychologist acquainted with the case offered the following comments by way of explanation of Joey's transformation:

> Mr. and Mrs. Perez knew how to cope with the world as blind people. And that's what they taught their son . . . But the normal mother leads her son to the window and says, "See the bird." Or she says, "Bring me the red book." Or, "Just look what you've done to that jacket" . . . His helplessness and his mother's,

---

35. Jhan and June Robbins, "The Boy Who Found the Sun," *Redbook*, December 1966, 48.

however, added up to an education in how to be successfully blind—for a boy who could see! Every day he looked at the world—colors, shapes, faces—and had no idea what to make of it all. The messages that come through his eyes were, indeed, on the level of a two-year-old—bewildering, uncatalogued impressions. And he couldn't turn to his parents and say, "What's that?"[36]

Of course, neither Gary nor Monselue had cerebral palsy, and, as a result, both were able to play outdoors with neighborhood children. In other words, they had access, as Joey did not, to a sighted social context, and, as a consequence, they learned a different way of being in the world.

With respect to speaking (Victor's case), one might well say, "Of course extended contact with humans is necessary for a child to learn to speak. After all, only humans possess language, so language cannot be acquired elsewhere." Visual perception, however, is shared by all mammals, not just humans, and seems to be more a matter of general biology than of human social development. Thus, we are tempted to think that visual perception is automatic, that it functions independently of others. But at least in Joey's case, not only were other humans necessary for him to learn to see, but *seeing* humans were necessary.

Polanyi points out that "the capacity to see external objects must be acquired, like the use of probes and the feats of subception, by a process of learning that can be laborious." Essential to learning to see is the act of looking. As Maurice Merleau-Ponty says, "The facts show above all else that sight is nothing unless the subject is more or less used to using his eyes."[37] That's because, he notes, "Apart from the probing of my eye or my hand, and before my body synchronizes with it, the sensible is nothing but a vague beckoning."[38] He adds, "In the gaze we have at our disposal a natural instrument analogous to the blind man's stick. The gaze gets more or less from things according to the way in which it questions them, ranges over or dwells on them."[39]

Seeing, like hearing, speaking, moving, and feeling, is an intentional act, although, by and large, the intentionality involved is operative rather than active. As intentional, however, such acts are motivated. Normally, the initial motivation for learning to see comes from the parents, who dangle shiny or colorful objects in front of the child and say, "See the pretty toy." Or, they place their faces close to the baby's face while speaking to it, then move away, drawing the baby's gaze after them, leading it into the world.

To learn to see, then, is not simply to trigger a preestablished circuitry but to acquire a "new use of one's own body; it is to enrich and recast the body image."[40] Put differently and more dramatically, to learn to see—or to hear or speak or feel—is to become a new self, a self that includes (as the previous self

36. Michael Polanyi, *The Tacit Dimension* (Garden City, New York: Doubleday Anchor, 1967), 14–15.

37. Maurice Merleau-Ponty, *Phenomenology of Perception*, trans. Colin Smith (London: Routledge and Kegan Paul, 1962), 223.

38. Ibid., 214.

39. Ibid., 153.

40. Ibid.

did not) perceiving, speaking, or feeling. This new self emerges at the instigation of other selves already possessing the requisite dimensions of human existence. Just as there are no teachers without students, no husbands without wives, no parents without children, so there are no human selves without human others. For the same reasons, there is no unchanging, independent self. Self and other are nondual. It is as true to say that their relationship creates both self and other as to say that self and other enter into and create a relationship.

This picture of self and other as nondual, however, was not arrived at by philosophical dialectics focused on the meaning of the terms "self" and "other" but by a narrative account of the biological-psychological-social-cultural-existential interplay of self and other in the world. Even Erikson's more abstract theory of stages can be read as a generalized narrative that is exemplified in a variety of ways and in different degrees by particular individuals.

Here, then, is a genuinely Buddhist understanding of self as expressed in the doctrines of *anatman* (no fixed, permanent self), *dependent co-origination* (interdependence, co-causality), and *sunyata*. At the same time, there is nothing in it that is alien, exotic, inscrutable, or life-denying. It has been created by thoroughly Western methods and expressed entirely in Western terms. Beyond that, it is also consonant with ancient pre-philosophical Hebraic thought as characterized in Chapters 2 and 3.

The human self, of course, is not the only ontological or metaphysical subject for which we are seeking a Western middle way. It is, however, a fairly accessible one. Vastly more difficult is the topic of God or transcendence, which has been so large a part of the Western philosophical and theological tradition. Surely in this case, a middle way will elude us. Here, too, however, we may be in for a surprise.

Chapter 7
Nondual Immanence and Transcendence[1]

Reality has no comparison, because there is nothing to which it may be likened: the body of reality is not constructed and does not fall within the scope of any category.[2]

Pai-Chang

Fish don't hold the sacred liquid in cups!
They swim the huge fluid freedom.[3]

Rumi

Metaphysical dualism, as we have seen, has taken a variety of forms in the West. In addition to those forms often applied to illuminate the nature of the self (self and other, mind and body, freedom and determinism, psychology and logic), there are those of a more comprehensive sort. Included among them are creator and creation, God and world, heaven and earth, the supernatural and natural, being and becoming, change and stasis, and transcendence and immanence. In his *Mediated Transcendence: A Postmodern Reflection*, Jerry Gill attempts to classify the multitude of schools of thought regarding these dualisms into two broad categories.[4] The first is naturalism (which rejects transcendence and espouses the horizontal dimension only), and the second is dualism (which adds to the naturalistic view a

---

1.   The bulk of this chapter appeared originally in Milton Scarborough, "In the Beginning: Hebrew God and Zen Nothingness" in *Buddhist-Christian Studies*, 20, 2000, 191–216.

2.   Thomas Cleary, trans., *Classics of Buddhism and Zen*, Vol. 1 (Boston, Massachusetts: Shambala, 1997), 264.

3.   Coleman Barks, John Moyne, A. J. Arberry, and Reynold Nicholson, trans., *The Essential Rumi* (San Francisco, California: HarperSanFrancisco, 1995), 123.

4.   Jerry H. Gill, *Mediated Transcendence: A Postmodern Reflection* (Macon, Georgia: Mercer University Press, 1989).

separate and vertical transcendent, supernatural, and otherworldly dimension).[5] But from the Mahayana Buddhist perspective, even naturalism is tacitly a form of dualism insofar as it defines itself over and against supernaturalism and is, thus, parasitically dependent upon the latter.

In the 1960s, during the heyday of the so-called Marxist-Christian dialogue, Leslie Dewart, one of the participants in the exchange, delivered himself of what I took to be a stunning and memorable utterance: "To put it lightly: the *whole* difference between Marxist atheism and Christian theism has to do with the existence of God."[6] Now, at the beginning of a new millennium, we are several decades into a Buddhist-Christian dialogue, precipitated by a shrinking globe, the growing presence of Buddhist communities and institutions in the West, and the philosophical initiative of the Kyoto School of Zen Buddhism. The dialogue has occurred along a variety of fronts. In terms of monastic life, for example, monks from the two traditions have discovered that they often feel a more powerful bond with each other than with laypersons of their own faiths. Some years ago I was a visitor at Gethsemane Abbey, a Trappist monastery in central Kentucky. Looking down from the sanctuary's balcony, where laypersons and other guests were required to sit, I noticed three Tibetan Buddhist monks in the choir, surrounded by Trappists and engaged in chanting the Christian liturgy, something that Christian non-monks were not permitted to do at the time. In the domain of ethics, similarities and differences between Buddhist compassion (*karuna*) and Christian love (*agape*) have been carefully noted. In soteriology, comparisons have been made between Christ as savior and the *bodhisattva* as savior.

Nevertheless, when it comes to an examination of ultimate reality in the two religions, the differences are obvious and stark. Traditionally, and still today for the most part, Christians are committed to some variety of theism. On the other hand, Masao Abe observes, "Unlike Christianity, however, Buddhism is *fundamentally* not theistic and does not accept one personal God as the ultimate reality but *sunyata* . . . In Buddhism there is nothing permanent, self-existing, and absolutely good."[7] In this regard, I am tempted to parallel Dewart's comment by saying, "The *whole* difference between Buddhist atheism and Christian theism has to do with the existence of God."[8]

---

5. Gill includes in the category of naturalism the following: scientific materialism, reductionism, atheistic materialism, logical empiricism, expressionism, absurdism, minimalism, phenomenology, and deconstruction. Dualism includes creationists, fideists, neo-Thomists, Reformed theologians, some conservative political thinkers, some radical peace activists, and back-to-basics educators. Of course, there are exceptions to these generalizations, and he makes no mention of existentialism, which comes in both religious and nonreligious varieties.

6. Leslie Dewart, *The Future of Belief: Theism in a World Come of Age* (New York: Herder and Herder, 1966), 62.

7. Masao Abe, "Kenotic God and Dynamic Sunyata" in John Cobb, Jr. and Christopher Ives, eds., *The Emptying God: A Buddhist-Jewish-Christian Conversation* (Maryknoll, New York: Orbis Books, 1990), 48.

8. What I mean here—and what I take Dewart to mean concerning Marxist-Christian dialogue—is not that this is the only difference but that all other differences can be seen to flow from this one.

The parallel, however, is not entirely accurate because more recently some members of the Kyoto School of Zen have shown a willingness to speak of God, most notably Masao Abe himself. On the other hand, they contend that God might be described better in conceptual categories other than "being," which has been habitually used in the West. Abe, for example, has proposed a reformulation of the idea of God in terms of *sunyata*. Like many other participants in the Buddhist-Christian dialogue, he finds an initial justification for such a reconceptualization in Philippians 2.5–8, where Christ's self-emptying (*kenosis*) has its biblical grounding. According to traditional Christian theological understanding, between the incarnation and the resurrection Christ either abandoned, concealed, or restrained—these words represent variant interpretations—his divine nature, such as his attributes of omniscience, omnipotence, and omnipresence, in order to condescend to his humanity and, hence, to ours.

This leads to the heart of Abe's proposal, which consists of bringing to bear on the trinitarian view of God Mahayana Buddhism's ample resources for critiquing the ideas of substance, essence, and identity, in which the traditional version of the doctrine is cast. Just as the Buddha attacked the Brahmanical doctrine of the *Atman*, a spiritual substance underlying the self of all things, and Nagarjuna attacked the Sarvastivadin notion of *svabhava*, a material substance underlying all *dharmas* (fundamental elements constituting reality), so Abe provides a critique of the Christian view of God as three persons in one *ousia* or substance. Both the three persons of the trinity, on the one hand, and the relation of the Trinitarian God to the rest of the universe, on the other, he understands as interdependent and coexistent rather than as independent and self-existent. Thus, the theory of the trinity is purged of the Greek concept of substance and its implications.[9]

Abe's proposal represents, in my estimation, a significant step forward in the dialogue between the two religions and can justifiably be regarded as having met Christianity at least halfway. Its merit consists not only in exorcising the Greek philosophical framework that has led to so many insoluble problems in Christian theology but also in focusing narrowly on what some Christians would judge to be the very heart of Christian belief, namely, the trinity and christology.

His suggestion, however, like any other, is not without limitations. The Philippians passage is a better starting point for Buddhism than for Christianity. First, historically, *kenosis* has been the concern primarily of a few professional theologians belonging to the Lutheran and Roman Catholic communions. It has not been, nor is it now, I suspect, part of the religious consciousness of most theologians of other Christian communions or of most laypersons of any Christian communion. It is found in none of the major creedal statements of Christendom; appears only briefly in the first of the five volumes of *The Christian Tradition* by Jaroslav Pelikan, who for many years was a Lutheran; and has no listing at all in the index of Mircea Eliade's 15-volume *Encyclopedia of Religion*.

9. "Substance" is not an exact equivalent to either "*atman*" or "*svabhava*." The latter, for example, means "own-being," something like "self-nature" or "self-identity." Substance can be thought of as a Western way of fixing self-nature. Scholars sometimes use "substance" as a rough-and-ready equivalent of the two Buddhist terms.

These facts suggest that Abe's proposal may not reach far into the consciousness of the majority of Christians.[10]

Second, because the Philippians passage refers to "Christ Jesus," the connection of *kenosis* to God requires the introduction of the doctrine of the trinity, which contributed to the split of Christianity into Roman Catholicism and Eastern Orthodoxy. For many Protestants, it is a late accretion with scant support in the biblical sources. At the outset, the doctrine eliminates from interreligious conversation about God not only Jews and Muslims, but also the many Christians who are Unitarian, genuinely pluralistic, or who otherwise find it unnecessary to divinize Jesus of Nazareth in the Greek fashion in order to adopt him as a model and source of inspiration for living the Christian life. For this last group, the trinity is simply of little or no importance.

My intention in pointing out these drawbacks is not to propose curbing philosophical or theological creativity either in interpreting the Philippians passage or in approaching Buddhist-Christian dialogue more generally. Indeed, it is the opposite, namely, to suggest that the engagement between Buddhists and Christians (and Jews and Muslims, as well) can be broadened and deepened if it occurs at many places along the spectrum of views to be found within both religions, even though each such engagement will have its own limitations.

One of my purposes in what follows is to attempt to draw into the dialogue on the Christian side persons in addition to Roman Catholic monks, Roman Catholic theologians, and process philosophers, the groups that have carried the bulk of the dialogue thus far. I propose to do that by addressing the atheism/theism issue from a different angle. That angle consists of what might be termed three "substitutions." First, I will substitute the P-account of creation in Genesis (1.1–2.4a) for the Philippians passage as the textual locus of this attempt at dialogue. The former has the advantage of being a passage significant to Christians of all descriptions, as well as to Jews and Muslims.

Second, methodologically speaking, I will rely largely on the existential phenomenology of Maurice Merleau-Ponty rather than process philosophy, traditional metaphysics, or negative theology. Elsewhere I have claimed that existential phenomenology, which is closer than other Western philosophical methods to Hebraic ways of thinking, is itself, as are contemporary academic theories in a wide range of fields, including the sciences, tacitly dependent upon Genesis as well as *Timaeus*.

Finally, to make the connection to Buddhism I will examine the Genesis passage in relation to Zen Nothingness rather than *sunyata* alone. One inspiration for so doing is Hebraic nondualism as characterized in Chapters 2 and 3.

---

10. According to some dictionaries of Christianity, Paul borrowed the text of Philippians 2.5–9 from a hymn sung in Palestinian churches. Its literary style and content are based on the so-called suffering servant passages in Deutero-Isaiah. Although *kenosis* was known in Platonic times, it acquired some importance only in the sixteenth century among Lutherans and was revived and developed into a Christological theory by a few nineteenth-century Lutheran, Anglican, and Russian Orthodox theologians. In the twentieth century, it was treated by Lutheran Karl Barth and Roman Catholic Karl Rahner, among others.

My intention is neither to set forth a full-blown doctrine of God nor to address all the issues generated in Buddhist-Christian dialogue by the juxtaposition of rival visions of ultimate reality. From impulses more philosophical and literary than theological I hope to suggest an avenue for further fruitful discussion. Let us see if by means of this approach Christianity can meet Buddhism halfway while continuing to be true to itself or perhaps even recovering a more authentic self.

The Neo-Platonic and Christian "Misunderstanding"

Previously, I noted that while some Buddhist thinkers, despite Buddhism's traditionally atheistic orientation, are willing to speak of God, they do not conceive of God either as a being or Being. If Christianity most frequently does so conceive God, it is because early on its destiny became linked to cultural forms prepared centuries in advance. Parmenides laid the foundations of Greek metaphysics with two principles. The first is that "what is, is; what is not, is not."[11] This statement implies that whatever is subject to change is unreal; the real is the unchanging. His second principle is the equivalence of being and intelligibility.[12] Put into more familiar language, it says that the real is the rational, and vice versa. Taken together, the two postulates establish an equivalence among reality, being, permanence, and intelligibility.[13]

Appearances, on the other hand, seem to provide overwhelming support for Heraclitus' opposing view that everything is characterized by change. As I indicated earlier, Plato, faced with a choice between these diverse accounts he had inherited, solved the problem by positing two worlds, a hidden world of unchanging, intelligible forms, which is accessible to the intellect, and a world of changing material objects, which is given to the senses. Having subscribed to the Parmenidean premise that the unchanging and intelligible are the real, Plato was led inevitably to the conclusion that the hidden, transcendent world of intelligible forms is the real world and that the sensible world is illusory. Plato's privileging of Parmenides over Heraclitus in this way proved decisive for the development of Western intellectual history in general and the theology of Latin Christendom in particular.

As indicated earlier, all of the Parmenidean themes—being, reality, permanence, and intelligibility—converge in Plato's theory of ideal forms. The principal textual vehicle for the diffusion of the theory of forms, especially as it affected the interpretation of the creation accounts in Genesis, was *Timaeus*. The story of the centuries-long interplay between Genesis and *Timaeus* is told by Jaroslav

---

11. Parmenides' dictum bears a striking resemblance to the following lines from the *Bhagavad-Gita*: "The unreal never is; the real never is not" (2:16).

12. This principle, located in *Fragment 3* states: "That which can be thought is identical with that which can be."

13. I am appealing here to the received view of Parmenides, the one that would have affected subsequent intellectual history in the West. Currently, there are revisionist views about Parmenides, for example, Peter Kingley's *Reality* (Inverness, California: Golden Sufi Center, 2003).

Pelikan in his *What Has Athens To Do with Jersualem: Timaeus and Genesis in Counterpoint*, which he says is devoted to a history of the "misunderstanding" earlier mentioned by Jowett:

> The influence which the *Timaeus* has exercised upon posterity is due partly to a misunderstanding. In the supposed depths of the dialogue the Neo-Platonists found hidden meanings and connections with the Jewish and Christian Scriptures, and out of them they elicited doctrines quite at variance with Plato. Believing that he was inspired by the Holy Ghost, or had received his wisdom from Moses, they seemed to find in his writings the Christian Trinity, the Word, the Church, the creation of the world in a Jewish sense, as they really found the personality of God or of mind, and the immortality of the soul.[14]

The effect of the misunderstanding on Judaism and Christianity began with the use of Platonic terms in the translation of the Hebrew Bible into Greek. Perhaps the most crucial move was the Septuagint's translation of God's name in the burning bush passage (Exod. 3.14) by Plato's Parmenidean term for the Demiurge: "he who is" (ὁ ὤν). Next, the *Book of Wisdom*, of which Pelikan notes that 20 percent of its vocabulary is *not* found in the Hebrew Bible and much of which *is* found in the *Timaeus*, spoke of God as "him who is" (τον οντα). With Philo of Alexandria, the reading together of Genesis and *Timaeus* became more deliberate and systematic. He, too, has God identify himself/herself as ὁ ὤν in the burning bush passage so as to make clear that God is the one "to whom alone existence belongs."[15]

Crucial to the understanding of creation was Philo's depiction of God as an architect in whose eternal mind the archetypal pattern of the cosmos preexisted the material copy made in its likeness. Pelikan notes that Philo

> was able to superimpose on the cosmogony of Genesis—or to find in it as he would have preferred to say—an entire systematic theory of pattern and copy derived from the cosmogony of *Timaeus* and based on the pre-supposition that God, being God, assumed that a beautiful copy . . . would never be produced apart from a beautiful pattern.[16]

From Plato's distinction between an archetypal pattern, accessible to the intellect alone, and a material copy, accessible to the senses, and from the assumption that the pattern in God's mind must have preexisted the copy, Philo concluded that there must have been two creations, one for the pattern and another for the copy.

In terms of anthropology, Philo connected the two creations to *Timaeus*'s distinction between an immortal soul and a mortal body, associating the former with the P-account of creation in Genesis (1.1–2.4a) and the latter with the J-account

---

14. Quoted in Jaroslav Pelikan, *What Has Athens to Do with Jerusalem: Timaeus and Genesis in Counterpoint*, the Thomas Spencer Jerome Lectures (Ann Arbor: The University of Michigan Press, 1997), 24. This misunderstanding affected the reading of *Genesis* as much as that of the *Timaeus*.

15. Ibid., 69.

16. Ibid., 79.

of creation (Gen. 2.4b–25). While Pelikan judges this application to be "brilliant," on the one hand, he also points out that the "very device from *Timaeus* that helped make sense of the double creation of man in Genesis appeared to introduce a fundamental metaphysical cleavage into the doctrine of man as the crown of creation and thus, by extension, into the entire doctrine of creation."[17]

With the ascendancy of Christianity in the fourth century to the status of the official religion of the Roman Empire, the center of theological speculation shifted from Jewish Alexandria to Christian Constantinople. By that time, however, as Pelikan notes,

> the equating of the God of Moses with Plato's ὁ ων was by now an assumption that it was not necessary to substantiate, that it was indeed not possible to controvert; for it was emblazoned in the most "towering text" of the entire Septuagint, the self-designation of the God who spoke to Moses from the burning bush in the words εγω ειμι ὁ ων.[18]

Thus, the early church fathers, especially those in the Latin West, had no apparent reservations in speaking of God as ουσια as they worked out the orthodox trinitarian conception of God as three persons in one substance.

It is not the intention of this chapter to trace the history of the reliance by Christian theology on Parmenides and Plato for understanding God as being; however, the reader will have no difficulty in seeing how the continuation of this line of thought led to Aquinas' notion of God as *Actus Purus* (pure actuality). The negative consequences for theology of building on Parmenides' foundation are perhaps nowhere more scathingly articulated than in Charles Hartshorne's comments on the traditional illustration (the relation of a donkey and a post) of the medieval distinction between internal and external relations.

The donkey is *externally* related to the post (the post is not aware of or capable of responding to the donkey). By contrast, the post is *internally* related to the donkey (the donkey is aware of and capable of taking account of the post). The donkey's awareness and responsiveness, which the post lacks, makes it superior to the post. Hartshorne observes that in Aquinas' application of this distinction to the relation of God to the world, he places God in the position of the post.[19] God as pure being, pure actuality, self-existing, and self-sufficient, is unaware of and indifferent to creation's concrete particularities. Both Protestant theology and much of Roman Catholic theology now find such a doctrine of God highly problematic. This traditional picture is the God of the philosophers, not the God of the Bible.

Over and beyond theology, however, post-structuralism, deconstruction, constructive postmodernism (process thought), and existential phenomenology are critical of the Enlightenment, whose emphasis on rationality, necessity, universality, and essence is of itself rooted in the Parmenidean-Platonic assumptions.

---

17. Ibid., 82.
18. Ibid., 92.
19. Charles Hartshorne, *The Divine Relativity: A Social Conception of God* (New Haven: Yale University Press, 1982), 7–8.

There is, of course, no time machine by means of which to return to the past and undo the "misunderstanding" of the early philosophers and theologians. On the other hand, I find no good and compelling reasons to perpetuate it into the future and many reasons not to do so.

A far back as the 1960s, Catholic thinker Leslie Dewart, dreaming of a possible alternative to a theology based on Greek metaphysics, said:

> The Christian theism of the future might not conceive of God as *a being*. I place the stress not merely on the indeterminate article *a* but also on the substantive *being*. In Scholastic philosophy God is not conceived as *a being*, but is nevertheless conceived as *being* (*ens*). We might go beyond this as well, if the methodological principle which may be operative in one future concept of God should transcend that which in Greek metaphysics and, later, in Christian thought has always been at work. I refer again to the *metaphysical* method, which rests on Parmenides' postulate of the convertibility of being and intelligibility. If reality is not assumed to be constituted by intelligibility—or by any (possible or actual) relation to mind—reality can no longer be identified with that-which-is . . . To be sure, reality will still be as a matter of fact intelligible. But its intelligibility will now be a matter of fact, not of necessity.[20]

Dewart, relying on Gabriel Marcel and Karl Rahner, among others, proposes a concept of God as presence. Since those times, however, the concept of presence itself has become a target of criticism by those who find absence to be more resonant with their own religious experience. Whatever the merits or limitations of such a critique may be, perhaps the moment has come, especially in view of the ongoing Buddhist-Christian dialogue, to consider an alternative.

As a positive alternative to Western metaphysics, Heidegger believed that there is an ancient neglected wisdom contained within the Western tradition. This ancient wisdom consists of neglected possibilities that can be retrieved and actualized in the present. Like Nietzsche before him, however, Heidegger sought that wisdom among the Pre-Socratic philosophers. In turning to Greece he exhibited a long-standing conditioned reflex among Western philosophers. If the reform of Western philosophy and theology is one's aim, however, there may be a better place to look.

The incorporation of Greek culture into Christianity occurred at the expense of Hebraic culture. This is true despite the fact that the central figure of Christianity was Jewish and that all the canonical books of the Bible were authored by Jews. If Babylon was the Jews' first exile and the Diaspora was the second, then the replacement of Hebraic by Greek patterns of thinking was the third. The importance of retrieving long-lost ancient possibilities, including Hebraic ones, is heightened if they hold out, at the same time, the prospect of enhancing Buddhist-Christian dialogue. This would be all the more true if we were to discover that the Hebrew God of *Genesis* is permeated by a generous dose of Buddhist *sunyata* and/or Zen Nothingness, concepts that entail nondualism.

20. Dewart, 174.

God and Sunyata

According to Keiji Nishitani, another member of the Kyoto School of Zen Buddhism, theism's inadequacies are related to its conception of God as a trans-historical being defined by consciousness, personality, intellect, and will.[21] From the Buddhist point of view, each one of these terms characterizing God is problematic. They result in a self-centered God who, instead of helping to eliminate self-centeredness in humans, inevitably, if unwittingly, grounds a religious endorsement of it. Presumably, Zen Nothingness offers an antidote to Christianity's flaws. Is it possible that by eliminating the "misunderstanding" of the early Church Fathers and returning to Hebraic modes of thinking as understood from the point of view of existential phenomenology, God and Nothingness can be conceived together? It certainly appears to be a tall order.

According to Thomas P. Kasulis, Zen Nothingness is comprised of two strands, emptiness and nonbeing-as-source.[22] The first and better-known strand is that of *sunyata* or emptiness, a concept that arose in India and that became central to Mahayana Buddhism through its development at the hands of Nagarjuna. The doctrine of *sunyata*, as we saw in Chapter 1, involves at least three claims. First, things are empty of any underlying, permanent "own-being" or substance or essence (*svabhava*). Second, things are causally conditioned by other things (*pratityasamutpada* or dependent co-arising) and hence are interdependent rather than independent. Indeed, in his *Mulamadhyamikakarika* 24:18, Nagarjuna equates *sunyata* with the Buddha's concept of dependent co-arising. Finally, words or concepts are relationally defined and, therefore, are not, as usually understood, always a reliable clue to the nature of reality. This point results simply from extending the concept of dependent co-arising to language.

Can anything like *sunyata* be found in the depiction of God in the P-account of Genesis? Perhaps phenomenology's concepts of being-in-the-world and the life-world (*Lebenswelt*) can help us answer in the affirmative. A concept first proposed by the later Husserl, then taken up by existential phenomenologists, the life-world is an oriented, pre-objective, lived world, which precedes and underlies reflection. For Maurice Merleau-Ponty at least, the life-world must be distinguished from the universe. The latter is the result of an attempt by means of theoretical reflection to produce an explicit and objective understanding of the cosmos. The universe is what can be arrayed before the attentive intellect. The world, by contrast, is the ultimate context, horizon, or concrete frame of reference in which all acts, intellectual or otherwise, are performed and in and by which they make whatever sense they do.

Being-in-the-*world*, then, is not a location in the geometric space (Euclidian or otherwise) of the universe. It cannot be plotted on the x and y axes forming a set of Cartesian coordinates. Nor is the "in" of being-in-the-world an external relation,

---

21. Keiji Nishitani, *Religion and Nothingness*, trans. Jan van Bragt (Berkeley: University of California Press, 1982), 202–203, 214–215, 233, 236, 251.

22. T. P. Kasulis, *Zen Action/Zen Person* (Honolulu: University of Hawaii Press, 1981), chapters 2 and 3.

as is Descartes's analogy of the pilot in a ship he used to explain the mind's relation to the body. "Being-in-the-world" expresses a *primordial* situatedness in an ambiguous, ultimately unspecifiable, and thus bottomless context by which we are surrounded and permeated and in and by which we live, move, and have our being. This situatedness means that there were not originally two things, a being and a world, which were at some time brought together. Always it is the case that already they are together. Thus, incarnation in this life-world is prior to, during, and subsequent to all philosophical activity. As Merleau-Ponty puts it, "There is no inner man, man is in the world, and only in the world does he know himself."[23] In other words, the alleged transcendental ego or self of much Western thought is exploded and dispersed through a body into the pre-reflectively appropriated and lived "system" of self-other-nature, which is the ambiguous life-world.

Moreover, the nature of existence in this world is that of a project, both in the sense of imaginatively projecting before oneself possible ways of being-in-the-world from which to choose, of transcending oneself forward and toward the future, but also in the sense of an enterprise that, although already underway, always remains unfinished. Now, with the aid of these two existential phenomenological concepts, let us turn to the task of understanding Elohim in Genesis.

Interpretation amounts to summoning an upsurge of meaning prompted by what one might call "wonder in the face of a text," a modification of phenomenologist Eugen Fink's famous definition of one of the steps of the phenomenological method as "wonder in the face of the world."[24] A lifetime of sedimented acts is put at the disposal of the intention to understand a text so that in the coition between them and the text an interpretive meaning arises that can be reflectively affirmed as fitting the text. This way of putting the matter eschews both a purely subjective and a purely objective understanding of the interpretive act and allows for a contribution from both text and interpreter. One could understand it as the nonduality of text and interpretation.

Given the foregoing, if an existential-phenomenological interpretation is to succeed in any measure, the Elohim of Genesis 1.1–2.4a must be viewed as a being-in-the-world. How is this possible, especially in a textual setting in which God is depicted as *creating* a world, not *living* in one? Here phenomenology's methodological practice of sweeping away, to the extent possible, any preconception that would prevent a fair intuiting/describing/interpreting of phenomena comes into play. The obstructive preconception in this instance is the traditional theological doctrine of *creation ex nihilo*—not itself a Socratic or Pre-Socratic Greek doctrine but one invented by early church fathers to eliminate problematic features of Plato's concept of matter—which denies the presence, prior to God's creative acts, of any matter that could serve as raw material for the creation. The elimination of this preconception allows an interpreter to take seriously the references in Genesis 1.2 to an "abyss," "waters," "earth," and "wind," which are three of the

---

23. Maurice Merleau-Ponty, *Phenomenology of Perception*, trans. Colin Smith (London: Routledge & Kegan Paul, 1962), xi.

24. Cited in ibid., xii.

four basic building blocks of the cosmos identified by Empedocles and utilized by Plato's craftsman (in *Timaeus*) in making the lower, material world. Nor is there even a hint in the biblical text of any prior act of creating materials out of nothing. On the contrary, the interpretation that Elohim made use of preexisting materials is also supported by the fact that "*barah*," the Hebrew term for God's creative act, means "to cut out and put into shape" rather than "to bring into being out of nothing." The former clearly implies the presence of something that can be cut out and shaped.

Having eliminated creation out of nothing, the way is now clear to connect the P-account of creation to *sunyata* in several ways. First, the purpose of the traditional Christian doctrine *creation ex nihilo* was to reject both the Neo-Platonic view of matter as inherently evil and its implication that an independent, chaotic matter could resist the will of God as God attempted to shape it. Such matter would undermine God's omnipotence. If Christendom's exposition was unsound and if the text supports both the presence of preexisting matter and God's use of it, then it is clear that God is, in fact, *dependent* on such matter, at least insofar as ordering a world is concerned.

On the other hand, if the internal resources of matter are chaotic, then matter alone has no possibility on its own of achieving order and form. In other words, matter is dependent upon God for its manifestation as order and form. It might also be helpful to say, borrowing language from Aristotle, that matter functions as a material cause while God functions as an efficient cause. Thus, dependency and causality run in both directions—from the world to God and vice versa. Such a way of speaking would also be misleading, of course, if taken to be about two absolutely distinct entities, God and the world. Here, however, the distinction is merely a relative one in the light of the previous statement of their *primordial* interrelation in being-in-the-world. Thus, this fundamental interdependency and co-causality fulfill Nagarjuna's definition of *sunyata* as *pratityasamutpada* (dependent co-origination).

But how, one might ask, does the fact that Elohim and matter "need" each other permit speaking of God as a being-in-the-world? The description of earth, water, abyss, and wind as "without form and void" is, in the language of existential phenomenology, saying that they are pre-objective. Objective thought embraces what Merleau-Ponty has called the "constancy hypothesis," according to which the universe contains things wholly determinate and fixed in their natures. A cube, he points out, is believed to have its six sides, all of which are perfect squares of exactly the same size. He notes, however, that in perceptual experience such cubes never make an appearance. As given to an actual, embodied, perceiving subject, phenomena are always more fleeting, less clear, less block-like, less Euclidean, more porous to other objects and to human intentionality, less solid, more ambiguous, more shifting, and more contextual than objective thought imagines or acknowledges. For experience, the world is never a plenitude. If the matter of Genesis is understood objectively, then relations between God and matter can be external only and being-in-the-world is not possible. As pre-objective, however, matter can be integrated into the world of Elohim, understood as a pre-objective life-world. Matter, then, even prior to God's creating activity—assuming, for the moment, that there was a beginning to God's creative activity—constitutes the world of God's being-in-the-world. The interdependency of God and matter, then, is not merely external but more fundamental and intimate.

Beyond that, if God is primordially a being-in-the-world, then God is neither simply transcendent nor immanent in relation to the world. Such a dichotomy is an inappropriate oversimplification produced by objective thought. To parallel Merleau-Ponty's rejection of the inner man, one might say, as might a Hebrew acquainted with existential phenomenology, "There is no transcendent God, God is in the world, and only in the world does God know God's self." Put in terms of the theme of this chapter, God and the world are nondual. In the context of Genesis, such a world, beyond the distinction between immanence and transcendence, would also be the nondual life-world of the Hebraic covenantal community.

God's interdependency with the world obtains not only before and during creation but also subsequent to the onset of creation. Indeed, strictly speaking, apart from a relation to the world, God cannot be God. "God," as was pointed out in Chapter 3, is a relational and functional term. In order to be God, Elohim must function as a God and do so in relation to something else, namely, the world, the creation, the creatures. Used of a solitary being, apart from any others, "God" is a meaningless term. Here again, God is seen to be *sunya*.

According to the existential phenomenological approach we are currently employing, God is not simply a being-in-the-world (the phenomenological emphasis), but is also a project-in-the-world (the existential emphasis). Not only does God create a more orderly and formful *world* from the chaotic, formless matter that constitutes the pre-objective life-world of God's being-in-the-world, but by the same creative acts God also creates God's self. The creation story is an account not simply of humankind's emerging from a state of dreaming innocence, but also the story of God's own emergence from the shadows of relative inaction, non-identity, and dreaming to undertake a project. In so doing, God launches a history that is simultaneously and ambiguously the history of creation and God's own autobiography. This assertion is consistent with the Hebraic understanding of reality as historical in a broader and premodern sense. In other words, God has no eternal essence, but by actions in the world, God, like us, is creating a "historical identity." This interpretation amounts to abandoning the Greek categories of substance and essence for understanding God's mode of existence. In Buddhist terms, God's existence is empty of *svabhava*; rather, it is *sunyata* in the sense that God's self is shaped by God's project-in-the-world, namely, the compassionate practice of bringing all things into a more meaningful and harmonious relationship.[25]

Finally, if, in the chronology of the biblical text, Elohim's first appearance is as Creator of the world, then a reader might legitimately conclude that as a project-in-the-world, the general nature of God's project is, as process thought claims, creating. This claim is supported by an alternative biblical manuscript in which Genesis opens with the words, "In the beginning of God's creating." The gerund

---

25. I am indebted for this insight to Peter Hershock, who was on the faculty at the East-West Center in Honolulu, Hawaii, where I was a fellow in November of 1998.

can be read as implying that God's creative activity may extend beyond a mere beginning, that it may be ongoing or continuous creating. This interpretation is homologous with that of Whitehead and, more recently, Gordon Kaufman.[26] Moreover, this implication is consistent with alternative translations of God's self-naming in the burning bush passage, namely, "I will cause to be what I will cause to be" or "I will be what I will be." In existentialist terms, one can understand God as saying something like, "If you want to know who I am, watch and see what I do, because it is in doing that my identity is being both formed and revealed."

God and Nonbeing

The other element of Zen Nothingness is nonbeing as source, an idea Ch'an and Zen Buddhism borrowed from Taoism. Although Masao Abe, borrowing from Christians Meister Eckhart and Jacob Boehme, speaks of *Nichts* and *Ungrund* as the Godhead, his focus is on what unifies the three persons of the trinity rather than on simply pointing to their source.

The typical Westerner understands nonbeing as the absence of anything, a total vacuum or void. The nonbeing of Taoism, Ch'an, and Zen, however, is not the $\mu\eta\ o\nu$ of Aristotle; rather, it designates a formless potential. Chinese "*wu*" and "*yu*" in their Taoist (not Ch'an) sense can be translated as "non" and "have," respectively, although they are often rendered in English as "non-being" and "being," respectively. They reflect the Chinese effort, consistent with the practice of nonduality, to avoid dilemmas posed by the dichotomy of being and *not*-being, a dichotomy explicitly rejected by the Buddha. If, however, the two terms constitute an unacceptable dichotomy, how is the dichotomy overcome? The answer is threefold.

First, a distinction is made between relative and absolute nonbeing. Second, absolute nonbeing is understood as indeterminate—neither determinate being, on the one hand, nor what is determined to be nothing at all, on the other. Nishitani speaks of "a field of indeterminateness or inexhaustible possibility" and recalls the Zen reference to "the inexhaustible storehouse with not a single thing in it."[27] The description of indeterminate being amounts to an Asian pre-ontology.

Third, absolute nonbeing is seen as the source of both determinate being and relative nonbeing. Kasulis, who finds these elements in both Taoist and Zen thought, illustrates them by reference to a temple bell.[28] The bell's metal casting represents being. The emptiness inside the casting represents relative nonbeing. Without the former, the bell can make no sound. Without the latter, the bell will have no ring, only a dull thud. Both are temporary and possess a determinate form. Rusting will eventually dissolve the casting, and both the casting and the

---

26. See Kaufman's *In the Beginning . . . Creativity* (Minneapolis, Minnesota: Augsberg Fortress, 2004).

27. Nishitani, 267.

28. Kasulis, *Zen Action/Zen Person*, 34–36.

space inside will return to the indeterminate space, which was their source. This indeterminate space represents absolute nonbeing.

The Taoist-Zen idea of the indeterminate as source is not, however, totally foreign to the West but appears in a different context in the existential-phenomenological concept of *Fundierung*, described as follows by Merleau-Ponty, who sometimes also refers to the indeterminate as the "ambiguous."

> The relation of reason to fact, or eternity to time, like that of reflection to the unreflective, of thought to language or of thought to perception is this two-way relationship that phenomenology has called *Fundierung*; the founding term, or originator—time, the unreflective, the fact, language, perception—is primary in the sense that the originated is presented as a determinate or explicit form of the originator . . . and yet the originator is not primary in the empiricist sense and the originated is not simply derived, since it is through the originated that the originated that the originator is made manifest.[29]

In relation to Taoism-Zen one can say that absolute nonbeing is a form of the originator and that both being and relative nonbeing parallel the originated. Let us see how this discussion facilitates an interpretation of the P-account of creation in Genesis.

The "without form and void" of Genesis 1.2 can be construed as nonbeing, understood as the pre-objective, indeterminate source of being, where being is understood as particular, formed, ordered things. If this construal is granted, then already God's being contains nonbeing since pre-objective matter, as part of the indeterminate and pre-objective life-world of Elohim, is part of God's being-in-the-world.

Nonbeing in God is, however, even more pervasive and more central than that. To see how this is so it is necessary to resort once again to phenomenology's practice of sweeping away preconceptions. In this case, the preconception obstructing a more adequate interpretation of Genesis is Philo of Alexander's notion, based on the *Timaeus* and subsequently taken for granted by the theologians and philosophers of Christendom, that in creating the world God was an architect who made use of eternal archtypes or forms, located within the divine mind.[30] It is part of what Jowett first and Pelikan more recently termed a "misunderstanding." As the mythical foundation of the logocentrism descried by deconstructionism, this preconception may be even more important than the one mentioned earlier. In the Hebraic account there is neither an explicit mention nor a veiled allusion to any such intelligible forms. The use by Elohim of Platonic-like forms is totally without textual support. How, then, can we understand Elohim's creative speech-act? The phenomenological concept of "intentionality" can help.

Intentionality is an alternative to the characterization of consciousness as consisting of ideas or representations. On the basis of phenomenological intuition

---

29.   Merleau-Ponty, 394. The concept of *Fundierung* applies to Polanyi's from-to relation, despite the fact that he never speaks of a to-from relation.

30.   Some scholars are of the view that, in his later writings, Plato abandoned the theory of ideas. See, for example, Anthony Kenny, *A Brief History of Western Philosophy* (Oxford: Blackwell Publishers, Inc., 1998), 49–55.

and description, which are part of the phenomenological method, phenomenology, like much of analytic philosophy, understands that consciousness is not a thing but an act of directedness toward an object, whether mental or material. Existential phenomenologists, however, take advantage of the distinction, drawn by the later Husserl, between active and operative intentionality. Whereas the former is conceived as a reflective, intellectual act directed toward a narrow, limited object, the latter is a pre-reflective intention directed toward a world. This spontaneous, naïve, ante-predicative, pre-positional, non-thetic[31] operative intentionality belongs to the phenomenological body, what Merleau-Ponty views as the body-as-subject rather than the usual body-as-object. Through it, we are primordially in coition with the life-world, in which, as beings-in-the-world, we are and which we are. In other words, we are in the life-world and the life-world is in us. It has similarities (naturalness, spontaneity, being beyond willing) with Zen's *mushin* (no-mind or without-thinking). For Merleau-Ponty in particular, perceiving, feeling, motility, and speaking are, first of all, partially differentiated modes of the subject's operative intentionality, which is incarnate in a body and world. This complex of "anonymous powers," always at work ahead of thought, constitutes a pre-personal subjectivity beneath personality and will. Moreover, whereas active intentionality is intermittent, operative intentionality is continuous, even (to some extent) during sleep. Finally, operative intentionality underlies and makes possible active intentionality. Indeed, there is no active intentionality without operative intentionality. The reverse is not true. (Again, Polanyi's focal and explicit awareness are intermittent, while the subsidiary and tacit awareness that make them possible are relatively continuous.)

Freed from the *Timaeus*-influenced model of Elohim as an architect gazing at eternal and wholly intelligible forms, we can now take seriously the statement of the text that God spoke the world into being. In the P-account of Genesis the creation takes the form of a speech-act, perhaps a kind of oral poetry. If God is a being-in-the-world and if God's speech is rooted in an operative intentionality, then Elohim's "Let there be" falls somewhere between the rather routine, form-guided craftsmanship of the Demiurge of the *Timaeus*, on the one hand, and the virtually accidental act of Kumokums, the aboriginal being of the Modocs, on the other.

Since the material world was merely a copy of preexisting and fixed patterns, wholly intelligible because primordially distinct and separated from obscuring matter, the Demiurge knew *essentially*—the only kind of knowing that counted for Plato—what the cosmos was going to be like before it was made. Given that for Plato the archetypal patterns are eternal, the world made by the Craftsman in using them was necessary, that is, it was impossible that he use any other patterns

---

31. The last three terms mean "prior to making judgments of affirmation or denial," "prior to taking a position on an issue," and "prior to making a dogmatic assertion," respectively (although the prefixes "pre" and "ante" can mean "prior to any reflection"). Perhaps "non" would be better so as to include the operative intendings that follow reflection. Sometimes, as in the learning of a martial art, unselfconscious action follows long periods of deliberate, self-conscious practice.

and thus impossible that the world could be *essentially* different. Moreover, any genuine novelty in the future is ruled out.

Alternatively, Kumokums accidentally created the world while playing in the mud. Utterly astonished by the outcome, he exclaimed, "I didn't know it would do that."[32] Elohim, by contrast, has more than Kumokums' idle curiosity and doodling hands. He has serious intentions.

If Elohim's intentions are not the merely operative ones of Kumokums, neither are they the purely active ones of the craftsman. To the extent that they were active, however, that is, to the extent that Elohim deliberately and self-consciously decided to create a world and a particular world, his intentions were subtended by operative ones. And there is no reason to assume that the active intentionality was constant. Because Elohim had no access to preexisting and fixed patterns, he/she did not know in advance of uttering it the outcome of "Let there be." Only subsequently, after looking at the actual creation, could God render the judgment, "It is very good." In the J-account God is even more radically different from the Neo-Platonic architect. There, the creation has been characterized by some biblical scholars as "experimental" and a process of "trial-and-error."[33]

One could, of course, raise the objection that even if Elohim had no fully explicit architectural blueprint, model, or pattern for creating, he/she must have had, unlike Kumokums, at least some vague image, visual or verbal, from which to make a beginning. The point is well taken. But then the question arises: from whence came the image or images? There is no basis for supposing that they were eternally present in God's mind. They, too, were an upsurge of Elohim's creativity, which, from the perspective of this chapter, is not in this respect unlike human creativity or even common speech.

Suppose that you and I are unselfconsciously engaged in a conversation about some topic of mutual interest. As you speak, I attend subsidiarily to your physiognomy, gestures, and words with an intention (probably operative) to understand you. I both retrotend (intending the past) the meaning of your previously uttered words while protending (intending the future) the direction in which your words seem to be headed. As I listen in this way, already a reply is prereflectively beginning to take shape, and when you pause, "my" words are launched toward you from the tip of my tongue without my having previewed them in advance. In other words, in replying to you, I have no experience whatsoever of visiting a storeroom (the memory?) of my mind and picking out, with the aid of some principle or explicit pattern, the appropriate words from the storeroom shelves, whereon they are neatly ordered (alphabetically?) and arranging those words with the aid of the same principle in order to construct an intelligent, cogent sentence or sentences. My words, in fact, did not originate in transparency and light at all but were an upsurge from some dark or hidden region of my self (whose "boundaries" and

---

32.   Alice Marriott and Carol Rachlin, *American Indian Mythology* (New York: New American Library, 1968), 45.

33.   Christian E. Hauer and William A. Young, *An Introduction to the Bible: A Journey into Three Worlds*, 4th ed. (Upper Saddle River, New Jersey: Prentice-Hall, 1986), 61–62.

resources are indeterminate and, therefore, are nonbeing-as-source) and issued from my mouth to be heard by *me* for the first time at the same moment that *you* also hear them for the first time. That is why sometimes I can be as surprised by what I say as you are. And yet, at least most of the time, the words that I let go into public space make sense to both of us because they are called forth in the first instance by the sense of the context, namely, the mutually intended conversation underway between us.

In the absence of the preconception, based on the *Timaeus*, of eternal archetypes, this account of speaking is applicable to the speech-act of Elohim in Genesis. To imagine Elohim as creating by writing rather than speaking would yield the same conclusion. Even if I deliberately take up a pen or sit at a computer with the active intention of writing, I can but invite the wished-for words to appear. The inviting itself may sometimes involve great effort, as when I search for a suitable rhyming word to complete the limerick I am composing. And when the summoned words do appear, we testify to their arrival from nowhere, from out of nothing, when we say, as we sometimes do, "The piece wrote itself in me." Its author was not, in the first instance, my reflective ego.

On this reading, then, the creation arose or is continuing to arise, from what is ultimately a background even to God. For Elohim, as for us, the whence of his or her words is unknown. And, as the story of Noah and the flood makes clear, the creation contained surprises, even for the creator. Thus, the matter from which creation was or is being made is indeterminate and the whence of God's intention in making it, given that fundamentally the intention is an operative one, is ultimately unknown, also.

This double indeterminacy infects and affects the whole of creation, depriving it of an *essential* intelligibility while allowing for the emergence in history of a *de facto*, partial, presumptive intelligibility. But this hidden, dark, indeterminate, prereflective background from which the relatively more determinate comes forth into light and into contingent, dependent being is precisely what Zen Buddhists mean by nonbeing-as-source.

The foregoing proposal addresses all of Nishitani's objections to Christendom's picture of God. Accordingly, God cannot be conceived simply as a personal being possessed of consciousness, intellect, and will. God's life, like that of humans, inheres fundamentally in a world constituted by an ultimately unspecifiable interrelatedness and interdependency. Thus, since both God and humans are beings-in-the-world, what Merleau-Ponty says of the human self applies also to the divine self, namely, that God "cannot say 'I' absolutely." This proposal also delivers those engaged in Buddhist-Christian dialogue from the stark contrast between an atheistic Nothingness, on the one hand, and the traditional God of Christendom, on the other.

Cosmology, Time, and History

To say that the entire difference between atheistic Buddhism and theistic Christianity has to do with the existence of God, however, is to say more than that the two religions differ in their conceptions of ultimate reality. Insofar as both religions possess a more or less coherent system of doctrines, commitment to Nothingness or to God also draws one to an interconnected range of other views. For both Nishitani and Abe, the God of Christendom is implicated in Western views of time and history. Nishitani says, "In the West, then, the problems of time and eternity, of the historical and the transhistorical, in the end always come to be combined with the concept of will."[34] With respect to Christianity, this means fundamentally the will of God. Already, however, we have seen a way of conceiving of God in terms of an operative intentionality at work beneath will. Thus, the retrieval of the ancient Hebrew God, carried out with the help of existential phenomenology, contains the possibility of resolving at least some, if not all, Buddhist and Christian differences concerning time. Before exploring these issues, however, let us address the matter of cosmology, which is part of the context in which, in this chapter, some of those time differences arise.

Traditionally, cosmology has never been of central importance to Christianity and has been even more peripheral to Buddhism. The creation story in Genesis was a relatively late addition to the text, and cosmology was of little importance to Judaism and Christianity until their contact with Islam. Dante helped draw attention to it in dramatic fashion in his *Divine Comedy*, and the Reformation elevated the importance of the Genesis account as part of its attempt to exorcise Aristotle from theology. Genesis became an urgent matter in the debates over evolution in the latter part of the nineteenth century and during virtually all of the twentieth century. In the 1950s and 1960s neoorthodox, existentialist, and ordinary language theologians tried, by means of their distinct methods, to secure for theology a refuge safe from scientific criticism by separating essential religious meaning from purely scientific claims and reading this distinction back into the biblical texts. The author or authors of Genesis was/were said to have had no cosmological intentions, only distinctly religious ones. This anachronistic approach, which was based ultimately on the very nonbiblical and Cartesian metaphysical dichotomy between inner and outer realities, which severely limited the scope of God's activity and which deprived religion of the support of a comprehensive worldview, was criticized by more traditional theologians, environmental thinkers, and process thinkers alike.

In Asia, Taoism was only marginally interested in cosmology, and while Buddhist schools—most notably Hua Yen—developed cosmological views, Zen did not. As Kasulis puts it, "Zen is interested not in the source of the universe, but in the source of our experience of the universe."[35] Such language, however, which distinguishes subject from object or scheme from reality or experience from the experienced, must be understood as merely heuristic. Such distinctions became largely discredited in Ch'an and Zen. Beyond that, if the Buddhist universe and the sentient beings inhabiting it are unoriginated (no beginning in time) and conditioned by *karma*, then, as Peter Hershock explains, "the typography of both

---

34. Nishitani, 236.
35. Kasulis, *Zen Action/Zen Person*, 37.

experience and the experienced are co-implicated with karma," a consideration which "fuzzies the line between the personal and the cosmic."[36]

Ch'an and Zen can, of course, take the tack of saying that cosmological concepts, along with other apparently metaphysical concepts, are simply skillful means to encourage practice and to lead to Nirvana. If, however, Buddhism generally continues to expand into the West and if the Kyoto School of Zen in particular wishes to engage both Christian theology and Western philosophy in dialogue, as it does, then one wonders if Buddhists can avoid eventually coming to grips with so-called modern science, whose telescopes and satellites probe the skies for clues to astral evolution and whose theories about the big bang and the steady state have become part of popular imagination.

A related difficulty is that Christianity has taken Genesis, whether read literally or otherwise, to be about an absolute beginning of the universe. By contrast, Buddhism denies such an absolute beginning. This was not always the case. One of the early discourses depicts the Buddha in conversation with Malunkyaputta:

> Accordingly, Malunkyaputta, bear always in mind what it is that I have not explained and what it is that I have explained. And what, Malunkyaputta, have I not explained? I have not explained, Malunkyaputta, that the world is eternal; I have not explained that the world is finite; I have not explained that the world is infinite . . .
>
> And why, Malunkyaputta, have I not explained this? Because, Malunkyaputta, this profits not, nor has to do with the fundamentals of religion, nor tends to aversion, absence of passion, cessation, quiescence, the supernatural faculties, supreme wisdom, and Nirvana.[37]

The Buddha's statement, however, is ambiguous with respect to an absolute beginning. It leaves open the possibility that he had knowledge or believed himself to have knowledge of these matters but chose not to disclose it for the reasons given.

Another early story says that by employing his super-normal powers the Buddha had sought to discover the origins of his *karma*. He reports having looked back through countless numbers of his previous incarnations but did not reach a beginning. This, too, is ambiguous. Hence, some Buddhist thinkers raised the question as to whether or not the beginning might not lie just beyond the point where the Buddha ceased to look. The position that prevailed in the end was that in the absence of any evidence for a beginning none should be assumed. The burden of proof, they might say, lies with the other side. The Buddhist view, then, appears to have evolved from silence or agnosticism to denial, but the claim contained in the denial, it should be pointed out, remains merely presumptive.[38]

36. Peter Hershock, an email message to Milton Scarborough, January 19, 1999.

37. E. A. Burtt, ed., *The Teaching of the Compassionate Buddha* (New York: New American Library, 1982), 35–36.

38. Such Buddhist terms as "bottomless," "infinite openness," "boundless," and "limitless" should be read as grounded in experience. In other words, "bottomless" should be understood as "So far, I have not experienced a bottom." That is why, for existential phenomenology, such terms and the statements containing them are presumptive.

Although it may be easier to read it as doing so, Genesis makes no explicit claim about an absolute beginning. Already, prior to God's creative acts, there were, as we have seen, water, earth, an abyss, wind, and Elohim, and there is no hint that these things themselves were the products of any previous act of creation. Is there then a beginning to God's project of meaningfully ordering the chaos? Such a reading certainly seems to be the case, but again the text does not say so explicitly. One could *speculate* that Elohim may have launched other, earlier projects, perhaps in other galaxies or clusters of galaxies and that Genesis is simply describing the most recent project or the one on this planet or in this galaxy. Although there may be value in such a purely speculative view, understood as the interpretation of the text of Genesis, it exhibits excessive exegesis or eisegesis. Process thought, for its part, takes the view that God is eternally involved in creating.

As for scientific cosmology, the prevailing theory is that of the big bang, which can be and has been read as supporting an absolute beginning. On the other hand, according to the oscillation theory, the big bang may be but the latest in an unending series of merely relative beginnings. In turn, these scientific views, as physicists Frederick Hoyle and Stephen Hawking admit, and as I have argued elsewhere, are themselves influenced in part by myths.[39]

The wisest move may be simply to adopt the humility implicit in Socrates' observation that none of us was there at the (alleged) beginning. Moreover, given that the earliest traditions in both Buddhism and Christianity were silent or agnostic about an absolute beginning, leaving the question open seems to be a legitimate position to take and one that eliminates or softens a potentially divisive issue between the two religions. All that Christianity need claim is that Genesis reveals God's fundamental intention in relation to the Creation, namely, to bring about a more meaningfully ordered world.

If cosmology and the question of absolute beginnings are peripheral to both Buddhism and Christianity, they lead, nevertheless, to more central concerns. One of those is history, which presumably, creation sets in motion. Buddhism rejects both traditional Christian and secular Western understandings of and emphasis on time and history. Christian orthodoxy is concerned with developing patterns in time, which explain things as they are now and intimate what they can or should become. Hence, it is oriented toward the future, wherein lies the goal of history, predetermined by the will of a transcendent God as part of a divine plan. History, then, is possessed of a beginning and an ending, is teleological or eschatological, linear, irreversible, and immanent.

To highlight the contrasts between their own view and that of Christianity, Buddhists sometimes speak of time as eternal, circular, non-teleological, non-eschatological, and reversible, but the situation is more complex. Both Abe and Nishitani hold that time is actually ambiguous. The ambiguity consists in time's having two aspects, one of which is historical, linear and irreversible, and the other of which is eternal, transhistorical, without beginning and ending, circular, and reversible. Of the two aspects, however, Buddhism's primary

39. Scarborough, *Myth and Modernity: Postcritical Reflections* (Albany, New York: State University of New York Press, 1994) 54–56.

concern is directed downward, as it were, toward history's eternal ground in Nothingness.

From the point of view of existential phenomenology, the Buddhist critique of Christian and Western views of time and history contains much that is cogent. Yet Christianity, like Buddhism, is not monolithic. It has had and presently contains a diversity of views. The Christianity characterized above is the Christianity of Christendom, Christianity as expressed in the Hellenistic world largely in Neo-Platonic philosophical categories and according to a style of thinking erected on a Greek foundation and, therefore, partaking of the "misunderstanding" already described. If such a "misunderstanding" is to be corrected, then Christianity's Hebraic roots must be retrieved. That Hebraic understandings may be closer to Buddhism is all the more reason to do so. Eschatology can provide an example.

Abe and Nishitani understand eschatology primarily as the end of history, and such a view of eschatology is, indeed, to be found in the Bible. Yet, the Bible contains a variety of views of the future, which developed, according to R. J. Weblowsky, when the preaching of the prophets of the Hebrew Bible about a golden age lying either in the past or the future,

> subsequently merged with Persian and Hellenistic influences and ideas. Prophecy gave way to apocalypse, and eschatological and messianic ideas of diverse kinds developed. As a result, alternative and even mutually exclusive ideas and beliefs existed side by side; only at a much later stage did theologians try to harmonize these into a coherent system.[40]

Yet, according to Weblowsky, the earlier use by the Hebrew prophets of such terms as *aharit* ("end") and *aharit yamim* ("end of days") originally referred to a more or less distant future (that is, to history) and not to the cosmic and final end of days.[41] It is this original and neglected possibility that Christian theologian Harvey Cox seeks to revive when he criticizes teleology and apocalypticism in favor of what he calls a "prophetic" view of history, according to which mankind is "a historical creature, called by a God who acted in historical events and who required him to take responsibility for himself and his world on the way to an open future."[42] Perhaps this is what Abe means by "open teleology."[43]

The foregoing, however, does not rule out the idea that God sets goals, but it does preclude history as teleological, if that means, as it apparently does for Abe, Nishitani, and much of traditional Christianity, that history moves forward toward a fixed and precise goal, predetermined by an utterly transcendent and totally independent God and imposed on history and creation from without or built into creation from an absolute beginning. Such a teleological view is also incompatible with the Hebrew God as retrieved with the help of existential

40. R. J. Zwi Weblowsky, "Eschatology," *The Encyclopedia of Religion*, 5, Mircea Eliade, ed. (New York: Macmillan Publishing Company, 1987), 150.

41. Ibid.

42. Harvey Cox, *On Not Leaving It To The Snake* (New York: The Macmillan Company, 1967), 41.

43. Abe, 61.

phenomenology in Chapter 2. Elohim or Yahweh is not omniscient. God's aims originate ultimately in an upsurge of creativity, not merely as a reflective application of eternal intelligibilities such as Plato's forms. Moreover, the resulting creation is not utterly intelligible and the future is neither revealed nor certain, even for Elohim, as the trial-and-error creation of the J-account, the multiple covenants (Noah, Moses, Abraham, and David), and the story of Noah's flood make clear.

Beyond that, the biblical God is not omnipotent and cannot absolutely guarantee the fulfillment of his or her aims and promises. Such plans as Elohim or Yahweh may make can fail and may have to be changed. As a being-in-the-world and a compassionate one, Elohim does not adopt a goal independently of all things but with and for all things in virtue of their being the context *in* which God's being is and which it *is*. The implementation of God's plans for history requires, as Chapter 3 makes clear, the involvement of humans as God's coworkers. For all these reasons, there is no teleology in the sense of an inevitable unfolding in time of a formal cause present at the beginning of time, and there is no inevitable progress.

Both Abe and Nishitani, along with Buddhism as a whole, reject also the Western view of time as linear. For Nishitani, time is both linear and circular. For Abe, it is neither linear nor circular. The merely apparent difference can be reconciled if, according to the Buddhist doctrine of the two truths, we understand Nishitani to be speaking conventional truth and Abe ultimate truth. Nishitani sees history as occurring on a ground of *sunyata*, producing a "stratified formation of simultaneous time systems."[44] While the stratum of history is characterized by such temporal distinctions as past, present, and future, the stratum of *sunyata* beneath it collects all time into an eternal present. This eternity lies *within* time rather than beyond it. Similarly, existential phenomenology describes stratified intentionalities, which apprehend and inaugurate time differentially. Active, reflective intentionality draws distinctions but is subtended by an operative, prereflective intentionality, which at every moment retrotends the past and protends the future from and into the always changing right now. For Merleau-Ponty, "eternity is the atmosphere of time," and this collection of all time into a present eternity is merely presumptive; it is never grasped as a plenitude.

To existential phenomenology, which, like Nishitani, regards time as ambiguous, Abe's rejection of both "linear" and "circular" is preferable. The terms are intended as a contrast, but they share much in common. It is not often noticed that both are linear: one is rectilinear ("linear") while the other is curvilinear ("circular"). Both are terms drawn from plane geometry, the use of which is characteristic of a Pythagorean approach to ontology. Euclidean geometry is a highly refined distillate of the rich, lived spaces of mind/bodily being-in-the-world, but it seems even more remote from and ultimately unsuitable for describing lived time: the thick, shifting, concrete, tension-filled and feeling-filled movements that constitute our lives. Both terms imply predictability since lines and circles can be generated and explained by reference to fixed formulas and precise definitions;

44. Nishitani, 219.

they can be extrapolated and plotted on a set of Cartesian coordinates. The same would be true of a spiral, one attempt to combine rectilinear and curvilinear forms. Yet the course of history, populated by people possessing some measure of freedom, cannot be so precisely predicted. Indeed, it is largely unpredictable and often surprising. The fixed formulas of Pythagoras contributed to the development of the fixed forms and essences of Plato and Aristotle, which were employed by the theologians of Christendom to develop a teleological view of history, which, when linked in the nineteenth century to Darwinian biology, gave rise to both secularized and Christian notions of inevitable progress.

More problematic for Christians in particular and Westerners generally is the view, held by both Abe and Nishitani, that time is reversible. First, there seems to be no traditional Buddhist doctrine of the reversibility of time. Perhaps the view arose as a result of encountering Western views on the subject. Second, there seems to be a logical problem with simultaneously rejecting a linear view of time and also holding to the reversibility of time since reversibility in its ordinary sense is also linear. Whether an automobile is moving straight ahead or straight backward, its movement is linear. Indeed, Abe grants that Buddhist reversibility is "different from the type of reversibility exhibited when we reverse a movie."[45] For Nishitani, the problem is partially resolved if we understand that reversibility applies not to time but to the "intersection" of time and eternity. He says that "there we have a field where irreversible time, without ceasing to be irreversible, becomes reversible."[46] He offers the following illustration:

> For example, in the case of the "original sin" that marks the "beginning" of history, it is said that in the sin of Adam all men have sinned simultaneously, and, conversely, that the sin of Adam is still at work in the home-ground of existence as the inheritance of all men.[47]

Most Westerners would interpret this as meaning merely that once a cause appeared, the effect became inevitable and that the effect continues in the present. On the other hand, the characterization of this inevitability as a simultaneity is understandable, given that the effect is found in the past and present and will be found in the future. In fact, "simultaneity," rather than "reversibility," is the term Nishitani almost always uses. It expresses the previously mentioned view of all time as being gathered into the present.

For Abe, on the other hand, "reversibility" seems to mean that from the present a past event can be changed. Perhaps Abe is simply claiming that the *meaning* of past events can change. Suppose, for example, in anger I shoot and kill another person. At that moment I take the other person to be evil and regard my own act as just. Later, however, I may come to understand my act as jealous, egoistic, and unjust and the victim as merely stupid. Or maybe the point is that the terrible karmic consequences created for me by the murder can be ameliorated by my present, political activity on behalf of gun control. Neither Westerner nor Christian

---

45. Abe, 190.
46. Nishitani, 270.
47. Ibid., 269.

is likely to disagree that such shifts of meaning or modification of consequences can and do occur. The latter seems little different from the position of the Hebrew prophet (*nabi*) who, unlike the seer (*ro'eh*), did not predict the future but warned of future doom in order to change people's present conduct so that they could avoid the full consequences of their past and present unfaithfulness to Yahweh.

Abe, however, rejects the distinction between fact and meaning so that it becomes the meaning-fact that changes. To be sure, there can be no absolute separation of meaning and event or value and fact, but the rejection of an absolute separation does not entail an absolute identity either. Here, Abe's view perhaps contains a trace of Zen Idealism. Neither the change of meaning nor the modification of karmic consequences can erase the fact that someone was killed and by me.

In sum, although existential phenomenology concurs with Zen's judgment as to the inadequacy of the concept of "irreversibility" alone to describe the ambiguities of time, I can detect no sufficient reason for using the term "reversibility" for the examples Abe gives, even when applied to history's bottomless depth and ground in Nothingness. Nothingness would seem ultimately to preclude both reversibility and irreversibility. There is, of course, an appropriate use of "reversibility" in relation to history, namely, when the trend of a decade, century, or generation (toward less violence, fewer diseases, less hunger and homelessness, or a higher standard of living, for example) turns around (more violence, homelessness, disease, and hunger).

The remaining difficulty has to do with Nishitani's criticism that history cannot ground itself, that is, provide its own meaning. According to Nishitani, Nietzsche's concept of eternal return was the "sledgehammer" that smashed the secular/scientific view of history as continuous and inevitable progress. Yet Nietzsche's own view leaves us with an unending round of meaningless events. In both cases history is merely immanent and groundless, that is, devoid of the resources for making sense of itself. Grounding history requires transcendence of history. Christianity purports to provide such a transcendent grounding in the form of a supernatural being, whose essence is will. Nishitani objects that to speak of a transcendent, supernatural, super-historical God who, nevertheless, acts immanently in history, is a contradiction since it requires God to be both transhistorical and historical at once.[48] Both Nishitani and Abe regard the Zen alternative to Christian transcendence to be the trans-decendence[49] of history by *sunyata*.

Several responses to this objection are possible. First, it should be noted, as previously indicated, that the objection is framed in terms of pairs of opposites whose meanings are mutually exclusive: transcendent-immanent, eternal-temporal, supernatural-natural, suprahistorical-historical. Neither these terms

---

48. See Thomas P. Kasulis, "Whence and Whither: Philosophical Reflections on Nishitani's View of History," in *The Religious Philosophy of Nishitani Keiji*, ed. Taitetsu Unno (Berkeley, California: Asian Humanities Press, 1989), 276.

49. This term is meant to provide a contrast with "transcendent," which is usually understood as pointing upward, above history, to God. "Transdecendence" points downward, beneath history, to nothingness.

nor their meanings expressed in other terms, however, are anywhere found in the biblical literature. Their provenance is Greek metaphysics. The style of thinking that they express and reinforce is a style of thinking that began entering Judaism and Christianity with the use of Platonic language in the Septuagint and that was more systematically employed by the author of the *Book of Wisdom*, Philo, and the Neo-Platonic theologians of Christianity. Such binaries reflect the contradictory positions of Parmenides and Heraclitus, which Plato attempted to resolve by conceiving of two metaphysically distinct worlds. As applied to the biblical worldview, they are part of the "misunderstanding" spoken of earlier in this chapter. Against such dualism, absorbed into the theology of Christendom, the Buddhist critique is an apt one.

Second, we have already seen that when the presupposition of Elohim's use of Platonic-like forms is eliminated, existential phenomenology can interpret Elohim as a being-in-the-world, situating God's existence in relation to a world *in* which God is and which God *is* primordially. Moreover, God's existence consists of the continuous operative intendings and intermittent active intendings with which God continues to create God's own self and the world. In this conception, God's concrete existence is beyond the abstract distinctions subsequently drawn by the theologians of Alexandria, Rome, and elsewhere. Consequently, as indicated in Chapter 2, the Hebraic God is neither simply transcendent nor immanent, neither simply eternal nor temporal. God is beyond the oppositions of Greek dualism. Relative to such oppositions, God as a being-in-the-world, is, like humans themselves, ambiguous and amphibian.

The history created and the history lived by such a God is, therefore, not the merely immanent history of secular or scientific thought. It is the richer and more ambiguous history that neo-orthodox and existentialist theologians tried unsuccessfully to express by speaking in dualistic terms of a transcendent salvation history (*Heilsgeschichte*) superimposed on a merely immanent history (*Historie*).

In this chapter, however, history is made even richer and more ambiguous by virtue of the claim that it arises from operative intentionalities. In other words, given the interpretation of God as ambiguous in nature, God can be said to contain aspects of both transcendence (an upward vector) and transdecendence (toward Nothingness, a downward vector). Such a God is capable of simultaneously grounding history in the mystery of the compassionate interconnectedness of all things, of providing reflective guidance grounded in a global pre-comprehension of the bottomless world, and functioning as a coworker and leader in the ongoing creation of a more meaningful order for all, which includes justice for all.

Although such a reading is obviously a contemporary one, it is not, for all that, completely alien to the West's roots in the past. The Hebrews themselves practiced a kind of nondualism, as Chapters 2 and 3 have already shown. British philosopher John MacMurray argues the point when he observes that ancient Hebrew culture

shows no need, in all of its classical literature, of a doctrine of immortality or of a belief in another world. The belief in immortality and in another world expresses, when it is essential to any religion, the incapacity to think of common experience religiously. If the world is thought contemplatively or pragmatically, there is no room in it for the satisfaction of the religious impulse. The religious demands of human nature, and the religious assertion to which they give rise require another world for their reference and for their realization. The achievement of the Hebrews lies in the fact that they retain, through the process of their development, the capacity to think *this* world religiously. In consequence, they feel no need to look beyond this world for a meaning and a significance which is not contained, at least potentially, in it . . .

There is hardly a trace in the Old Testament even of anything that could be construed as a hope of immortality, while the realization of the Kingdom of God in this world and in a thoroughly "this-world" sense, is what is looked for in its place. Old Testament religion is clearly about this world, and about nothing else.

. . . Indeed, the whole history of the Jews as described in the Old Testament, is the story of a continuous struggle to overcome the continuous tendency toward dualism.[50]

While this quote is helpful in rejecting a purely transcendent God, it remains dualistic, despite its explicit rejection of dualism. Chapter 2 of this volume, I believe, sketches a more genuinely nondualistic view of ancient Hebraic thought.

It is true, of course, that Hebraic literature contains no explicit statement of a principle of nonduality. Hebraic thought is, as we say, "pre-philosophical," although this description perhaps blinds us to its sophistication and subtlety. Implicit though it may be, however, the nondualism can be found there.

MacMurray sees nondualism not only in the absence of both another world and the doctrine of immortality but also in the complete integration of action and reflection, of the ideal and the actual, and of the spiritual and the material. Socially, it is expressed in the prophetic fight against kingship and against the establishment of a distinct priestly class. Laws concerning the year of Jubilee and prophetic utterances on behalf of the poor militate against the formation of an aristocracy of wealth. MacMurray sees it also in the conception of God as a fellow worker alongside the creatures rather than as an aloof, remote thinker.[51]

Victoria Scarborough notes that the Hebrew God "inhabits mountains, burns bushes, passes by in storms. He makes barren women fertile and raises their children from the dead. He wrestles with men and dislocates their hips. He talks to men and makes their faces shine."[52] These are dramatic ways of making the point, in language prior (both logically and historically) to the distinction between the metaphorical and the literal, that God is not separated from humans by a metaphysical gulf but has direct access to creation, to which from "the beginning" (because God is a being-in-the-world) there is an intimate relation beyond the dichotomies of internal and external, transcendent and immanent, eternal and temporal.

50. John MacMurray, *The Clue to History* (New York: Harper & Brothers Publishers, 1939), 30–31.

51. Ibid., 31–33.

52. Victoria Scarborough, "In Search of an Ancient God," a paper given at Shared Silence in Danville, Kentucky, March 14, 1999.

Paul's language in the New Testatment about spirit and flesh, which was mistakenly read by Neo-Platonic theologians as a metaphysical dualism of spirit and matter, is understood in its Hebraic context as an ethical-soteriological-ontological characterization. In anthropology, the Bible knows no Cartesian dualism. Even the apocalyptic picture of the Book of Revelations of a new heaven descending to earth makes no sense whatsoever if one presupposes with Plato an eternal, metaphysical dualism of worlds; the two could simply not be integrated. For the Hebrews, however, the picture represents the healing of longstanding tensions within a single, yet differentiated, reality.

In this Hebraic nondualism there is much promise for Buddhist-Christian dialogue. Heidegger says that "the greater a revolution is to be, the more profoundly must it plunge into its history."[53] To overcome the internalized "misunderstanding" lying at its core, Christianity and the West to which it played midwife, must return to and retrieve its root and source in ancient Hebraic thought. Retrievals of the past, of course, are inevitably selective. Any retrieval of ancient Hebrew culture must select against its patriarchy, its depiction of Yahweh as warlike, and its notion of a chosen people (if understood as exclusive). Indeed, such selectivity is consonant with a God who also learns from the past and for whom, consequently, revelation and God's own self develop in time.

Objections and Replies

In this chapter it has been my purpose neither to develop a full-blown theological doctrine or philosophical theory of God nor to try to resolve all the issues separating Buddhist nondualism from Christian or Western dualism. Rather, I have simply attempted to broaden Buddhist-Christian dialogue in particular and Asian-Western dialogue in general by proposing a different textual locus (Genesis) and, with the help of a different philosophical method (existential phenomenology), offering a different interpretation of the text, one that narrows the gap between Buddhist and traditional Christian (and perhaps Jewish and Muslim) understandings of ultimate reality by addressing Buddhism's objections (as represented by Nishitani and Abe) to God as a transcendent, personal will. All of these efforts, in turn, are ways of demonstrating the efficacy in the realm of metaphysics of a new form of nondualism.

Does the outcome of this effort favor one side or the other? Some might assert that I have gone more than halfway to meet Buddhism, perhaps too far. Almost certainly, even Buddhists who might accept the God depicted herein, if asked "From whence did everything come?" will still answer, "From Nothingness." And Western theists will object that if creation comes ultimately from Nothingness, then isn't Nothingness more fundamental than God? Is not God secondary? Doesn't Buddhism or Zen win?

---

53. Cited in Michael Levin, *The Body's Recollection of Being: Phenomenological Psychology and the Deconstruction of Nihilism* (London: Routledge & Kegan Paul, 1985), 72.

In principle, the answers to these critical questions are contained in several points already made. First, the questions are based on a misunderstanding. God and nonbeing (or God and nothingness) are not two separate realities, one of which can be superior to the other. They stand in a relation of essential interdependence. Elohim as God is an *ek-stase* (standing out from) from a field of *sunyata*, and the being and nonbeing, the existence and nonexistence that characterize the field of *sunyata* are, therefore, in God. God, like human "beings," is a being-in-the-world in which the world is ultimately nothingness, that is, interdependent and not finally specifiable, traceable, or explicable. If from habit Buddhism places greater emphasis on the aspect of nothingness or *sunyata* than on God or history, that is to say, if Buddhism is interested in the "root" of history rather than its "fruit" (the West's or Christianity's interest),[54] then perhaps it needs to be reminded of the Buddhist admonition to practice the "emptiness of emptiness" or the nothingness of nothingness. In other words, Buddhism itself may need to refrain from absolutizing and becoming attached to emptiness or nothingness.

Moreover, to ignore the historical aspect of time in favor of the emptiness aspect, from which the former arose, can be construed as a kind of *de facto* genetic reductionism, comparable in some ways to the claim that because humans arose from apes, they are nothing but apes. Emergent realities are, nevertheless, realities or, rather, parts of the greater reality. Provided that they are attuned and responsive to their ground and source, they are worthy of relative affirmation. Both root and fruit, as I previously insisted, are abstracted parts of the plant as a whole.

Second, and finally, negation of conventional dualities is the primary way Buddhism distinguishes itself from and offers a critique of Western ways of thinking, but negation is not, for Buddhism, the middle way. Recall from Chapter 1 that Nagarjuna rejects the earlier identification of emptiness with absolute truth. He equates emptiness with conventional truth (purged of *svabhava*) and the middle way. An increased emphasis on the importance of the middle way would reduce misunderstanding and eliminate the distance between the two religions.

A response in more Western terms to the questions raised above can be given by adverting to and adapting the language of Merleau-Ponty about *Fundierung*: "The originator (nothingness) is primary *in the sense* that the originated (being, creation, God) is presented as a determinate or explicit form of the originator" (emphasis and parentheses added). In the beginning (perhaps a continuing beginning) God steps forth from relative silence, inaction, purposelessness, and lack of identity to speak creation and history into being.

Yet Merleau-Ponty qualifies the first statement by a second: "The originator is *not* primary in the empiricist sense and the originated is not simply derived

---

54. Kasulis, "Whence and Whither," 278. In my own view, the difference of focus is explicable by the theory that every religion privileges a particular embodied act essential to its founding. This act becomes the paradigm for all activities of the religion. In Zen, that act would be *zazen*, seated meditation, from which place nothingness is most readily apprehended. For Christianity, by contrast, the paradigm would be Jesus' going about doing good, a way of being-in-the-world that emphasizes history.

since it is through the originated that the originator is made manifest" (emphasis added). In other words, it is only as God stepped forth to launch creation and history that the background or whence or nothingness of that step is disclosed.

The choice presented to Jews, Christians, and Muslims, then, is not God or nothingness but rather which of two versions of God accords with human experience and scriptural tradition: one conceived as absolute, infinite, transcendent, utterly independent and unresponsive or one whose absolute self is exploded and plunged primordially into the life-world with us, beyond the dichotomy of immanence and transcendence, to lead and share in the work of us all—*tikkun olam* (the repair or the healing of the whole of reality).

In order to stimulate class discussion I used to tell students that human minds do not exist. Immediately, they took me to be a materialist, and few of them raised objections. Then I would add the statement that human bodies do not exist either, except perhaps as corpses. What is real, I would affirm, are persons. Both minds and bodies are reified abstractions from persons. Recall that in Chapter 3 of this volume I argued that for some ancient Hebrews, both God and the people of Israel were but parts of a comprehensive reality, namely, the covenantal community.

By analogy to these two examples, I am inclined to say that God and the world, like the transcendent and the immanent, are parts of something more comprehensive and nondual, which I call "Reality." One consequence that could be drawn from this understanding is that partnership with God in repairing Reality, rather than worship of God, is more appropriate as one's fundamental attitude and orientation. This view accords with the biblical depiction of God as turned always toward the world and acting in and with it for the common good of all, God included.[55]

Some might classify this view as panentheism. If it is, it differs from the panentheisms of Whitehead and Hartshorne, for example, in a variety of ways. First, whereas I use "God" in only a single way, both Process philosophers speak of God in a double sense. Whitehead, for his part, distinguishes God's "primordial nature" (excluding the world) from God's "consequent nature" (including the world), while Hartshorne distinguishes God's "abstract essence" (excluding the world) from God's "concrete existence" or "the Supreme" (including the world). For Whitehead, both divine natures, at times, seem to be concrete; hence, their unity is not always readily apparent. For Hartshorne, one use of "God" is abstract, the other concrete, and the concrete includes the abstract. For Hartshorne, God's abstract essence (that which transcends the world) is necessarily externally related

---

55. Prior to the reforms of Vatican II, the priests at Roman Catholic altars stood with their backs to their congregations. Presumably, the priests were facing God. This orientation is consonant with the God of Christendom. If I were to imagine in an anthropomorphic way the Hebrew God, the picture would look something like this: I would be standing on a hill overlooking a city. God would be standing behind me (not visible). God's left hand would be placed on my left shoulder. God's right arm would be extended over my right shoulder and pointing to the town below. I would hear a barely audible whisper, saying, "Are you ready now? Let's go help out." Such a God could be the "father" of Jesus.

to and absolutely independent of the world, although the reverse is not true. Recall the donkey and post analogy.

For me, God and the world are fundamentally interdependent. For me, God is abstract relative to Reality as a whole, but the same is true of what is called "this world" (the binary opposite of "other world"). My use of "abstract" is based on etymology: "tract" is related to a word meaning "draw" and "ab" is "away" or "from." The concrete, then, is the larger, richer reality from which a lesser reality is abstracted or drawn out by creative simplification. Moreover, what is concrete or abstract is determined by context. A human individual is often understood as concrete but could also be regarded as abstract when considered completely apart from his or her dependent relations to the social and natural environment. The same is true for God or world; both can be regarded as abstract relative to Reality, or the All.

To articulate the relation of transcendence to immanence Jerry Gill borrows from William James a material (rather than a social) model, namely, an aquarium filled with water and shot through with light.[56] God, or the transcendent, is the light; water is the world in which God is immanent. What remains unclear, however, is whether or not Gill is assuming that light is a separate, independent reality that enters the water from outside.

My own view with respect to this model is that, as beings-in-the-world, our standpoint is inside an aquarium whose water is already illuminated. We have no experience of light's entering the aquarium; both light and water are experienced as always already together. Water and light are distinguishable but not separable from each other. Both are abstract relative to the aquarium as a whole.

And if God, also, is a being-in-the-world of the kind adumbrated earlier in this chapter, then there can be no dualism of transcendence and immanence. The aquarium metaphor is especially appropriate here, given that Buddhists sometimes speak of reality as a whole as an ocean, in which we are always already immersed.[57] In the end, Gill's view does seem to accord with my own when he says that the transcendent and the immanent "are fundamentally two foci of the same reality."[58]

Finally, for the two Process thinkers, God's primordial nature or abstract essence consists of purely intelligible ideas or patterns. It is here that one sees most clearly the shadow of Plato in the background. Both philosophers accept the form-matter, essence-existence, actual-potential, and eternal-temporal conceptions of Plato, Aristotle, and Christendom as the terms in which God must be understood to be a rational architect.

God and world, transcendent and immanent, heaven and earth, sacred and profane are quasi-abstractions (more or less abstract or concrete, depending upon the context). They are abstractions from the more comprehensive Reality, beyond simple unity or simple differentiation.

---

56. Gill, 21.

57. See, for example, Kenneth K. Tanaka, *Ocean: An Introduction to Jodo-Shinshu Buddhism in America* (Berkeley, California: Wisdom Ocean Publications, 1997).

58. Ibid., 47.

The foregoing solution to finding a middle way between God and nothingness remains vulnerable to other possible objections. One is that in my attempt to offer a novel interpretation of Genesis and to answer criticisms by Abe and Nishitani of the Christian or Western view of God or the transcendent, I have not translated biblical or theological language sufficiently thoroughly into categories purged of their mythological, anthropological, and personal residue. Many philosophers, if they are willing to speak of God at all, prefer to do so in an impersonal language allegedly freed of all anthropomorphism and myth.

First, let me address the matter of anthropomorphism. Earlier, I noted that both "linear" and "circular" (sometimes used of theories of time) refer to lines. In one case the lines are rectilinear; in the other, curvilinear, yet both are linear. "Linearity" does not name an abstraction but the more ambiguous, nondual, pre-objective phenomena that include the linear and the circular and are given to what Merleau-Ponty will call (in Chapter 8 of this volume) "naïve perception." Likewise, in Chapter 5 we saw Polanyi assert that Ptolemy's cosmology reflects an anthropocentrism of the senses while that of Copernicus displays an anthropocentrism of reason. Both are forms of anthropocentrism. In both instances, beneath the genuine but often superficial differences lies a common grounding or source.

Can we not say something similar for anthropomorphism as it relates to human language? Presumably, language developed from bodily gestures, to grunts and groans, to single words, to sentences. As language forms grew more stable and more universal, grammatical rules were abstracted from linguistic practice, and those rules eventually assumed control over much subsequent speaking, thinking, and writing. Anthropomorphic language was prominent in such narrative and originally oral forms as myth, saga, and legend. Allegedly non-anthropomorphic forms dominated language born of abstract thought, to which the advent of writing served as midwife. Hence, narrative speaks of Jane Doe, while discourse generates abstract definitions of the entire class of humans (rational animal). Perhaps, then, we can speak of an anthropomorphism of narrative and an anthropomorphism of discourse. They are not identical, yet beneath the differences both were created by humans and, in that sense, possess a human or anthropomorphic form. Both are human ways of understanding and articulating experience. Hence, anthropomorphism of some kind cannot be avoided.

Second, speaking of God as simply a grander version of a person is, of course, problematic. Too often it leads to runaway conceptions. God becomes both the sole cause and explanation of everything—the disaster of Hurricane Katrina, the spread of AIDS, and the winner of sporting events and television game shows. Faced with such abuses and trivializations, I understand the preference of some for impersonal conceptions exclusively and even for adopting Paul Tillich's proposed moratorium on the use of "God" for at least a century.[59]

Nevertheless, personal and impersonal terms are not inherently incompatible. For example, both are applied unproblematically to people. Humans consist of

59. Cited in John Shelby Spong, *Why Christianity Must Change or Die: A Bishop Speaks to Believers in Exile* (San Francisco, California: HarperSanFrancisco, 1998), 65.

realities studied by physics (atoms), chemistry (molecules), biology (cells, organs), psychology (affectivity), logic (rational thought). All of these constituents and disciplines require impersonal language. On the other hand, biography, autobiography, history, and ethics require personal terms. Yet persons are microcosmic wholes; they comprehend both their impersonal and personal aspects. If the impersonal constituents are eliminated, the person also vanishes.

With respect to God, one can say that God has personal aspects without claiming that God is a person. We speak this way of mammals when we say they are conscious and intelligent; possess tool-making skills; and exhibit humor, courage, and loyalty. If there is any legitimacy in speaking of God as a being-in-the-world (as I have done) and if the world contains persons (as it does), then God's nonessentialist form of being necessarily includes persons: the persons that inhabit the world are part of the being of God. In other words, a concrete and exhaustive account of God (if such were possible) would require both personal and impersonal language. Impersonal terms alone would not be adequate. If both intellectual maturity and spiritual growth involve an increasingly comprehensive self-identification with reality and if one conceives of the self as a person comprising both personal and impersonal aspects, then that self-identification is likely to be more profound and effective if reality (including God) is understood to include the personal as well as the impersonal.

It has been noted by scholars of religion that, generally speaking, whether ultimate reality is conceived as personal or impersonal has something to do with whether one is Asian or Western. Although Asian traditions do have personal gods, such traditions tend to favor impersonal language and an impersonal ultimate reality. Almost certainly, that fact is related to how Asians conceive of the self. Such traditions surely form a significant part of the sediment that both shapes experience and its reflective interpretation. The same is true for the Christian, Jewish, and Muslim West's preference, in most instances, for understanding ultimacy in personal terms.

Beyond that, whether one prefers personal or impersonal language for God can be explained, at least partially, in terms of a differential reliance upon the sources the West has identified over the centuries for knowledge about God. One such codification is the Wesleyan Quadrilateral, which identifies four such sources: (1) revelation (scripture), (2) reason (Plato, Aristotle), (3) tradition (papal encyclicals, councils of bishops, the theology of early church fathers), and (4) personal experience. Traditionally, Protestants have given greater weight than others to scripture. Catholics have favored reason and tradition. Mystics and religious liberals look primarily to experience. Philosophers tend to rely on reason and experience, variously defined.

Generally speaking, appealing to scripture and tradition when reflecting on the transcendent correlates with personal language, while relying more heavily on reason or meditative experience correlates with impersonal language. Most people, I suspect, are not purists but eclectic in their reflections and move easily enough back and forth between the two.

In any event, we do not have to choose between a nonsensical and runaway personalism, on the one hand, or a reductionistic, materialistic, or idealistic impersonalism, on the other. Both Einstein and philosophical theologian Paul Tillich attempted to point to a middle way by speaking, however awkwardly, of God as "superpersonal" or "suprapersonal," by which they meant to deny that God is a person (conceived as a grander version of a human being) but also to affirm that God has personal qualities as well as impersonal ones. One might, taking a cue from the Kyoto school of Zen, simply employ the phrase "impersonal *soku* personal," which is to say that God is personal in some respects and impersonal in others. Even better, one might say that with respect to this issue God is nondual—beyond the personal and impersonal.

Third, my reply with respect to myth is to say that mythic influence is inescapable. The mythic legacy of a culture forms part of the sediment tacitly carried forward toward the future and is, consequently, a Wordsworthian *a priori* (prior to reflection but not prior to experience) for all theoretical reflection. Myth courses through our veins. In Polanyian terms, it is part of the "from" of the from-to structure of all feats of knowing, described in Chapter 5. This implies that philosophy itself, while certainly not identical to myth, is inevitably myth-dependent. The same is true for science. Myth is part of what gives to abstract thought of whatever kind such intelligibility as it has and, at the same time, gives expression to the deeper significance that eludes rational categories. That is why Plato, despite his negative assessment of poetry, continued to appeal to myth at problematic junctures in his philosophy.

More recently, the dependency of philosophy on myth has been argued by several thinkers. One is Lawrence J. Hatab, whose *Myth and Philosophy: A Contest of Truths*, shows that early Greek philosophy is a rationalized form of the myths of Homer and Hesiod.[60] Another is Stephen Daniel, whose *Myth and Modern Philosophy* demonstrates the reliance on myth by seventeenth- and eighteenth-century philosophers, even those who were overtly hostile to myth.[61] Kevin Schilbrack's edited collection *Thinking Through Myths: Philosophical Perspectives* is yet another.

Elsewhere I have argued that essentialism and existentialism in philosophical anthropology, covering law and continuous series theories of explanation in the philosophy of science, steady state and big bang theories in scientific cosmology, and phenomenology of religion and history of religion in religious studies are myth-dependent, the former of each pair indebted more heavily to *Timaeus* and the latter to Genesis.[62] The list could easily be extended. Excluding the role played by myth in reflection is one more way in which the West, in typical fashion, ignores the root and focuses on the fruit of things.

Very likely, an as yet unspoken reason for rejecting personal, anthropomorphic, and mythic language and conceptions is that they are merely metaphorical, not literal. But this introduces yet another problematic dualism. The terms "literal" and "metaphorical" acquire their meanings in virtue of the way they differ

---

60. Lawrence J. Hatab, *Myth and Philosophy: A Contest of Truths* (LaSalle, Illinois: Open Court, 1990).

61. Stephen Daniel, *Myth and Modern Philosophy* (Philadelphia, Pennsylvania: Temple University Press, 1990).

62. Scarborough, *Myth and Modernity: Postcritical Reflections*, chapter 4.

from each other. But as several critics have pointed out, "literal" is a metaphor. William Poteat, for example, says:

> We have seen that there can be only a metaphorical hence no literal meaning of the word "literal," since, to be etymologically strict, a literal meaning would be "taken by the letters." But l.i.t.e.r.a.l. are not a word. If then I were to wish to say, "He was literally at the end of his rope," and mean and you took me to mean, "He was hanging by a strand of twisted hemp," this would occur only because you and I have tacitly agreed to take "literally" metaphorically, that is, to take the mere letters, l.i.t.e.r.a.l., as a word.[63]

If, then, all words, including literal ones, are metaphorical, then what happens to literal? And if there are no literal words, then can there be any metaphorical ones? Both terms make sense only insofar as they are included in a more ambiguous and prereflective meaning prior to their reflective differentiation, what Owen Barfield once called "figural" meaning. All of our utterances, then, have just the meaning they do. Their logical force and our personal backing of them are in no way diminished when others characterize them by means of the literal/metaphorical distinction.

When Plato taught the West that the only true objects of knowledge were the forms of the intelligible world, all of which were impersonal, non-anthropomorphic, and, presumably, non-mythic, he was also instructing the West in the inherent superiority of such language and conceptions. Freed from these arbitrary, Greek-based intellectual standards, perhaps we can now rely on options that more fully echo the fullness of our experience.

Concluding Comments

At a minimum, to speak of either God or Reality as a whole is to assert that neither the technical language of science nor our more commonsense vocabulary about tables, chairs, trees, mountains, mule deer, okra, computers, and people, etc., adequately describes or defines or alludes to all there is. This is known by the humblest athlete who, when asked how it feels to win the championship game, replies, "I can't begin to put it in words." Moreover, it is proverbial that experience collides with the limitations of language when lovers try to speak of their love. And then there are the women who, miraculously, give birth to children.

Reality outruns all our conceptualizations of it, however precise, subtle, or intricate. To say "world" is but to offer a relatively more adequate name for our experience of the relatively more determinate, definable, and phenomenal aspects of Reality. To say "God" is to speak humbly and haltingly of our experience of those more elusive, less determinate, less definable, and sublime dimensions of Reality, especially those that summon us to compassion, justice, courage, and

---

63. William H. Poteat, *Polanyian Meditations: In Search of a Post-Critical Logic* (Durham, North Carolina: Duke University Press, 1985), 163–164. For a longer treatment of the difficulties of the literal-metaphorical distinction see Scarborough, *Myth & Modernity*, 90–93.

creativity; that motivate, empower, comfort, and sustain us along life's journey; and that prompt surprising upsurges of gratitude and joy.

Our knowledge of Reality is inherently limited, a knowing-as-learning that everywhere relies on tacit clues and intimations. As we move (in reflection, meditation, or ecstasy) beyond the perceptible and relatively more palpable features of Reality to the less tangible ones, awareness increasingly involves imagination and/or feeling. Ultimately, all the faculties or powers of a person, integrated into a single organ of apprehension, open up to intimations that beckon to us from the farthest, most inclusive horizons of experience—a boundless experience beyond personal and impersonal, beyond presence and absence. These intimations invite us to take the risk of incorporating them into ourselves and to rely on them as clues to a more comprehensive, ambiguous, and nondual "entity" that some call "God" and I am calling "Reality" and to future meaningful adventures in the world, adventures whose outcomes we cannot presently divine. This integration of clues deriving from a variety of sources does not, as in traditional thought, culminate solely in luminous theoretical or doctrinal formulations but occurs primarily in an ongoing tacit integration of one's mindbodily-being-in-the-world.

It is an irony of the nondualistic position I have suggested that by distancing ourselves from Parmenides, Plato, Christendom, and the modern West, we may not only correct the "misunderstanding" of the Septuagint, the *Book of Wisdom*, Philo, and the Neo-Platonic church fathers and move closer to Buddhism, but also recover our own Hebraic, biblical roots.

So, let us see where we have arrived in our search for a middle way. One simple way to do that—perhaps overly simple—is by means of the table below.

EXTREME (abstract)	MIDDLE (concrete)	EXTREME (abstract)
from*	from-to	to
subsidiary*	subsidiary-focal	focal
tacit*	tacit-explicit	explicit
root*	plant, eco-system	fruit
prereflective*	being-in-the-world	reflective
blind faith	personal knowledge	reason
ignorance	learning (finite knowledge)	knowledge
body	person	mind
subjective	being-in-the-world	objective
inside	being-in-the-world	outside
operative intentions	intentionality	active intent
originator	existence	originated
relative	finite	absolute
living	learning	knowing
practice	practice-theory (learning)	theory
reductionism	emergentism	apexism
immanent	Reality	transcendent
nature, world	Reality	God
zig	middle	zag
Ur	journey	Canaan

It is important to understand that while the terms in the middle column represent in all instances the middle way between extremes, the extremes themselves are of varying provenance. "Root" and "fruit" are Asian binaries, but they also sometimes reflect distinctions drawn by the West. Asia privileges the former, the West the latter. "Tacit" and "explicit," on the other hand, are Western terms that, nevertheless, have Asian applications. Again, Asia prefers the "tacit," while the West prefers the "explicit." In fact, the first five pairs of extremes (the concepts, if not the terms denoted by asterisks) are found in both Asia and the West in some form. Asian preferences are expressed in the left-hand column; Western preferences are in the right-hand column. Hence, in those five cases, the middle or Middle Eastern or Hebraic lies between East and West. The remainder of the terms in the "extreme" columns express Western binary oppositions and/or dualisms. Hence for them, the middle or Hebraic column represents a Western middle way. Reductionism, apexism, and emergentism will be treated in the following chapter.

Notice the frequent hyphenations in the middle column. Such a device is necessary because there are too few ready-to-hand terms in either Asia or the West that express the appropriate middle way. Dualism, of course, would regard the extremes as concrete rather than as abstract, whereas I regard the extremes as abstract derivatives from the more inclusive and ambiguous middle.

By now, however, the reader may be asking, "So what? Are there implications, ramifications, actions, and practices that flow from such nondual ideas as have been adumbrated in the preceding pages?" I believe there are.

It may be worth remarking that the meanings of the following terms, although far from identical, do have significant affinities and/or overlappings: dependent co-orgination (from the Buddha), emptiness (from Nagarjuna); nothingness (from Zen); life-world, being-in-the-world, the pre-reflective, ambiguity, intentionality, body-as-subject (from existential phenomenology); the tacit dimension, body, the from- to structure of tacit knowing/doing (from Polyani); and convenant (from the ancient Hebrews).

Chapter 8
Setting Out In and Toward the Middle

Just stop dualism; stop suppositions of being and nonbeing, of neither being nor nonbeing.[1]

Pai-Chang

Live in the nowhere that you came from, even though you have an address here.[2]

Rumi

"Just do it."

Nike

Hopeful Signs?

On November 9, 2006, two days after mid-term elections in the United States, the Business Roundtable ran a full page announcement in *The New York Times*. The page was dominated by two images of Planet Earth, one colored red, the other blue. The caption beneath them read, "THE REAL WORLD IS NEITHER RED NOR BLUE." The ad called for the nation's leaders, both Republican and Democrat, to find a "common view" in order to serve the "common good." Two days earlier, at a victory announcement to his supporters, Connecticut Senator Joe Lieberman said that the outcome of the election proved the wisdom of his running "in the middle." Each of those last three words was uttered slowly and was punctuated by a jab in the air with his fist. Weeks later, incoming chairman of the House Energy and Commerce Committee, Rep. John Dingell, D-Michigan,

---

1. Thomas Cleary, trans., *Classics of Buddhism and Zen*, vol. 1 (Boston, Massachusetts: Shambala, 1997), 264.
2. Coleman Barks, John Moyne, A. J. Arberry, Reynold Nicholson, trans., *The Essential Rumi* (San Francisco, California: HarperSanFrancisco, 1995), 75.

announced that he intended to conduct the committee's business "in the middle."[3] The strategy of ignoring the center of the American body politic while whipping up the fervor of one political extreme had apparently failed after having been pursued successfully for 6 years by Karl Rove, President Bush's campaign advisor, worsening the polarization of the nation and the world. Former White House counsel Lanny Davis and author of *Scandal: How "Gotcha" Politics is Destroying America*, said in an NPR interview that the mid-term election was a "revolt of the center."[4] Even before the elections, Jim Wallis' *God's Politics: Why the Right Gets It Wrong and the Left Doesn't Get It* had become a bestseller. And a year after the elections Ron Brownstein's *Second Civil War: How Extreme Partisanship Has Paralyzed Washington and Polarized America* appeared.[5]

Beyond electoral politics, widely respected sociologist Robert Bellah revised the preface to his still-popular book *Habits of the Heart*. In speaking of the place of religion in a democratic society, he said that he would "try to steer a sometimes difficult course between" the extremes of the "Enlightenment fundamentalists," who want no religion in public discourse, and "religious fundamentalists," who hold that there is only one true view, namely, a religious one. On a less serious note, Cornell University professor Brian Wansink, author of *Mindless Eating, Why We Eat More than We Think We Eat*, stated that people would lose more weight if they obsessed about it less. The answer lies, he says, "not in counting calories, not in legislating, but in the middle range of what we can do by changing some of our habits."[6]

Such references to the center, the middle, the in-between seem omnipresent these days. Everywhere they gush from mouths and leap up from the written page. Much of the appeal of the Obama campaign stems from his hope to unify America. Perhaps this moment offers an opening for moderation, for common sense, for a middle way, a way for which so many Americans and people around the globe appear to be longing. Is it, in fact, the beginning of a major shift in orientation? Or is it but a momentary enthusiasm?

Obstacles

The Flatland[7] of Plane Geometry

There are, at the very least, imaginative and conceptual obstacles to the fulfillment of such hopes. I shall mention three that are related to the concerns of this chapter. First, while the common ground that politicians and others seek

---

3. *The Lexington Herald*, November 27, 2006, A4.

4. The interview was broadcast on November 25, 2006.

5. Ronald Brownstein, *The Second Civil War: How Extreme Partisanship Has Paralyzed Washington and Polarized America* (New York: Penguin Group, 2007).

6. Reported by Michael Hill, *The Lexington Herald*, November 6, 2006.

7. Edwin A. Abbott, *Flatland: A Romance of Many Dimensions* (Boston, Massachusetts: Little, Brown and Company, 1899).

is certainly a good thing and perhaps never so desperately needed as now, the image "common ground" has its limitations. For many in the West, the idea of the middle is conceived as lying, along with the extremes, on a single plane, as it were. This is perhaps due in no small measure to the fact that "ground" suggests imaginatively a flat surface on which Boolean circles (two overlapping circles that create three distinct areas) could be drawn to indicate precisely the boundaries separating what is common, neutral, between, or middle (in the Western sense), on the one hand, from the differences at the extremes, on the other. In imagination, we remain a largely visualistic culture and are heavily indebted, as noted in Chapter 5, to geometry, even for our conceptions of lived space.

The concept of grounding or groundedness, by contrast, connotes a dimension of depth and perhaps of pilings or roots going downward and disappearing from sight. Common ground contains only what is common and excludes what is not common. Common grounding includes both what is common and what is not common because both are encompassed by its more comprehensive reality. It conjures up a sense of a larger reality and deeper unity that does not ignore disagreements at the surface but, nevertheless, softens them, renders them relative, and devalues them somewhat by understanding them as belonging to a larger, prior, unitary, and more significant context. It more readily enables adversaries to grasp the basic reality to which they both belong and to understand that this reality takes precedence over differences and mere similarities, which are less fundamental.

Given flatland as an imaginative context for conceiving the middle or the common and given overlapping Boolean circles as a governing image for that flatland, there is no reason to value the central area over those at its left or right. Even if one imposes upon this image the notion that the left and right areas represent extremes that oppose each other, the middle can be grasped only as a kind of balance or tension between opposites or as a distinct domain in tension with both extremes. For resolving conflicts conceived in this way, one is left with altruism (one person gives up his or her interests entirely in favor of the other), compromise (those at both extremes give up something), or a protracted tug-of-war in which each side is always digging in its heels and pulling in the opposite direction from the other. None of these options is very satisfactory, even initially, and none is likely to constitute an enduring solution.

By contrast to the West, Asian and Hebraic nondualisms require (if we stick to geometric analogies) an additional plane, as it were, a dimension of depth, a nothingness, or a more ambiguous and comprehensive whole from which the extremes and the middle (in the Western sense) are abstractions rather than discrete, concrete realities. In such a conception, the superior value of the concrete, comprehensive whole is immediately grasped. The bearing of such a conception on reality is grasped, however, only by actually experiencing that greater, deeper, or prior reality from which the sometimes helpful but always somewhat misleading oppositions and commonalities are drawn by abstract thought. When that greater reality is experienced, differences or distinctions will not vanish altogether and neither will disagreements. Yet the tension and polarization will be reduced as the overriding significance of that hitherto unnoticed unity is disclosed. At the very least, it gives people the requisite reason, cause, or motive to persist in the dialogue that seeks to bring people together. Moreover, it makes sense of two lessons journalist William Raspberry says he has learned: (1) that with respect to significant public controversies we secretly believe both sides and (2) that others can disagree with us without being either scoundrels or fools.[8] Absent the experience of such a deeper unity, the efforts to effect harmony or agreement on the basis of the middle, the between, and the common ground of flatland too readily become enervated and ineffective. For Asia, the middle is this deeper reality.

Process thinker John Cobb makes a similar point by offering an illustration of what he terms "creative transformation." He imagines that a young man of conservative moral principles becomes part of a group whose attitude to morality is more "carefree and casual." How is the young man to negotiate his way forward within the group in the light of such differences? Cobb describes five possibilities.

First, he can simply block out any consideration of the differences, ignoring them and postponing indefinitely a decision about what his stance ought to be. Cobb calls this option "anesthesia." Second, after reflection, he may make the decision to stick to his guns, to persist in holding onto his principles. Third, he may abandon his principles and take up the attitude and behavior of his new friends. Fourth, he may compromise, acting according to his principles in designated situations while ignoring them on other occasions. Finally, Cobb describes what, for him, is the preferred option, namely, "creative transformation":

> He may perceive that both moral rigor and carefree spontaneity have their value from a larger perspective that understands and appreciates both. This larger perspective will be enriched by their inclusion and the quality of experience that embodies it will be stronger or more intense. In this case something genuinely new has been introduced.
>
> What before were mutually exclusive elements are now contrasts that jointly contribute to the whole. He has not abandoned his own past convictions, but by being set into a new and larger context these convictions are creatively transformed.[9]

Cobb's solution is distinctively Western because of its emphasis on novelty, creativity, and a prospective orientation. The more comprehensive reality and perspective were not previously there, but were created. Buddhist nonduality, as indicated earlier, points to an always already existing unity grounded in nothingness. Yet these two approaches need not be construed as an Asian-Western dualism, since the possibility of creating Cobb's larger perspective arises from and depends upon prior intimations arising from the nothingness (Polanyi's tacit dimension) of an even more comprehensive interdependence, of which Buddhism speaks. In either case, a realistic hope for finding a middle way depends upon experiencing a more comprehensive and unifying context. Such experiencing, in turn, requires a new way of seeing. We will address that new way shortly.

A slightly different example is more Asian in nature because it appeals to a comprehensive reality already there, although belatedly recognized. In Chapter 1

---

8.   William Respberry, convocation lecture at Centre College, February 8, 2007.
9.   John B. Cobb, Jr. and David Ray Griffin, *Process Theology: An Introductory Exposition* (Philadelphia, Pennsylvania: The Westminster Press, 1976), 99–100.

I suggested that in the segregated American South of the past, African Americans were regarded by many whites as virtually a separate species. The extremely negative consequences of such a dualism led many blacks to flee to the urban centers of the North. In the 1970s, however, once legal segregation had been eliminated, a trickle of African Americans began returning to the South. By the 1990s, the trickle had swollen to a river of millions. Why did they return to a place inextricably linked in their memories to oppression, knowing that it was likely that merely the *de jure* segregation had disappeared, not the *de facto* one?

One way to answer that question is to list the values Southern blacks shared in common with Southern whites. Scholars have identified some of them, including a preference for fried food, an attachment to the land, manners, morals, folk beliefs, material culture, core values (religion and morality), saying grace before meals, blended musical forms, church attendance, family, and common historical experiences. On this view, Southern blacks returned because they realized that, quantitatively, they had more in common with Southern whites than with Northern whites; the two races shared common ground.

Yet the enumeration of common values is merely the product of a reflection that seeks to explain rationally the persistent and ineradicable tug of a whole, of a place that is greater than the sum of its features—the South. It is an explanation in the *lingua franca* of flatland. Put simply, the more fundamental "reason" for their return is that Southern blacks living in the North realized they were Southerners. Oscar-winning film star Morgan Freeman, who could live anywhere in the world, returned to live in Clarksdale, Mississippi (pop. 22,000). He said, "I have deep genetic roots in Mississippi."[10] The South, then, is the already-lived, encompassing whole that links blacks and whites to each other beyond their differences or enumerated commonalities. In Polanyian terms, this tacitly lived whole is what both prompted and guided the explicitation of specifically shared values. The dichotomy of black vs. white, then, is but an abstraction from that more comprehensive reality.

W. J. Cash could have been illustrating Buddhist *sunyata* when he said that in the South, "Negro entered into white man as profoundly as white man entered into Negro." Ralph Ellison echoed that observation when he stated that "you can't be Southern without being black and you can't be a black Southerner without being white."[11]

Root and Fruit: East, West, and Middle East

The first obstacle to nonduality was in conceiving the problem in terms of a single plane. We might call it the "horizontal" problem. Once a second plane is acknowledged, however, another problem can arise, namely, excessively privileging one plane over the other. This privileging is the "vertical" problem.

10.   Morgan Freeman, quoted in Nancy Griffin, "Home Again" *AARP The Magazine*, November/December 2007, 60.

11.   James Cobb, *Away Down South: A History of Southern Identity* (New York: Oxford University Press, 2005), 288.

Several times I have called attention to the distinction drawn by Buddhists between "root and branch" or "root and fruit." While Buddhism does not explicitly deny the existence of the fruit, the strong and persistent emphasis on the former obscures and devaluates the latter. The West, by contrast, privileges the branch or fruit and either dismisses the root as insignificant or refuses to acknowledge it all.

In ontology, for example, Buddhism points unrelentingly and almost exclusively to the emptiness or nothingness that grounds all beings. While the West often alleges that beings (human or otherwise) are independent, persisting realities with fixed essences, in fact, say Buddhists, they appear from out of nothing, change, and vanish back into nothing. Buddhism's critique is, in my view, correct and appropriate. Yet Buddhism says little more. By almost exclusively emphasizing source or ground, Buddhism pays too little attention to emergent realities, for example, biological differences or differences across the evolution of the inorganic into the organic. Its focus is on the lowest common ontological denominator.

To be sure, traditional Buddhist cosmology does conceive of six realms—those of the devils, hungry ghosts, animals, humans, deities, cosmic Buddhas—that are ordered hierarchically in terms of karma, but in the end the differences among them are not permanent or ultimately real. Karma, too, changes and disappears. Some other Buddhists understand such a cosmology to be nothing more than a mythology to be used as a skillful means (*upaya*) for encouraging devotees along the path.

Hua-Yen Buddhism, from which other Buddhist schools often borrowed their cosmology, would say, for example, that a human is no more significant than a fruit fly in the sense that both contribute equally to the totality of interacting causes. Such a perspective brings Buddhism close to radical ecologists in the West. It explains, at least partially, why Buddhism, faced with the question raised in Chapter 1 about whether to save—if it is possible to save only one—a drowning puppy or a drowning human infant, has no answer but must turn for one to Confucian ethics.

The West, on the other hand, has constructed atop the shifting and ambiguous phenomena of perceptual experience the constant, well-defined, theoretical object—the cube with six square faces of equal size, the triangle whose interior angles total 180 degrees—and has either chosen to forget the origin of those theoretical objects or presumed to find them hidden in or beneath perception. The West has also often espoused an ontological hierarchy in which humans are not only ensconced at the top, but, as a consequence, are regarded as entitled to treat all beings lower in the hierarchy as having no intrinsic value. Such value as lower beings may have is derived solely from their utility to humans.

In such a hierarchy, nature is but raw material for self-centered human projects. Hillsides may be strip-mined for coal, nature preserves may be exploited for oil, waters may be fished to extinction, manatees may be killed by recreational boaters, rivers may be turned toxic by industrial waste, and air may be polluted by the emission of carbon dioxide. Only relatively recently have environmentalists and ecologists challenged such a stance.

On the basis of the view that people alone possess immortal souls, rationality, moral sensibility, or the capacity to make tools, humans were separated by an ontological gulf from all lower beings. Even the theory of evolution can be hijacked by proponents of the "anthropic principle" to give apparent scientific credibility to human egotism by depicting a primordial slime evolving from the start in the direction of *homo sapiens* as the apex and final goal of cosmic evolution. We might say, then, that whereas in the main the West holds both in theory and practice to a kind of apexism, in practice Buddhism holds to a kind of reductionism.

Epistemologically, the West has, for the most part, made its intellectual home at one extreme, emphasizing autonomous, positive reason, whether in contemplation of theories, speculative construction of theories, or theoretical analysis. Often it has taken for granted that universal, absolute truth exists and can be precisely defined and otherwise expressed unproblematically in human language.

By contrast, India, according to Nakamura, has a preference for the negative and is generally extremist.[12] East Asia in general has been reticent in its development and use of abstractions, but Taoism and Zen Buddhism have been especially skeptical of language, not only for its inherent inadequacy to speak of the most significant matters in life but also for its role in artificially fragmenting the unity of reality and for creating an artificial, conceptual barrier between the knower and the known. They urge a more spontaneous (Taoism) or disciplined but unreflective activity (Zen) in relation to the world. Ironically, Zen texts rail frequently against texts, study, thinking, scholarship, and words because all of them are alleged to lead adepts astray from the true path and delay the arrival of *nirvana*. New Rinzai, the form of Zen to which D. T. Suzuki introduced America, constantly emphasized the contrast between intuition and thinking and encouraged the former as a universal human capacity that is superior to rationality.

Finally, although Nagarjuna himself is clear that the two truths of which he speaks, the absolute and the conventional, are absolutely identical, some Buddhists have privileged the former over the latter. Given that absolute truth is often expressed in negative terms, such an emphasis fosters nihilism. Moreover, Rinzai Zen's practice of presenting Zen teaching from the perspective of a non-enlightened person, while intended to provoke an existential crisis (the "great doubt" leading to the "great death"), also creates an anti-intellectualist, nihilistic image of the religion for outsiders. Indeed, Buddhism is sometimes compared to the skeptical tradition in the West.

Steven Laycock, for example, identifies the middle way with the great doubt, which for him is not simply a matter of negation but a state of "equipoise" in which there is neither affirmation nor denial.[13] For Hakuin, however, the Zen master who introduced the idea of the great doubt and incorporated it into the training program he devised for Rinzai Zen, the great doubt was merely a first step toward enlightenment. Describing his own experience of such doubt, he says, "It was as though I were frozen solid in the midst of an ice sheet extending tens of

---

12.   Hajime Nakamura, *Ways of Thinking of Eastern Peoples: India, China, Tibet, Japan*, ed. and rev. Philip P. Wiener (Honolulu: University of Hawaii Press, 1968), 142.

13.   Steven W. Laycock, *Mind as Mirror and the Mirroring of Mind: Buddhist Reflections on Western Phenomenology* (Albany: State University of New York Press, 1994), 150.

thousands of miles . . . I was out of my mind."[14] Such a disturbed state is clearly not liberation, equipoise, or the middle way.

The second step, surpassing and terminating the great doubt, was the great death, understood as the final dissolution of the ego. No more than the great doubt is this great death characterized by the cessation of affirmation and denial or by nihilistically turning the Buddha's "right view" into "no views,"[15] as Laycock does, but rather by the Buddha's nonattachment to views. The middle way does involve equipoise, but that means that one has overcome addiction to views, obsession with theories, and reliance upon post-experiential constructions of reality as a way of sustaining egoism. It means that one's life remains grounded and unshakable in the midst of life's exigencies, including the affirmations and denials that life necessarily entails. It does not prohibit views and theories per se.

In Chapter 5 I proposed a Western epistemological (and non-nihilistic) middle way based on the from-to structure of all feats of knowing, from the most mundane to the most sublime and adventurous. The from-pole (subsidiary awareness or the tacit dimension) that underlies all such acts of knowing-as-learning corresponds to the epistemological features of Nagarjuna's emptiness or Zen Nothingness. The to-pole (focal or explicit awareness) reflects the goal, object, or universal intent of those same acts.

A consequence of this middle way is that while acknowledging the limitations of language and thought, one is, nevertheless, free to make full use of rational analysis for human projects, including the organization, planning, and implementation of acts of compassion on a larger scale than the one-to-one interchanges that ancient Buddhist texts most often describe. Thus, compassion can be brought to bear not only on localized and particular problems of individuals but also on structural problems confronting society.

With respect to ontology, a Western middle way is emergentism, which rejects the extremes of reductionism, on the one hand, and apexism, on the other. Like, apexism, emergentism acknowledges a hierarchy among the outcomes of the evolutionary process. Unlike apexism, however, it rejects the concept of discrete levels within the hierarchy; there are no absolute gaps among levels. For emergentism, it is true that the higher or more advanced level has emerged from lower levels, but it is also true that the lower levels have been incorporated into the higher levels. "Higher" and "lower" are interdependent (*sunya*).

The argument against reductionism is based on the different laws operating at each level and the impossibility of predicting the higher from the lower ones. For Michael Polanyi, the particulars of any level are governed by two sets of laws, both the set that operates at the level in question and the set that operates at the next higher level. The latter cannot be deduced from the former, and this fact is itself an indication of an emergence.

---

14. Philip B. Yampolsky, trans. *The Zen Master Hakuin: Selected Writings* (New York: Columbia University Press, 1971), 118. Cited in T. P. Kasulis, *Zen Action/Zen Person* (Honolulu: University of Hawaii Press, 1989), 107.

15. Laycock, 107.

A lawn mower, for example, is constructed of a certain material, steel, let's say. Steel has certain properties—ductility, conductivity, melting point, tensile strength, etc. These properties or particulars, which obey the laws of physics and chemistry, specify the natural boundary conditions within which engineers set the artificial boundaries required by the design of the lawn mower. Hence the laws of physics and chemistry, which contain no principles of engineering, cannot explain the operation of the lawn mower.

Moreover, Polanyi would note that the most thorough scrutiny of the physico-chemical particulars of the lawn mower cannot identify the machine as a lawn mower or even as a machine. "Machine" and "lawn mower" are not terms in the technical vocabulary of physics and chemistry. The proper functioning of the lawn mower is explained by the principles of engineering, which are imposed by engineers on top of the laws of physics and chemistry and within the boundary conditions of the material used in making the mower. The laws of physics and chemistry can, however, explain why the lawn mower breaks down. For example, if the heat generated by mowing exceeds the melting point of steel, the parts of the machine will melt, become deformed, and cease to function properly.

The same logic is at work in biological organisms. Polanyi argues that the human form takes shape according to the laws of morphologenesis, which are studied by embryology. Nutrition, growth, and reproduction (vegetative functions) obey the laws of physiology, as do sensori-motor activities. Conscious behavior, intellectual operations, and moral behavior are the provinces of ethology, psychology, and ethics, respectively. These operations, laws, and disciplines represent an emergent hierarchy that is not deducible from the laws governing the operations of the lower levels.[16]

On the other hand, emergentism agrees with Buddhist *sunyata* (emptiness) or *mu* (nothingness) that all particulars are valuable, all preach *dharma* or display the Buddha nature. It disagrees with them, however, by saying that not all particulars are equally valuable, certainly not at every place and time. Thus, emergentism, like apexism, would, in most instances, support saving the drowning child rather than the dog.

Emergentism, then, is in harmony with Hebraic pre-ontology, according to which all things made by Elohim are "very good," yet humans, as the final and highest creation possess emergent properties, namely, the "image" of God. Hence emergentism is what I am calling a "Middle Eastern" ontological middle way between the theoretical reductionism of Hua Yen Buddhism and the practical reductionism of Zen, on the one hand, and the Apexism of the modern West, on the other.

Habits

The third obstacle, which is related to the first two, is that dualistic language is a long-established cultural tradition, and dualistic thinking is a deeply rooted intellectual habit. When we attempt to speak or think about experience, we reach

---

16. My position is that the lower levels are taken up into the higher levels. Polanyi's position on this is not clear.

for the language patterns that are ready-to-hand, and they are almost always dualistic. The result is that we lose our grip on the nondual experience of reality, and, consequently, the tendency to acritical reliance on dualistic language and concepts is reinforced.

In the West, for example, the hopeful and inspiring statement "THE REAL WORLD IS NEITHER RED NOR BLUE" will likely be read as meaning that the world is neither wholly red nor wholly blue and, therefore, Republicans and Democrats must be understood either as in a tug-of-war in which neither side has a critical advantage or as sharing a few political positions in common despite their many differences.

Asian thinkers, however, will adopt a more profound interpretation, recognizing immediately that "THE REAL WORLD IS NEITHER RED NOR BLUE" exhibits the form of the fourth lemma of Nagarjuna's tetralemma and points, however inadequately, to a nondual reality in which both red and blue are enveloped. What is required, then, is the elimination of habits of distortion (Buddhists call them "*samskaras*") so that the greater reality can be experienced.

Habits, of course, are established initially by human action introducing change. That fact implies that habits are not inherent, natural, fixed, or inevitable but are susceptible to further change by further and alternative human action. We must create new habits of perceiving, thinking, and acting that mitigate the bifurcation of experienced reality at the prompting of binary oppositions. In other words, we must undergo a transformation, the self-transformation of self. But before new habits can be established, we must take notice of the greater reality beyond binary oppositions, that is, we must experience the emptiness, nothingness, or the more comprehensive whole from which such oppositions are derived. We must become convinced that such reality exists.

Looking and Seeing

Imagine that blossoms begin to appear on cherry trees in both Tokyo and at the tidal basin in Washington, D.C. The editor of an American magazine hires a photographer to take a photo of one of the Washington trees for publication in the next issue. The photographer is well-known for employing a particular method in his work. He arrives at the tidal basin, quickly selects a particular tree, and begins to unload his equipment—tripods, camera bodies, lenses, filters, lights, etc. Then he sets about rendering the tree in accordance with his own distinctive and recognizable style.

The session proceeds in a routine sequence through the high-angle shot; the low-angle shot; the eye-level shot; the wide-angle shot; the telephoto shot; shots with polarizing filters and various colored filters; and shots that are back-lit, side-lit, and front-lit. Later in the day, the photographer will print the several hundred exposures made with multiple rolls of film and select three or four images to submit to the editor.

The editor of a Tokyo magazine also engages the services of a photographer, who arrives at a tree bursting with fresh blossoms and who sits down before it, quietly contemplating the tree for a time. Then, she moves to another spot, sits again, and resumes drinking in the scene from the new location. Over the course of an hour or so she manages to circle the tree in this fashion. Finally, she returns to one of the previous spots, raises her camera, makes a single exposure, and then leaves.[17] Her approach also is an established one.

These two stories illustrate the difference between what Zen master Joshu Sasaki Roshi calls "looking" and "seeing," which he distinguishes in the following way.

> If we continue to live our lives assuming that our apparent individual identity is a fixed constant, if we continue on with this false assumption, then we will find that our relationships are not fulfilling. But, as you know, most people do indeed live assuming their apparent individuality is a fixed constant; they do not surrender themselves profoundly at all. So in the situation of the flower, they never see the flower; they're always only looking at flowers. And on this basis they say, "Oh, the flowers are lovely. I love flowers, etc." and they deny themselves union with the flower.[18]

The American photographer merely looks at the tree; he never sees it. His is an egoistic approach that focuses on the distinctive cluster of techniques he brings to the tree and on efficiently imposing his signature photographic style upon the tree. The tree is given little or no voice in the outcome of the encounter. In some sense, the photographer (like Plato's Craftsman but unlike Elohim) knows in advance what the photo should look like.

By contrast, the Japanese photographer unites with the tree and opens herself up to guidance from the tree, allowing the tree, as it were, to show her the vantage point from which it can most fully disclose itself. Neither photographer is omniscient. Both bring with them to the trees the basic wherewithal necessary to perceive and photograph them. Both exhibit the from-to structure of finite knowing/learning. Both see from a particular location, with the aid of a sedimented and tacit dimension.

They differ, however, in that looking involves a dualism of subject (photographer) and object (tree), an understanding that is reflected in the American photographer's actions. His approach to the tree is laden with a battery of techniques and conceptions that get in the way of his perceiving and appreciating the tree; they keep the self aloof and the tree at bay. These techniques serve the ego's desire to order the perceptual field and bring the tree under control. That is not to say that the photographs produced in this way are not beautiful or interesting; they well may be. They are less likely, however, to communicate to one looking at the photograph the tree as it appears to a sensitive perceiver. To say so, however, is not to claim that all sensitive perceivers will have identical perceptions.

The Japanese photographer's approach is nondualistic. Relatively unrestrained by her preestablished program, she is freer to experience the tree, to become one

---

17.   The basic outline of this story is not my own. I cannot, however, recall the source. The details of the story and its use to illustrate Joshu Sasaki's distinction are mine.

18.   Years ago, I attended the Seminar on the Sutras at Cornell University. Joshu Sasaki Roshi lectured there. So far as I can remember, the quote appeared (along with another) on a handout acquired there.

with it, to blur the subject-object dichotomy. The tree is less muzzled and can make a greater contribution to the perception. In Joshu Sasaki's terms, she *sees* the tree. But how is such seeing to be achieved? How is nondual reality to be experienced?

Practice

In India, the classical philosophical systems were accompanied and undergirded by practices. For example, Yogacara, a school of Buddhist philosophy, was linked to the practice of a specific form of yoga. The Western intellectual tradition, however, has largely eschewed any connection to practice. Practice, as we have noted in Chapter 4, has often been linked in binary opposition to theory, from which it is sharply distinguished. Such a view is related to the form-matter dualism of Plato and the mind-body dualism of Descartes. To this day, Russian glass artists, for example, merely *design* works of art, leaving the actual *making* of them to craftsmen, who are held to be of lesser status. Supposedly, artists rely on mind (a higher and separate reality); craftsmen rely on mere body. Moreover, the artist's task is to create form; the task of the craftsman is to shape matter to fit the preexisting form.

Already in this volume, however, I have expressed my agreement with those who are critical of the practice-theory dichotomy. In Chapter 5 I noted Polanyi's view that every actual feat of knowing relies upon tacit skills, an understanding that blurs the distinction between knowing and doing. The nonduality of theory and practice does not mean, of course, that relative, contextual distinctions between them are to be eliminated altogether, so long as their fundamental inseparability is acknowledged.

In what follows I intend to rely largely on existential phenomenology, which has frequently described itself as a method (and thus is, at least potentially, a kind of practice) but which at the same time is an intellectual project. Because the subject that experiences is a mind/bodily-being-in-the-world and not a subject utterly transcendent of object or world, such phenomenology has an affinity with nondualism. Also, in virtue of affirming the reality of time, avoiding constructivism, embracing finitude, and appealing to experience, existential phenomenology displays its divergence from Plato and exhibits its indebtedness to and continuing consonance with Hebraic culture, which I have characterized in Chapters 2 and 3 as a pre-philosophical version of nondualism.

Practice and Perception

One way to experience reality is through perception. Modern, constructivist[19] theories of perception, however, have constituted a hindrance to experiencing reality as nondual. Descartes, for example, reported that whereas he could not be certain that his leg hurt, he could be sure that he *thought* his leg hurt. Because

---

19. Constructivism is reading back into pre-reflective experience the products of reflective analysis and trying to reconstruct pre-reflective experience out of those abstract products.

he believed that thought yielded certainty and because certainty was the goal of his passionate quest, he was led to reconceive perception as thought about perception. Just as Kant accepted the conclusions of physics as true and attempted to conceive a theory of knowing that led precisely to those conclusions, so theorists of perception in the modern era have often accepted the existence of objects that possessed all the constancy, clarity, and distinctness with which abstract thought has constructed them. Perceiving, then, was conceived as an operation or act that led precisely to the aforementioned objects. As a consequence, perceiving has often been understood in the modern West as a form of thinking. The inherent dualism of such thinking obscures nondual reality.

Existential phenomenologist Merleau-Ponty rejects both "the constancy hypothesis" (the view that the object of perception is constant in possessing the attributes thought knows it has) and the understanding of perception that is in collusion with it, calling instead for a "naïve" perception that seeks "a direct and primitive contact with the world, and endowing that contact with philosophical status."[20] This naïve perception is an existentialist version of phenomenological intuiting, the first step in the phenomenological method.[21] It is a giving of oneself up to and wonder before the ongoing and mysterious upsurge of pre-reflective experience. As noted earlier, Merleau-Ponty calls perception a "communion" that involves the very attitude Joshu Sasaki indicates is essential for seeing, namely, surrender. Merleau-Ponty says, "I surrender part of my body, even my whole body, to this particular manner of vibrating and filling space known as blue or red."[22] Later, he adds, "As I contemplate the blue of the sky . . ., I abandon myself to it and plunge into this mystery."[23] This characterization of perception diverges sharply from Descartes's admonition to direct one's eyes "attentively to single points, and by practice to acquire a capacity to adequately distinguish things which are subtly minute."

Let's try a bit of phenomenology and see what we can learn. Focus attentively on a small object, a coin perhaps. Notice that while the edges of the coin appear clear and sharp, they do so within a surrounding area that is quite blurred. This blurriness is not a defective or problematic state to be eliminated by blinking one's eyes, by rest, by donning spectacles, or by surgery. The greater clarity of the coin is purchased at the cost of blurriness elsewhere in the field, much as order in one area of a thermodynamic system is "sucked" from another area.

Now breathe deeply and relax. When you do, your gaze will shift on its own to a global view of what lies before you, and focusing will cease. Such relaxed, global awareness is, perhaps, the default position in perception. Notice that both the central clarity and the surrounding blurriness disappear. They are replaced by a relatively more uniform and intermediate degree of clarity. One could say, perhaps, that a high degree of surrounding blurriness is an ontological condition for a high degree of central clarity and that a certain degree of intermediate clarity is an ontological condition for global perception.

20. Maurice Merleau-Ponty, *Phenomenology of Perception*, trans. Colin Smith (London: Routledge & Kegan Paul, 1962), vii.

21. Herbert Spiegelberg, *The Phenomenological Movement: A Historical Introduction*, vol. II, (The Hague: Martinus Nijhoff, 1971), 659.

22. Merleau-Ponty, 212.

23. Ibid., 214.

Perhaps more importantly, a global view results not only in a relatively uniform degree of intermediate clarity, but also in a reduction in sharp boundaries that distinguish coins, tables, chairs, walls, etc. from each other. It is as if boundaries soften and partially merge. Here the perceiver neither thinks nor says, "That is a table" or "That is yellow." This state is what Nishitani meant when he spoke of "the inexhaustible storehouse with not a single thing in it."[24] Nevertheless, the global perceptual field is not a single, monochrome, uniform canvas comparable to a photographer's gray card; rather, all is characterized by ambiguity—neither clear nor unclear, neither distinct objects nor an utter absence of differentiation. Even if I reach out for my cappuccino and take a sip, as I did just a moment ago, the cup does not emerge from its perceptual ambiguity unless I focus on it specifically. Ambiguity, then, is a positive phenomenon.[25] It is not what Descartes calls a "confused mind." It belongs to nondual, naive perception. If a brightly colored bird flies by, however, it summons our attention and polarizes the visual field. Pre-reflective focusing is prompted by the bird.

Pre-reflective, naïve perception occurs prior to any attempt to describe in language the contents of the perceptual field. This does not mean, as Derrida might be inclined to point out, that previous language usage has no effect on what we perceive. Almost certainly it does. Names are given to perceptual features that are deemed significant; as a result, we may become habituated to noticing those features rather than others. Insofar, however, as existential phenomenology is aware of such habits and seeks to bracket them by a deliberately cultivated naivety (a practice), the influence of language can be rendered largely insignificant in most instances.

To focus deliberately (not naively), however, to undertake perception at the direction and in the service of thought, as Descartes recommends, is to impose limitations on perception. It sets in motion an active intentionality of probing that creates/discovers a momentary object by carving it out from the ambiguous perceptual field. Reflection carries the process further, constructing an ideal and permanent object from the momentary, perceptual one. In both cases this carving out is at once an abstracting and a creating; it is not like a mere cutting out of paper dolls from already printed images of them. What such deliberate perception and/or reflection produces is more determinate and more precise than the matrix that is its source. Merleau-Ponty says:

> The positing of the object therefore makes us go beyond the limits of actual experience which is brought up against and halted by an alien being, with the result that finally experience believes that it extracts all its own teaching from

---

24. Keiji Nishitani, *Religion and Nothingness*, trans. Jan van Bragt (Berkeley: University of California Press, 1982), 267.

25. Merleau-Ponty makes this point by reference to the Muller-Lyer lines, an optical illusion well-known to psychologists of perception. To naïve perception, the lines are neither equal nor unequal in length. The question of the length is one raised in reflection. See Merleau-Ponty page 6. Spiegelberg points out that the term "ambiguity" has a less negative meaning in French than in English, that Merleau-Ponty placed an equal emphasis on clarity, and that the Merleau-Ponty understood ambiguity as having a positive sense, namely, the rejection of absolute knowledge. See Spiegelberg, 526.

the object . . . Obsessed with being, and forgetful of the perspective of my experience, I henceforth treat it as an object and deduce it from a relationship between objects.[26]

Naïve perception and phenomenological intuiting dissolve the sclerosis of the constant, ideal object and place it back into the ambiguous matrix that is its source.

According to Tom Kasulis, this relaxed attentiveness is one instance of what Soto Zen master Dogen termed *"mushin"* (without thinking). To use phenomenological terminology, it is a "non-thetic" (not advancing a thesis) or "non-positional" (not advocating a position) awareness devoid of an active intentionality. The intentionality involved here is the operative intentionality of the body-as-subject-in-the-world. The objective pole of such an awareness, the ambiguous phenomenal field, is an instance of what Soto Zen master Dogen calls *"genjokoan"* (the "presencing of things as they are"). This ambiguous field in which no object is found can be characterized as Nothingness, the unity of *sunyata* (emptiness, interdependence) and nonbeing-as-source. The upsurge of pre-reflective experience is the nonbeing-as-source from which both the extremes of blurriness and clarity of focused perception and the objects of thought are created/discovered.

Returning to relaxed, global, "naïve" awareness is not only phenomenological intuiting but also a form of meditation and, therefore, a practice. The practice of this meditation leads to contact with the nondual reality beyond, beneath, or prior to any reality described in binary oppositions. The practice of returning to an experience of nondual reality destabilizes and de-absolutizes already existing dualisms, prevents an overvaluing of binary oppositions, and forestalls the hardening of such oppositions into fresh dualisms. The experience of nondual reality, however, is not limited to relaxed, global *visual* perception. It is also found in any pre-reflective experience.

Notice also, that even in visual perception there is no sharp boundary at the periphery of the visual field; rather, there is an indeterminate horizon, which shifts with each movement of the head and which extends outward from the body in all directions. This omni-directional visual horizon accords with what is more readily understood from aural perception, namely, that as perceivers, we are surrounded by, indeed embodied in, a phenomenal field.

Reality, however, keeps outrunning all boundaries imposed upon it by finitude. Hence, the phenomenal field sweeps on toward an ever-receding horizon, to wider and wider contexts, to what Merleau-Ponty calls a "world" but what I prefer to call "Reality," the pre-reflectively lived and nondual "system" of self-other-nature. Merleau-Ponty characterizes it variously as the "context of all contexts," the "field of all fields," the "horizon of all horizons." He characterizes it further as "an open and indefinite multiplicity of relationships which are of reciprocal implication,"[27] the "vague theater of all experiences,"[28] and "the cradle of meanings, the direction of all directions, and ground of all thinking."[29]

26. Merleau-Ponty, 70.
27. Ibid., 23.
28. Ibid., 343.
29. Ibid., 430.

Such a world has obvious similarities to Buddhist ideas. The "open and indefinite multiplicity of relationships" accords with *sunyata* (emptiness). The Taoist conception of nonbeing-as-source is reflected in his statement that the world is the "inexhaustible reservoir from which things are drawn"[30] and that things "emerge from a background of formlesness."[31] The following passage from Merleau-Ponty is even redolent of the Dainichi Buddha, the cosmological Buddha of Hua-Yen:

> From the very start I am in communication with one being, and one only, a vast individual from which my own experiences are taken, and which persists on the horizon of my life as the distant roar of a great city provides the background of everything we do in it.[32]

Naïve perception is part of the nondualistic "seeing" of which Sasaki Roshi spoke. Insofar as existential phenomenology calls attention to and endows naïve perceiving with philosophical significance, the practice of phenomenological intuiting unthaws habits of dualistic looking, replacing them with nondualistic seeing. The practice of *zazen* (seated meditation in Zen) can do the same. Both involve an attunement, without active intentionality, to the phenomenal field. The difference between the two is that phenomenological intuiting is usually undertaken in anticipation of eventually providing the verbal description necessary for doing philosophy. Ordinarily, *zazen* has no such anticipation.

Nihilistic forms of Buddhism seem to aim at the total elimination of all habits (*samskaras*) and of all intentionality. Laycock, for example, regards intentions as thoughts laced with desire and directed toward specific goals. They become problematic when superimposed upon perceptions and actions[33] and, consequently, must be relinquished. By equating intentions with thoughts, he seems to be describing what the later Husserl and Merleau-Ponty refer to as "active intentionality." He never mentions, however, what they call "operative intentionality," the prereflective intentionality essential to our inherence in a life-world.

The radical aim of expunging *all* intentions would result in an inability to sit, stand, walk, speak, perceive, eat—in short, an inability to live. Meditation, also, would be impossible; it is, to be sure, the cessation of active intentions, but not all intentions. Perhaps meditation is best described in terms Merleau-Ponty uses to describe phenomenological intuiting: "it slackens the intentional threads which attach us to the world and brings them to our notice."[34] According to Merleau-Ponty, even our ability to awake from sleep is due to the body-subject's ongoing attunedness to or operative intending of the world, a kind of standby mode of being-in-the-world. And Laycock's own acknowledgement of our "tending toward universality"[35] (analogous to Polanyi's "universal intent") is itself a form

---

30. Merleau-Ponty, 344.
31. Ibid., 441.
32. Ibid., 328.
33. Laycock, 107–108.
34. Merleau-Ponty, xiii. Merleau-Ponty is explicating the phenomenological reduction, also known as "bracketing" or the "epoche."
35. Ibid., 133.

of intentionality. Philosopher David Kalupahana, himself a Theravada Buddhist, asserts that despite the elimination of some *samskaras* (intentions made habitual), we always remain conditioned and that to eliminate all habits or dispositions whatsoever would result in death.[36] Such an asceticism is no middle way.

In Speech and Reflection

Reflection is to thought what focusing is to perception, namely, a limitation of the scope of attention in the service of a project. Philosophers and non-philosophers alike move beyond mere perception to verbal description and then on to reflective analysis of naïve experience. Both steps take the abstraction process (which began with focusing) further. The latter step in particular, especially in philosophical reflection, creates a fixed idea of the object and endows it with a defined essence. Imagine the following: the perception of a person, a photograph of the same person (using a 50 mm lens—a focal length that approximates that of the human eye), a realistic painting of the same person, a recognizable caricature of the person, and a stick-figure drawing of the person. The items in this series are increasingly abstract, increasingly omitting the particularities that link them to the original perception, and increasingly creating new forms embodying the abstraction. In the case of the stick figure there may well be almost nothing left that can single out a particular individual. Such abstracting can be performed skillfully or unskillfully, and the resulting abstractions are not necessarily complete distortions, but whatever may be the advantages they bring, they exhibit an increasingly tenuous hold on concrete experience.

An analogous kind of abstracting is carried out by thinking. Verbalization, whether silent, spoken, or written, draws the distinctions that turn so readily into dualisms. In Buddhism, *manas* (the mind, the sixth sense) performs this same operation and is, consequently, identified as the culprit in producing obstacles to liberation (the *atman*, for example) and the consequent suffering.

Consider Figure 8.1. If the left-most symbolizes the content of naïve perception, then the other three symbolize reflection on that content in an effort to clarify it. The result, however is that reflection alters the content of perception, making it more precise, more determinate. The more indistinct figure is transformed into perfectly round circles that are described by narrow, precise lines, and the ambiguity of the border area is dispelled by three different possible interpretations.

Yet in reflection also, as in perception, there is ambiguity, emptiness, and nothingness. Recall from Chapter 5 that verbal expressions arise from we-know-not-where and have the meaning they do in virtue of our reliance on a tacit dimension of ultimately unspecifiable habitual operative intentions and sedimented meanings. Recall also that the definitions of words are interdependent and that developed thought is inescapably embodied in language. Hence, thinking never outruns the emptiness (*nothingness*) that is its ground and source.

---

36. David J. Kalupahana, *The Principles of Buddhist Psychology* (Albany: State University of New York Press, 1987), 86.

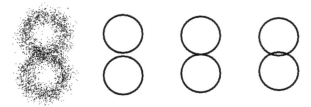

Figure 8.1 *Relation of abstract reflection to ambiguous perception.*

Despite the distinctions and oppositions they inevitably involve, we do and must engage in speaking and thinking. This circumstance is not, as Buddhist rhetoric sometimes seems to suggest, a fate to be fought or deplored but an opportunity to be seized. After all, reflection vs. no reflection is itself a dualism. Human projects more complex than momentary and spontaneous responses often require careful reflection, a fact Zen Buddhism in particular has sometimes overlooked. This need for reflection holds true even of projects of compassion, which often require research, analysis, and planning. Compassion asks more of us than a spontaneous and positive response to a woman's request to be carried across a stream. A variety of circumstances must be examined, distinctions must be drawn, methods employed, and results critiqued. Such reflective activities are indispensable for a task done well.

Here, too, there is a practice that can prevent, or at least reduce the likelihood, of our being led astray. It involves, first of all, vigilance in detecting the appearance in thought or speech or action, our own or that of others, of binary oppositions. Just as in simple breath meditation one must, time and time again, bring one's attention back to one's breathing in order to become habituated to awareness of breathing, so one who wishes to elude the dangers of binary opposites must make a habit of noticing them, recalling their limitations and dangers, and searching for and attuning herself or himself to the greater reality that encompasses them both. This, along with meditation and phenomenological intuiting, is practicing the middle way.

We can also work at eliminating from our rhetorical habits the uncritical use of the universal quantifiers "all" or "no," reserving them for the few instances in which they may be appropriate and substituting for them the more nuanced terms "some," "a few," "most," "many," etc. Steven Laycock, for example, says that distinctions "have *no* purchase on experience" and that models, and metaphors "have *no* purchase on reality"[37] (emphasis added). Apparently, there's no room here even for a Derridian trace, which was discussed in Chapter 4. Such claims are not offhand but occur in the context of a discussion of the relation of language to reality. A contemplative, nihilist extreme wins out over nuance and the middle way.

Teachers who have helped students formulate good thesis statements for their term papers will understand the pitfalls of claiming the following: Muslim women

37. Laycock, 52, 125.

are required to wear the veil. Presented with such a proposed thesis, I am inclined to ask several questions. In Saudi Arabia, Iran, Morocco, Indonesia, the United States? In the seventh century, the seventeenth century, the twenty-first century? Among Sunnis and Shi'ites?

Finally, instead of describing the status of a scientific theory as either "confirmed" or "unconfirmed," one could say that theory X is *partially* confirmed or that it is *"relatively* more confirmed than theory Y." Doubtless, there are other ways we can adopt to prevent the bifurcation of ambiguous and shifting reality into static, black-and-white pigeonholes and to forestall the negative consequences that flow therefrom.

In the end, however, as Buddhism would attest, what is required is something more profound, namely, a transformation of the self; and indispensable to such a transformation is the transformation of one's understanding of the nature of the self. Self-transformation capitalizes on a basic feature of human selfhood, namely, that humans are not simply in time but are fundamentally constituted as temporal. This idea, conceived by Zen master Dōgen, is expressed in Japanese by the term *"uji,"* which is often translated as "being-time." For existential phenomenology and ancient Hebrew thought, transformation of self, then, is a matter of transcending oneself forward toward the future, that is, transcending one's old self in favor of a new self in a way roughly analogous to the ongoing identity development Erikson has described for us in Chapter 6.

Compassion

According to Buddhism, one of the fruits of a self-transformation grounded in nothingness is compassion. Compassion (*kuruna*), although present in Hinayana Buddhism, is more prominent in and more often associated with Mahayana Buddhism, where it is central to the *bodhisattva* ideal. A bodhisattva is a person who, motivated by compassion for sentient beings, undertakes the quest for Buddhahood so as to increase his or her power to perform compassionate acts in this world on behalf of those other beings. To that end the bodhisattva refuses to enter *nirvana* (as understood dualistically by Hinayana), choosing to be reborn again and again into this world (*samsara*), and vows to continue to do so until all sentient beings have been saved. Sometimes the vow to save others is extended to cover even the blades of grass. The Dalai Lama, who belongs to the Vajrayana tradition, has said that if there were an absolute to be found in Buddhism (there is not), it would be compassion.[38]

One who takes the vow to become a bodhisattva practices the Mahayana perfections. One list names six of them; another names ten. In any case, one of the most important of them is wisdom (*prajna*), understood to mean "saving insight." What wisdom sees is *sunyata*, life's interdependence, its interconnectedness, its oneness. Emptiness entails that a person is an ongoing cause and ongoing effect

---

38. Paul Williams, *Mahayana Buddhism: The Doctrinal Foundations* (London: Routledge, 1989), 198.

of everything else in the universe. In that sense, one *is* everything else. Such an insight turns one's egoistic passion for oneself (the little self) into compassion for one's big self, namely, all sentient beings (Indian and Tibetan Buddhism) or all sentient beings plus non-sentient things (East Asian Buddhism). Compassion, then, is both a cause and an effect of wisdom. In other words, wisdom and compassion are themselves nondual.

There are remarkable stories in Buddhist texts of the astonishing lengths to which bodhisattvas, acting from compassion, have gone in order to alleviate the suffering of others. In one, King Maharatha and his three sons (Mahapranada, Mahadeva, and Mahasattva) visit a beautiful park. The three sons come upon a mother tigress and her five cubs. All the tigers are weak from hunger and are near death. The mother has not eaten in days and can no longer produce milk for her young. As the princes discuss the situation, noting that tigers live on flesh and blood, Mahasattva says:

> Holy men are born of pity and compassion. Whatever the bodies they may get, in heaven or on earth, a hundred times will they undo them, joyful in their hearts, so that the lives of others may be saved . . . Now the time has come for me to sacrifice myself . . . From deep compassion I now give away my body, so hard to quit, unshaken in my mind.[39]

Having brought along no sword or knife, he slits his own throat with a piece of sharp bamboo and, covered with blood, lies down near the mother tigress, who devours him, enabling her to feed her cubs.

As inspiring as such tales are, Buddhist compassion has not been immune from criticism, even by Buddhists themselves. Traditionally and generally, it has been spontaneous and reactive. Mahasattva sacrificed himself only because he came upon the tigers. The Theravada monk who stoops to remove a snail from the path so that it won't be stepped on, does so only because he happened upon the snail. The Zen monk who carries a woman across the stream does so in response to their meeting and to her request. These compassionate reactions were spontaneous, intuitive, on the spot, not reflective and deliberate.

Traditionally and for the most part, then, Buddhist compassion has operated in small-scale, one-to-one situations. It has not often engaged in larger-scale projects requiring analysis, planning, and organization in order, for example, to move bald eagles from the endangered list to a healthy and sustainable population, to eliminate AIDS, or to rebuild the Gulf Coast in the wake of Hurricane Katrina. It has not concerned itself with social justice—that is, changing those structures of society at large that determine how goods, power, and opportunity are allocated within society and whether all or only some groups within society have access to the crucial decision-making processes.

Burt Wolf, formerly the host of the television program "A Taste for Travel," attempted to explain traffic patterns in Taiwan in terms of Taoist philosophy.

---

39. Cited in "The Bodhisattva and the Hungry Tigress" in *Buddhist Scriptures*, selected and translated by Edward Conze (Baltimore, Maryland: Penguin Books, 1959), 25–26.

He contrasted an American highway, with its painted lane lines and parallel streams of cars, with a Taiwan intersection in which pedestrians, scooters, bicycles, cars, trucks, and buses entered from all four directions simultaneously, filling the streets from curb to curb. Each person or vehicle spontaneously adjusted and readjusted to the movement of every other person and vehicle to produce an efficient and harmonious flow. This traffic model of Taoist and East Asian Buddhist ethics seems to ignore the fact that trucks and buses (like corporations or governments) possess a power to intimidate that a person cycling or walking lacks. Power is not equitably distributed here, leaving ample openings for injustice and oppression.

More recently, however, Buddhism has been moving beyond traditional ethical patterns as it becomes "engaged" in dealing with social problems and social structures both in Asia and in the West.[40] A particularly noteworthy example is Buddhism's mission to the inmates of prisons in the United States through the Prison Dharma Network.[41]

Although the West is also familiar with the concept of compassion, its highest virtue or perfection is love. The single English term covers *eros*, *philia*, and *agape*, which derive from Greece, as well as many other meanings. The prominence of love in the West, however, is due largely to the importance given to it by Judaism and Christianity. The Tanak (the Hebrew Bible), for example, employs five Hebrew words for love, the most important of which is *hesed*, which was mentioned in Chapter 2 of this volume. It can mean "kindness," "loving kindness," "loyalty," "mercy," and "steadfast love." And although it can apply to the love of humans for each other or for God, it is most often associated with God's attitude toward and behavior on behalf of God's creatures. Presumably, it distinguishes the God of Israel from the fickle, irresponsible, immoral deities of other ancient religions.

In the New Testament, Paul's famous paean to love in I Corinthians 13, ends thus: "In a word, there are three things that last forever: faith, hope, and love; but the greatest of them all is love." An epistle of John actually identifies God with love. Perhaps most influential of all, however, is Jesus's "great commandment" or "the love commandment." When asked by a Pharisee what is the greatest of the commandments, Jesus, drawing upon the Tanak, replies:

> "Love the Lord your God with all your heart, with all your soul, with all your mind." That is the greatest commandment. It comes first. The second is like it: "Love your neighbor as yourself." Everything in the Law and the prophets hangs on these two commandments. (Mt. 22.37–40)

Whatever the source, the various meanings of "love" relate to differences in both kind (romance, friendship, concern) and degree (affection, tenderness, passion).

---

40. See Christopher S. Queen and Sallie B. King, eds., *Engaged Buddhism: Buddhist Liberation Movements in Asia* (Albany: State University of New York Press, 1996) and Christopher S. Queen, ed. *Engaged Buddhism in the West* (Boston, Massachusetts: Wisdom Publications, 2000).

41. See Kobai Scott Whitney, *Sitting Inside: Buddhist Practice in America's Prisons* (Boulder, Colorado: Prison Dharma Network, 2002).

What they share in common is the attachment, however qualified or character-ized, of one being (a person or animal) to another (a person, animal, or object). In other words, love is dualistic; there is the lover and the object of love.

Love in the West has, by contrast to traditional East Asia, motivated both orga-nized and reflective activity on behalf of individuals and classes of beings. In the latter case love has prompted the building of general hospitals as well as spe-cialized ones for children or persons with particular diseases. It has prompted the construction of schools, the organization of childcare services for working parents, and the creation of recreation or enrichment programs for children. It has also given rise to nursing homes for the elderly and hospices to care for the dying.

In addition, the legacy of the ancient Hebrew prophets' concern for justice and the example of Jesus have inspired concerted action to challenge economic and political structures that are unfair to the poor. Both the Social Gospel movement of the early twentieth century and recent Liberation Theology, with its "prefer-ential option for the poor," have made social justice the focus of their activities. Racial groups, women, homosexuals, Muslims, and immigrants have benefited from efforts, motivated by love, to see that they are treated justly.

Beyond the fact that, when considered separately, they have been understood largely within the context of individualism and dualism, love and justice have often been conceived together as standing in a relation of opposition to each other. St. Thomas Aquinas understood justice, which is known by reason, to relate to natural law and the four classical virtues (temperance, justice, courage, and pru-dence). He saw love, however, as belonging among the three theological virtues (faith, hope, and love) and as requiring revelation. Of the two, love is higher than justice. Some Social Gospel advocates, on the other hand, tended uncritically to identify love with justice. Some sectarian groups (the Mennonites, for instance) regarded justice as inevitably involving the use of violence or force and, in the name of love, refused to hold public office, fight in wars, or serve as executioners. Evangelical and Reformed churches, along with Lutherans, held that love and jus-tice stand in a relation of paradox. Reinhold Niebuhr held that love, understood as self-sacrificial agape, is an ideal impossible of realization, at least in politics; yet it provides a measuring rod by which to critique justice and to thwart its perversion. Finally, Augustine, Calvin, and Wesley believed that justice must be transformed by grace to prevent the classical virtues from serving evil ends.

The widespread dualistic, individualistic interpretation of love in Western cul-ture has led to an ultimately unsatisfactory reliance on several ethical options. Eschewing the extreme of selfishness, one can become an altruist, sacrificing one-self completely for the other. One can act from self-interest in some situations and selflessly in others. One can become a do-gooder, one who is perhaps not altogether clear about his or her own motives and who, perhaps unthinkingly, imposes inappropriate or otherwise unwanted "good works" on others.

What is needed is a middle way, not only between the obvious dualities within the West, but also between the extremes represented by Asia and the West. How might one sketch the contours of such a middle? In agreement with Asia, it would, first of all, embrace *sunyata* (emptiness) or nothingness as the ultimate context of all thought/action—the most comprehensive and fully interdependent. Second, this context would include not only human beings, but also, animals, plants, minerals,[42] and the divine. Third, compassion would be the highest moral perfection or virtue, providing the most fundamental motivation for moral and ethical action. After all, "compassion," unlike "empathy," "sympathy," "pity," or "love," includes the meaning "the inclination to give aid or support," that is, it moves one beyond mere feeling and toward action. It does so because, at least in its Buddhist usage, it avoids the West's inner-outer dualism that permits love to be understood as merely a matter of internal feeling.

In agreement with the West, it would, first of all, make use of reason understood as embodied and finite. Second, it would not simply react but also be proactive. Third, it would seek justice motivated and guided by compassion. Fourth, it would acknowledge an emergent ontological hierarchy and would have a corresponding differential valuation of the interdependent constituents of Reality while, nevertheless, valuing them all.

Already, ancient Hebrew religion, at least as I have interpreted one strain of it in the preceding chapters (especially Chapter 3) constitutes a precedent for such a middle way. It lacks only a more explicit inclusion of minerals among the interconnected elements of Reality—there is already an implicit inclusion of them in God's pronouncement that the creation is "very good."

As I have depicted it so far, Hebrew religion lacks the virtue of compassion. In fact, however, compassion (*rahamim*) is found in both the Tanak and the Talmud. According to the *Anchor Bible Dictionary*, it describes the fundamental relation of God and Israel within the covenant. It is also meant to characterize the proper relation of humans to each other and to animals. An example of the latter case is given in Exodus 23.5 and Deuteronomy 22.4, where compassion requires helping to its feet an enemy's ox or ass otherwise incapable of standing up with its load.

Especially interesting in juxtaposition to Buddhism is the fact that "*rahamim*" (a noun) and its verbal forms come from the same root as "*rehem*," which means "womb." Some scholars have suggested that "*rahamim*" means the brotherly feeling of those born from the same womb.[43]

The womb appears in Mahayana Buddhism in the concept of the *Tathagata-Garbha*, according to which all sentient beings contain within them the Buddha essence (*Dharmakaya*) or the potential to become a Buddha. The Gelugpa school of Vajrayana Buddhism, the Sanskrit version of the *Ratnagotravibhaga*, and some passages in the *Mahaparinirvana Sutra* understand the *Tathagata-Garbha* to be empty (*sunya*) of inherent existence or aseity (existence not dependent on anything else).[44] As we have seen in Chapter 2, the ancient Hebrews have no concept

---

42. It may seem strange to speak of compassion for minerals, but I recall reading somewhere about the spontaneous and momentary twinge of sadness some people have upon seeing and hearing a stone break.

43. *Encyclopedia Judaica*, Vol. 5 (Jerusalem: The Macmillan Company, 1971), 855–856.

44. The Chinese version of the *Ratnagotravibhaga*, the *Srimaladevivisimbanada Sutra*, the *Mahaparinirvana Sutra*, and the *Jo nang pa* school of Vajrayana see the womb as an eternal, absolute, and ultimate reality. See Paul Williams, *Mahayana Buddhism*, 96–115. For a discussion of these differences see Jamie Hubbard and Paul L. Swanson, eds., *Pruning*

of an eternal reality. Hence, for both the Hebrews and Vajrayana, the womb is a symbol of *sunyata*, knowledge (wisdom) of which leads to or is nondual with compassion.

Even the Great Commandment can be interpreted in a nondualistic fashion, provided one places God, neighbor, and self into a context of ancient Hebraic assumptions. The God referred to by Jesus is not any God but the God who created the world, regards the creation as fundamentally good, and loves the creation, including all selves and their neighbors. In other words, self and neighbor are internally related to God. Hence to love God well (with all one's heart, mind, soul, and strength) is to love what God creates, loves, and regards as good, including neighbor and self. Self and neighbor are also internally related to each other in that they are "children" of the same parent (from the same "womb," as it were), and they cocreate each other through their interactions in history. Hence, for self and neighbor to love each other well, they must love God, the parent who created, sustains, and loves both neighbor and self. In other words, God, neighbor, and self are internally related to each other and interdependent with each other. This interaction extends, as I have indicated, even to cocreating each other. God needs the creation (self and neighbor) in order to be a creator, just as God needs children in order to be a parent. Speaking of divine relationality, Martin Buber puts the matter more dramatically: "God needs you—in the fullness of his eternity needs you."[45] In short, to love any one of the three well, is to love the other two. Perhaps from this perspective, the commandment to love God, neighbor, and self is really the commandment to be mindful of and respond to the interconnectedness (*sunyata*) that always already unites them.

If Reality, then, is the ongoing interconnectedness, interdependence, internal relatedness, and emptiness of all things in the universe, then not only is everything impinging upon, affecting, and creating us, but we are, willy-nilly and for better or worse, impinging upon, affecting, and creating everything else. And if this *prajna*, insight, wisdom, knowledge (learning or knowledge-in-process) is inevitably linked to compassion (which includes "the inclination to give aid or support"), then our larger practice or mission in life is *tikkun olam*—that is, the repair, nurture, restoration, or mending of the universe through our local upsurge from it and embodiment in it, a repair that includes expanding and deepening the knowledge of our fundamental interrelatedness and the achievement of a justice motivated by and occurring within a context of compassion. To that end, we are to make use of the full range of our native capacities and skills, both noncognitive and cognitive, including our finite and empty rationality. Other practices are valuable insofar as they serve this Grand Practice of nondual wisdom and compassion.

the Bodhi Tree: The Storm over Critical Buddhism (Honolulu: University of Hawaii Press, 1997).

    45. Martin Buber, *I and Thou*, trans. R Gregor Smith; 2nd ed. (New York: Charles Scribner's Sons, 1958), 18, 82. Cited in C. Eric Mount, Jr., "It Takes a Community—or at Least an Association" in Patrick D. Miller and Dennis P. McCann, eds., *In Search of the Common Good* (New York: T&T Clark, 2005), 171.

"*Tikkun*," however, understood as "repair" or "nurture" or "restoration," seems to presuppose a static universe, as if we are to keep repairing the one universe God completed back "in the beginning." In Chapter 7, however, we saw that Genesis can also be interpreted as suggesting a notion of God's continuing creation. Consistent with that interpretation, God's image in humans can be and has been understood as meaning that we are to share in God's project of creativity. Here, Process Thought has latched onto a significant insight, one that concurs at many points with Buddhism's understanding that the universe is constantly changing and that all things are interdependently involved in co-origination. In light of these reflections, the ultimate aim of compassionate action is nothing less than the ongoing cocreation of a universe that is ever richer in justice, harmony, peace, and meaning.

Yet are nondual wisdom and compassion, as urgent and grand as they are, enough? Are they all there is?

Celebration

In his enormously popular *The World's Religions* Huston Smith sums up the vast literature and endlessly divergent practices of Hinduism as affirming, in essence, "You can have what you want."[46] Initially, most people want pleasure, and Hinduism stands ready to provide instruction for acquiring it. The well-known *Kama Sutra*, for example, is part of that instruction. Pleasure, however, soon palls, and people inquire if there is something more. Next, Hinduism points them to the quest for wealth, power, and fame, which involves them more broadly in the world and provides a longer-lasting satisfaction. After a few lifetimes, however, this quest, too, becomes meaningless. For Hinduism, these first two goals belong to the "path of desire."

The most enduring satisfactions, however, lie on the "path of renunciation," the renunciation of the ego that comes only after the inadequacy of the path of desire has been experienced. The first of these is service to others. Here one finds a profound satisfaction, one that persists across many incarnations. Yet, in the end, even this goal is found wanting because its object is limited. Smith has the seeker stand once again before Hinduism to ask, "Is that all there is?" Finally, the seeker is ready for the ultimate goal, that of realizing a relationship to the Infinite through yoga.

The yogas, however are plural in number. For *jnana* and *raja* yogas, the goal is nondual identity with *Brahman*, becoming a part of God's infinite being (*sat*), awareness (*chit*), and joy (*ananda*). In other words, people want to become an eternal consciousness of joy, which, essentially, they always were. Hinduism's emphasis on joy is consonant with Process thought's recognition of the centrality of enjoyment for all beings, including God. Such a monumental goal is attainable merely by the realization that one's deepest self is, in fact, identical with the

46.   Huston Smith, *The World's Religions* (New York: HarperSanFrancisco, 1991). 13.

eternal essence of the universe and always has been. By contrast, *Karma* (usually) and *bhakti* yogas are dualistic and urge the worship of God, regarded as a separate being.

If the compassion we discussed previously is roughly analogous to the third Hindu goal, that of serving others, then what is analogous to the fourth? And if wisdom and compassion are not enough, what is lacking? Both Buddhist *anicca* (impermanence) and Hebraic myth and history rule out the possibility of an unchanging *Brahman* with which to identify. And Chapter 7 of this volume downplayed the dualistic worship of God, as in *Bhakti* yoga and most of Christianity. Is there some other possibility?

Around midnight on Friday, July 7, 2000, an extraordinary event took place in bookstores all across America and England. Children, dressed in round, black-rimmed glasses; capes; and tall, pointed hats; and bearing lightning marks on their foreheads, awaited the countdown to the sale of J. K. Rowling's latest Harry Potter novel—*Harry Potter and the Goblet of Fire*. Harry, a subteenaged boy, is a student in the Hogwarts School of Witchcraft and Wizardry, where he learns about the magical world all around him, a world that adults and other "muggles" cannot see. Allegedly, however, there was a time when nobody was afflicted with muggle-itis.

In our ancient, animistic past both children and adults believed the world to be populated with a host of elves, witches, wizards, monsters, demons, fairies, and dragons. Regarded as real, these imaginary creatures were a daily concern of most people. With the appearance of the monotheisms of Judaism, Islam, and Christianity and the great religions of Asia, however, that changed. In the West the notion of a single deity acted as a secularizing force to clear the forests, jungles, mountains, waters, skies, and adult minds of such fantastical beings.

As a result, magic and fantasy are confined largely to childhood, where they are generally regarded as harmless. Parents may even tolerate temporarily a child's imaginary playmate, so long as it does not become an excuse for getting into trouble or interfere with schoolwork or normal socialization. Many parents even contribute to their children's love of fantasy by reading to them books, taking them to movies, and buying them videos and computer games, all containing fantasy material. Most of us can recall our own childhood appreciation of fairy tales. I can remember clearly seeing the movie *The Wizard of Oz* starring Judy Garland and reading comic books about Batman and Superman. My children, in turn, read *The Chronicles of Narnia* and Tolkien's *The Hobbit*. Today, there are entire television channels devoted to cartoons and other kinds of programming populated with fantastical beings too numerous to name.

As children move into the teenaged years, however, society expects this preoccupation with fantasy to give way to an increasing adjustment to adult reality. This does not mean that adults must lose a sense of wonder but that the source of the wonder can shift to religion, and for some, to the one transcendent deity of theism in particular. For poets like Gerard Manley Hopkins, evidence of this God abounds in the world. In his poem "God's Grandeur" he wrote, "The world is charged with the grandeur of God. / It will flame out like shining from shook foil; / It gathers to a greatness, like the ooze of oil / Crushed."

But in our age the transition from childhood to adulthood does not always go smoothly. Already in the nineteenth century Wordsworth, for example, lamented in his "Ode: Intimations of Immortality from Recollections of Early Childhood":

> But trailing clouds of glory do we come
> From God, who is our home.
> Heaven lies about us in our infancy!
> Shades of the prison-house begin to close
> Upon the growing Boy . . .
> At length the Man perceives it die away,
> And fade into the light of common day.

Although of different centuries, the two poets seem to agree that the loss of wonder in adulthood is due to an insensitivity born of a preoccupation with worldly affairs. Wordsworth says:

> The world is too much with us; late and soon,
> Getting and spending, we lay waste our powers . . .
> We have given our hearts away, a sordid boon! . . .
> For this, for everything, we are out of tune:
> It moves us not.

Hopkins puts it this way:

> Generations have trod, have trod, have trod;
> And all is seared with trade; bleared, smeared with toil;
> And wears man's smudge and shares man's smell; the soil
> is bare now, nor can foot feel, being shod.

It is a lament at least as old as Ecclesiastes, which begins: "Emptiness, emptiness, says the Speaker, emptiness, all is empty. What does man gain from all his labour and his toil here under the sun?" (Eccl. 1.1)

By the 1960s, Beat poet Lawrence Ferlinghetti could announce, "I am waiting, perpetually and forever, a renaissance of wonder,"[47] (commas added) a wonder that had long since vanished. More recently, philosopher and theologian Karl Rahner wrote, "Your God-distance is in truth only the disappearance of the world before the dawning of God in your soul."[48] Wordsworth, Hopkins, Ferlinghetti, and Rahner seem to be in agreement that the world is the culprit, that somehow it obscures wonder and throttles us.

While I recognize the malaise these thinkers and others describe, I cannot agree with their diagnosis of its cause or with their solution. Wordsworth is mistaken, I believe, in saying that "the world is too much with us." If he means merely to

---

47. Lawrence Ferlinghetti, "I am Waiting," in *A Coney Island of the Mind: Poems by Lawrence Ferlinghetti* (New York: New Directions Books, 1959), 53.

48. Karl Rahner, "Peace" in *Prayers & Meditations: An Anthology of the Spiritual Writings by Karl Rahner*. Edited by John Griffiths (New York: Crossroad, 1981), 106.

urge us to reduce our involvement in the commerce of the industrial revolution and spend more time exploring and appreciating the enchantments of nature, which he so loved, then I can hardly disagree. But in this instance his rhetoric, if not his intention, is dualistic. It suggests that we should shift our gaze from *this* world to something else.

As for Hopkins, his poem "God's Grandeur" says that "the world is charged with the grandeur of God." If we assume that the expression "grandeur of God" is intended to be understood along the lines of the subjective genitive case in Latin (the grandeur is a quality or attribute of God) rather than the objective genitive case (grandeur is an object that God owns or possesses), then the world is charged not simply with grandeur but also with God. Indeed, it is because the world is charged with God that it is also charged with grandeur. But what if God were discharged from the world? That possibility appears later in the poem when Hopkins writes that "the Holy Ghost over the bent World broods with warm breast and with ah! bright wings." The "over" suggests God is distinct from the world. In that case, then, does the world exhibit any grandeur? Does it have any grandeur of its own? The answer is not clear, but we are nowhere led to think that it does.

By contrast, Psalms 19.1 affirms that the "heavens declare the Glory of God and the firmament showeth his handiwork." To be sure, God's having created the world is the cause of its ability to declare God's glory; nevertheless, once the world has been created in that way, then even if God vanished or died, the grandeur or glory of the creation that announces God's glory would remain. In other words, in that instance the world is wonderful in its own right, not simply when God invades and saturates it or is personally present to it. Precisely because the world is itself full of wonder can its creator be seen as wonderful. Moreover, if one were to claim that the world has no value, beauty, goodness, or wonder of its own, that claim would appear to contradict the pronouncement in Genesis, in which God is depicted as judging that the creation is "very good."

I wonder if Hopkins would be willing to add another line to his poem that said the following: "God is also charged with the grandeur of the world." I doubt it. If he would, then it would no longer be necessary, in order to experience magic, either to enter another world or conceive of this world as invaded by a magic-bearing being. Both alternatives imply that this world, considered in itself (either as one of a pair of dualities or in abstraction from a nondual reality that includes God and the world) is dull, prosaic, mundane, profane, uninteresting, of little value, or, at worst, even evil or unreal.

If, as supposedly clear-eyed adults, we are to experience life's magic, then it is precisely in *the* world, not some dualistic *other* world opposed to *this* world, that we must immerse ourselves more fully. In other words, the world is *too little* with us! Far from attempting to make the phenomenal world disappear, we should open ourselves up to experiencing it more fully and to celebrating it as an aspect of nondual Reality. Indeed, that is why Zen instruction calls for the eyes to remain partially open during meditation—the phenomenal world must not, contrary to what Rahner suggests, disappear. To experience Reality nondually as emptiness (*sunyata*) or nothingness is to experience wonder, for if everything is constituted by everything else, everything is always more, unimaginably more, than it initially appears to be.

What wisdom and compassion—practices already discussed—are lacking is the celebration of the wonder of Reality. This celebration is nondualistic. Both theistic worship and some versions of mystical identification focus on God, and both are dualistic. The former places God outside the world, while the latter reduces God to the essence of the universe. If God and humans are covenantal partners in the repair/creation of the world, then both God and humans participate in the celebration. Or, to use less personal language, if God (whatever the term may mean) and humans are interdependent, then the object of celebration is Reality and everyone, including God, is always already invited to the celebration.

If we could but see it, wonder is everywhere. Wonder fills the forest the way the smell of honeysuckle permeates the air in late spring and early summer. It pops up suddenly and miraculously like wild flowers in a meadow. It thunders down at Niagara or Victoria or Iguazu Falls. It saturates the night sky, as do the stars in Arizona or above the flanks of Kilimanjaro. It emerges from between the legs of women in childbirth. It splatters us in the form of compassionate acts, such as that of the white, middle-aged, middleclass, female teacher who gave one of her kidneys to a poor, black, male, elementary student she hardly knew or Dr. Paul Farmer's leaving Harvard Medical School to open a clinic in the disease-ridden countryside of impoverished Haiti. It gushes into the streets like the freedom-loving people of Belgrade as they overthrew a repressive regime. And it will stun us one day when the Palestinians and Israelis "beat their swords into plowshares and their spears into pruning hooks" and drink thick, dark coffee together at cafes inside the old city of Jerusalem, smilingly showing each other digital photos of their grandchildren.

But there are more homely, and therefore more significant, illustrations. Pick up a piece of Styrofoam from a littered street or a piece of gravel from a driveway or rural road. Styrofoam, a product of chemistry, merely keeps coffee or food hot for a few minutes and is then discarded. Gravel is merely a commercial resource, something to be sold, an ingredient in concrete, or something to prevent a vehicle from getting stuck in mud or snow. Or so we think. But is that not egoistic, dualistic looking rather than seeing? Is that all there is to it?

Years ago, while teaching a senior seminar in philosophy, I brought to the first meeting of the class a handful of pebbles hurriedly picked up from here and there. There was nothing obviously special about them. I gave one to every student in the course and asked the students to describe the pebbles as thoroughly as possible on a 6 × 4 inch card. Although I set no time limit for this exercise, most students were done in 10 minutes. They wrote about the size, shape, color, pattern, weight, smell, texture, and even the taste of their pebbles. After taking up the cards, I instructed the students that over the course of the term they were to keep the pebbles with them at all times—in class, on a date, even when taking a shower. I provided them no reason for this requirement.

At the end of the term, I returned the cards to the students and asked them if they still regarded their original descriptions as adequate. None did; all had more to write. New features had been noticed. Moreover, the pebbles had become endowed with a significance they previously lacked. Some students had given them proper names, even before the "pet rock" craze.[49] Yet there is still more to be said.

Some 520 million years ago, in the Cambrian Period of the Paleozoic era, long before there were humans, before there were apes, before there were dinosaurs or fish or even trilobites and brachiopods, the earth's crust consisted of old rocks such as basalt and granite. Year after year, decade after decade, century after century, millennium after interminable millennium, drop by drop erosion by water and other forces began to remove from the rocks calcium ions. At the same time, rain began to cleanse the atmosphere, thick with carbon dioxide. In water the carbon dioxide became carbonate. Here and there the calcium ions from the earth's crust and the carbonate mixed together to form calcium carbonate.

In the Ordivician period of the Paleozoic era, some 440 millions of years ago, still before anything but primitive shelled sea creatures, the calcium carbonate began to precipitate out of the water and solidify to form limestone. Since then, for hundred of millions of years, the original limestone deposits have been breaking up into smaller and smaller units under pressure from the same forces that produced the calcium ions. One result is gravel. Yet in the light of its rich and incomprehensibly ancient pedigree and its slow, cumulative travail the appearance of gravel is no longer an uninteresting, insignificant fact. It's a miracle!

But the significance of stone is not found simply in its past or in its future as part of a rock fence, a concrete highway, or even a monument to dead soldiers. There is a still unnoticed and unappreciated depth dimension to stone. I am reminded of Mircea Eliade's account of the special powers ancient peoples saw in stones.[50] They were regarded as dwelling places for the dead, as witnesses to a covenant between God and humans, as having a heavenly origin, as manifestations of gods, as possessing the power to cause rain, as markers of sacred boundaries between the divine and the earthly, and as possessing the power to cause pregnancy. Traditionally, Jews, Christians, and Muslims regard "rock" as a metaphor for God.

Even for supposedly clear-eyed postmoderns, the significance of stone cannot be confined to its surface meaning. Stone contrasts sharply with our human mode of existing and puts it into relief. Our bodies, consisting largely of water, are soft. At death, however, *rigor mortis* sets in and we become like stone. Hence Moses (a.k.a. Charlton Heston) can speak of anti-gun advocates having to pry his gun from his "stone cold hand." Stone represents our destiny. Despite its long evolutionary history, we are inclined to think of stone as what our hit-or-miss perceptions tell us it is, namely, unchanging. As Eliade says, "Above all, stone *is*. It always remains itself." We who are alive, who are self-moved movers, who are constantly shape-shifting, growing, and developing, are destined to become like stone, to cease all movement and become fixed.

49.   In 1975, Gary Dahl, a California entrepreneur with a sense of humor, marketed "pet rocks" to customers across America. The rocks were wrapped in excelsior and shipped in a box made to look like a carrying case for an animal. With each pet came a training manual. Pet rocks may still be bought today on e-Bay.

50.   Mircea Eliade, *Patterns in Comparative Religion*, trans. Rosemary Sheed (New York: New American Library, 1958), chapter 6.

Again, speaking of humankind, Eliade says:

> Rock shows him something that transcends the precariousness of his humanity: an absolute mode of being. Its strength, its motionlessness, its size, and its strange outlines are none of them human; they indicate the presence of something that fascinates, terrifies, attracts and threatens, all at once. In its grandeur, its hardness, its shape and its colour, man is faced with a reality and a force, that belongs to some world other than the profane world of which he is himself a part.[51]

To me, the most eerie quality of stone is its indifference, its total absence of an iota of anxiety, its utter imperturbability. It has no doubts. It has no decisions to make. It cannot make mistakes; it is faultless. It is a quality that, when we are caught in the agony and ecstasy and stupidity and triviality of the human tragedy-comedy, we can envy. This utter equanimity, serenity, tranquility, and imperturbability is what Buddhism calls the "adamantine nature" or "diamond nature" of a Buddha. Substituting "gravel" for Kasulis' "shit and piss," a Buddhist might say, "Even gravel preaches Dharma." If such ordinary magic is present in a discarded plastic spoon, a Styrofoam cup, or kitty litter, what of a dandelion, a wild rose, a thoroughbred, a book, old friends, a lover, one's own child?

When Beat poet Lawrence Ferlinghetti wrote that he was "perpetually and forever awaiting a rebirth of wonder," he seemed, like most moderns, not to know that it is everywhere in the middle way, even right in the middle of the road, where another poet, Elizabeth Bishop, found it.

In the Middle of the Road

> In the middle of the road there was a stone
> there was a stone in the middle of the road
> there was a stone
> in the middle of the road there was a stone.
>
> Never should I forget this event
> in the life of my fatigued retinas.
> Never should I forget that in the middle of the road
> there was a stone
> there was a stone in the middle of the road
> in the middle of the road there was stone.[52]

---

51. Eliade, 216. From a longer perspective, of course, mountains move. Author James Still, inspired by Psalm 114.4, writes, "These hills is jist dirt waves, washing through eternity." See his *River of Earth* (Lexington: The University Press of Kentucky, 1978), 76. Zen master Dogen says that "the Green mountains are always walking," that "they walk more swiftly than the wind," and that "all mountains walk with their toes on all waters and splash there." See "Mountains and Waters Sutra" in Kazuaki Tanahashi, ed. *Moon in a Dewdrop: Writings of Zen Master Dogen* (New York: North Point Press, 1985), 97, 98, 101.

52. Elizabeth Bishop, *The Complete Poems, 1927–1979/Elizabeth Bishop* (New York: Farrar Straus Giroux, 1983), 259.

A fortiori, Reality, which includes that stone—indeed, all stones and everything else besides—is worth celebrating!

To say that Reality is worth celebrating is not to affirm with Leibniz that there is a preestablished cosmic harmony or with Pangloss that "this is the best of all possible worlds" or with Pope that "whatever is, is right." We cannot close our eyes to the fact that war and terrorism rage in many countries. Disease, like a medieval scythe, cuts down vast numbers of people and animals. And much of the world's population suffers from tsunamis, tornados, floods, hurricanes, earthquakes, mudslides, abject poverty, political oppression, discrimination, hunger, and ignorance. There is no reason, desire, or capacity to celebrate these tragedies, but one can surely celebrate the good.

One may well ask, however, whether it is appropriate or possible to celebrate the good in the midst of so much tragedy and suffering, especially if one is a compassionate person. Even the ancient Hebrews could not sing the Lord's song in Babylon. There are two reasons I believe we must try. First, unless we can celebrate, at least sometimes, we will lack the personal wherewithal to carry on in the repair/creation of the world. Wisdom, compassion, and celebration are nondual. All of us know people who have found sufficient strength, joy, and gratitude to celebrate their own lives despite the fact that their bodies are riddled with cancer. Analogously, at least sometimes we can celebrate Reality, despite the tragedy it contains. Second, if we cannot celebrate life in the world, as children's playwright Mary Hall Surface has pointed out, our children will never come to believe the world is worth saving.[53] What is needed, then, beyond the practice of wisdom and compassion, is celebration.

The Path of All Paths is the Path of No-Path

Of all the terms used by religions to speak of themselves, perhaps the most common is "way" or "path." In Hinduism, a synonym for "yoga" is "*marga*," which means "path." Confucianism, Buddhism, Sufism, Christianity, and Islam, also, offer self-designations that employ one or both of the two terms. In many respects the terms are apt ones. Let's see why.

On the third day of a hike of the Torres del Paine Circuit in remote Chilean Patagonia, two friends (father and son) and I reached a fork in the path. One friend (Eddy, the father) went to the left, the other (Todd, the son) went right, and I stayed put. My expectation was that both would return to the fork in a few minutes with information that would help us determine which way to go. After the passage of some time, I called out in each direction. Both hikers replied, but their replies were faint and grew progressively fainter. Eventually, it became clear that neither intended to return to the fork, and I was forced to make a choice. I went left.

Some time later, I caught up with Eddy at the edge of a fen (a marsh with flowing water) to which the left-hand trail had led. Very reluctantly, we moved

53. A conversation with Mary Hall Surface at Centre College, Danville, Kentucky, in 2006.

forward, entering the fen; there seemed to be no good alternative. As our feet sank into the thick mud, water came over the top of our boots and filled them. The Goretex lining, rather than keeping the water out, held it inside! After approximately 45 minutes we came to dry land but discovered that there was still no path in sight. For another hour we followed pseudo-trails of bent grass made by other wayward souls that had preceded us. The "trails" went only in circles. It was then that we realized and admitted to each other that we were lost.

We sat under a tree to rest, eat, and think. We had no map and no compass. The sun was completely hidden from view, so we could not orient ourselves. We were concerned about the approach of darkness and the possibility of dangerous animals. I had a sleeping bag and a one-person tent. Eddy had a bag only. We disagreed about what to do. Our mood, which had been gradually turning sour, turned grim.[54]

Eventually, prompted by the adage that doing something is better than doing nothing (the reverse of Navajo wisdom, incidentally), Eddy decided to bushwhack, and I agreed to go with him. The ground was flat but covered with bushes head-high or higher. It was not easy going. Often, Eddy simply bulled his way forward through the thick growth, the branches grabbing at his clothes. I followed in his wake. Suddenly, we came upon a path, but quickly realized that we did not know in which direction to follow it. We sat again to mull the options, and after a few minutes, miraculously, along the trail came three Belgian backpackers. They had a map and knew where they were going. At once relieved and joyous, we joined them all the way to the day's intended destination.

The story illustrates why paths are so highly valued. Doubtless, the knowledge, safety, encouragement, and camaraderie we felt when we found the trail and hooked up with the Belgians is similar to what is felt by people who find a religious path. When a group of early Muslims fled to Abyssinia to escape the persecution occurring in Mecca, their spokesman, a cousin of Muhammad, told this story to the Abyssinian ruler:

> We were folks immersed in ignorance, worshipping idols, eating carrion, given to lewdness, severing the ties of kinship, bad neighbors, the strong among us preying the weak; thus were we till Allah sent us a messenger of our own, whose lineage, honesty, trustworthiness and chastity we knew, and he called us to Allah that we should acknowledge His unity and worship Him and eschew all the stones and idols that we and our fathers used to worship beside Him.[55]

Now, they had some sense of spiritual direction, and it promised to lead to something better than they had hitherto known. And they had supportive companions.

Even philosophical schools and methodologies can, I would argue, be construed as paths, at least in some limited sense. In fact, Asia, unlike the West,

---

54. Eddy, who has now heard me tell this story, denies being as distressed as I have indicated.

55. *The Meaning of the Glorious Koran*, An explanatory translation by Mohammed Marmaduke Pickthall (New York: New American Library), 220.

has never distinguished philosophy from religion. Neo-Thomism, Existentialism, Phenomenology, Deconstruction, Process Thought, and the Analytical School are at least ways of thinking, ways of moving in the direction of knowledge.

Recall, too, that the Wesleyan Quadrilateral names the four sources for doing theology: revelation, tradition, reason, and experience. These sources are also paths. Philosophy shares, differentially, the same four sources. Revelation is simply the digested pre-reflective communal experience of ancient peoples (religious or otherwise). Tradition is congealed communal reflection on revelation. Reason is distilled reflection on tradition. And experience is what happens to us in our own lifetimes rather than what has happened to others in the past. In the end, philosophy, like theology, is simply elucidated experience. The principal difference between the two is that theology is more likely to consult in a deliberate fashion all four sources, even when according them different values. Philosophy, on the other hand, explicitly focuses on reason and/or experience; revelation and tradition are left to affect it tacitly. Actually, the situation is a bit more complex. Philosophy may well deliberately consult ancient Greek and traditional philosophical texts, while these sources may affect theology tacitly.

Inevitably, however, two crucial questions arise: (1) how many paths are there and (2) which one, if any, is the right one. As for the first question, I would borrow Shakespeare's line, "Let me count the ways." The Christian gospels depict Jesus as saying, "I am the way, the truth, and the life. No man cometh to the father but by me." So is there but one way? Some conservative Christians used to hold up an index finger to indicate that the answer is "yes." But is that way the Christian one or, given that Jesus remained a Jew, the Jewish one? And is there only one Christian interpretation? Some more liberal Christians take it to mean that Jesus's way is the only way to Jesus's understanding of God; other ways lead to other understandings of divinity. Islam refers to "people of the book," a designation that includes Judaism, Christianity, and Islam. So are there three ways? Islam, however, refers to itself as "the straight path," implying that perhaps Judaism and Christianity are crooked ways in virtue of the corruption of their textual revelations from God. Patanjali's *Yoga Sutras* describes the four classic yogas of Hinduism: *Jnana* (the way of intellectual knowledge), *Bhakti* (the way of devotion), *Karma* (the way of consecrated action), and *Raja* (the way of meditation or of mystical quest). Dale Cannon argues in his *Six Ways of Being Religious* that the number is at least six.[56] To the four classic Hindu yogas he adds (1) the way of ritual and (2) the way of shamanic mediation. For him, however, ways are broader than religions.

The various religious paths envision and move toward different destinations. Buddhists seek nirvana. Hindus pursue knowledge leading to *moksha* (ultimate liberation from this world, *samsara*). Jains believe themselves to be headed, following voluntary self-starvation (*sallakhana*), to *Isatpragbhara*, a place atop the human-shaped cosmos where souls are restored to their natural state of knowledge, brightness, and joy. And although Jews, Christians, and Muslims seek a

---

56.   Dale Cannon, *Six Ways of Being Religious: A Framework for Comparative Studies in Religion* (Belmont, California: Wadsworth Publishing Company, 1996), 69–70.

life in heaven, each religion conceives it somewhat differently. Some nonreligious paths foresee the end as complete annihilation of selfhood. Existentialism sees it as the point at which human essence finally becomes fixed because we can no longer act to change it. The notion that religions are but many paths that converge at the top of a single mountain is difficult to maintain, as S. Mark Heim so effectively argues.[57]

Some hiking trails—those in national or state parks in the United States, for example—are usually well marked. Others, like those in England's Lake District, are confusing. Trail booklets provided by tourist offices make references to fells, tarns, barns, or particular trees (sometimes no longer there) as markers. In the Alps, rocks bearing painted designs indicate the proper direction, while in Patagonia guidance is a cairn or sometimes a dab of orange paint on a single stone. On stony ground or scree the trails often disappear temporarily. Some trails provide substantial bridges over streams, while others offer only rope bridges, a tree trunk, or a few stepping stones. Some offer nothing at all.

Religious paths, also, are variously marked and provisioned. Some—Islam, for instance—are well-marked and simple. The practice of the five "pillars" (creed, prayer, fasting, charity, and pilgrimage) constitutes the religion for Sunnis, the majority sect. In that respect, it resembles a self-guided trail. Others, like Zen, are not well-marked at all; consequently, a teacher or guide becomes important. Hinduism allows people to choose from its variety of paths or to create a new one. The latter option is, we might say, a kind of spiritual bushwhacking. Some have creedal statements or sacred texts; others do without one or both.

If, however, we assume that each religion is a way, then the number of paths swells dramatically. According to David Barrett, editor of the two-volume *World Christian Encyclopedia*, published by Oxford University Press, there are 9,900 "separate and distinct religions in the world, increasing by two or three religions every day."[58]

But even when a trail is well-worn and/or well-marked, no two travelers step in exactly the same spots. Some cut across switchbacks in an effort to shorten the distance, and some go off-trail temporarily to bypass a recently fallen tree or newly formed mudhole. The bypass may eventually become the trail. This is neither surprising nor deplorable. After all, each of us has a unique fingerprint, voice print, eye print, DNA sequence, and sedimented experience. How can our paths be absolutely identical? Considered in the most concrete terms possible, there are, then, as many paths as there are individuals.

The absence of an absolute identity of paths does not mean, however, that there are no similarities among them or that we cannot or should not form and participate in broader communities. In fact, given the political, cultural, military,

57. S. Mark Heim, *Salvations: Truth and Difference in Religion* (Maryknoll, New York: Orbis Books, 1995).

58. Cited in Toby Lester, "OH, GODS!" in *The Atlantic Monthly*, 289 (February, 2002), 37–43. Lester notes that Barrett and the scholars helping him have, apparently, abandoned the distinction between cults and religions and also count Baptists, Presbyterians, and Methodists, etc., as separate religions.

and religious tensions in our world today, finding such common grounding as we can is vital. Even when the prospects for convergence appear nonexistent, we are sometimes surprised by unsuspected breakthroughs.

Given the current violence that engulfs Judaism and Islam and involves Christians, for example, some thinkers (some Muslims among them) have urged seeking unity among the three religions by emphasizing their connection in the Qur'an as "people of the book." Others urge emphasizing the figure of Abraham, which is shared by all three religions. There is much wisdom in doing so. The reader will recall that Chapter 5 of this volume proposes Abraham as a paradigm for a nondual epistemology, but he might also serve as a paradigm for a more comprehensive way or path.

Yet the adoption of Abraham as a paradigm is not without problems. The most obvious of these is that my proposal to adopt him as a paradigm, both an epistemological one and now a broader one, is made with universal intent, despite the fact that Abraham is not a part of the non-Semitic religions and of few philosophies anywhere. Clearly, that hardly makes sense. But can some sense be made of it? I believe the answer is "yes."

First, I do not, as do others, understand Abraham primarily as the patriarch of a racial or religious family of which some are remote descendents while others are not. Nor is he primarily the source of a cultural or religious history of which I, but not others, am a legatee far downstream. I see him as a paradigm for a fundamental orientation to life that is potentially universal. And what is that orientation?

Here, it is important to notice that Hebrews 11.8, which I cited in Chapter 5, says that Abraham "left Ur of the Chaldees not knowing where he was going" (King James) or "left home without knowing where he was to go." (NEB) His being the father of faith, then, consists of two elements: an action (leaving Ur) and a condition (not knowing where he was going). Recall, however, that in Chapter 5 his "not knowing" was interpreted not as complete ignorance (the binary opposite of knowing) but as "non-knowing," a middle way. In other words, he was willing to rely on intimations from his experience, both present and sedimented, in the courageous pursuit of a greater destiny.

The key, however, to discovering Abraham's presumptively universal implications for religion and philosophy—Asian and Western—is noticing that no reference whatsoever is made to a path, way, road, trail, highway, corridor, or thoroughfare. This is both striking and significant! In other words, what makes Abraham the "father of faith;" not only to Judaism, Christianity, and Islam but to the non-Western religions/philosophies as well; is not that he followed an established path, one differing from and/or excluding other paths. It is not even that he bushwhacked a trail that eventually became an established path. Both "path" and "way" are primarily spatial in connotation and easily give rise to forms of territoriality. The heart of the matter is not the path but the setting out, the leaving, the undertaking of a journey. "Journey" is primarily temporal in connotation and, consequently, less likely to harden, to succumb to sclerosis, to generate fundamentalism. To take up any religion, any philosophy is to set out in search of something. To follow this "path of setting out" is to follow the "path" of Abraham, which we can do no better than call a "non-path" or "the path of no path."

Annie Dillard seems to agree. She writes:

> "Spiritual path" is the hilarious popular term for those night-blind mesas and flayed hills in which people grope, for decades on end, with the goal of knowing the absolute. They discover others spread under the stars and encamped here and there by watch fires, in groups or alone, in the open landscape; they stop for a sleep, or for several years, and move along without knowing toward what or why. They leave whatever they find, picking up each stone, carrying it for awhile, and dropping it gratefully and without regret, for it is not the absolute, though they cannot say what is. Their life's fine, impossible goal justifies the term "spiritual." Nothing, however, can justify the term "path" for this bewildered and empty stumbling, this blackened vagabondage—except one thing: They don't quit. They stick with it.[59]

Her assessment, however, seems excessively bleak and Sisyphusian when she states that "the planet turns under their steps like a water wheel rolling; constellations shift without anyone's gaining ground" and that "decade after decade they see no progress." She admits that such wayfarers do cease to worry about doctrines and cease to doubt that the journey is "a reasonable way to pass one's life," but she does not acknowledge this as progress. Moreover, the journey she depicts is absent of any sense of joy or adventure.

The problem lies in several of her apparent assumptions: that the goal is "knowing the absolute," that the goal does not change during the course of the journey, and that no active creation of the goal on the part of the wayfarer is required. As we have seen, however, for Buddhists and ancient Hebrews, there are no absolutes. So, if one set out to know the absolute and, subsequently, came to the realization that the ultimate reality is beyond the dualism of absolute and relative, that would constitute significant progress. The promised land, as we saw in Chapter 5, is not like an Easter egg, hidden in advance for one to find, but a reality to be cocreated from circumstances that are merely suitable. And while the absence of a sense of joy and adventure are, indeed, common features of life's journey, a more complete description would need to include them, also.

The all important setting out begins, as Huston Smith says in describing Sufism, "in institutions, in corridors countless other have trod before him, but it will open soon enough on the trackless waste where each person must be his own scout."[60] We could, then, equate paths with those institutional corridors. Dillard's night-blind mesas and flayed hills, then, might correspond to the trackless waste.

Setting out, however, is not even necessarily a self-conscious matter; willy-nilly, we all set out or find ourselves already set out. Recall from Chapter 6 that, according to Erikson, the newborn child must develop a basic trust in the new world into which it has been thrust and that this trust is modified in each of the eight stages of the life cycle, becoming the basis of religion. In one sense, then,

---

59. Annie Dillard, *For the Time Being*, a Vintage Book (New York: Random House, Inc., 2000), 169–171.
60. *The Sufi Way*, a videotape narrated by Huston Smith (New York: The Hartley Film Foundation, 1971).

it is from birth that we set out. Hence, there can be no dualism of those who have set out and those who have not. Later, of course, it may be that some take an extended rest stop while others take up the journey in a more reflective, deliberative, and passionate way.

Based on the work of Erikson (identity development), Lawrence Kohlberg (moral development), and Jean Piaget (cognitive development), James Fowler proposed a six-stage theory of faith development.[61] Initially (ages 0–3), a child has merely an undifferentiated and unconscious disposition toward the world. At ages 3–7 a child's "intuitive-projective" faith amounts to introjecting the actions, examples, moods, and words of its parents. Next comes the "mythic-literal" stage in which a child accepts its parents beliefs, taken literally. Puzzlement over conflicts among authorities leads to a "synthetic-conventional" faith in which one conforms to the expectations and judgments of others. According to Fowler, most people stop here. These stages, too, could be seen as corresponding to Smith's institutional corridors. Perhaps the remaining stages more closely correspond to the "trackless waste, where each person must be his own scout," to the moment when the setting out becomes self-conscious, more individualized and adventurous.

So what about the second question raised above, namely, which path is the right, correct, or true one? The conclusions already reached in Chapter 5 dictate the following answer: "We cannot say *absolutely*." We can, of course, give our reasons and point to evidence in the conviction that some reasons and some evidence are better than others. But we must do so with the understanding that nobody is omniscient and nobody is utterly ignorant. Nobody has finally arrived; all are always yet on the way. All, like Abraham, are between Ur and the Land of Promise, a land that all of us can share in creating. Hope remains because almost nobody is finally lost. Humility, seeking, and cooperation continue because nobody is totally saved. And although some may have bivouacked in one spot too long, all tread the middle way.

Travel guide writer Rick Steves ends each installment of his television show with the words "Keep on traveling." Applied to the whole of life, his advice is redundant; we really have no other option. But we can press on with renewed understanding, learning to share the journey peaceably with others, engaging without reservation in the compassionate transformation of Reality (including ourselves) by repairing, nurturing, and creating it in the direction of increased justice, harmony, and joy for all beings, celebrating (as we are able) each adventurous step.

61. James W. Fowler, Robin W. Lovin, Katherine Ann Herzog, Brian Mahan, Linell Cady, and Jonathan P. Gosser. *Trajectories of Faith: Five Life Stories* (Nashville, Tennessee: Abingdon, 1980).

Bibliography

Abbot, Edwin A. *Flatland: A Romance of Many Dimensions.* Boston, Massachusetts: Little, Brown and Company, 1899.

Abe, Masao. "Kenotic God and Dynamic Sunyata." In *The Emptying God: A Buddhist-Jewish-Christian Conversation*, John Cobb, Jr. and Christopher Ives, eds. Maryknoll, New York: Orbis Books, 1990.

Armstrong, Karen. *Buddha.* New York: Penguin, 2001.

Auerbach, Eric. "Odysseus' Scar." In *Mimesis: The Representation of Reality in Western Literature.* Princeton, New Jersey: Princeton University Press, 1953.

Austin, J. L. *How to Do Things with Words.* Cambridge, Massachusetts: Harvard University Press, 1962.

Barbour, Ian G. *Issues in Science and Religion.* Englewood Cliffs, New Jersey: Prentice-Hall, Inc., 1966.

___. *Myths, Models, and Paradigms: A Comparative Study of Science and Religion.* New York: Harper & Row, 1974.

___. *Religion and Science: Historical and Contemporary Issues.* San Francisco, California: HarperSanFrancisco, 1997.

Bellah, Robert and Richard Madsen, William M. Sullivan, Alan Swidler, and Steven M. Tipton. *Habits of the Heart: Individualism and Commitment in American Life.* Berkeley and Los Angeles, California: University of California Press, 1996.

Berry, Wendell. *A Continuous Harmony: Essays Cultural and Agricultural.* New York: Harcourt Brace Jovanovich, 1970.

Bishop, Elizabeth. *The Complete Poems, 1927–1979/Elizabeth Bishop.* New York: Farrar, Straus and Giroux, 1983.

"Bodhisattva and the Hungry Tigress." In *Buddhist Scriptures*, selected and translated by Edward Conze. Baltimore, Maryland: Penguin Books, 1959.

Bowra, Cecil M. *The Greek Experience.* New York: New American Library, 1957.

Brownstein, Ronald. *The Second Civil War: How Extreme Partisanship Has Paralyzed Washington and Polarized America.* Penguin Group, 2007.

Brueggemann, Walter. *The Prophetic Imagination.* Minneapolis, Minnesota: Fortress Press, 1978.

Buber, Martin. *I and Thou.* 2nd ed. New York: Charles Scribner's Sons, 1958.

Burtt, Edwin A. *The Metaphysical Foundations of Modern Physical Science.* rev. ed. Garden City, New York: Doubleday and Company, Inc., 1932.

___, ed. *The Teaching of the Compassionate Buddha.* New York: New American Library, 1982.

Cannon, Dale. *The Six Ways of Being Religious: A Framework for Comparative Studies in Religion.* Belmont, California: Wadsworth Publishing Company, 1996.

Caputo, John. "Beyond Sovereignty: Many Nations Under the Weakness of God." In *Soundings: An Interdisciplinary Journal* 89 (Spring/Summer 2006).

Carol, Rebecca. "Senate Apologizes for Anti-lynching Failures." In *The Advocate-Messenger.* Danville, Kentucky (June 14, 2005).

Cobb, James. *Away Down South: A History of Southern Identity.* New York: Oxford University Press, 2005.

Cobb, John B., Jr. and David Ray Griffin. *Process Theology: An Introductory Exposition.* Philadelphia, Pennsylvania: The Westminster Press, 1976.

Cooey, Paula. *Family, Freedom, and Faith: Building Community Today.* Louisville, Kentucky: Westminster John Knox Press, 1966.

Cox, Harvey. *On Not Leaving It to The Snake.* New York: The Macmillan Company, 1967.

Cullman, Oscar. *Immortality of the Soul or Resurrection of the Dead?* New York: Macmillan, 1958.

Daniel, Stephen. *Myth and Modern Philosophy.* Philadelphia, Pennsylvania: Temple University Press, 1990.

Derrida, Jacques. *Deconstruction in a Nutshell: A Conversation with Jacques Derrida,* edited and with commentary by John D. Caputo. New York: Fordham University Press, 1997.

___. *Speech and Phenomena,* translated by D. B. Allison. Evanston, Illinois: Northwestern University Press, 1973.

Descartes, René. "Discourse on Method." In *Descartes's Philosophical Writings,* translated and edited by Norman Kemp Smith. New York: The Modern Library, 1958.

___. *The Principles of Philosophy,* translated by Valentine Rodger Miller and Reese P. Miller. Dordrecht Holland, Boston, Massachusetts, London, England: D. Reidel Publishing Company, 1983.

___. "Rules for the Direction of the Mind." In *Descartes's Philosophical Writings,* selected and translated by Norman Kemp Smith. New York: The Modern Library, 1958.

Dewart, Leslie. *The Future of Belief: Theism in a World Come of Age.* New York: Herder and Herder, 1966.

Dillard, Annie. *For the Time Being.* New York: Random House, Inc., 2000.

Eagleton, Terry. *Literary Theory: An Introduction.* Minneapolis: University of Michigan Press, 1983.

Elazar, Daniel J. "Covenant as the Basis of Jewish Political Tradition." In *The Jewish Journal of Sociology* 20 (June 1978): 5–37.

___. "Federal Models of (Civil) Authority." In *Journal of Church and State* 33 (Spring 1991): 231–254.

Eliade, Mircea. *Patterns in Comparative Religion,* translated by Rosemary Sheed. New York: New American Library, 1958.

Encyclopedia Judaica. Vol. 5. Jerusalem: The Macmillan Company, 1971.

Erikson, Erik. *Childhood and Society.* rev. ed. New York: W. W. Norton & Company, Inc., 1963.

___. *Identity, Youth and Crisis.* New York: W. W. Norton & Company, Inc., 1963.

___. *Insight and Responsibility: Lectures on the Ethical Implications of Psychoanalytic Insight.* New York: W. W. Norton & Company, 1964.

Esposito, John L., Darrel J. Fasching, and Todd Lewis. *World Religions Today.* New York: Oxford University Press, 2002.

Farley, Edward. *Divine Empathy: A Theology of God.* Minneapolis, Minnesota: Fortress Press, 1996.

___. *Good & Evil: Interpreting a Human Condition.* Minneapolis, Minnesota: Fortress Press, 1990.

Fausto-Sterling, Anne. "The Five Sexes: Why Male and Female are Not Enough." In *The Sciences* (March/April 1993): 20–25.

Ferlinghetti, Lawrence. "I am Waiting." In *A Coney Island of the Mind: Poems by Lawrence Ferlinghetti.* New York: New Directions Books, 1959.

Foster, Michael. "The Christian Doctrine of Creation and the Rise of Modern Natural Science." In *Creation: The Impact of an Idea,* edited by Daniel O'Connor and Francis Oakley. New York: Charles Scriber's Sons, 1969.

Fowler, James W., Robin W. Lovins, Katherine Ann Herzog, Brian Mahan, Linell Cady, Jonathan P. Gosser. *Trajectories of Faith: Five Life Stories.* Nashville, Tennessee: Abingdon, 1980.

Gale, George. *Theory of Science: An Introduction to the History, Logic, and Philosophy of Science.* New York: McGraw-Hill Book Company, 1979.

Gandhi, Mohandas K. *Gandhi: An Autobiography: The Story of My Experiments with Truth,* translated from Gujarati by Mahadev Desai. London: Phoenix Press, 1949.

Garfield, Jay. *The Fundamental Wisdom of the Middle Way.* New York: Oxford University Press, 1995.

Gill, Jerry H. *Mediated Transcendence: A Postmodern Reflection.* Macon, Georgia: Mercer University Press, 1989.

Gilson, Étienne. *Etude sur le role de la pensée médiévale dan la formation du systeme cartésien.* Paris: J. Vrin, 1930.

___. *Index scholastico-cartésien.* Paris: F. Alcan, 1913.

Griffin, Nancy. "Home Again." In *AARP The Magazine.* (November/ December 2007).

Hakuin, Zenji. *The Zen Master Hakuin: Selected Writings,* translated by Philip B. Yampolsky. New York: Columbia University Press, 1971.

Hall, David L. and Roger T. Ames. *Thinking Through Confucius.* Albany, New York: State University of New York Press, 1987.

Hartshorne, Charles. *The Divine Relativity: A Social Conception of God.* New Haven, Connecticut: Yale University Press, 1982.

Hatab, Lawrence J. *Myth and Philosophy: A Contest of Truths.* LaSalle, Illinois: Open Court, 1990.

Hauer, Christian F. and William A. Young. *An Introduction to the Bible: A Journey into Three Worlds.* 4th ed. Upper Saddle River, New Jersey: Prentice Hall, 1998.

Hayes, John. *Introduction to the Bible.* Philadelphia, Pennslyvania: The Westminster Press, 1971.

Heim, S. Mark. *Salvations: Truth and Difference in Religion.* Maryknoll, New York: Orbis Books, 1995.

Heschel, Abraham Joshua. *Between God and Man: An Interpretation of Judaism,* selected, edited, and translated by Fritz A. Rothschild. New York: The Free Press, 1959.

Hubbard, Jamie and Paul L. Swanson, eds. *Pruning the Bodhi Tree: The Storm over Critical Buddhism.* Honolulu: University of Hawaii Press, 1997.

Humphrey, George. "Introduction." In Jean-Marc-Gaspard Itard. *The Wild Boy of Aveyron,* translated by George and Muriel Humphrey. New York: The Century Co., 1932.

Inada, Kenneth K. *Nagarjuna: A Translation of his Mulamadhyamikakarika with an Introductory Essay.* Tokyo: Hokuseido, 1970.

Itard, Jean-Marc-Gaspard. "First Development of the Young Savage of Aveyron." In *The Wild Boy of Aveyron,* translated by George and Muriel Humphrey. New York: The Century Co., 1932.

___. "A Report Made to His Excellency the Minister of Aveyron." In *The Wild Boy of Aveyron,* translated by George and Muriel Humphrey. New York: The Century Co., 1932.

Kalupahana, David J. *Nagarjuna: The Philosophy of the Middle Way.* Albany: State University of New York Press, 1986.

___. *The Principles of Buddhist Psychology.* Albany: State University of New York Press, 1987.

Kasulis, T. P. *Intimacy or Integrity: Philosophy and Cultural Difference, the Gilbert Ryle Lectures.* Honolulu: University of Hawaii Press, 2002.

___. "Whence and Whither: Philosophical Reflections on Nishitani's View of History." In *The Religious Philosophy of Nishitani Keiji*, edited by Taitetsu Unno. Fremont, California: Asian Humanities Press, 1989.

___. *Zen Action/Zen Person.* Honolulu: University of Hawaii, 1981.

Kaufman, Gordon. *God Mystery Diversity.* Minneapolis, Minnesota: Fortress Press, 1996.

___. *In the Beginning . . . Creativity.* Minneapolis, Minnesota: Augsburg Fortress, 2004.

Kenny, Anthony. *A Brief History of Western Philosophy.* Oxford: Blackwell Publishers, Inc., 1998.

Kim, Hee-Jin. *Dogen Kigen—Mystical Realist.* Tucson: University of Arizona Press, 1975.

___. "The Reason of Words and Letters: Dogen and Koan Language." In *Dogen Studies*, edited by William LaFleur. Honolulu: University of Hawaii Press, 1955.

King, Sallie and Christopher S. Queen, eds. *Engaged Buddhism: Buddhist Liberation Movements in Asia.* Albany: State University of New York Press, 1996.

Kingsley, Peter. *Reality.* Inverness, California: Golden Sufi Center, 2003.

Laycock, Steven W. *Mind as Mirror and the Mirroring of Mind: Buddhist Reflections on Western Phenomenology.* Albany: State University of New York Press, 1994.

Lehman, Paul. *The Decalogue and a Human Future: The Meaning of the Commandments for Making and Keeping Life Human.* Grand Rapids, Michigan: Eerdmans, 1995.

Lester, Toby. "OH, GODS!" In *Atlantic Monthly* 289, 2 (February 2002): 37–43.

Levin, Michael. *The Body's Recollection of Being: Phenomenological Psychology and the Deconstruction of Nihilism.* London: Routledge & Kegan Paul, 1985.

Loy, David. "Dead Words, Living Words, and Healing Words." In *Healing Deconstruction: Postmodern Thought in Buddhism and Christianity*, edited by David Loy. Atlanta, Georgia: Scholars Press, 1996.

MacMurray, John. *The Clue to History.* New York: Harper & Brothers Publishers, 1939.

McBride, S. Dean, Jr. "Polity of the Covenant People: The Book of Deuteronomy." In *Interpretation* 41 (July 1987): 232–234

Magliola, Robert. *Derrida on the Mend.* West Lafayette, Indiana: Purdue University Press, 1984.

Maritain, Jacques. *Three Reformers: Luther—Descartes—Rousseau.* New York: Charles Scribner's Sons. n.d.

Marriott, Alice and Carol Rachlin. *American Indian Mythology.* New York: New American Library, 1968.

The Meaning of the Glorious Koran, translated by Mohammed Marmaduke Pickthall. New York: New American Library.

Meredith, James. *Three Years in Mississippi.* Bloomington: Indiana University Press, 1966.

Merleau-Ponty, Maurice. *Phenomenology of Perception*, translated by Colin Smith. London: Routledge & Kegan Paul, Ltd., 1962.

Miller, Patrick D. *The Religion of Ancient Israel.* Louisville, Kentucky: Westminster John Knox Press, 132.

___. "'That It May Go Well with You': The Commandment and the Common Good." In *In Search of the Common Good*, edited by Dennis P. McCann and Patrick D. Miller. New York: T&T Clark, 2005.

Mount, Eric Jr. *Covenant, Community, and the Common Good: An Interpretation of Christian Ethics.* Cleveland, Ohio: The Pilgrim Press, 1999.

___. "It Takes a Community—or at Least an Association." In *In Search of the Common Ground*, edited by Patrick D. Miller and Dennis P. McCann. New York: T&T Clark, 2005.

Myers, Carol. "The Family in Early Israel." In *Families in Ancient Israel*, edited by Joseph Blinkinsopp, John J. Collins, Carol Meyers, and Leo G. Perdue. Louisville, Kentucky: Westminster John Knox Press, 1997

Nakamura, Hajime. *Ways of Thinking of Eastern Peoples: India, China, Tibet, Japan*, edited and revised by Philip P. Wiener. Honolulu: University of Hawaii Press, 1968.

Nietzsche, Friedrich. *The Birth of Tragedy and the Genealogy of Morals*, translated by Francis Golffing. Garden City, New York: Doubleday & Company, Inc., 1956.

Nishitani, Keiji. *Religion and Nothingness*, translated by Jan van Bragt. Berkeley: University of California Press, 1982.

Ong, Walter. *The Presence of the Word: Some Prolegomena for Cultural and Religious History.* New Haven, Conneticut: Yale University Press, 1967.

Ortega y Gasset, José. *The Modern Theme*, translated by James Clough. New York: Harper and Row Publishers, 1961.

Pelikan, Jaroslav. *What Has Athens to do with Jerusalem: Timaeus and Genesis in Counterpoint.* Ann Arbor: The University of Michigan Press, 1997.

Philo. *De vita Mosis*, 1.75.

Plato. *The Dialogues of Plato*, 4 vols., 4th ed., trans. and ed. Benjamin Jowett. Oxford: Oxford University Press, 1953.

Polanyi, Michael. "Faith and Reason." In *The Journal of Religion* 41, 4 (October 1961): 237–247.

___. *Personal Knowledge: Towards a Post-Critical Philosophy.* New York: Harper and Row, 1958.

___. "The Structure of Tacit Knowing." Lecture at Duke University, February 17, 1964.

___. *The Tacit Dimension*, Anchor Books edition. Garden City, New York: Doubleday & Company, Inc., 1967.

Poteat, William H. "On First Sitting Down to Read *Personal Knowledge* . . . An Introduction." In *Intellect and Hope: Essays in the Thought of Michael Polanyi*, edited by Thomas A. Langford and William H. Poteat. Durham, North Carolina: Duke University Press, 1968.

___. "Persons and Places: Paradigms in Communication." In *The Primacy of Persons and the Language of Culture*, edited and with an introduction by James M. Nickell and James W. Stines. Columbia: University of Missouri Press, 1993.

___. *Polanyian Meditations: In Search of a Post-Critical Logic.* Durham, North Carolina: Duke University Press, 1985.

Queen, Christopher S., ed. *Engaged Buddhism in the West.* Boston, Massachusetts: Wisdom Publications, 2000.

Rahner, Karl. "Peace." In *Prayers & Meditations: An Anthology of the Spiritual Writings by Karl Rahner.* Edited by John Griffiths. New York: Crossroad, 1981, 106.

Ramsey, Ian T. *Models and Mystery.* London: Oxford University Press, 1964.

Raspberry, William. A convocation lecture at Centre College, February 8, 2007.

Robbins, Jhan and June. "The Boy Who Found the Sun." In *Redbook* (December 1966).

Rorty, Richard. *Philosophy and the Mirror of Nature.* Princeton, New Jersey: Princeton University Press, 1979.

Scarborough, Milton. "In the Beginning: Hebrew God and Zen Nothingness." In *Buddhist-Christian Studies*, 20 (2000): 191–216.

___. *Myth and Modernity: Postcritical Reflections.* Albany, New York: State University of New York Press, 1994.

Scarborough, Victoria. "In Search of an Ancient God." Paper presented in Danville, Kentucky, March 14, 1999.

Smith, Huston. *The World's Religions.* New York: HarperSanFrancisco, 1991.

Spiegelberg, Herbert. *The Phenomenological Movement: A Historical Introduction,* II. The Hague: Martinus Nijhoff, 1971.

Spong, John Shelby. *Why Christianity Must Change or Die: A Bishop Speaks to Believers in Exile.* San Francisco, California: HarperSanFrancisco, 1998.

Sprung, Mervyn. *The Magic of Unknowing: An East-West Soliloquy.* Peterborough, Canada: Broadview Press, 1987.

Still, James. *River of Earth.* Lexington: The University of Kentucky Press, 1978.

"The Sufi Way," a videotape narrated by Huston Smith. New York: The Hartley Film Foundation, 1971.

Tanahashi, Kuaki, ed. *Moon in a Dewdrop: Writings of Zen Master Dogen.* New York: North Point Press, 1985.

Tanaka, Kenneth. *Ocean: An Introduction to Jodo-Shinshu Buddhism in America.* Berkeley, California: Wisdom Ocean Publications, 1997.

Tarnas, Richard. *Cosmos and Psyche: Intimations of a New World View.* Viking, 2006.

Teilhard de Chardin, Pierre. *The Phenomenon of Man.* New York: Harper & Row, 1964.

The Torah: A Modern Commentary, edited by W. Gunther Plaut and David E. S. Stein. New York: Union for Reform Judaism Press, 2005.

Waters, Frank. *Masked Gods: Navaho and Pueblo Ceremonialism.* New York: Ballantine Books, 1970.

Weblowsky, R. J. Zwi. "Eschatology." In *The Encyclopedia of Religion,* 5, edited by Mircea Eliade. New York: Macmillan Publishing Company, 1987.

Welwood, John. "Double Vision: Duality and Nonduality in Human Experience." In *The Sacred Mirror: Nondual Wisdom and Psycho-Therapy,* edited by John Prendergast, Peter Fenner, and Sheila Krystal. St. Paul, Minnesota: Paragon House, 2003.

Whitney, Kobai Scott. *Sitting Inside: Buddhist Practice in America's Prisons.* Boulder: Prison Dharma Network, 2002.

"Wild Child: The Story of Feral Children." A video documentary produced by Optomen Television for the Discovery Channel.

Williams, Paul. *Mahayana Buddhism: The Doctrinal Foundations.* New York: Routledge, 1989.

Wissler, C. "Depression and Revolt." In *Natural History,* 41, 2 (1938).

Wittgenstein, Ludwig. *Prototractatus: An Early Version of Tractatus Logico-Philosophicus,* (ed.) B. F. McGuinness, T. Nyberg, G. H. von Wright, with a translation by D. F. Peaars, B. F. McGuinness, an historical introduction by G. H. von Wright and a facsimile of the author's manuscript (Ithaca, New York: Cornell University Press , 1971), 6.53.

Wright, G. Ernest and Reginald H. Fuller. *The Book of the Acts of God.* Garden City, New York: Doubleday & Company, 1960.

INDEX